THE EARLIEST
PRINTED LAWS
OF DELAWARE
1704 - 1741

THE COLONY LAWS OF NORTH AMERICA SERIES

General Editor: JOHN D. CUSHING

THE EARLIEST PRINTED LAWS OF DELAWARE 1704 - 1741

With an Editorial Note
by
JOHN D. CUSHING

Michael Glazier, Inc.
Wilmington, Delaware

This edition published in 1978 by:

MICHAEL GLAZIER, INC., 1210A King Street
Wilmington, Delaware 19801

Copyright © Editorial Note 1978 by John D. Cushing

Library of Congress Catalog Card Number 78-60459

International Standard Book Number 0-89453-093-3

Publisher's Note

Every effort has been made to produce exact
facsimiles of the original documents. Some
pages have faded with the passing of the
centuries, but we have decided to reproduce
them as they stand as the meaning of the text
is quite clear.

Printed in the United States of America

TABLE OF CONTENTS

Note: The above page numbers reflect those
found at the bottoms of the pages.

Editorial Note

The Swedish colony at Wilmington was established in 1633 under a charter from the Swedish South Company and was, for all practical purposes, a military expedition. The charter provided for a governing council, but inasmuch as the governor was a military commander, and most of the settlers were either employees of the company or exiles, there was little need to distinguish between military and civil affairs; the governor's word was law. Indeed, Johan Printz, who was appointed governor in 1642, was specifically vested with all governmental powers, as was his successor Johan Rising, and it was not until some twenty years after the settlement was first established that judges were appointed to interpret all colonial regulations according to Swedish law. The only other source of law in the area was a series of directives issued by the council of the South Company, subject to royal approbation.

After the initial settlement had developed into a series of separate communities and a significant number of settlers had arrived, gubernatorial orders continued to establish general policy, but the stability of the colony rested to a large extent upon the rules, regulations and customs developed at the local level and accepted by common consent. The system proved to be adequate to the needs of the times, and when the colony came into the hands of Peter Stuyvesant and the Dutch, little change took place. Municipal regulations provided for the day-to-day needs of most settlers, while general legislative, administrative and judicial powers were exercised by Stuyvesant and his council at New York.

In 1664, when title to the Delaware area passed to the Duke of York under a charter from Charles II, there was but little change in the *status quo*. The first formal change took place a dozen years later when Colonel Richard Nicholls compiled a rudimentary code known as "The Duke of York's Laws," drawn up for use throughout the Duke's vast North American holdings. Immediately following its promulgation, Governor Edmund Andros excerpted sections applicable to the Delaware area and sent copies to the newly appointed justices of the court at Newcastle. Known simply as the "Instructions," the dozen articles were devoted chiefly to establishing a formal government and a court system for the area. They can scarcely be considered as a code of laws and, in effect, brought little change other than to provide that appeals of litigation need no longer be carried to New York.

The "Duke's Laws" worked reasonably well for the colony and remained in force when, in 1682, the Duke of York conveyed title to his Delaware lands to William Penn. The Pennsylvania government eventually provided for a separate general assembly for the "lower counties," as the Delaware settlements were known, and such an assembly was finally established in 1704. The *Charter of Privileges* granted by William Penn, however, remained the basic charter document for both jurisdictions, and the Governor of Pennsylvania continued to serve as chief executive, approving or disallowing all legislation enacted by the separate legislature.

The laws enacted at the earliest sessions of the Delaware assembly appear to have been kept in ledgers designated "A" through "E." It would also appear from the scanty surviving evidence that many acts were never entered in those ledgers, that some of them were actually lost and their text unknown. It is difficult to determine when the assembly undertook to have the laws properly arranged and compiled for printing. But in 1734, more than a century after the first settlement, a 24 page publication issued from the press of Benjamin Franklin at Philadelphia (Evans #3762). It contained two acts; one regulating insolvent debtors, the other regulating attachments, and was the first issue of printed Delaware laws. Because the only available copy will not reproduce well, and because its contents were repeated in a subsequent compilation, it has not been included in this facsimile edition. Another issue, consisting of 20 pages, also printed by Franklin, appeared the following year (Evans #3895) but no copy appears to have survived.

Sometime between 1735 and October of 1738, attempts were made to have the laws of the three counties arranged in some useful format and printed, but the work languished and a committee appointed to prepare the material for the press could do no more than present a few acts for the approval of the assembly and Governor George Thomas. The latter, pressed by the Lords Commissioners for Trade and Plantations to send copies of all existing legislation to London, was dismayed by the haphazard approach of the assembly to the problem and urged the compilation of a body of laws according to some "proper methods." By October of the following year, 44 separate acts had been approved and a committee contracted with Benjamin Franklin to print twenty-one copies for the use of the government and as many more as he might desire for his own account.

Available records do not indicate when Franklin began work on the compilation, but it is clear that during the year 1741 he had completed 21 copies of 178 unbound pages for sale in his own shop, and 21 copies of 282 bound pages for his Delaware clients. In all copies examined, page 178 is signed Yy^2 and contains no catchword, suggesting that it was intended to be the final page of the compilation. Page 179, signed Zz, is actually a continuation of the first part. That bibliographical oddity may possibly be explained by the fact that in October of 1741, the governor was still prodding the assembly to complete the work, and a month later a committee was appointed to revise some 60 additional acts and prepare them for the press. Thus one may speculate that pages 179-282 may even have been printed in 1742 and were simply added to the first portion.

The work was a retrospective compilation of all then viable legislation enacted between 1704 and 1741 but, regretably, the compilers did not see fit to indicate the original date of each act. The present facsimile edition, slightly reduced in size in order to accommodate the format of the Colony Laws of North America Series, consists of the Penn Charter, the 282 page *Laws of the Government of New-Castle, Kent and Sussex Upon Delaware*, and a three page table.

This volume has been made available through the kindness of Mr. Murphy Smith of the American Philosophical Society Library in Philadelphia.

THE
CHARTER
OF
PRIVILEGES,

Granted by

WILLIAM PENN, Efq;

TO THE

Inhabitants of *PENSILVANIA*
and Territories.

MERCY JUSTICE

PHILADELPHIA:
Printed and Sold by *B. FRANKLIN.*
M DCC XLI.

THE
CHARTER
OF
PRIVILEGES, &c.

WILLIAM PENN, Proprietary and Governor of the Province of *Penfilvania* and Territories thereunto belonging, To all to whom thefe Prefents fhall come, fendeth Greeting. WHEREAS King *CHARLES the Se-* Preamble. *cond*, by His Letters Patents, under the Great Seal of *England*, bearing Date the *Fourth* Day of *March*, in the Year *One Thoufand Six Hundred and Eighty*, was gracioufly pleafed to give and grant unto me, and my Heirs and Affigns for ever, this Province of *Penfilvania*, with divers great Powers and Jurifdictions for the well Government thereof.

AND WHEREAS the King's deareft Brother, *JAMES Duke of YORK and ALBANY*, &c. by his Deeds of Feoffment, under his Hand and Seal duly perfected, bearing Date the *Twenty-Fourth* Day of *Auguft*, *One Thoufand Six Hundred Eighty and Two*, did grant unto me, my Heirs and Affigns, all that Tract of Land, now called the Territories of *Penfilvania*, together with Powers and Jurifdictions for the good Government thereof.

AND WHEREAS for the Encouragement of all the Freemen and Planters, that might be concerned in the faid Province and Territories, and for the good Government thereof, I the faid WILLIAM PENN, in the Year *One Thoufand Six Hundred Eighty and Three*, for me, my Heirs and Affigns, did grant and confirm unto all the Freemen, Planters and Adventurers therein, divers Liberties, Franchifes and Properties, as by the faid Grant, entituled, *The FRAME of the Government of the Province of* Penfilvania, *and Territories thereunto belonging, in* America, may appear ; which Charter or Frame being found in fome Parts of it, not fo fuitable to the prefent Circumftances of the Inhabitants, was in the *Third* Month, in the Year *One Thoufand Seven Hundred*, delivered up to me, by *Six* Parts of *Seven* of the Freemen of this Province and Territories, in General Affembly met, Provifion being made in the faid Charter, for that End and Purpofe.

AND WHEREAS I was then pleafed to promife, That I would

I would restore the said Charter to them again, with necessary Alterations, or in lieu thereof, give them another, better adapted to answer the present Circumstances and Conditions of the said Inhabitants ; which they have now, by their Representatives in General Assembly met at *Philadelphia*, requested me to grant.

KNOW YE THEREFORE, That for the further Well-being and good Government of the said Province, and Territories ; and in Pursuance of the Rights and Powers before-mentioned, I the said *William Penn* do declare, grant and confirm, unto all the Freemen, Planters and Adventurers, and other Inhabitants in this Province and Territories, these following Liberties, Franchises and Privileges, so far as in me lieth, to be held, enjoyed and kept, by the Freemen, Planters and Adventurers, and other Inhabitants of and in the said Province and Territories thereunto annexed, for ever.

FIRST.

No Person believing in One GOD, &c. shall be molested on Account of his Religious Persuasion ;

BECAUSE no People can be truly happy, though under the greatest Enjoyment of Civil Liberties, if abridged of the Freedom of their Consciences, as to their Religious Profession and Worship : And Almighty God being the only Lord of Conscience, Father of Lights and Spirits ; and the Author as well as Object of all divine Knowledge, Faith and Worship, who only doth enlighten the Minds, and persuade and convince the Understandings of People, I do hereby grant and declare, That no Person or Persons, inhabiting in this Province or Territories, who shall confess and acknowledge *One* almighty God, the Creator, Upholder and Ruler of the World ; and profess him or themselves obliged to live quietly under the Civil Government, shall

Nor be compelled to frequent or maintain any Worship contrary to his Mind, &c.

be in any Case molested or prejudiced, in his or their Person or Estate, because of his or their consciencious Persuasion or Practice, nor be compelled to frequent or maintain any religious Worship, Place or Ministry, contrary to his or their Mind, or to do or suffer any other Act or Thing, contrary to their religious Persuasion.

Christians of all Denominations are capable of Offices, promising Allegiance to the King, &c.

AND that all Persons who also profess to believe in *Jesus Christ*, the Saviour of the World, shall be capable (notwithstanding their other Persuasions and Practices in Point of Conscience and Religion) to serve this Government in any Capacity, both legislatively and executively, he or they solemnly promising, when lawfully required, Allegiance to the King as Sovereign, and Fidelity to the Proprietary and Governor, and taking the Attests as now established by the Law made at *New-Castle*, in the Year *One Thousand and Seven Hundred*, entitled, *An Act directing the Attests of several Officers and Ministers*, as now amended and confirmed this present Assembly.

II.

An Assembly shall be chosen yearly.

FOR the well governing of this Province and Territories, there shall be an Assembly yearly chosen, by the Freemen thereof, of, to confift of *Four* Perfons out of each County, of moft Note for Virtue, Wifdom and Ability, (or of a greater Number at any Time, as the Governor and Affembly fhall agree) upon the *Firft* Day of *October* for ever; and fhall fit on the *Fourteenth* Day of the fame Month, at *Philadelphia*, unlefs the Governor and Council for the Time being, fhall fee Caufe to appoint another Place within the faid Province or Territories : Which Affembly fhall *Their Powers* have Power to chufe a Speaker and other their Officers; and *and Privileges.* fhall be Judges of the Qualifications and Elections of their own Members; fit upon their own Adjournments; appoint Committees; prepare Bills in order to pafs into Laws; impeach Criminals, and redrefs Grievances; and fhall have all other Powers and Privileges of an Affembly, according to the Rights of the free-born Subjects of *England*, and as is ufual in any of the King's Plantations in *America*.

AND if any County or Counties, fhall refufe or neglect to *Two Thirds* chufe their refpective Reprefentatives as aforefaid, or if chofen, *met fhall have* do not meet to ferve in Affembly, thofe who are fo chofen *the Power of* and met, fhall have the full Power of an Affembly, in as ample *the whole.* Manner as if all the Reprefentatives had been chofen and met, provided they are not lefs than *Two Thirds* of the whole Number that ought to meet.

AND that the Qualifications of Electors and Elected, and all *The Qualifica-* other Matters and Things relating to Elections of Reprefentatives *tions of Elec-* to ferve in Affemblies, though not herein particularly expreffed, *tors and E-* fhall be and remain as by a Law of this Government, made at *lected.* *New-Caftle* in the Year *One Thoufand Seven Hundred*, entitled, *An Act to afcertain the Number of Members of Affembly, and to regulate the Elections.*

III.

THAT the Freemen in each refpective County, at the Time *Power to chufe* and Place of Meeting for Electing their Reprefentatives to ferve *Sheriffs and* in Affembly, may as often as there fhall be Occafion, chufe a *Coroners.* double Number of Perfons to prefent to the Governor for Sheriffs and Coroners, to ferve for *Three* Years, if fo long they behave themfelves well; out of which refpective Elections and Prefentments, the Governor fhall nominate and commiffionate one for each of the faid Offices, the *Third* Day after fuch Prefentment, or elfe the *Firft* named in fuch Prefentment, for each Office as aforefaid, fhall ftand and ferve in that Office for the Time before refpectively limited; and in Cafe of Death or Default, fuch Vacancies fhall be fupplied by the Governor, to ferve to the End of the faid Term.

PROVIDED ALWAYS, That if the faid Freemen fhall at any Time neglect or decline to chufe a Perfon or Perfons for either or both the aforefaid Offices, then and in fuch Cafe, the Perfons that are or fhall be in the refpective Offices of Sheriffs
b or Co-

or Coroners, at the Time of Election, shall remain therein, until they shall be removed by another Election as aforesaid.

Clerk of the Peace to be nominated by the Justices, &c.

AND that the Justices of the respective Counties shall or may nominate and present to the Governor *Three* Persons, to serve for Clerk of the Peace for the said County, when there is a Vacancy, one of which the Governor shall commissionate within *Ten* Days after such Presentment, or else the *First* nominated shall serve in the said Office during good Behaviour.

I V.

Stile of the Laws.

THAT the Laws of this Government shall be in this Stile, viz. *By the Governor, with the Consent and Approbation of the Freemen in General Assembly met*; and shall be, after Confirmation by the Governor, forthwith recorded in the Rolls Office, and kept at *Philadelphia*, unless the Governor and Assembly shall agree to appoint another **Place.**

V.

Criminals may have Council, &c.

THAT all Criminals shall have the same Privileges of Witnesses and Council as their Prosecutors.

V I.

None shall be obliged to answer, but in ordinary Course of Justice.

THAT no Person or Persons shall or may, at any Time hereafter, be obliged to answer any Complaint, Matter or Thing whatsoever, relating to Property, before the Governor and Council, or in any other Place, but in ordinary Course of Justice, unless Appeals thereunto shall be hereafter by Law appointed.

V I I.

Tavern-keepers, &c. to be recommended before licensed.

THAT no Person within this Government, shall be licensed by the Governor to keep an Ordinary, Tavern or House of publick Entertainment, but such who are first recommended to him, under the Hands of the Justices of the respective Counties, signed in open Court; which Justices are and shall be hereby impowered, to suppress and forbid any Person, keeping such Publick-House as aforesaid, upon their Misbehaviour, on such Penalties as the Law doth or shall direct; and to recommend others from time to time, as they shall see Occasion.

V I I I.

The Estate of Persons destroying themselves, shall descend to their Heirs.

IF any Person, through Temptation or Melancholy, shall destroy himself; his Estate, real and personal, shall notwithstanding descend to his Wife and Children, or Relations, as if he had died a natural Death; and if any Person shall be destroyed or killed by Casualty or Accident, there shall be no Forfeiture to the Governor by Reason thereof.

No Law, &c. shall alter this Charter, without &c.

AND no Act, Law or Ordinance whatsoever, shall at any Time hereafter, be made or done, to alter, change or diminish the Form or Effect of this Charter, or of any Part or Clause therein, contrary to the true Intent and Meaning thereof, without the Con-

Confent of the Governor for the Time being, and *Six* Parts of *Seven* of the Affembly met.

BUT becaufe the Happinefs of Mankind depends fo much upon the Enjoying of Liberty of their Confciences as aforefaid, I do hereby folemnly declare, promife and grant, for me, my Heirs and Affigns, That the *Firft* Article of this Charter relating to Liberty of Confcience, and every Part and Claufe therein, according to the true Intent and Meaning thereof, fhall be kept and remain, without any Alteration, inviolably for ever.

The Article relating to Liberty of Confcience, fhall be inviolable for ever.

AND LASTLY, I the faid *William Penn*, Proprietary and Governor of the Province of *Penfilvania*, and Territories thereunto belonging, for myfelf, my Heirs and Affigns, have folemnly declared, granted and confirmed, and do hereby folemnly declare, grant and confirm, That neither I, my Heirs or Affigns, fhall procure or do any Thing or Things whereby the Liberties in this Charter contained and expreffed, nor any Part thereof, fhall be infringed or broken : And if any thing fhall be procured or done, by any Perfon or Perfons, contrary to thefe Prefents, it fhall be held of no Force or Effect.

The Proprietary folemnly confirms this Charter.

IN WITNESS whereof, I the faid *William Penn*, at *Philadelphia* in *Penfilvania*, have unto this prefent Charter of Liberties, fet my Hand and broad Seal, this *Twenty-Eighth* Day of *October*, in the Year of Our Lord *One Thoufand Seven Hundred and One*, being the *Thirteenth* Year of the Reign of King *WILLIAM the Third*, over *England*, *Scotland*, *France* and *Ireland*, &c. and the *Twenty-Firft* Year of my Government.

Date.

AND NOTWITHSTANDING the Clofure and Teft of this prefent Charter as aforefaid, I think fit to add this following Provifo thereunto, as Part of the fame, *That is to fay*, That notwithftanding any Claufe or Claufes in the above-mentioned Charter, obliging the Province and Territories to join together in Legiflation, I am content, and do hereby declare, that if the Reprefentatives of the Province and Territories fhall not hereafter agree to join together in Legiflation, and that the fame fhall be fignified unto me, or my Deputy, in open Affembly, or otherwife from under the Hands and Seals of the Reprefentatives, for the Time being, of the Province and Territories, or the major Part of either of them, at any Time within *Three* Years from the Date hereof, that in fuch Cafe, the Inhabitants of each of the *Three* Counties of this Province, fhall not have lefs than *Eight* Perfons to reprefent them in Affembly, for the Province ; and the Inhabitants of the Town of *Philadelphia* (when the faid Town is incorporated) *Two* Perfons to reprefent them in Affembly ; and the Inhabitants of each County in the Territories, fhall have as many Perfons to reprefent them in a diftinct Affembly for the Territories, as fhall be by them requefted as aforefaid.

Provifo, that the Province and Territories may feparate in Legiflation ;

NOT-

And shall nevertheless enjoy separately the Privileges granted to them jointly.

NOTWITHSTANDING which Separation of the Province and Territories, in Respect of Legislation, I do hereby promise, grant and declare, That the Inhabitants of both Province and Territories, shall separately enjoy all other Liberties, Privileges and Benefits, granted jointly to them in this Charter, any Law, Usage or Custom of this Government heretofore made and practised, or any Law made and passed by this General Assembly, to the Contrary hereof, notwithstanding.

WILLIAM PENN.

Acceptation.

THIS CHARTER of PRIVILEGES *being distinctly read in Assembly; and the whole and every Part thereof, being approved of and agreed to, by us, we do thankfully receive the same from our Proprietary and Governor, at* Philadelphia, *this* Twenty-Eighth Day *of* October, *One Thousand Seven Hundred and One. Signed on Behalf, and by Order of the Assembly,*

per Joseph Growdon, *Speaker.*

Edward Shippen,	*Griffith Owen,*	} Proprietary and Governor's Council.
Phineas Pemberton,	*Caleb Pusey,*	
Samuel Carpenter,	*Thomas Story.*	

LAWS

OF THE

GOVERNMENT

OF

New-Castle, *Kent* and *Sussex*

Upon *Delaware*.

Published by Order of the ASSEMBLY.

PHILADELPHIA:

Printed and Sold by B. FRANKLIN, at the *New Printing-Office*, in *Market-Street*.

M,DCC,XLI.

An ACT *obliging the Officers of this Government to give Security.*

NOTHING being more juft nor reafonable, than *Preamble:* that Thofe, who by Virtue of any Publick Office in this Government enjoy Profit and Truft, fhould for the refpective Offices to the refpective Counties give good and lawful Security.

BE IT THEREFORE ENACTED by the Honourable *CHARLES GOOKIN*, Efq; by and with Her Majefty's Royal Approbation, Lieutenant-Governor of the Counties of *Newcaftle, Kent* and *Suffex* upon *Delaware*, and Province of *Pennfylvania*, by and with the Advice and Confent of the Freemen in Affembly met, and by the Authority of the fame, That all Perfon and Perfons who by Virtue of any Commiffion, poffefs and enjoy any Poft or Office of Profit or Truft within this Her Majefty's Go- vernment, fhall at the next Quarter-Seffions within their *Officers to give* refpective Counties, after Publication hereof, give Security *Juftices, &c.* to the Juftices of the Peace for the Time being, or to the *Security to the* Treafurer of the faid County, for their refpective Offices; and that all Perfon or Perfons who fhall hereafter hold or enjoy any Poft of Profit or Truft, fhall at the next Quarter- Seffions to be held for their refpective Counties, after the Receipt of his or their Commiffion, give to the Juftices of the Peace, or to the Treafurer of the faid County, Security as abovefaid; and any Perfon or Perfons in any Poft or Commiffion, refufing to give Security as above ordained, *On Penalty of* fhall for fuch Contempt forfeit his faid Poft or Office, *forfeitures their* and is hereby debarred from enjoying and poffeffing the *Offices, &c.* fame or any other Poft within this Government, for the Space of Three Years.

PROVIDED ALWAYS, and it is hereby En- acted, That the Juftices of the Peace, or Treafurer for the refpective Counties, to whom the faid Securities fhall be given,

given, shall not, nor are hereby impovered to take more
Security not to exceed 500 l. nor be less than 300 l. than *Five Hundred Pounds* current Money, nor less than *Three Hundred Pounds* Money aforesaid, for any of the said Officers Security, which shall be by Recognizance with one good Surety.

PROVIDED ALWAYS, That all Officers within this Government, who have already given Security, are not comprehended within this Act.

What Officers are to give Security. PROVIDED ALSO, That nothing in this Act mentioned, shall extend to any other Officers, except Register, Recorder, Clerk, Treasurer, and High Sheriff.

Signed by Oder of the House,

JOS. ENGLAND, *Speaker.*

An ACT *for Establishing a Great Seal for this Government.*

Preamble. WHEREAS great Inconveniency has insued to the People of these Counties for want of a Publick Seal in many Acts of Government, which ought to be kept and remain within the Jurisdiction of these Territories, to be used by the Governor as Occasion shall require: For quieting therefore the Minds of the People, by preventing for the future the Disputes which have frequently arisen on this Subject between us and our good Neighbours in the Province of *Pennsylvania,*

BE IT ENACTED by the Honourable *WILLIAM KEITH,* Esq; with His Majesty's Royal Approbation Lieutenant-Governor of the Counties of *New-Castle, Kent* and *Suffex* on *Delaware,* and Province of *Pennsylvania,* and by and with the Advice and Consent of the Freemen of the said Counties in General Assembly met, and by the Authority of the same; That from and after the Rising of this present Sessions of Assembly, a certain Silver-Seal, now in the

the Governor's Cuſtody, with the King of *Great-Britain*'s Arms cut upon it, and the Inſcription DELAWARE round it, ſhall be held and deemed to be the Great Seal of Government in theſe Counties and Territories, to be made uſe of and affixed to all Judicial Writs, of whatſoever Kind iſſued in the King's Name, and made returnable into the Supreme Court of this Government; alſo to all Charters, Patents, Commiſſions, Privileges or Authorities, which the Governor for the Time being, by Virtue of his Commiſſion and Power may or can lawfully grant. AND to the End that the ſaid Seal may have the full Force and Effect to all Intents and Purpoſes, as that of a Great Seal of Government in any other of His Majeſty's Colonies and Plantations in *America*; BE IT ENACTED by the Authority aforeſaid; That all Writs, Charters, Patents, Commiſſions, *&c.* to be hereafter granted by the Governor as aforeſaid, ſhall not be in Force or have any Effect in Law to the Purpoſes therein reſpectively mentioned, until the Sanction of the ſaid Publick Seal be thereunto reſpectively affixed, in the Manner after-mentioned, *that is to ſay,* Either by the Governor for the Time being himſelf, who is hereby and always underſtood to be the principal and ſole Keeper of the ſaid Great Seal of Government; or by ſuch Perſon or Perſons as he ſhall think fit to appoint from time to time under him, ſuch Perſon or Perſons firſt obtaining a Warrant under the Governor's Sign Manual and Seal at Arms, for affixing each Stamp or Impreſſion of the ſaid Great Seal reſpectively, before he or they ſhall preſume to execute that Part of their Office, ſuch Warrant granted by the Governor from time to time as aforeſaid, to be carefully preſerved upon a File in the Office, where the ſaid Great Seal is kept. AND if any Perſon or Perſons ſhall either by Stealth, or by any pretended Authority whatſoever, preſume or dare to affix the Impreſſion of the ſaid Great Seal unto any Parchment or Paper, or otherwiſe, than by Warrant under the Governor's Sign Manual and Seal at Arms, as aforeſaid to be kept in the Office, as a Voucher for their ſo doing; he or they ſhall ſorfeit the Sum of *Two Hundred Pounds,* to be levied for the Governor's Uſe, and ſhall be declared for ever incapable of any publick Truſt, and undergo the Puniſhment inflicted by Law in the Caſe of Perſons convict of Forgery. AND for Defraying the neceſſary Charges which the Governor muſt be at, not only in providing this Seal with the Utenſils, or Parchment, Paper, Wax and Wafers, *&c.* but alſo in keeping an Office of Record, ſuitable to the Authority of a Great Seal, with a

Uſe of the Seal.

Writs, Charters, &c. not to be of Force until ſealed, &c.

The Governor is principal Keeper of the Seal.

The Officer appointed by him, not to affix the Seal without his Warrant.

Penalty on affixing the Seal without the Governor's Warrant.

B 13 ſufficient

fufficient Clerk or Clerks to give conftant Attendance on that Duty; BE IT ENACTED by the Authority aforefaid, That for each Impreffion of the faid Seal iffuing out of that Office, there fhall be paid by the Party at whofe Defire or for whofe Benefit the faid Seal is granted, to the Clerk of the Office, or other Perfon appointed by the Governor for the fame, the Sum of *Twenty Shillings* for the Governor's own proper Ufe, as a Recompence for the Expence and Trouble of keeping the Office of the Great Seal of this Government.

Fee to the Governor's Ufe for each Impreffion of the Seal.

Signed by Order of the Houfe,

JOHN FRENCH, *Speaker.*

An ACT obliging all Non-Refidenters within this Government to give Security to the Prothonotaries of thefe Counties, before any Writ can iffue from their faid Offices for the Payment of the Cofts.

BE IT ENACTED by the Honourable *WILLIAM KEITH*, Efq; by and with His Majefty's Royal Approbation, Lieutenant-Governor of the Counties of *New-Caftle*, *Kent* and *Suffex* on *Delaware*, and Province of *Pennfylvania*, by and with the Advice and Confent of the Reprefentatives of the faid Counties in General Affembly met, and by the Authority of the fame; That no Prothonotary or Clerk of any County of this Government, fhall grant or iffue any Writ to any Perfon whatfoever, who is not an Inhabitant within this His Majefty's Government, without caufing and obliging every fuch Perfon firft to give Security for the Cofts and Charges that may accrue by fuch Writ or Action; which faid Security fhall be by a fubftantial Inhabitant of that County where fuch Action is commenced.

No Prothonotary, &c. to grant a Writ to a Non-Refidenter without Security, &c.

AND BE IT FURTHER ENACTED by the Authority aforefaid, That every Attorney who

fues

sues out any Process for any Person not an Inhabitant, and who has not given Security as aforesaid, shall be liable and made answerable for the Costs and Charges of the said Action to such Prothonotary where the said Office is kept.

Attornies suing out Process for a Non-Resident without Security, shall be answerable for Costs, &c.

AND BE IT FURTHER ENACTED by the Authority aforesaid, That every Prothonotary or Clerk who issues out any Writ without such Security as above mentioned, shall be liable for the Charges and Costs himself; any Law, Custom or Usage to the contrary in any wise notwithstanding.

And the Prothonotary, &c. issuing Writs without Security, shall be liable for Costs, &c.

Signed by Order of the House,

JOHN FRENCH, *Speaker.*

An ACT *for reducing the Interest of Money from Eight to* Six *per Cent. per annum.*

BE IT ENACTED by Sir *WILLIAM KEITH,* Baronet, Governor of *New-Castle, Kent* and *Sussex* Counties upon *Delaware,* and Province of *Pennsylvania,* by and with the Advice and Consent of the Representatives of the Freemen of the said Counties in General Assembly met, and by the Authority of the same; That no Person shall, directly or indirectly, for any Bonds or Contracts to be made after the Publication of this Act, take for the Loan or Use of Money, or any other Commodities, above the Value of *Six Pounds,* for the Forbearance of *One Hundred Pounds,* or the Value thereof, for One Year, and so proportionably for a greater or lesser Sum; any Law, Custom or Usage to the contrary notwithstanding.

No Person shall take above 6 l. for Forbearance of 100 l. one Year.

AND BE IT FURTHER ENACTED, That if any Person or Persons whatsoever do or shall (after the Publication of this Act) receive or take more than *Six Pounds per Cent. per annum,* on any such Bond or Contract as aforesaid; upon Conviction thereof, the Person or Persons so offending shall forfeit the Money, and other Things lent, the

Penalty.

the one Half thereof to the Governor, for the Support of Government, and the other Half to the Person who shall sue for the same, by Action of Debt, Bill, Plaint or Information, in any Court of Record within this Government, wherein no Essoign, Protection or Wager of Law, nor any more than one Imparlance, shall be allowed.

Signed by Order of the House,

JOHN FRENCH, *Speaker.*

An ACT for the Advancement of Justice, and more certain Administration thereof.

Preamble. WHEREAS the common Law is justly esteemed to be the Birth-Right of *English* Subjects, and ought to be regarded in this Government as the safest Rule of our Conduct; and whereas Acts of Parliament have been adjudged not to extend to these Plantations, except when they are particularly named in the Body of such Act; And forasmuch as some Persons have been encouraged to transgress certain Statutes against Capital Crimes, and other Enormities, because those Statutes have not been hitherto fully extended to this Government; And also, that His Majesty's good Subjects the Inhabitants thereof, have not yet been so happy as to obtain the Royal Confirmation of any Law for the better Establishment of their Constitution and Government : For the preventing therefore any Failure for the future, in that Behalf, may it please the Governor that it may be Enacted;

AND BE IT ENACTED by *WILLIAM KEITH*, Esq; by and with His Majesty's Approbation and Appointment, Lieutenant and Governor of the Counties of *New-Castle*, *Kent* and *Sussex* upon *Delaware*, and Province of *Pennsylvania*, by and with the Advice and Consent of the Freemen of the said Counties in General Assembly met, and by the Authority of the same; That all Inquests and Trials of High-Treason shall be according to due Order and

and Course of Common Law, observing the Directions of the Statute-Laws of *Great-Britain*, relating to the Trials, Proceedings and Judgments in such Cases. *Trials of High-Treason.*

AND BE IT FURTHER ENACTED, That the Enquiries and Trials of all Petty-Treasons, Misprisions of Treasons, Murders, Man-slaughters, Homicides, and all such other Crimes and Misprisions, as by this Act, or any other Act of Assembly of this Government, are or shall be made Capital, or Felony of Death, which have been or shall be done, committed, perpetrated, or happen within this Government, shall be as by this Act is directed. *Trials of Petty-Treason, &c.*

AND WHEREAS the several Crimes declared by this Act to be Felonies of Death, are by the Course of the Laws of that Part of *Great-Britain* called *England*, to be enquired of, and tried by Justices, Juries, and Witnesses upon their Oaths; but forasmuch as many of the Inhabitants of this Government are such, who for Conscience sake cannot take an Oath in any Case, yet, without their Assistance, Justice cannot be well administred, and too great a Burthen will fall upon the other Inhabitants; BE IT THEREFORE ENACTED by the Authority aforesaid, That all and all Manner of Crimes and Offences, Matters and Causes whatsoever, to be enquired of, heard, tried and determined by Virtue of this or any other Law of this Government, or otherwise shall and may be enquired of, heard, tried and determined by Judges, Justices, Inquests and Witnesses, qualifying themselves according to their conscientious Persuasions respectively, either by taking a corporal Oath, or by taking the solemn Affirmation allowed by Act of Parliament to those called *Quakers* in *Great-Britain*; which Affirmation of such Persons as conscientiously refuse to take an Oath, shall be accounted and deemed in the Law to have the full Effect of an Oath, in any Case whatsoever in this Government. And that all such Persons as shall be convicted of falsly and corruptly Affirming or Declaring any Matter or Thing, which, if the same had been upon Oath, would by Law amount to wilful and corrupt Perjury, shall incur the same Penalties, Forfeitures and Disabilities, as Persons convicted of wilful Perjury do incur by the Laws of *Great-Britain*. And that upon all Trials of the said Capital Crimes, lawful Challenges shall be allowed, and learned Council assigned to the Prisoners, and shall have Process to compel Witnesses to appear for them upon any of the said Trials; but *All Crimes to be tried upon Oath or Affirmation.* *Affirmation to have the Effect of an Oath.* *False Affirmations to be punished as Perjury.* *Challenges to be allowed to Prisoners, &c.*

before such Witnesses shall be admitted to depose or give any Manner of Evidence, they shall first take an Oath or Affirmation to say the Truth, the whole Truth and nothing but the Truth, in such Manner as the Witnesses for the King are by the Laws of this Government obliged to do;

Witnesses con-
victed of Perju-
ry shall be puni-
shed accordingly.
and if convicted of any wilful Perjury in such Evidence, shall suffer all the Punishments, Penalties, Forfeitures and Disabilities, which by any of the Laws and Statutes of *Great-Britain* are or may be inflicted upon such Persons convicted of wilful Perjury. But if any of the said Pri-

Persons stand-
ing mute, &c.
suffer as Felons
convict, &c.
soners shall upon their Arraignment for any of the said Crimes, stand mute, or not answer directly, or shall per-emptorily challenge above the Number of Twenty Persons returned to serve of the Jury; he or they so offending shall suffer as a Felon Convict, and shall lose the Benefit of the Clergy and of this Act, in the same Manner as he or they should have done if they had been indicted, arraigned, and found guilty, if it appear to the Justices, before whom such Felons be arraigned, by Evidence given before them or by Examination, that the same Felonies, whereon they are so arraigned, had been such Felonies by reason where-of they should have lost the Benefit of their Clergy. And when any Person or Persons shall be so, as aforesaid, con-victed or attainted of any of the said Crimes, they shall suffer as the Laws of *Great-Britain* now do or hereafter

Justices to give
Judgment ac-
cordingly.
shall direct and require in such Cases respectively. And it shall and may be lawful for the Justices of the Court, where any of the said Attainders or Convictions shall happen, to give and pronounce such Judgment or Sentence against the Persons so attainted or convicted, as their Crimes respectively require, according to the Manner, Form and Direction of the Laws of that Part of *Great-Britain* called *England*, in the like Cases; and thereupon to award and order Execu-tion to be done accordingly.

AND BE IT FURTHER ENACTED

Persons convict
of Sodomy, &c.
shall suffer as
Felons.
by the Authority aforesaid, That if any Person or Persons shall commit Sodomy, or Buggery, or Rape, or Robbery, which Robbery is done by assaulting another on or near the Highway, putting in Fear, and taking from his Person Money or other Goods, to any Value whatsoever; he or they so offending, or committing any of the said Crimes within this Government, their Counsellors, Aiders, Com-forters and Abettors being convicted thereof, as aforesaid; shall suffer as Felons, according to the Tenor, Direction, Form and Effect of the several Statutes in such Cases re-

spectively

spectively made and provided in *Great-Britain* ; any Act or Law of this Government to the contrary in any wise notwithstanding.

AND BE IT FURTHER ENACTED by the Authority aforesaid, That if any Woman shall be delivered of any Issue of her Body, Male or Female, which being born alive, should by the Law be deemed a Bastard, and that she endeavours privately, either by Drowning, or secret Burying thereof, or any other Way, by herself or the procuring of others, so to conceal the Death thereof as it may not come to Light, whether it were born alive or not, but be concealed ; in every such Case the Mother so offending, being convicted thereof according to the usual Course of Proceeding in Capital Crimes within this Government, shall suffer Death, as in Case of Murder, except such Mother can make Proof by one Witness at the least, that the Child, whose Death was by her so intended to be conceal'd, was born dead. And if any Person or Persons shall counsel, advise or direct such Woman to kill the Child she goes with, and, after she is delivered of such Child, she kills it ; every such Person so advising or directing, shall be deemed Accessary to such Murder, and shall have the same Punishment as the Principal shall have.

Women concealing the Death of their Bastards to be deemed Murderers.

Accessaries to such Murder:

AND BE IT FURTHER ENACTED by the Authority aforesaid, That the Statute against Stabbing, made in the First Year of the Reign of King *JAMES the First*, Chapter the Eighth, entituled, *An Act to take away the Benefit of the Clergy for some kind of Manslaughter* ; shall be duly observed and put in Execution in this Government, and be of like Force and Effect as if the same Act were here repeated and enacted : But that all such Persons as shall happen to be present and aiding to the stabbing another, which by the said Act is made Murder, shall not be deemed Principals, but Accessaries to such Stabbing.

The Statute against Stabbing extended here.

AND BE IT FURTHER ENACTED by the Authority aforesaid, That if any Person or Persons on Purpose, and of Malice fore-thought, and by lying in Wait, shall unlawfully cut out, or disable the Tongue, put out an Eye, slit the Nose, cut off the Nose or Lip, or cut off or disable any Limbs or Members of any of the King's Subjects, with Intention in so doing to maim or disfigure in any of the Manners before mentioned, such his Majesty's Subjects ;

Persons convicted of cutting out or disabling the Tongue, &c. shall suffer as Felons.

19

Subjects; that then and there in every such Case the Person or Persons so offending, their Counsellors, Aiders and Abettors, knowing of and privy to the Offence as aforesaid, shall suffer Death, as in Cases of Felony, without Benefit of the Clergy.

The Statute against Conjuration, &c. extended. AND BE IT FURTHER ENACTED by the Authority aforesaid, That another Statute, made in the First Year of the Reign of King *JAMES the First*, Chapter the Twelfth, entituled, *An Act against Conjuration, Witchcraft, and dealing with evil and wicked Spirits*, shall be duly put in Execution in this Government, and of like Force and Effect as if the same were here repeated and enacted.

Burglary how to be punished. AND BE IT FURTHER ENACTED by the Authority aforesaid, That if any Person or Persons shall be so, as aforesaid, convict of Burglary, which is a Breaking and Entering into the Dwelling-House of another in the Night-time, with an Intent to kill some reasonable Creature, or to commit some other Felony within the same House, whether the felonious Intent be executed or not, he or they so offending within this Government, being convicted thereof as aforesaid, shall suffer Death, without Benefit of Clergy; any Law of this Government to the contrary notwithstanding.

Burning of Houses. AND if any Person or Persons shall be so, as aforesaid, convicted of maliciously and voluntarily Burning the Dwelling-House, Barn, Stable, or Out-House of another, having Corn or Hay therein; he or they so offending within this Government, shall suffer Death; any Law of this Government to the contrary notwithstanding.

AND BE IT FURTHER ENACTED by the Authority aforesaid, That if any principal Offender in any Capital Crime, which by the Laws of this Government for the Time being is made Felony of Death, shall be convicted of any such Felony, or shall stand mute, or peremptorily challenge above the Number of Twenty Persons returned to serve of the Jury; it shall and may be *Accessaries to Capital Crimes how to be proceeded against.* lawful to proceed against any Accessary, either before or after the Fact, in the same Manner as if such principal Felon had been attainted thereof, notwithstanding any such principal Felon shall be admitted to the Benefit of his Clergy, pardoned or otherwise delivered before Attainder;

and

and every such Accessary shall suffer the same Punishment, if he or she be convicted, or stand mute, or peremptorily challenge above the Number of Twenty Persons returned to serve of the Jury, as he or she should have suffered if the Principal had been attainted.

AND BE IT FURTHER ENACTED by the Authority aforesaid, That if any Person or Persons shall receive, harbour or conceal any of the said Robbers or Burglars, Felons or Thieves, or shall receive or buy any Goods or Chattels that shall be feloniously taken or stolen by any such Robbers or Burglars, Felons or Thieves, knowing the same to be stolen, and being so, as aforesaid, convicted of either of the said Offences; if he or they pray to have the Benefit of this Act in Lieu of Clergy, Judgment of Death shall not be given against them upon such Conviction, nor Execution awarded upon any Outlawry for such Offence, but they shall be Burnt in their Hands, in Manner as herein after directed. *Persons concealing Robbers, Burglars, &c. to be burnt in the Hand.*

PROVIDED ALWAYS, That if any such principal Robber or Burglar, Felon or Thief cannot be taken, so as to be prosecuted and convicted for any such Offence, nevertheless it shall be lawful to prosecute and punish every such Person and Persons, buying or receiving any Goods stolen by any such principal Felon, knowing the same to be stolen as for a Misdemeanor, to be punished by Fine and Imprisonment, or other such corporal Punishment, as the Court shall think fit to inflict, although the principal Felon be not before convict of the said Felony; which Punishment shall exempt the Offender from being punished as Accessary, if such principal Felon shall be afterwards taken and convicted. *Accessaries to be punished by Fine, &c. if the Principal cannot be taken.*

AND BE IT FURTHER ENACTED by the Authority aforesaid, That if any Person or Persons who have been indicted or appealed, or hereafter shall be indicted or appealed for any of the said Crimes, did not or will not appear to answer such Indictment or Appeal, the Justices before whom the same hath been or shall be taken, shall award a Writ, called *Capias*, against every such Offender, directed to the Sheriff of the County where the Party indicted or appealed are by such Indictment or Appeal supposed to be conversant or inhabit, returnable before the Justices of that Court, where such Party is or shall be so indicted or appealed at the Supream or Provincial Court *If Persons indicted do not appear, Capias shall be awarded.*

D

21

next

next after the taking such Indictment or Appeal; by which Writ of *Capias* the same Sheriff shall be commanded to take the Body of him or them so indicted or appealed, if he or they can be found in his Bailiwick; and if he or they cannot be found, the Sheriff shall make Proclamation in every Court of Quarter-Sessions, which shall be held for the said County where the said Party indicted or appealed is supposed to inhabit or be conversant as aforesaid; That he or they, being so indicted or appealed, shall appear before the said Justices at the said Supream Court, on the Day of the Return of the said Writ of *Capias*, to answer our Lord the King, or to the Party, of the Treason, Felony or Trespass whereof he or they are so indicted or appealed. Which Writ shall be delivered to the said Sheriff or Sheriffs Three Months before the Return thereof; after which Writ of *Capias* so served and returned, if he who is so indicted or appealed, comes not at the said Day of Return of the said *Capias*, and yield his Body to the Sheriff, he shall be by the Justices of the said Supream Court pronounced outlawed and attainted of the Crime, whereof he is so indicted or appealed as aforesaid; and from that Time shall forfeit and lose all his Lands and Tenements, Goods and Chattels. Which Forfeiture, and all other Forfeitures expressed or implied by the Judgments to be given upon the said Capital Offences mentioned in this Act, after such Criminals just Debts and the reasonable Charges of their Maintenance in Prison, are deducted, shall go one Half to the Governor for the Time being, towards Support of this Government, and for defraying the Charges of Prosecution, Trial, and Execution of such Criminals; and the other Half, or Residue thereof, shall go to such Criminal's Wife and Children equally: But if he leaves no Wife or Children, then to the next of his Kindred, not descending lower than the second Degree, to be claimed within Three Years after the Death of such Criminals; otherwise the same shall go to the Governor, as aforesaid; any Law or Usage to the contrary notwithstanding.

The Sheriff to make Proclamation,

That the Offender appear, &c.

Forfeitures.

PROVIDED ALWAYS, AND BE IT FURTHER ENACTED, That where any Person or Persons charged, committed to Prison, or convicted of any of the said Capital Crimes, being justly indebted to any other Person or Persons; he or they so indebted may be arrested, or their Goods and Chattels attached, to answer the Suits of their respective Creditors; who, making due Proof that the Debts or Sums demanded are really and without

Criminals to answer for their Debts.

without Fraud due, ſhall recover Judgment for the ſame, and Executions may be awarded againſt the Lands, Goods and Chattels of ſuch Defendants, as is uſual in other Caſes.

PROVIDED ALSO, That he or they who ſhall happen to break Priſon, ſhall not have Judgment of Life or Member for Breaking of Priſon only; except the Cauſe for which he or they were taken and impriſoned, did require ſuch Judgment, had he been convict according to Law.

Breakers of Priſons.

AND BE IT FURTHER ENACTED by the Authority aforeſaid, That if any Perſon be convicted of any ſuch Felony as is hereby made Capital, for which he ought by the Laws of *Great-Britain* to have the Benefit of his Clergy, and ſhall pray to have the Benefit of this Act; he ſhall not be required to read, but without any Reading ſhall be allowed, taken and reputed to be, and puniſhed as a Clerk Convict, and burnt, if for Murder, with an M upon the Brawn of the Left Thumb, and if for any other Felony, with a T in the ſame Place of the Thumb; which Marks are to be made by the Goaler in open Court, as is uſual in *Great-Britain*; which ſhall be effectual to all Intents and Purpoſes, and be as advantageous to him, as if he had read as a Clerk; any Law or Uſage to the contrary notwithſtanding.

Such as by Law have Benefit of Clergy, to have the Benefit of this Act,

And without Reading be as Clerks Convict, and burnt in the Hand.

AND that the ſaid Juſtices, before whom ſuch Offender or Offenders ſhall be tried and convicted, ſhall alſo at their Diſcretion award and give Judgment, That ſuch Offender and Offenders ſhall be committed to ſome Houſe of Correction, or publick Work-Houſe, within the County, Hundred or Place where ſuch Conviction ſhall be, there to remain and be kept without Bail or Mainprize for ſuch Time as ſuch Juſtices ſhall then judge and award, not leſs than Six Months, and not exceeding Two Years, to be accounted from the Time of ſuch Conviction, and an Entry thereof ſhall be made of Record, purſuant to ſuch Judgment and Award; and ſuch Offender and Offenders ſo judged and awarded to remain and be kept in ſuch Houſe of Correction or publick Work-Houſe, ſhall be there ſet at Work and kept at hard Labour, for and during ſuch Time as ſhall be ſo adjudged and awarded: And in Caſe ſuch Perſon or Perſons ſhall refuſe or neglect to work and labour, as they ought to do, the Maſter or Keeper of ſuch Houſe of Correction or publick Work-Houſe reſpectively,

Juſtices may commit them to ſome Houſe of Correction, &c.

is

is hereby required to give such Persons such due Correction as shall be fit and necessary in that Behalf.

If they escape, and be retaken, to be kept longer. AND BE IT FURTHER ENACTED by the Authority aforesaid, That in Case any such Offender or Offenders shall, after such Judgment given, escape out of Prison, or out of such publick Work-House or House of Correction, as he, she or they shall be committed unto, as aforesaid; such Person or Persons being afterwards retaken, shall be brought before one or more of the Provincial Judges, or before two or more of the Justices of the Peace, of such County, Hundred or Place, where such Offender or Offenders shall be so retaken, which Judge or Justices are hereby required to commit such Offender and Offenders to some House of Correction, or publick Work-House, within such County, Hundred or Place, where he, she or they shall be so retaken, there to remain without Bail or Mainprize, for any Time, not less than Twelve Months, and not exceeding Four Years, to be accounted from the Time of such Retaking, and there be set at Work and kept at hard Labour, and receive such due Correction as aforesaid.

The Master of such House neglecting his Duty shall be removed. AND in Case any Master or Keeper of any House of Correction, or publick Work-House, shall neglect to do his Duty, as above directed; any Judge or Justice of Goal-Delivery, upon Complaint and due Proof thereof, upon the Oath or Affirmation of one or more Witnesses to him made, shall be and is hereby impowered to remove such Person from his said Office.

Women convicted of Felony, &c. AND BE IT FURTHER ENACTED by the Authority aforesaid, That where a Man being convicted of any Felony for which he may demand the Benefit of his Clergy; if a Woman be convicted for the same or like Offence, upon her Prayer to have the Benefit of this Act, Judgment of Death shall not be given against her upon such Conviction, or Execution awarded upon any Outlawry for such Offence, but shall suffer the same Punishment as a Man should suffer, that has the Benefit of his Clergy allowed him in the like Case, *That is to say*, Shall be burnt in the Hand, in Manner aforesaid, and further to be kept in Prison for such Time as the Justices in their Discretion shall think fit, so as the same do not exceed **One Year.**

BUT

BUT if any Man er Woman, who have once had the Benefit of this Act, as aforesaid, and shall be again convicted of any other Felony, hereby made Capital or Felony of Death for which a Man might have the Benefit of his Clergy; every such Man and Woman shall be and are hereby totally excluded from having any Benefit or Advantage of this Act, but shall suffer Pains of Death, as in Cases where the Benefit of Clergy is by Law taken away.

No Person to have the Benefit of this Act more than once.

AND BE IT FURTHER ENACTED by the Authority aforesaid, That where any Murder or Felony hath been or hereafter shall be committed in one County of this Government, and one or more Persons shall be Accessary or Accessaries to any such Murder or Felony in another County; that then an Indictment found or taken against any such Accessary or Accessaries, upon the Circumstance of such Matters before Justices of the Peace, or other Justices or Commissioners to enquire of Felonies in the County where such Offences of Accessary or Accessaries in any Manner have been or shall be committed or done, shall be as good and effectual in Law, as if the said principal Offence had been committed or done within the same County where the Indictment against such Accessary hath been or shall be found.

Felonies committed in one County, and Accessaries in another, &c.

AND BE IT FURTHER ENACTED, That the Justices of the said Supream Court, or Two of them, upon Suit to them made, shall write to the Keepers of the Records, where such Principal is or shall be hereafter attainted or convict, to certify them, whether such Principal be attainted, convicted or otherwise discharged of such principal Felony; who upon such Writing to them or any of them directed, shall make sufficient Certificate, in writing under their Seal or Seals to the said Justices, whether such Principal be attainted, convicted, or otherwise discharged or not: And after they, who have the Custody of such Records, do certify that such Principal is attainted, convicted, or otherwise discharged of such Offence by the Law; then the Justices of Goal-Delivery, or Oyer and Terminer, shall proceed upon every such Accessary in the County where he or they became Accessary, in such Manner and Form as if both the said principal Offence and accessary had been committed and done in the same County where the Offence of Accessary was or shall be committed or done. AND that every such Accessary, and other Offenders above expressed, shall answer upon their Arraignments, and receive

Justices to certify, whether such Principal be convicted, &c.

Accessaries how to be judged.

E   25   such

such Trial, Judgment, Order and Execution, and suffer such Forfeitures, Pains and Penalties, as is usual in other Cases of Felony; and as the Statute, made in the Second and Third Year of King *EDWARD the Sixth*, Chapter the Twenty-fourth, entituled, *An Act for the Trial of Murders and Felonies committed in several Counties*, doth direct in such Cases; which Statute shall be observed in this Government, any Law or Usage to the contrary notwithstanding.

Subornation of Perjury.

AND BE IT FURTHER ENACTED by the Authority aforesaid, That every Person who shall unlawfully and corruptly procure any Witness to commit wilful and corrupt Perjury in any Matter or Cause depending in Suit and Variance in any of the Courts of Judicature within this Government, or shall unlawfully and corruptly procure and suborn any Witness to testify upon Oath or Affirmation, in any Matter, Cause or Thing whatsoever; *Penalty,* such Offender shall forfeit the Sum of *Forty Pounds*, one Half thereof to the Governor, for the Support of this Government, and the other Half to the Party grieved: But for want of Lands, Goods or Chattels, to satisfy the said *Forty Pounds*, every such Offender being convicted or attainted of Perjury or Subornation aforesaid, shall for his said Offence suffer Imprisonment by the space of Six *Imprisonment, Pillory.* Months, without Bail, and stand on the Pillory the space of One whole Hour, in some Market or publick Place, where the Offence was committed; and shall suffer all the other Punishments, Penalties, Forfeitures and Disabilities, which are inflicted upon such Offenders by any Law or Statute of *Great-Britain*. AND that the Statute, made in the Fifth Year of Queen *ELIZABETH*, Chapter the Ninth, entituled, *An Act for Punishment of such Persons as shall procure or commit any wilful Perjury*, shall be observed in this Government, and be duly put in Execution, as well against those that shall falsify their Affirmations, as those who shall falsify their Oaths, or be convicted of Subornation of Perjury.

Justices of Goal Delivery may give Judgement of Death against Persons reprieved.

AND BE IT FURTHER ENACTED by the Authority aforesaid, That in all Cases where any Person or Persons have been, or shall be found guilty of any of the said Crimes for which Judgment of Death should or may ensue, and shall be reprieved to Prison, without Judgment at that time given, him, her or them so found guilty; that those who now are or hereafter shall be assigned Justices, or deliver the Goal, where any such guilty Persons shall remain, are hereby impowered and authorized to give Judgment

ment

ment of Death, and award Execution againſt ſuch **Perſons** ſo found guilty and reprieved, as the ſaid Juſtices **before** whom ſuch Perſon or Perſons was or we:e found guilty, might have done before ſuch Reprieve. AND that no manner of Proceſs or Suit made, ſued or had before any of the King's Juſtices of the Supream or Provincial Court, Goal Delivery, Oyer and Terminer, Juſtices of the Peace, or other of the King's Commiſſioners in this Govenrment, ſhall not in any wiſe be diſcontinued by making and pub-liſhing of any new Commiſſion or Aſſociation, or by alter-ing the Names of the Juſtices of the ſaid Supream **Court**, Goal-Delivery, Oyer and Terminer, Juſtices of the **Peace**, or other the King's Commiſſioners; but that the new Juſ-tices of the Supream Court, Goal Delivery, and of the **Peace**, and other Commiſſioners may proceed in every reſpeٕ, **as** if the old Commiſſions and Juſtices and Commiſſioners had ſtill remained and continued unaltered. AND that no Proceſs, Pleas, Suits, Aٕions or Proceedings whatſoever, which now are, or at any time hereafter ſhall be commenced, ſued, brought or depending before any of the ſaid Juſtices of the Supream Court, Juſtices of the Courts of Common Pleas, or other the King's Juſtices, Commiſſioners or Ma-giſtrates in this Government, ſhall be diſcontinued or put without Day, by reaſon of the Death or Removal of the Lieutenant Governor of this Government, or by the Death, new Commiſſion, or not Coming of the ſaid Juſtices or Commiſſioners, or any of them ; but ſhall ſtand good and effeٕual in Law to all Intents and Purpoſes, notwithſtand-ing the Death or Removal of the ſaid Governor, or of the Death, new Commiſſion, Aſſociation, or not Coming of the ſaid Juſtices, or any of them.

No Proceſs to be diſcontinued by reaſon of any new Commiſ-ſions or Alter-ation of Magi-ſtrates, &c

Nor by the Death or Re-moval of the Governor, &c.

AND BE IT FURTHER ENACTED by the Authority aforeſaid, That in caſe of any Officer be-ing a *Quaker*, that notwithſtanding he be ſuch, yet any Oath at the Requeſt of the ſaid Officer, taken before any Magiſtrate, ſhall be deemed equal and full to the Purpoſe, as if adminiſtred by the ſaid Officer, any Law or Uſage to the Contrary notwithſtanding.

Oath adminiſ-tred at the Re-queſt of a Qua-ker, Officer, &c.

PROVIDED ALWAYS, AND BE IT FURTHER ENACTED by the Authority aforeſaid, That no Indiٕment, Preſentment or Inquiſition, or any Proceſs whatſoever now depending in any Court within this Government for any of the Crimes or Offences mentioned in this Aٕ, ſhall be diſcontinued, abated or

No Judgment, &c. now de-pending ſhall be diſcontinued.

27   quaſhed

quafhed for or by reafon of this Act, or any thing therein contained; but that the Judges and Juftices of the refpective Courts within this Government fhall proceed to hear, try and determine the faid Offences in fuch Indictments, Prefentments and Inquifitions mentioned to be committed againft any Act or Acts of Affembly of this Government as were in Force at the Time of finding, making or taking the faid Indictments, Prefentments and Inquifitions, and thereupon to give Judgment and award Executions according to the Directions of the faid refpective Acts of Affembly, upon which the faid Indictments, Prefentments or Inquifitions are founded, as if the fame Act or Acts of Affembly were by a fpecial Claufe in this Act continued for that Purpofe; any thing herein contained to the contrary notwithftanding.

Signed by Order of the Houfe,

JOSEPH ENGLAND, *Speaker.*

An ACT *for eftablifhing Orphans Courts.*

Preamble.

WHEREAS feveral Matters. of great Importance are directed to be done by the Orphans Courts of this Government; but upon Perufal of the Law directing the Doing thereof, the fame appears to be very deficient, and divers Orphans and Perfons concerned for them or entrufted with their Eftates, labour under great Inconveniences: BE IT THEREFORE ENACTED by the Honourable Sir *WILLIAM KEITH*, Baronet, with his Majefty's Royal Approbation, Governor of the Province of *Pennfylvania*, and Counties of *New-Caftle*, *Kent* and *Suffex* on *Delaware*, and by and with the Advice and Confent of the Freemen of the faid Counties, in General Affembly met, and by the Authority of the fame, That the Juftices of the Court of General Quarter-Seffions of the Peace in each County of this Government, or fo many of them as are or fhall be from time to time enabled to hold thofe Courts, fhall have full Power, and are hereby impowered, in the fame Week that they are or fhall be by Law directed to hold the fame Courts,

Juftices of Quarter-Seffions to hold the Orphans Court.

or

or at such other Times as they shall see occasion, to hold and keep a Court of Record in each of the said Counties, which shall be stiled, *The Orphans Court*; and to award Process, and cause to come before them all and every such Person and Persons, who as Guardians, Trustees, Tutors, Executors, Administrators, or otherwise are or shall be entrusted with or any wise accountable for any Lands, Tenements, Goods, Chattels or Estate belonging, or which shall belong to any Orphans or any Persons under Age, and cause them to make and exhibit, within a reasonable time, true and perfect Inventories and Accounts of the said Estates, and to cause and oblige the Register, or such Person or Persons as for the time being shall have the Power of Probate of Wills and granting Letters of Administration in this Government, or their Deputies, upon Application made in that Behalf, to bring or transmit into the Orphan's Court true Copies or Duplicates of all such Bonds, Inventories, Accounts, Actings and Proceedings whatsoever, now or hereafter remaining or being in the respective Offices or elsewhere within the Limits of their Authority, as do or shall concern or relate to the said Estates, or any of them, and to order the Payment of such reasonable Fees for the said Copies, and for all other Charges, Trouble and Attendance which any Officer or other Person shall necessarily be put upon in the Execution of this Act, as they shall think equitable and just; and if upon Hearing or Examination thereof it appears to the Justices of the said Court that any of the said Officers have misbehaved themselves to the Prejudice of any Minor, or any concerned for them as aforesaid, the said Justices are hereby required to certify the same accordingly, which shall be good Evidence for the Party grieved to recover his Damages at Common Law. And where any Letter of Administration shall be granted, and no Bond with Sureties given, as the Law in that Case requires, such Letters of Administration shall be and are hereby declared to be void and of none Effect; and that the Officer or Person that grants the same, and his Sureties, shall be, *ipso facto*, liable to pay all such Damages as shall accrue to any such Person or Persons by occasion of granting such Administration; and the Party to whom the same shall be so granted may be sued as Executor in his own wrong, and shall be so taken and deemed in any Suit to be brought against him for or by reason of his said Administration. Or if upon such Examination it appears that any of the said Officers have not taken sufficient Sureties where the Administrators may not be of Ability to answer or

And may award Process, &c.

Letters of Administration without giving Bond, are void.

F 29 make

make good the Value of what the Decedent's Estate doth
or shall amount to ; then the said Justices of the Orphans
Court are hereby impowered and required to call all such
Administrators to give better Security to the Register by
Bonds, in Manner and Form as the Law prescribes, and
under such Penalties, and with such Sureties as the said
Justices after they have heard the Objections of Creditors
or Persons concerned (if any such be made to the Court)
shall approve of. And if it appears that any of the said Administrators have imbezzled, wasted or misapplied or suffered so to be, any Part of the Decedent's Estates, or shall
neglect or refuse to give Bonds with Sureties as aforesaid,
then, and in every such Case, the said Justices shall forthwith, by their Sentence, revoke or repeal the Letters of
Administration granted them, and thereupon the said Register, or other Person then impowered to grant Administration as aforesaid, where such Occasion happens, are hereby
required to grant Letters of Administration to such Person
or Persons (having Right thereto) as will give Bonds in
Manner and Form aforesaid, who may have their Actions
of Trover or Detinue for such Goods or Chattels as came
to the Possession of the former Administrators, and shall be
detained, wasted, imbezled or misapplied by any of them,
and no Satisfaction made for the same.

If Security given by Administrators be not sufficient, they shall give better.

In case of Im-bezzlement or Refusal of suffi-cient Surety &c. Letters of Ad-ministration may be revoked, and granted to others, &c.

AND BE IT FURTHER ENACTED,
That when any Complaint is made to any of the said
Justices, that an Executrix having Minors of her own, or
being concerned for others, is married, or like to be espou-
sed to another Husband, without securing the Minors Portions or Estates ; or that an Executor or other Person
having the Care and Trust of Minors Estates, is like to
prove Insolvent, or shall refuse or neglect to exhibit true
and perfect Inventories, or give full and just Accounts of
the said Estates, come to their Hands or Knowledge ; then
and in every such Case the same Justices are hereby required forthwith to call an Orphans Court, who shall cause
all and every such Executors and Trustees, as also such
Guardians or Tutors of Orphans or Minors, as have been
formerly appointed or shall at any Time hereafter be appointed by the said Court, to give Security to the Orphans
or Minors, by Mortgage or Bonds, in such Sums and with
such Sureties as the said Court shall think reasonable, conditioned for the Performance of their respective Trusts, and
for the true Payment or Delivery to and for the Use and
Behoof of such Orphans as they are concerned for (or such

In case Minors Estates be in Danger by Ex-ecutors, &c. the Orphans Court shall cause such to give Security.

as shall legally represent them) the Legacies, Portions, Shares and Dividends of Estates, real and personal, belonging to such Orphans or Minors, so far as they have Assets, as also for their Maintenance and Education, as the said Court shall think fit to order for the Benefit and Advantage of such Orphans, as is usual in such Cases.

AND BE IT FURTHER ENACTED, That any of the said Executors, Administrators, Guardians or Trustees, may by the Leave and Direction of the Orphans Court, put out their Minors Money to Interest, upon such Security as the said Court shall allow of; and if such Security so taken *bona fide* and without Fraud, shall happen to prove insufficient, it shall be the Minors Loss : But if no Person, who may be willing to take the said Money at Interest (with such Security) can be found by the Persons so as aforesaid concerned for the Minors, nor by any others, then the said Executors, Guardians, Administrators or Trustees shall in such Cases be responsible for the principal Money only until it can be put out at Interest as aforesaid. *Minors Money may be put out to Interest,*

PROVIDED ALWAYS, That the Day of Payment of the Money so to be put out to Interest, at any one time shall not exceed Twelve Months from the Date of the Obligation or other Security given for the same, and so *toties quoties*, when and so often as the said Money shall be paid or come to the Hands of the said Executors, Guardians or Trustees. *Not exceeding 12 Months at one time.*

PROVIDED ALSO, That no Executors, Administrators or Guardians, shall be liable to pay Interest, but for the Surplusage of the Decedent's Estate, remaining in their Hands or Powers, and belonging to the Minors, when the Accounts of their Administration are or ought to be settled and adjusted before the Orphans Court or Register respectively.

AND BE IT FURTHER ENACTED, That the Justices of the said Orphans Court, in the said respective Counties, shall by Virtue of this Act have full Power and Authority, to exercise all the Powers, Authorities and Jurisdictions granted or mentioned, or intended to be granted to the Orphans Court, in and by a Law of this Government, entitled, *An Act for the better settling Intestates Estates*; and to do, execute and perform all such Matters and Things as the Orphans Court in the said Act mentioned, *Farther Authority of the Orphans Court.*

might

might or ought to have done or performed according to the true Intent and Meaning thereof; with Power also to admit Orphans or Minors, when and as often as there may be Occasion to make Choice of Guardians or Tutors, and to appoint Guardians next Friends, or Tutors over such as the Court shall judge too young, or uncapable according to the Rules of the Common Law, to make Choice themselves; and at the Instance and Request of the said Executors, Administrators, Guardians or Tutors, to order and direct the binding or putting out of Minors Apprentices to Trades, Husbandry or other Employments, as shall be thought fit; and that all Guardians and Prochein Amies, which shall be appointed by any of the said Orphans Courts, shall be allowed and received without further Admittance to prosecute and defend all Actions and Suits relating to the Orphans or Minors, as the Cause may require in any Court or Courts of this Government.

Persons summoned and not appearing, &c. may be punished by Imprisonment, &c.

AND if any Person or Persons, being duly summoned to appear in any of the said Orphans Courts Ten Days before the Time appointed for their Appearance, shall make Default, the Justices may send their Attachments for Contempts, and may force Obedience to their Warrants, Sentence or Orders concerning any Matter or Thing cognizable in the same Courts, by Imprisonment of Body or Sequestration of Lands or Goods, as fully as any Court of Equity may or can do.

Persons aggrieved may appeal to the Supream Court.

PROVIDED ALWAYS, That if any Person or Persons shall be aggrieved with any definitive Sentence or Judgment of the said Orphans Court, it shall be lawful for them to appeal from the same to the Governor for the time being, in Equity, which Appeal, upon Security given as is usual in such Cases, shall be granted accordingly.

Discharges for Money, &c by Executors, are binding to the Orphans.

AND if any of the said Executors, Administrators, Guardians or Trustees did or shall receive and give Discharges for any Sums of Money, Debts, Rents or Duties belonging to any Orphan or Minor, for whom they were or are intrusted; It is hereby Declared and Enacted, That all such Discharges or Receipts shall be binding to and upon the Orphan or Minor, when he or she attains to full Age, and shall be most effectual in Law to discharge the

Bonds how to be cancelled.

Person or Persons that take the same. And when any of the said Minors attain to full Age, and the Person or Persons so as aforesaid entrusted or concerned for them, having

rendered

rendered their Accounts to the Orphans Court according to the Direction of this and the said other Acts, and paid the Minors their full Due; then such Minors shall acknowledge Satisfaction in the said Court : But in case any of them refuse so to do, then the said Court shall certify how the said Persons concerned have accounted and paid, which shall be a sufficient Discharge to the Guardians or Tutors, and to the Trustees, Executors or Administrators, who shall so account and pay; and thereupon all Bonds entered into for Payment of such Orphans Portions, shall be delivered up and cancelled.

PROVIDED ALWAYS, AND BE IT FURTHER ENACTED, That none of the said Orphans Courts shall have any Power to order or commit the Tuition or Guardianship of any Orphans or Minors, or to bind them Apprentices, to any Person or Persons of a Religious Persuasion, that shall be different from what the Parents of such Orphan or Minor professed at the time of their Decease, or against the Minor's own Mind or Inclination, so far as he or she has Discretion and Capacity to express and signify the same, or to Persons that are not of good Repute, so as others of good Credit and the same Perswasion may or can be found.

What Persons may have the Charge of Orphans or Minors.

PROVIDED ALSO, that the Justices of the said Courts, and all others, concerned in the Execution of this Act, shall have due regard to the Direction of all last Wills and Testaments, and to the true Intent and Meaning of the Testators, in all Matters and Things that shall be brought before them concerning the same.

Due Regard to be had to Wills &c.

AND BE IT FURTHER ENACTED, That all such Bonds or Obligations as are by this Act, or by any other Law of this Government, directed and required to be given to the Governor, and all such Bonds as by any Law are directed to be given by the Register, or by any other Officers or Persons in Office whatsoever in this Government, for the due Execution of his or their respective Offices or Imployments, ARE HEREBY DECLARED to be to, and for the Use of, and in Trust for the Person or Persons concerned; and that the Benefit thereof shall be extended, from time to time, for the Relief and Advantage of the Party grieved by the Mis-feazance or Non-feazance of the Officers that did or shall give the same: And that when any of the said Bonds shall be put in Suit, and

Bonds directed to be given by any Law, &c. to be for the Use of the Persons concerned, &c.

G
33
Judgment

Judgment thereupon obtained, the Judgment shall remain in the same Nature the Bonds were, and that no Execution issue out thereupon, before the Party grieved shall by Writ of *Scire Facias* summon the Person or Persons, against whom the said Judgment is obtained, to appear and shew Cause why Execution shall not issue upon the said Judgment; and if the Party grieved shall prove what Damages he sustained, and thereupon a Verdict be found for him, the Court of Common Pleas (where such Suits is) shall award Execution for so much as the Jury shall then find, with Costs, and no more. And the former Judgment is hereby declared still to remain Cautionary, for the Satisfaction of such others as shall legally prove themselves damnified, and recover their Damages in the *Clerks of Courts &c. required to give Copies of such Bonds, &c.* manner aforesaid: And the said Clerks of the Courts of Common Pleas and all others, in whose Hands the said Bonds shall be deposited or lodged, are hereby required to give any Person injured, that requests the same, a true Copy of any of the said Bonds, paying *Three Shillings* for the same, and to produce the Original in Court upon any Tryal that shall be had for the Breach of any of them, if required by the Court : And if the Person in whose Hands the said Bonds shall be lodged or come, shall refuse or delay to give Copies thereof, and produce the Original in Court as aforesaid, he or they shall forfeit and pay to the Party grieved, Treble Damages, to be recovered against the Officer that hath such Bonds, or his Sureties, by Action of Debt, Bill, Plaint, or Information, in any Court of this Government, where no Essoign, Protection, or Wager of Law, or any more than one Imparlance shall be allowed.

Signed by Order of the House,

JOHN FRENCH, *Speaker.*

An

An ACT *for the better settling Intestates Estates.*

BE IT ENACTED by the Honourable Sir *WILLIAM KEITH*, Baronet, with the Royal Approbation, Lieutenant Governor of the Province of *Pennsylvania*, and the Counties of *New-Castle*, *Kent*, and *Sussex*, on *Delaware*, by and with the Advice and Consent of the Freemen of the said Counties in Assembly met, and by the Authority of the same, That the Registers of the several Counties of this Government, having Power to grant Letters of Administration of the Goods and Chattles of Persons dying Intestate within this Government, shall upon their granting such Letters of Administration, take sufficient Bonds with two or more able Sureties (respect being had to the Value of the Estate) in the Name of the Governor for the time being, with the Condition in Manner and Form following, *mutatis mutandis* (viz.)

Registers granting Letters of Administration shall take sufficient Bonds, &c.

*T*HE Condition of this Obligation is such, That if the within-bounden A. B. Administrator of all and singular the Goods, and Chattles, and Credits of C. D. deceased, do make or cause to be made, a true and perfect Inventory of all and singular the Goods, and Chattles, and Credits of the said Deceased, which have or shall come to the Hands, Possession or Knowledge of him the said A. B. or unto the Hands and Possession of any other Person or Persons for him; and the same, so made, do exhibit, or cause to be exhibited into the Registers Office of the County of -------- at or before the -------- Day of -------- next ensuing; and the same Goods, Chattles and Credits of the said Decedant, at the Time of his Death, or which at any Time after shall come to the Hands or Possession of the said A. B. or into the Hands and Possession of any other Person or Persons for him, do well and truly Administer according to Law ; and further, do make or cause to be made a true and just Account of his said Administration at or before the -------- Day of -------- and all the rest and residue of the said Goods, Chattles and Credits which shall be found remaining upon the said Administrators Account (the same being first examined and allowed of by the Orphans-Court of the County where the said Administration is granted) shall deliver and pay unto such Person or Persons respectively, as the said Orphans-Court is

Form of the Condition.

in the respective County, by their Decree or Sentence, pursuant to the true Intent and Meaning of this Act, shall limit and appoint: And if it shall hereafter appear, that any last Will and Testament was made by the said Decedant, and the Executor or Executors therein named, do exhibit the same into the Register's Office, making request to have it allowed and approved accordingly: If the said A. B. within bounden, being thereunto required, do render and deliver the said Letters of Administration (Approbation of such Testament being first had and made in the said Register's Office) then this Obligation to be void and of none Effect, or else to remain in full Force and Virtue.

Which Bonds are hereby Declared and Enacted to be Good, to all Intents and Purposes, and pleadable in any Courts of Justice; and also that the said Orphans-Court in the respective Counties, shall and may, and are hereby *Orphans-Court* enabled to proceed and call such Administrators to account *may call Admi-* for and touching the Goods of any Person dying Intestate; *nistrators to* and upon Hearing and due Consideration thereof, to order *Account, and* *order Distribu-* and make just and equal Distribution of what remaineth *tion, &c.* clear, (after all Debts, Funerals and just Expences of every sort first allowed and deducted) amongst the Wife and Children, and Childrens Children (if any such be) or otherwise to the next of Kindred to the deceased Person, in equal Degree, or legally representing their Stocks, to every one his Right, according to the Laws in such Cases, and the Rules and Limitations hereafter set down: And the same Distributions to decree and settle, and to compel such Administrators to observe and pay the same, by the due Course of the Laws of this Government; saving to every one (supposing him or themselves grieved) their Right of Appeal to the Provincial or Supreme Court of this Government.

PROVIDED ALWAYS, That the said Orphans-Court in each County, which is by this Act enabled to make Distribution of the Surplusage of the Estate of any Person dying Intestate, shall distribute the whole Surplusage of such Estates in Manner and Form following, that is to say, One Third Part of the said Surplusage, to *Manner of Dif-* the Wife of the Intestate, and all the Residue, by equal *tribution.* Portions, to and among the Children of such Persons dying Intestate, and to such Persons as shall legally represent such Children, in Case any of the Children be then dead (other than such Child or Children who shall have any Estate by

the

the Settlement of the Inteſtate, or ſhall be advanced by him in his Life-time by Portion or Portions, equal to the Share which ſhall by ſuch Diſtribution be allotted to the other Children) to whom ſuch Diſtributions are to be made. And in Caſe any Child, who ſhall have any Eſtate by Settlement from the Inteſtate, or ſhall be advanced by the ſaid Inteſtate, in his Life-time by Portion, not equal to the Share which will be due to the other Children by ſuch Diſtribution, as aforeſaid, then ſo much of the Surpluſage of the Eſtate of ſuch Inteſtate, to be diſtributed to ſuch Child or Children as ſhall have any Land by Settlement from the Inteſtate, or were advanced in the Life-time of the Inteſtate, as ſhall make the Eſtate of all the ſaid Children to be equal, as near as can be eſtimated as aforeſaid.

Caſe of Children that have been advanced in the Inteſtate's Life-time.

AND in Caſe there be no Children, nor any legal Repreſentatives of them, then one Moiety of the ſaid Eſtate to be allotted to the Wife of the Inteſtate, and the Reſidue of the ſaid Eſtate to be diſtributed equally to every of the next Kindred of the Inteſtate, who are in equal Degree to thoſe who legally repreſent them.

Where there are no Children, the Wife to have one Moiety, &c.

PROVIDED, That there be no Repreſentatives admitted amongſt Collaterals, after Brothers and Siſters Children. And in Caſe there be no Wife, then all the ſaid Eſtate to be diſtributed equally to and amongſt the Children, the eldeſt Son to have *Two Shares* as aforeſaid.

If no Wife, eldeſt Son to have two Shares

AND in Caſe there be no Child, then to the next of Kindred, in equal Degree of or unto the Inteſtate, and their legal Repreſentatives, as aforeſaid, and in no other manner whatſoever.

PROVIDED ALSO, And to the End that a due regard be had to the Creditors, that no ſuch Diſtribution of the Goods of any Perſon dying Inteſtate, be made till after one Year be expired after the Inteſtate's Death. And that ſuch, and every one to whom any Diſtribution and Share ſhall be allotted, ſhall give Bond, with ſufficient Sureties, to the ſaid Orphans-Court, in the Name of the Governor for the Time being, That if any Debt or Debts, truly owing by the Inteſtate, ſhall be afterwards ſued for and recovered, or otherwiſe duly to be made appear, that then, and in every ſuch Caſe, he or ſhe ſhall reſpectively refund and pay back to the Adminiſtrator, his

No Diſtribution to be made till after one Year be expired, &c.

or her rateable Part of that Debt or Debts, and of the Costs of Suit and Charges of the Administrator, by reason of such Debts, out of the Part or Share, so as aforesaid allotted to him or her, thereby to enable the said Administrator to pay and satisfy the said Debt or Debts so discovered after the Distribution made, as aforesaid.

Proviso in Case of a Testament annexed to the Administration.

PROVIDED ALWAYS, AND BE IT FURTHER ENACTED by the Authority aforesaid, That in all Cases where the Register hath used heretofore to grant Administration, with a Testament annexed, he shall continue so to do ; and the Will of the Deceased, in such a Testament expressed, shall be performed and observed in such manner as it should have been if this Act had never been made.

Relations, &c. not laying Claim in seven Years, to be debarred forever.

PROVIDED ALSO, That all such of the Intestate's Relations, and Persons concerned, who shall not lay legal Claim to their respective Shares within *Seven* Years after the Decease of the Intestate, shall be debarred from the same forever.

Personal Estate not being sufficient to pay Debts, &c. Lands may be sold;

AND BE IT FURTHER ENACTED, by the Authority aforesaid, That if any Person or Persons shall die Intestate, being Owners of Lands and Tenements within this Government at the Time of their Death, and leave lawful Issue to survive them, but not a sufficient personal Estate to pay their just Debts and maintain their Children, Then, and in such Case, it shall be lawful for the Administrator or Administrators of such Decedents, to sell and convey such Part or Parts of the said Lands or Tenements for defraying their just Debts, Maintenance of their Children, and for putting them Apprentices, and teaching them to read and write, and for Improvement of the Residue of the Estate (if any be) to their Advantage, as the Orphans-Court of the County where such Estate lies, shall think fit to allow order and direct from time to time.

Except Lands, &c. contained in Marriage Settlements.

PROVIDED ALWAYS, That no Lands or Tenements contained in any Marriage Settlement, shall, by virtue of this Act, be sold or disposed contrary to the Form and Effect of such Settlement; nor shall any Orphans-Court allow or order any Intestate's Lands or Tenements to be sold, before the Administrator, requesting the same, doth exhibit one or more true and perfect Inventories

tories and confcionable Appraifment of all the Inteftate's *Proceedings in the Sale of Lands directed.* perfonal Eftate whatfoever; and alfo a juft and true Account, upon his or her folemn Affirmation, of all the Inteftate'sDebts which fhall be then come to his or her Knowledge; and if thereupon it fhall appear to the Court, that the Inteftate's perfonal Eftate will not be fufficient to pay the Debts and maintain the Children until the Eldeft of them attains to the Age of Twenty-one Years, or to put them out to be Apprentices or teach them to read and write, then and in every fuch Cafe, and not otherwife, the Court fhall allow fuch Adminiftrator to make publick Sale of the faid Lands, as the Court, upon the beft Computation they can make of the Value thereof, fhall adjudge neceffary for the Purpofes aforefaid, referving the Manfion-Houfe and moft profitable Part of the Eftate till the laft. But before any fuch Sale be made, the Court fhall order fo many Writings to be made by the Clerk upon Parchment or good Paper as the Court fhall think fit to fignify, and give Notice of fuch Sales, and of the Day and Hour when, and the Place where the fame will be, and what Lands are to be fold, and where they lie; which Notice fhall be delivered to the Sheriff or Conftables, in order to be fixt in the moft publick Places of the County, at leaft Ten Days before the Sale; and the Sheriffs or Conftables are hereby required to make Publication accordingly: And the Adminiftrator that makes fuch Sale, fhall bring his or her Proceeding therein to the next Orphans-Court after the Sale made. And if it fhall happen that any Lands be fold by virtue of this Act for more than the Court's Computation of the Value thereof, then the Adminiftrator fhall be accountable for the fame, as by this Act is required for the Inteftate's perfonal Eftates.

AND BE IT FURTHER ENACTED, *Surplufage upon Sale, how to be divided.* by the Authority aforefaid, That the Surplufage or remaining Parts of the Inteftate's Lands, Tenements and Hereditaments, not fold or ordered to be fold by Virtue of this Act, and not otherwife limited by Marriage Settlement, fhall be divided between the Inteftate's Children, or the Survivors of them, who fhall equally inherit, and make Partition as Tenants in common may or can do, the eldeft Son having a double Share.

BUT if the Inteftate leaves no Child, then fuch Widow *If no Child, the Widow to have one Moiety, &c.* or Relict fhall inherit one Moiety or half Part of faid Lands and Tenements, and the other Moiety fhall defcend

and

and come to the Inteftate's next Heir, according to the Courfe of the common Law.

If no Children living, the Heir at Law inherits the Lands, &c. BUT if the Inteftate leaves no Child living at the Time of his Death, or if the Children all die in their Minority, then the faid Lands and Tenements fhall defcend and come to the Inteftate's Heir at Law, according to the Courfe aforefaid.

Unlefs there be Iffue of Children. BUT if any of the Inteftate's Children dying before the Inteftate, fhall leave lawful Iffue, fuch Iffue fhall equally inherit the Inteftate's Lands and Tenements with their Uncles and Aunts, and make Partition as aforefaid.

Child having equal Share by Settlement, to have no Share of the Surplufage. PROVIDED ALWAYS, That no Child of any Inteftate having fo much Land by Settlement from the faid Inteftate, as by the faid Court's Computation of the Value thereof, fhall be equal to the Share or Purport of the Inteftate's Lands, which by this Act, are to be allotted to any of the other Children in manner aforefaid; then fuch Child fo provided for, fhall have no Share of the faid Surplufage of the Inteftate's other Lands.

If the Settlement does not amount to an equal Share, it fhall be made equal. BUT if the Value of the Lands fo settled by the Inteftate, fhall not, by the Computation aforefaid, amount to an equal Share, then the faid Court fhall allot to the Party fo much of the faid Land as fhall make the Shares or Eftates of all the faid Children equal, as near as can be eftimated, the eldeft Son having a double Share as aforefaid.

Widows of Inteftates fhall hold a Third Part of the Lands, &c. PROVIDED ALSO, That the Widows of Inteftates having Lands and Tenements in this Government, fhall hold and enjoy the full Third Part of all the Lands and Tenements of the Inteftate within this Government as her Dower, whereof her Husband died feized, which Dower fhe fhall hold as Tenants in Dower do in *England*; and the profitable Lands or Tenements, and the unimproved or rough Lands next adjacent thereto, fhall not be fold but for Payment of the Inteftate's Debts.

No Partition to be made, if the Heir at Law will pay the Value of Shares in Money, &c. PROVIDED ALSO, That no Partition of the Lands or Tenements which are to be divided by this Act, fhall be made by or for the younger Children of the Inteftate, if the Heir at Law will, within the fpace of Twelve Months, pay fo much Money, or other Effects, to the Perfon or Perfons demanding fuch Partition, as their refpective

Shares

Shares or Purports ſhall amount unto, by the Valuation of ſour or more Perſons indifferently choſen by both Parties, or by an Inqueſt appointed by the Orphans-Court, to value the ſame, where the Parties cannot otherwiſe agree. And the Perſon or Perſons (whether Minors or others) to whom or for whoſe Uſe Payment or Satisfaction ſhall be made for their reſpective Purports, by the Heir at Law, in manner aforeſaid, ſhall be forever debarred of all the Right, Title and Demand which he or they can or may have, of, in or to ſuch Share or Purports, by Virtue of this Act, but the ſame ſhall be held and enjoyed by the Heir at Law, as freely and fully as the Inteſtate held the ſame.

AND in Caſe the Inteſtate have no known Kindred but a Wiſe, then all his Lands, Tenements and Hereditaments, ſhall deſcend to his ſaid Wiſe, during her natural Life ; and after the Death of the ſaid Wiſe, then all his Lands, Tenements and Hereditaments, ſhall eſcheat or go to the immediate Landlord of whom ſuch Lands are held, his Heirs and Aſſigns : And all the Goods, Chattles and perſonal Eſtate whatſoever, of ſuch Perſons dying Inteſtate, and without Wiſe or Kindred as aforeſaid, ſhall go to the Governor or Commander in Chief for the Time being.

If the Inteſtate have no known Kindred but a Wiſe, the Lands, &c. to be hers during Life, and afterwards eſcheated, &c.

Perſonal Eſtate goes to the Governor;

BUT if any of the ſaid Inteſtate's Relations ſhall appear, and make their Claims to ſuch Inteſtate's perſonal Eſtate, within Seven Years after the Deceaſe of the Inteſtate, they ſhall be reſtored thereunto.

But ſhall be reſtored if Relations appear in 7 Years.

AND if the lawful Heir to any ſuch Lands or Tenements, ſhall at any Time within Twenty-one Years after the Inteſtate's Deceaſe, appear, he may traverſe the Inquiſition, or Office, found for the Lands ſo eſcheated, and recover the ſame, paying the Lord or Perſon in Poſſeſſion for the Improvements made thereupon, according to the Valuation of Twelve Men.

If an Heir at Law appear in 21 Years, he ſhall recover the eſcheated Lands, &c.

AND for the leſſening the Charge of dividing the Lands of Inteſtates amongſt their Children, BE IT ENACTED by the Authority aforeſaid, That the Juſtices of the Orphans-Court, of the County where the Lands lie, upon Application made to them by the Heir at Law, or any other Child, when he or ſhe ſhall attain to the Age of Twenty-one Years, ſhall, and are hereby empowered, to appoint Five honeſt and diſcreet Men of the County,

Diviſion of Lands to be made by five Men, &c.

I

upon

upon their Oaths or Affirmations, to go upon the Lands of the Inteſtate, and to divide the ſame equally amongſt the Children of the Inteſtate, according to the Directions and true Intent and Meaning of this Act; which ſaid five Men, or any three of them, agreeing, ſhall make return of ſuch Diviſion to the next Orphans-Court; and if ſuch Diviſion be approved of by the ſaid Court, the ſame ſhall remain firm and ſtable forever.

Return to be made of the Diviſion to the Orphans Court, &c.

PROVIDED ALWAYS, That ſuch Diviſion ſhall not debar the eldeſt Son from making a Purchaſe of the Share or Purport of his Brothers and Siſters, in the manner directed in this Act.

AND that an Act entitled, *An Act for the Settling Inteſtates Eſtates*, and directing the Deſcent of Lands of Perſons dying Inteſtate, having Lands in this Government, made in the Year of our Lord *One Thouſand Seven Hundred and Six*, ſhall be, and is hereby Repealed.

Repeal of a former Act.

Signed by Order of the Houſe,

JOHN FRENCH, *Speaker.*

An ACT *to encourage the Building of good Mills in this Government.*

Preamble.

WHEREAS a Law of this Government which was made in the Sixth Year of the Reign of his preſent Majeſty King *GEORGE*, for encouraging the Building of Griſt-Mills within this Government, hath been found very advantageous to the Inhabitants thereof, but by Reaſon of ſome Defect in the ſaid Law, it hath not anſwered all the good Ends and Purpoſes for which the ſame was deſigned : Therefore, for the greater Commodity and Advantage of the People of this Government, BE IT ENACTED, by *PATRICK GORDON*, Eſq; Lieutenant Governor of the Counties of *New-Caſtle*, *Kent* and *Suſſex* upon *Delaware*, and Province of of *Penfylvania*, by and with the Advice and Confent of the Freemen of the faid Counties, in General Affembly met, and by the Authority of the fame, That on whatfoever Creeks, Rivers or Runs, within this Government, any Water-Mills are built, or intended to be built, if on either Side of the faid Creeks, Rivers or Runs, the Owner or Proprietor of the faid Mill or Mills, have a real Property in a Part of the Land fit to be ufed for that Purpofe, or upon which he has already built a Mill or Mills, yet neverthelefs cannot perfeét or fecure the fame, without purchafing and obtaining fome other fmall fhare of adjacent Land, which at the Time may happen to be another Man's Property, in order to convey the Water conveniently to and from the faid Mill or Mills; or if any Perfon or Perfons before the *Fifteenth* Day of *March*, in the Year One Thoufand Seven Hundred and Twenty-fix, hath or have built a Mill or Mills upon any Land adjoining to any Creek, Run or River within thisGovernment, by the Licence or Confent of fuch Perfon or Perfons as were really the Owners of the faid Land, or had or was deemed to have any Eftate in the fame, at the Time of building fuch Mill or Mills ; or if any Perfon or Perfons having before the Time aforefaid, purchafed fuch Lands with the Conveniencies of Water, and thereon have built a Mill or Mills, but have not obtained a perfeét and compleat Title for the fame, and that fuch Title cannot be had by reafon of the Death, Abfence, Infancy, or other Inability or Incapacity of any Perfon or Perfons having, or that may have, any Right, Title or Intereft, in Poffeffion, Remainder or Reverfion, of, in or to the faid Lands, Creeks, Runs or Rivers, or where fuch Mill or Mills are built, whereby the Builder of fuch Mill or Mills may be in danger of lofing the faid Mill or Mills fo built and e-reéted at a great Charge and Expence, and the Country lofe the Benefit of the faid Mill : Then, and in fuch Cafe or Cafes, the Owner and Proprietor of fuch Mill or Mills, may apply himfelf to any two Juftices of the Peace of that County, and thereupon the faid Magiftrates are here-by required and direéted, by their Precept to the Sheriff, to caufe fix Freeholders to be fummoned before them, who fhall, upon their Oaths or Affirmations, determine the true and intrinfick Value of the faid adjacent Land, or the Lands on which any Mill or Mills are already built by the Licence or Confent of the Owner or fuch as had or were deemed to have any Right in the fame Lands, in Poffeffion, Remainder or Reverfion, of building or ereét-ing fuch Mills, not exceeding the Quantity of fix Acres

Method of Se-curing neceffary Land to the Owners of Mills &c.

in

in the County of *New-Castle*, and two Acres in each of the other Counties, on either side of the said Creeks, Rivers or Runs where such Mill or Mills are built or intended to be built; and also the Damage and Loss which they judge may be to the Owner of such adjacent Land, or any other Person or Persons whatsoever; or shall find the true Value for which the said Lands, upon which any Mill or Mills were built before the Time mentioned in this Act, were sold or agreed to be sold for; and after a Verdict given by the said Freeholders, the said Justices are likewise hereby commanded, by a certain Instrument under their Hands and Seals, to certify and return the Verdict and Determination of the said Freeholders unto the next County Court, where it shall remain upon Record, and shall, upon Payment of the Money (so found in the Verdict of the said six Freeholders) to the Owner or Owners of the Lands aforesaid, or Depositing the same in Court for the Use of such Owner or Persons having a Right in the same Lands, transfer forever a good Title in Fee of the said adjacent Lands, not exceeding the Quantities aforesaid, respectively so valued, to the Owner or Projector of such Mill or Mills, and also shall create a Debt upon the said Owner or Projector's Estate, for the said determined Value, unto him and his Heirs, from whom the said adjacent Lands were so judged and taken.

Signed

An ACT *for regulating Pedlars within the Government of the Counties of* New-Castle, Kent *and* Sussex *upon* Delaware.

Preamble. WHEREAS of late many idle and vagrant Persons are come into this Government, and under pretence of being Hawkers or Pedlars, and carrying Goods from House to House within the same to sell, have greatly imposed upon many People, as well in the Quality as in the Price of the Goods. AND WHEREAS many of the Persons now following the Business or Imployment of of Pedlars, Hawkers or Petty Chapmen, within this Government, have no fixt or fettled Place of Refidence, and thereby are exempted from paying Taxes and contributing towards the Support of this Government proportionably with others the Inhabitants thereof. For remedying which Inconveniences, and to the End that no Perfon may be admitted and allowed to follow the Bufinefs of Hawkers or Pedlars within this Government, but Perfons of known Honefty and civil Behaviour, BE IT ENACTED, by the Honourable *PATRICK GORDON*, Efq; Lieutenant Governor of the Counties of *New-Caftle, Kent* and *Suffex* upon *Delaware*, and Province of *Pennfylvania*, by and with the Advice and Confent of the Reprefentatives of the Freemen of the faid Counties in General Affembly met, and by the Authority of the fame, That after the firft Day of *January* next, no Perfon or Perfons whatfoever, *No Perfon to* fhall follow or employ him, her or themfelves in the Bufi- *follow Pedling,* nefs or Employment of a Hawker, Pedlar or Petty-Chap- *&c. until they* man, or in going from Town to Town or to other Mens *ed, licenced,* Houfes, and travelling with Horfe or Horfes, Afs or Affes, *and have given* Mule or Mules, or otherways within this Government of *Bond, &c.* the Counties of *New-Caftle, Kent* and *Suffex* upon *Delaware*, (except as herein after is excepted) or carry to fell or expofe to fale any Goods, Wares or Merchandizes, within the Government aforefaid, until fuch Perfon or Perfons fhall have obtained a Recommendation from the Juftices of the County Court, where he or fhe dwells, certifying their Opinion of the Honefty of the Perfon recommended, and that he or fhe is a Liver within this Government, and intends to travel with one, two or more Horfe or Horfes, or other Beafts of Burden, or on Foot, and fhall thereupon have obtained a Licence from the Governor, and fhall have given Bond in the Prothonotary's Office of the County Court, in His Majefty's Name, with one Surety at leaft, in any Sum not exceeding *Forty Pounds*, Conditioned that fuch Perfon or Perfons fhall be of good Behaviour, during the Continuance of the faid Licence, and fhall well and duly pay and fatisfy all fuch Taxes and Duties as fhall be legally affeffed upon him, her or them, within the County where he, fhe or they fhall obtain the faid Recommendation; for which Licence there fhall be paid to the *Fees to be paid* Governor, the Sum of *Twenty-five Shillings*, by every *for Licences.* Perfon obtaining a Licence to travel with a Horfe, Afs, Mule or other Beaft of Burden, and the Sum of *Fifteen Shillings* for every Perfon licenfed to travel on Foot.

AND if any Person or Persons, not being qualifyed as aforesaid, shall be found travelling, hawking and pedling from House to House, to sell Goods, as a Hawker, Pedlar or Petty-Chapman, he or she so offending, if travelling with one or more Horses, shall forfeit the Sum of *Fifteen Pounds*, and if travelling on Foot, the Sum of *Ten Pounds*, one Moiety thereof to the Governor for the the Support of Government, and the other Moiety to the Person who will sue for the same, by any Action of Debt, Bill, Plaint or Information, in any Court of Record within this Government, wherein no Essoign, Protection or Wager of Law, nor more than one Imparlance shall be allowed.

AND that every Person so trading, who, upon Demand made by any Justice of the Peace, Constable, or other Officer of the Peace, of any Town, Place or County within this Government, where he or she shall so trade, shall refuse to produce and shew unto such Justice or Officer of the Peace, his or her License for so trading, to be granted as aforesaid, that then the Person so refusing, shall forfeit *Forty Shillings*, to be recovered in manner aforesaid ; and for Non-payment thereof, shall suffer as a common Vagrant.

PROVIDED ALWAYS, AND IT IS HEREBY FURTHER ENACTED, That nothing herein contained, shall extend, or be construed to extend, to hinder any Person or Persons from selling or exposing to sale any sort of Goods or Merchandize in any publick Market or Fair within this Government, or to hinder any Persons from carrying about from Town to Town and from House to House, any Goods, Wares or Merchandizes, being of the Growth, Product or Linen Manufacture of this Government, but that such Person or Persons may do therein as they lawfully might have done before the making of this Act ; any thing herein before contained to the contrary notwithstanding.

AND BE IT HEREBY FURTHER ENACTED, That if any Dispute shall happen to arise concerning the said Goods, Wares or Merchandizes, the Person or Persons so carrying about or exposing the same to sale, in manner aforesaid, shall be obliged to declare upon Oath or Affirmation before any Justice of the Peace or other Magistrate of the County, Town or Place where he, she or they shall carry about or offer the same

to

to fale, whether fuch Goods, Wares or Merchandizes be
of the Growth, Product or Linen Manufacture of this
Government.

Signed by Order of the Houfe,

HEN. BROOKE, *Speaker.*

An ACT *for the eftablifhing Courts of Law and Equity within this Government.*

BE IT ENACTED by the Honourable
PATRICK GORDON, Efq; Lieutenant
Governor of the Counties of *New-Cafle, Kent* and
Suffex upon *Delaware,* and Province of *Pennfylvania,*
by and with the Advice and Confent of the Reprefentatives of the Freemen of the faid Counties in General Affembly met, and by the Authority of the fame, That
there fhall be a Court ftiled, *the General Quarter-Seffions
of the Peace and Gaol-Delivery,* holden and kept fourTimes
in every Year in each County of this Government, (*viz.*)
at *New-Cafle,* for the County of *New-Cafle,* on the third
Tuefday in the Months called *February, May, Auguft,* and
November. At *Dover,* for the County of *Kent,* on the fecond *Tuefday* in every of the fame Months. And at *Lewis-
Town,* for the County of *Suffex,* on the firft *Tuefday* in
every of the faid Months. And that there fhall be a competent Number of Juftices in every of the faid Counties,
nominated and authorifed by the Governor, or Lieutenant
Governor for the time being, by Commiffion under the
Broad Seal of this Government; which faid Juftices, or
any three of them, fhall and may hold the faid General
Seffions of the Peace and Gaol-Delivery, according to Law,
and as fully and effectually as any Juftices of the Peace,
Juftices of the Affize, and Juftices of Oyer and Terminer,
or of Gaol-Delivery, may or can do.

Courts of Quarter-Seffions to be held 4 times a Year in each County.

The Governor to commiffio-nate Juftices for that purpofe.

AND BE IT FURTHER ENACTED,
by the Authority aforefaid, That the faid Juftices of the
Peace

47

Which Justices may hold special Sessions;

And take Re-cognizance out of Sessions;

Which shall be certified into the next Quarter-Sessions, &c.

Peace of the respective Counties, or any three of them, may, pursuant to their said Commissions, hold special and private Sessions, when and as often as Occasion shall require; and that the said Justices, and every of them, shall have full Power and Authority, in or out of Sessions, to take all manner of Recognizances and Obligations to the KING, as any Justices of the Peace of *Great-Britain* may or can or usually do; and all Recognizances for the Peace, Behaviour or Appearances which shall be taken by any of the said Justices out of Sessions, shall be certifyed into their said General Sessions of the Peace, to be holden next after their taking thereof, and every Recognizance taken before any of them for Suspicions of any man of Felony or other Crime, not triable in the said Court of Quarter-Sessions of the Peace and Goal-Delivery, shall be certified before the Justices of the Supreme Court of Oyer and Terminer, at their next succeeding Court to be holden next after the taking thereof, without Concealment, Detainment or Imbezelling of the same: But in Case any Person or Persons shall forfeit his or their Recognizance of the Peace, Behaviour or Appearance for any Cause whatsoever, then the Justices of the said Court of Quarter-Sessions, shall make a Record of every such Default or Cause of Forfeiture, and issue Writs of *Scire Facias*, and all such other Process as shall be needful for the Recovery of the said Forfeitures.

PROVIDED ALWAYS, That the said Courts of General Quarter Sessions of the Peace, may be kept and continued for the Space of three Days in the Counties of *New-Castle, Kent* and *Sussex* aforesaid, respectively, at any of the said Times herein before appointed for the holding and keeping of the said Courts and Sessions in each of the said Counties.

Quarter-Sessions may continue 3 Days in each County.

AND to the End that Persons indicted or outlawed for Felonies or other Offences in one County or Town Corporate, who dwell, remove or be received into another County or Town Corporate, may be brought to Justice, BE IT FURTHER ENACTED, That the said Justices, or any of them, shall and may direct their Writs or Precepts, under the Seal of the proper County to which they belong, to all or any of the Sheriffs or other Officers of the said Counties or Towns Corporate within this Government, where need shall be, to take such Persons indicted or outlawed, and that it shall and may be lawful to and for the **said**

Writs under the proper Seal of one County, may be directed to the Officers of another County, &c.

said Justices, and every of them, to issue forth *Subpæna's* and other Warrants, under their respective Hands and Seals, into any County or Place of this Government, for summoning or bringing any Person or Persons to give Evidence in and upon any Matter or Cause whatsoever, now or hereafter examinable or in any wise triable before them, or any of them, under such Pains and Penalties as by *Subpæna's* or Warrants of that Kind usually are or ought by Law to be granted or awarded.

Subpæna's to be issued for summoning Evidence.

AND BE IT FURTHER ENACTED by the Authority aforesaid, That if any Person or Persons shall find him or themselves aggrieved with the Judgment of any of the said Courts of General Quarter-Sessions of the Peace and Gaol-Delivery, or any other Courts of Record within this Government, it shall and may be lawful to and for the Party or Parties so aggriev'd, to have his or their Writ or Writs of Error, which shall be granted them of Course, in manner as other Writs of Error, to be granted and made returnable to the said Supreme Court of this Government.

Persons aggrieved may have Writs of Error, &c.

AND BE IT FURTHER ENACTED by the Authority aforesaid, That there shall be holden and kept a Court of Record twice in every Year, in each of the Counties of this Government, that is to say, on the *Fifth* Day of *October*, and on the *Twenty-first* Day of *April* at *New-Castle*, for the County of *New-Castle*; and on the *Ninth* Day of *October* and the *Twenty-fifth* Day of *April* at *Dover*, for the County of *Kent*; and on the *Thirteenth* Day of *October* and the *Twenty-ninth* Day of *April* at the Town of *Lewis*, for the County of *Sussex*; and if the same Days, or either of them, happen to be the first Day of the Week, then in such Case, the said Courts shall be held on the next Days following, which said Court shall be called and stiled the *Supreme Court* of the Counties of *New-Castle*, *Kent* and *Sussex* upon *Delaware*; and that there shall be three Persons, of known Integrity and Ability, commissionated by the Governor, or his Lieutenant for the Time being, by several distinct Patents or Commissions under the Great Seal of this Government, to be Judges of the said Courts, one of whom shall be distinguished in his Commission by the Name of *Chief Justice*, and every of the said Justices shall have full Power and Authority by Virtue of this Act, when and as often as there may be occasion, to issue forth Writs of *Habeas Corpus*, *Certiorari*

Supreme Courts to be held twice a Year in each County,

By three Judges to be commissionated by the Governor, &c.

Who have Power to issue Writs of Habeas Corpus, &c.

and

and *Writs of Error*, and all remedial Writs or Process returnable to the said Court and grantable by the said Judges by Virtue of their Office, in pursuance of the Powers and Authorities hereby given them.

AND That the said Judges, or any two of them, *And to hear and determine Causes, &c.* shall have full Power to hold the said Courts, and therein to hear and determine all Causes, Matters and Things cognizable in the said Court, and also to hear and determine all and all manners of Pleas, Plaints and Causes in Law or Equity, which shall be removed or brought there from the respective General Quarter-Sessions of the Peace, to be held for the respective Counties of *New-Castle*, *Kent* and *Suffex*, by Writs of *Certiorari*, Writs of Error or Appeal, or from any other Court of Law or Equity of this Government, by Virtue of any of the said Writs or Appeal after final Judgment or Decree shall be given in the said Courts, and to examine and correct all and all manner of Errors of the Justices and Magistrates of this Government, in their Judgment, Process and Proceedings in the said Courts, as well in all Pleas of the Crown, as in all Pleas real, personal and mixt, and Suits in Equity, and thereupon to reverse or affirm the said Judgments or Decrees as the Law doth or shall direct, and shall be appeal- *And to correct the Errors of Justices, punish the Faults of Officers, award Process for Levying Fines, &c.* able to Equity, and also to examine, correct and punish the Contempts, Omissions and Neglects, Favours, Corruptions and Defaults of all or any of the Justices of the Peace, Sheriffs, Coroners, Clerks and other Officers within the said respective Counties: And also shall award Process for levying all such Fines, Forfeitures and Amerciaments, which shall be left, taxed and set in the said Supreme Courts, and not paid to the Uses they are or shall be appropriated: And generally shall minister Justice *And generally minister Justice as in the King's Bench in Great Britain.* to all Persons, and exercise the Jurisdictions and Powers hereby granted them, concerning all and singular the Premises according to Law, as fully and amply to all Intents and Purposes whatsoever, as the Justices of the Courts of King's-Bench and Common-Pleas at *Westminster*, or any of them, may or can do upon Writs of Error and other remedial Writs issuing out of the said Courts; saving to *Saving to all Persons their Right of Appeal.* all and every Person or Persons, his, her or their Heirs, Executors and Administrators, their Right of Appeal from the final Sentence, Judgment or Decree of any Court within this Government, to His Majesty in Council, or to such Court or Courts, Judge or Judges as by our Lord the King, His Heirs or Successors, shall be appointed in that

Part

Part of *Great-Britain* called *England*, to receive, hear and judge of Appeals from His Majefty's Plantations.

PROVIDED the Perfons appealing fhall, upon entring his or their Appeal in the Court where the Sentence, Judgment or Decree fhall be given in this Government, pay all the Cofts before that Time expended in the Profecution or Defending the faid Suit, and fhall further enter into Bond, with two good and fufficient Securities in double the Sum recovered (in the faid Court) to the Defendant in the Appeal, conditioned to profecute the faid Appeal with effect, within the Space of *Eighteen Months* next after the Entry of fuch Appeal, and to fatisfy the Judgment of the Court from whence he appeals; and further to pay all fuch Cofts and Damages as fhall be adjudged to him to pay, in Cafe a Sentence, Judgment or Decree pafs againft the faid Appellant, or in Cafe he, fhe or they fail to profecute their Appeal with Effect; and Execution fhall be fufpended until the final Determination of fuch Appeals, unlefs good and fufficient Security be given by the Appellee, to make ample Reftitution of all that the Appellant fhall have loft by means of fuch Judgment or Decree, in Cafe, upon the Determination of fuch Appeal, fuch Decree or Judgment fhould be reverfed, and Reftitution awarded to the Appellant.

Appellant to give Bond, &c.

Execution to be fuſpended, &c. unleſs the Appellee give Security, &c.

AND BE IT FURTHER ENACTED, That all the faid Writs fhall be granted of Courfe, and made in the Name and Stile of the King, His Heirs and Succeffors, and fhall bear Teft in the Name of the Chief Juftice for the Time being, but if he be Plaintiff or Defendant, in the Name of one of the other Juftices, and fhall be fealed with the judicial Seal of the faid Court, figned by one of the Judges, and made returnable to the next Court after the Date of fuch Writ.

Stile of the Writs.

PROVIDED ALWAYS, That none of the Judges of the faid Supreme Court, fhall fit judicially in any of the faid Courts of Common-Pleas, Quarter-Seffions, or and other inferior Court of this Government.

No Judge of the Supreme Court ſhall ſit in inferior Courts.

AND BE IT FURTHER ENACTED by the Authority aforefaid, that the faid Judges of the faid Supreme Court, or any two of them, fhall have Power, and are hereby authorifed and impowered, from time to time, when there fhall be Occafion, to deliver the

The ſaid Judges to deliver Goals &c.

the

the Goals, of all Perſons which now are or ſhall hereafter be committed for Treaſons, Murders, and ſuch other Crimes as by the Laws of this Government now are or hereafter ſhall be made Capital or Felonies of Death as aforeſaid, and for that End, from time to time, to iſſue forth ſuch neceſſary Precepts and Proceſs, and force Obedience thereunto, as Juſtices of Aſſize, Juſtices of Oyer and Terminer and Goal-Delivery, may or can do in the Realm of *Great-Britain.*

Fees in the Su- preme Court to be double, &c.

PROVIDED ALWAYS, That the Fees due to the Judges and Officers of the ſaid Court, for hearing any of the ſaid capital Offences, for any thing done there, ſhall be double the Fees uſually taken in the General Quarter-Seſſions held in any of the ſaid Counties in this Government ; any thing herein contained, or in any other Law of this Government, to the contrary notwithſtanding.

No Cauſe now depending before the Judges of the Supreme Court ſhall be diſcontinued, &c.

PROVIDED ALWAYS, AND BE IT FURTHER ENACTED, That no Cauſe removed from any of the other Courts of this Government into the ſaid Supreme Court, or any other Matter legally removed from any other Court, and now depending before the Judges of the ſaid Court, ſhall be diſcontinued, but that the ſame may be heard, tryed, and determined before the ſaid Judges, as fully as the ſame could have been heard, tryed, and determined before the making of this Act ; any thing herein contained to the contrary in any wiſe notwithſtanding.

Notice to be gi- ven the Judges when there ſhall be any Cauſes &c.

PROVIDED ALWAYS, That nothing herein contained, ſhall oblige the Judges of the Supreme Court, nor any of them, to go their Circuit, or hold a Court in any County of this Government, but when there ſhall be ſome Cauſe removed from ſome inferior Courts by Writ of *Error, Habeas Corpus, Certiorari* or *Appeal,* or ſome other Matter or Cauſe cognizable by them, which ſhall require their coming, whereof the Clerks of the reſpective Counties from whence ſuch Cauſe or Cauſes ſhall be removed, ſhall give Notice to each of the Judges, after any ſuch Writ of *Error, Habeas Corpus, Certiorari* or *Appeal* ſhall be made or brought, at leaſt Fourteen Days before the time of holding the ſaid Supreme Court; and that the ſaid Judges, upon Notice given them, ſhall cauſe the Sheriff of the reſpective County where ſuch Supreme Court is to be held, forthwith to warn the Juſtices, Coroners and

Conſtables

Constables to give their Attendance at the said Supreme Court, to be held according to the Directions of this Act.

AND BE IT FURTHER ENACTED by the Authority aforesaid, That a competent Number of Persons shall be commissionated by the Governor, or his Lieutenant for the time being, under the Broad Seal of this Government, who shall hold and keep a Court of Record in every County of this Government, which shall be stiled and called *the County Court of Common-Pleas*, and shall be holden four times in every Year, at the Times and Places where the General Quarter-Sessions of the Peace are directed, and shall be respectively kept in the said Counties (that is to say) at *New-Castle*, for the County of *New-Castle*, on the third *Tuesday* of *February*, *May*, *August* and *November*: And at *Dover*, for the County of *Kent*, on the second *Tuesday* in every of the same Months: And at *Lewis*, for the County of *Sussex*, on the first *Tuesday* in every of the said Months; which Justices, or any three of them (according to the Tenor and Direction of their Commissions) shall hold Pleas of Assize, *Scire Facias*, Replevins, Informations and Actions upon penal Statutes, and hear and determine all and all Manner of Pleas, Actions, Suits and Causes, civil, real, personal and mixt, according to the Laws and Constitutions of this Government, as fully and amply to all Intents and Purposes, as the Justices of the King's-Bench, Common-Pleas and Exchequer in *England*, or any of them may or can do.

Justices to be commissionated to hold Courts of Common-Pleas 4 times a Year in each County;

AND BE IT FURTHER ENACTED, by the Authority aforesaid, That every of the said Justices shall, and are hereby impowered, to issue forth *Subpœna's* under their respective Hands and Seals, into any County or Place of this Government, for summoning and bringing any Person or Persons to give Evidence in and upon the Tryal of any Matter or Cause whatsoever, depending before them, or any of them, under such Pains and Penalties as by the Rules of the Common Law and Course and Practice of the King's Courts at *Westminster* are usually appointed.

Who are impowered to issue Subpœna's, &c.

AND BE IT FURTHER ENACTED, by the Authority aforesaid, That if any Defendant or Defendants in any Suit or Action, by reason of his or their sudden Departure out of this Government, shall require

And to grant special Courts.

M

a more

a more speedy Determination in such Action or Suit, than can be obtained by the common or ordinary Rules of Proceeding in any of the said County Courts of Common-Pleas in this Government, the said Justices, upon Application made, shall grant to such Defendant or Defendants, special Courts, and shall proceed to hear and determine the Premises according to the Course and Practice of said County Courts of Common-Pleas, for the usual Fees therein taken.

The Defendant to give Bail, &c.

PROVIDED ALWAYS, That before such Justices shall grant such special Courts, or proceed to hear and determine the Premises, the Defendant shall give Bail to the Plaintiff's Action by Recognizance, according to the Course and Practice of the said County Courts of Common-Pleas.

Writs of Enquiry how to be Executed.

AND to prevent the excessive Charges that have sometimes arisen upon executing Writs of Enquiry for Damages, BE IT ENACTED, That the Justices, who give any Interlocutory Judgment, shall (at the Motion of the Plaintiff or his Attorney in the Action where the Judgment is given) make an Order in the Nature of a Writ of Enquiry, to charge the Jury attending at the same or next Court after such Judgment is given, to enquire of the Damages and Costs sustained by the Plaintiff in such Action, which Enquiry shall be made and Evidence given in open Court, and after the Inquest have considered thereof they shall forthwith return their Inquisition under their Hands and Seals, whereupon the Court may proceed to Judgment as upon Inquisitions of that kind returned by the Sheriffs.

Testatum Executions may be awarded where needful.

AND BE IT FURTHER ENACTED, by the Authority aforesaid, That it shall and may be lawful to and for the Justices of the said respective Courts of Common-Pleas within this Government, to award a a *Testatum* Execution in all Cases where the same is needful, and is or ought to be done by the Practice and Course of the Laws of *England*, and to amerce the Sheriffs or other Officers neglecting or refusing to execute and make Return of such Writ or Writs according to the Direction of the said Writs.

Courts of Equity to be held 4 times a Year.

AND BE IT FURTHER ENACTED by the Authority aforesaid, That there shall be a Court of Equity, held by the Justices of the said respective County Courts

Courts of Common-Pleas four times a Year at the respective Places, and near the said Times as the said Courts
of Common-Pleas are held in every County of this Government ; and that the Prothonotary of the Common- *Prothonotary of*
Pleas shall be the Register of the said Courts of Equity *the Common-*
in every County ; which said Justices, or any three of them, *gister.*
within the Limits of their Commissions and Authorities
to them appointed as is aforesaid, shall have full Power, *Power of the*
and are hereby impowered and authorised, to hear and de- *Court of E-*
cree all such Matters and Causes of Equity as shall come *quity.*
before them in the said Courts, where the Proceedings shall
be as heretofore by Bill and Answer, with such otherPlead-
ings as are necessary in Chancery Courts and proper in these
Parts, with Power also for the said Justices of the respective Courts of Equity, to issue forth all manner of *Sub-*
pœna's and all other Process as may be needful to oblige
and force Defendants to answer Suits there, as also to award
Commissions for taking Answers and examining Witnesses,
and to grant Injunctions for staying Suits in Law and stop-
ping Wastes as there may be Occasion, observing as near as
may be the Rules and Practice of the High Court of
Chancery in *Great-Britain*, with Powers to make Orders
and award all manner of Process, and do all other
Things necessary for bringing Causes to Hearing, and to
force Obedience to their Decrees in Equity, which may
be by Imprisonment of Bodies or Sequestration of Lands,
and admit Bills of Reviver as the Case may require.

AND if any Defendant or Defendants in any Suit *Cases in which*
which shall be commenced against them in one of the *Process may be*
said Counties, shall, after he or they are served with a *awarded out of*
Subpœna or other Process, remove into any other County *quity into other*
of this Government, all Process necessary to bring such *Counties.*
Defendants to answer, and all Commissions for taking
of their Answers and examining Witnesses, with all other
Process necessary to bring such Causes to a Hearing, shall
and may be awarded out of the Court where those Causes
or Suits shall be first commenced, into any other
County of this Government, as the Case may require.

PROVIDED ALWAYS, That no *Subpœna's*, *Before Sub-*
or other Process for Appearance, shall issue out of any of *pœna's or Pro-*
the said Courts of Equity, till the Bill is filed with the pro- *cess for Appea-*
per Officer, except Bill for Injunctions to stay Wastes or *rance issue, Bill*
Suits at Law. *to be filed, &c.*

PRO-

PROVIDED ALSO, That if any Perfon or Perfons shall find themfelves aggrieved with any Decree or Sentence made or given by the said Juſtices in Equity, it shall and may be lawful to and for him or them ſo grieved,

Perſons ag-grieved may appeal to the Supreme Court, &c.

forthwith to appeal or have recourfe to the Judges of the Supreme Court, to fet forth his or their Cafe by Petition, Bill or Plaint, ſo as the Sum adjudged to be paid by fuch Decree amount to *Ten Pounds* or upwards, and ſo as he or they, ſo appealing, firſt pay down the Court Charges, and either ſatisfy the Decree or Sentence ſo given, or depoſite with the Juſtices the Sum awarded, or give fufficient Security to profecute the said Appeal, and to pay all Coſts and Damages that shall be awarded againſt him or them; and then, albeit the Party appealing be impriſoned upon thatDecree or Sentence, he shall be inlarged; and that fuch Appeals shall fuperfede all other Procefs upon the Decree or Sentence appealed from, till the ſame be heard, tryed or difmiffed in the said Supreme Court.

PROVIDED ALSO, that nothing herein con-

Matters deter-minable by Common Law not to be heard in Courts of Equity.

tained shall give the said Juſtices any Power or Authority to hear, decree or determine in Equity, any Matter, Caufe or Thing wherein fufficient Remedy may be had in any other Court or before any other Magiſtrate or Judicature in this Government, either by the Rules of the Common Law or according to the Tenor and Directions of the Laws of this Government, but that when Matters determinable at Common Law shall be brought before them in Equity, they shall refer or remit the Parties to the Common Law; and when Matters of Fact shall hap-

When Matters of Fact arife, they are to be try'd in the Courts of Common Pleas.

pen to arife upon their Examination or Hearing of the Matters and Caufes to be heard and determined in the said Court, then, and in every fuch Cafe, they shall order the Matter of Fact to Iffue and Tryal at the Court of Common-Pleas for the proper County where the Fact arifeth, before they proceed to Sentence or Decree in the said Court of Equity.

AND BE IT FURTHER ENACTED

Atternies how to be admitted, &c.

by theAuthority aforefaid, That there may be a competent Number of Perfons of an honeſt Difpoſition and learned in theLaw, admitted by the Juſtices of the said refpective Courts to practice as Attornies there, who shall behave themfelves juſtly and faithfully in their Practice, and before they are ſo admitted shall take the following Qualification (*viz,*)

THOU

*T*HOU shalt behave thy self in the Office of an Attorney **The Qualifi-** within the Court according to the best of thy Learning **cation.** and Ability, and with all good Fidelity as well to the Court as to the Client: Thou shalt use no Falshood, nor delay any Person's Cause through Lucre or Malice.

AND if they misbehave themselves therein, they shall **Penalty on Mis** suffer such Penalties and Suspensions as Attornies at Law **behaviour.** in *Great-Britain* are liable to in such Cases. By which Attornies Actions may be entered, and Writs, Process, De- **Business of At-** clarations and other Pleadings ; and Records in all such **tornies.** Actions and Suits as they shall respectively be concerned to prosecute or defend from time to time, may be drawn, and with their Names and proper Hands signed ; which said Attornies, so admitted, may practice in all the Courts of this Government, without any further or other Licence or Admittance.

PROVIDED ALWAYS, That no Person, not being an Inhabitant of this Government or of the Pro- **Non-Resident** vince of *Pennsylvania*, shall be permitted to plead in any **Attornies shall** Court or Courts within this Government, without Licence **out a Licence** first obtained from the Governor for the time being, by **from the Gover-** the Recommendation of the Justices of one of the Coun- **50 s per Court.** ty-Courts of this Government; unless such Lawyer or Lawyers shall obtain the Court's Leave, and pay to the said Court, for the Use of the Governor, the Sum of *Fifty Shillings* for each Court he shall so plead, until licenced.

Signed by Order of the House.

A. HAMILTON, *Speaker.*

An ACT against Defacers of Charters, and Counterfeiting Hands and Seals.

*W*HEREAS the Security of Titles and Property in a great Measure depends on the Safety and and Certainty of Writing and Records, BE IT EN- ACTED by the Honourable *PATRICK GORDON,* Esq;

Esq; Lieutenant Governor of the Counties of *New-Castle*, *Kent* and *Suffex* upon *Delaware*, and Province of *Pennsylvania*, by and with the Advice and Consent of the Representatives of the Freemen of the said Counties in General Assembly met, and by the Authority of the same, That whosoever shall counterfeit the Hand and Seal, or Hand or Seal of any Person, with an Intent to defraud or hurt another, or shall counterfeit any publick Seal, or forge, deface, corrupt or imbezle any Charters, Gifts, Grants, Bonds, Bills, Wills, Conveyances or Contracts, or shall deface or falsify any Inrollments, Registry or Record within this Government, and shall be thereof legally convict, shall suffer the like Pains and Penalties as by the Laws of that Part of *Great-Britain* called *England* is provided against such Offences for the time being.

Punishment of Counterfeiting, Forging, &c.

Signed by Order of the House,

A. HAMILTON, *Speaker.*

An ACT against Speaking in Derogation of Courts.

BE IT ENACTED, by the Honourable *PATRICK GORDON*, Esq; Lieutenant Governor of the Counties of *New-Castle*, *Kent* and *Suffex* upon *Delaware* and Province of *Pennsylvania*, by and with the Advice and Consent of the Representatives of the Freemen of the said Counties in General Assembly met, and by the Authority of the same, That if any Person or Persons at any time or times hereafter, shall write or speak any Thing in Derogation of any Sentence or Judgment given in any Court of Record within this Government, by saying such Sentence or Judgment was given corruptly, partially or unjustly, and being thereof legally convict, shall forfeit for such Offence any Sum not exceeding *Five Pounds*, one half to the Informer, and the other to the Governor for the Support of Government ; and in Case any Person or Persons shall commit any Rudeness, or be guilty of any Misdemeanour in the said Courts, during the Sitting thereof, such Person, so offending, shall be fined at the Discretion of

Penalties on Speaking in Derogation, &c.

Rudeness or Misdemeanour in Court how punished.

of the said Court in any Sum not exceeding *Five Pounds*, for the Uses aforesaid.

Signed by Order of the House,

A. HAMILTON, *Speaker*.

An ACT *against Riots, Routs and unlawful Assemblies.*

BE IT ENACTED by the Honourable *PATRICK GORDON*, Esq; Lieutenant Governor of the Counties of *New-Castle*, *Kent* and *Sussex* upon *Delaware*, and of the Province of *Pennsylvania*, by and with the Advice and Consent of the Representatives of the Freemen of the said Counties in General Assembly met, and by the Authority of the same, That if any Persons to the Number of *three* or upwards, meet together within this Government, with Clubs, Staves or other hurtful Weapons, to the Terror of any of the peaceable People or Inhabitants of the same, and shall commit, or attempt to commit, Violence or Injury upon the Person or Goods of any of the said Inhabitants, they and every of them shall be reputed and punished as Rioters, and the Act of Terror or Violence, or Attempt to do Violence, shall be accounted and deemed a Riot; and such Persons so offending, as likewise all other riotous and unlawful Assemblies, shall be adjudged and punished according to the Laws and Statutes of *Great-Britain* against Riots and unlawful Assemblies. And whosoever shall introduce into this Government any riotous and unlawful Sports and Games, as Prizes, Stage-Plays, Masks or Revels, and shall practise the same, and be lawfully convicted thereof, such Person or Persons shall for every such Offence be reputed Breakers of the Peace, and shall forfeit and pay *Twenty Shillings*, or suffer *Ten* Days Imprisonment at hard Labour in the House of Correction.

What shall be deemed a Riot.

Riotous Sports, Revels, &c. how punished.

Signed by Order of the House,

A. HAMILTON, *Speaker*.

An

An ACT of Priviledge to a Freeman.

B B IT ENACTED by the Honourable *PATRICK GORDON*, Efq; Lieutenant Governor of the Counties of *New-Caftle*, *Kent* and *Suffex* upon *Delaware*, and Province of *Pennfylvania*, by and with the Advice and Confent of the Reprefentatives of the Freemen of the faid Counties in General Affembly met, and by the Authority of the fame, That no Freeman within this Government fhall be taken or imprifoned, or diffeized of his Free-hold or Liberties, or be out-lawed or exiled, or otherways hurt, damnified or deftroyed, nor to be tryed or condemned but by the lawful Judgment of his Twelve Equals, or by the Laws of *England* and of this Government.

Signed by Order of the Houfe,

A. HAMILTON, *Speaker*.

An ACT for affigning Bills and Specialties.

FOR the Encouragement of Trade and Commerce BE IT ENACTED by the Honourable *PATRICK GORDON*, Efq; Lieutenant Governor of the Counties of *New-Caftle*, *Kent* and *Suffex* upon *Delaware*, and of the Province of *Pennfylvania*, by and with the Advice and Confent of the Reprefentatives of the Freemen of the faid Counties in General Affembly met, and by the Authority of the fame, That all Bonds, Specialties and Notes in Writing, made or to be made payable to any Perfon or Perfons, his, her or their Order or Affigns, for any Sum of Money, may by the Perfon or Perfons to whom the fame is or are made payable, be affigned, indorfed or made over to any other Perfon or Perfons who will accept the fame ; and that fuch Affignee or Indorfee, their Executors, Administrators or Affigns, may

Bonds, Specialties, Notes, &c. may be affign-ed, &c.

may again, at their Pleasure, assign, indorse or make o- *Assignees may assign again:*
ver the same Bonds, Specialties or Notes to any other,
and so *Toties Quoties* as any Person shall be willing to accept of the same.

AND That such Assignee or Assignees, Indorsee or *And sue in their own Name.*
Indorsees, their Executors or Administrators, may in their
own Name or Names sue for and recover the Sums of
Money contained in any Bonds, Specialties or Notes so
assigned, indorsed or made over, for his or their own Use
or Uses, and at their own Costs and Charges, in like
Manner as the Person or Persons to whom the same were
at first made payable, might or could have done.

PROVIDED ALWAYS, That all Assignments *Assignment how to be made, &c.*
to be made of any Bonds or Specialties shall be under the
Hand and Seal of the Assignor, and at least before two
credible Witnesses; and that it shall not be in the Power
of the Assigners or Indorsers, their Executors or Administrators to release or discharge any of the Debts or Sums
of Money due by the said Bonds, Specialties or Notes,
after the Date of such Assignment; and that no Release,
Receipt or Discharge from the Assignor, his Executors or
Administrators, made after the Date of such Assignment,
shall be available to the Obligor or the Persons from whom
the Money was owing, his, her or their Executors or
Administrators.

Signed by Order of the House

A. HAMILTON, *Speaker.*

An ACT against Jurors absenting themselves, being lawfully summoned to attend the several Courts of Judicature within this Government.

BE IT ENACTED by the Honourable *PA-
TRICK GORDON*, Esq, Lieutenant Gover-
nor of the Counties of *New-Castle*, *Kent* and *Sussex* upon

O *Delaware*

Delaware and Province of *Pennsylvania*, by and with the Advice and Content of the Representatives of the Freemen of the said Counties in General Assembly met, and by the Authority of the same, That all Persons Freemen within this Government, being duely and legally summoned to appear at any Court established by Law, at least Ten Days before the holding such Court, to serve upon any Jury or any Inquest, and shall neglect or refuse to give their Attendance, shall be fined, by the respective Court where they were summoned to attend, in any Sum not exceeding *Twenty Shillings* each Court, for the Use of the Poor of *Fine on Jurors* the County where such Offender shall be convicted, unless *not attending.* at the next succeeding Court they shall render a reasonable Excuse for such their Absence to be allowed of by the Judges or Justices then present ; And that all Grand-Jury *Grand Jury-* Men, summoned as aforesaid, shall serve the space of one *men to serve one* whole Year, notwithstanding their being sworn at each re- *Year.* spective Court to attend that present Service only. And in Case a sufficient Number so summoned shall not appear, the Sheriff shall have Power to return such other Free- *A sufficient* holders of that County as he shall judge fit for that present *Number not ap-* *pearing, Sheriff* Service, to make up the said Number, altho' it be in Time *may return o-* of Court ; and any Person so summoned and refusing to *thers, &c.* serve accordingly, shall forfeit the Sum of *Twenty Shillings* for the Use of the Poor as above directed.

Signed by Order of the House,

A. HAMILTON, *Speaker.*

An ACT for Appraisment of Goods taken in Execution.

BE IT ENACTED by the Honourable *PATRICK GORDON*, Esq; Lieutenant Governor of the Counties of *New-Castle*, *Kent* and *Sussex* upon *Delaware*, and Province of *Pennsylvania*, by and with the Advice and Consent of the Representatives of the Freemen of the said Counties in General Assembly met,

met, and by the Authority of the fame, That the refpective County Courts within this Government, fhall and are
hereby impowered, as often as they fhall fee Caufe, to
nominate two or three fufficient honeft and difcreet Perfons,
whom they fhall fwear or atteft, to be Appraifers in their
feveral and refpective Counties, to value and appraife all
fuch Goods and Chattles as fhall be taken in Execution
by any Precept iffuing out of the refpective Courts of this
Government, as need fhall require; which Goods or Chattles
fhall not be difpofed of or fold until fuch Appraifement
be made by them as aforefaid, or any two of them, if they
will attend when required, nor till Thirty Days after Appraifement, to the End that the Party or Parties concerned
may, if they think fit, relieve the fame according as they
were appraifed; and the Appraifers fhall be allowed *four
Pence* per Pound for what they fhall appraife, and *two
Pence* each per Mile for Journey Fees, to be paid out of the
Value of the Effects or Goods fo appraifed; any Law,
Cuftom or Ufage of this Government, to the contrary
thereof in any wife notwithftanding.

County Courts impowered to nominate Appraifers, &c.

Goods, &c. not to be fold till 30 Days after Appraifment.

Allowance to the Appraifer.

Signed by Order of the Houfe,

A. HAMILTON, *Speaker.*

An ACT for taking Lands in Execution for payment of Debts.

TO the End that no Creditors may be defrauded of
their juft Debts due to them from the Perfons who
have fufficient real if not perfonal Eftates to fatisfy
the fame, BE IT ENACTED by the
Honourable *PATRICK GORDON*, Efq; Lieu-
tenant Governor of the Counties of *New-Caftle*, *Kent* and
Suffex upon *Delaware*, and of the Province of *Pennfylvania*, by
and with the Advice and Confent of the Reprefentatives
of the Freemen of the faid Counties in General Affembly
met, and by the Authority of the fame, That all fuch
Lands, Tenements or Hereditaments whatfoever within
this

this Government, where no sufficient personal Estate can be found, shall be liable to be seized and sold upon Judgment and Execution obtained.

PROVIDED ALWAYS, That it shall not be lawful for any Sheriff or other Officer, by Virtue of any Executions or of any Writ or Writs thereupon, to sell or expose to Sale any such Lands, Tenements or Hereditaments in this Government, which shall or may yield yearly Rents and Profits beyond all Reprizes, sufficient within the Space of seven Years to satisfy or pay such Debts or Damages with the Costs of Suit ; but that all those Lands, Tenements and Hereditaments shall by Virtue of the Writ or Writs of Execution, be delivered to the Party obtaining the same, until the Debt and Damages be levied by a reasonable Extent, in the same Method and Manner as Lands are delivered upon Writs of *Elegit* in *England.*

PROVIDED NEVERTHELESS, That if the clear Profits of such Lands or Tenements shall not be found, by the Valuation of two judicious and substantial Freeholders upon their Oaths or Affirmations, to be sufficient within seven Years to satisfy the Debt and Damages in such Executions, or if before the Extent be out, any other Debt or Damages shall be recovered against the the same Debtor or Defendant, his Heirs, Executors or Administrators, which, with what remains due upon that Extent, cannot all be satisfied out of the yearly Profits of the Lands and Tenements so extended within seven Years ; then, and in every such Case, the Sheriff or other Officer shall accordingly certify the same upon the return of such Executions, whereupon Writ or Writs of *Venditioni Exponas* shall issue forth, to sell such Lands or Tenements for and towards Satisfaction of what shall so remain due upon such Extent, as also towards Satisfaction of all the rest of the said Debts or Damages, in manner as is herein after directed concerning the Sale of other Lands.

AND BE IT FURTHER ENACTED by the Authority aforesaid, That it shall and may be lawful for the Sheriff or other Officer, by a Writ of *Levari* *Facias,* to seize all Lands in Execution which are unimproved, and all such Lands and Tenements which yield no yearly Profit, and thereupon, with all convenient speed, either with or without any Writ of *Venditioni Exponas,* to make

make publick Sale thereof for the moſt they will yield, and pay the Price or Value of the ſame to the Party towards Satisfaction of his Debt, Damages and Coſts: But before any ſuch Sale be made, the Sheriff or other Officer ſhall cauſe ſo many Writings to be made upon Parchment or good Paper as the Debtor or Defendant ſhall reaſonably deſire or requeſt, or ſo many without ſuch Requeſt as may be ſufficient to ſignify and give Notice of ſuch Sales or Vendues, and of the Day and Hour when and the Place where the ſame will be, and what Lands and Tenements are to be ſo ſold and where they lie, which Notice ſhall be given to the Defendant, and the ſaid Parchments or Papers fixt by the Sheriff or other Officer in the moſt publick Place of each Hundred in the County where the Land lies, at leaſt Ten Days before Sale, and upon ſuch Sale the Sheriff or other Officer ſhall make return thereof indorſed or annexed to the ſaid *Levari Facias*, and give the Buyer a Deed duly executed and acknowledged in Court for what is ſold, as has been heretofore uſed upon the Sheriff's Sale of Lands: But in Caſe the ſaid Lands and Hereditaments ſo to be expoſed cannot be ſold, then the Officer ſhall make Return upon the Writ, *That he expoſed ſuch Lands or Tenements to Sale, and the ſame remained in his Hands unſold for want of Buyers*; which Return ſhall not make the Officer liable to anſwer the Debt or Damages contained in ſuch Writ, but a Writ called *Liberari Facias* ſhall forthwith be awarded and directed to the proper Officer, commanding him to deliver to the Party ſuch Part or Parts of thoſe Lands, Tenements or Hereditaments, as ſhall ſatisfy his Debt, Damages and Intereſt from the time of the Judgment given, with Coſts of Suit, according to the Valuation of Twelve Men, to hold to him as his Free-Tenement in Satisfaction of his Debt, Damages and Coſts, or ſo much thereof as thoſe Lands, by the Valuation of Twelve Men as aforeſaid, ſhall amount unto; and if it fall ſhort, the Party may afterwards have Execution for the Reſidue, againſt the Defendant's Body, Lands or Goods, as the Laws of this Government ſhall direct and appoint from time to time concerning other Executions: all which ſaid Lands, Tenements, Hereditaments and Premiſes, ſo as aforeſaid, to be ſold or delivered by the Sheriff or Officer aforeſaid, with all their Appurtenances, ſhall and may be quietly and peaceably held and enjoyed by the Perſon or Perſons or Bodies Politick to whom the ſame ſhall be ſold or delivered, and by his and their Heirs, Succeſſors or Aſſigns as fully and amply, and for ſuch Eſtate and Eſtates, and under ſuch Rents

Ten Days Notice of Sale to be given.

The Sheriff to give the Buyer a Deed, &c.

Liberari facias.

Lands, &c. falling ſhort, Execution may be had for the Reſidue, &c.

P

and

and Services, as he or they, for whose Debt or Duty the same shall be so sold or delivered, might, could or ought to do at or before the taking thereof in Execution.

AND forasmuch as divers Persons have mortgaged their Lands and Tenements in this Government for securing the Payment of Monies, and some of them have died before the Time of Payment, and left others to succeed them that have proved Insolvent, and others have neglected to pay the Mortgage-Money, and so Mortgages are become no effectual Security, considering how low the annual Profits of Tenements and improved Lands are here, and the Discouragement which the Mortgagees meet with by reason of the Equity of Redemption remaining in the Mortgagors; BE IT THEREFORE ENACTED by the Authority aforesaid, That when Default or Defaults have been or shall be made or suffered by any Mortgagor or Mortgagors of any Lands, Tenements or other Hereditaments within this Government, or by his, her or their Heirs, Executors, Administrators or Assigns, of or in Payment of the Mortgage-Money or Performance of the Condition or Conditions which they or any of them should have paid or performed, or ought to pay or perform, in such Manner and Form, and according to the Purport, Tenor and Effect of the respective Proviso's Conditions or Covenants comprized in their Deeds of Mortgage or Defeazance, and at the Days, Times and Places in the same Deeds respectively mentioned and contained: That in every such Case it shall and may be lawful to and for the Mortgagee or Mortgagees, and him, her or them that grant the Deeds of Defeazance, and his, her or their Heirs, Executors, Administrators and Assigns, at any Time after the Expiration of Twelve Months next ensuing, the last Day whereon the said Mortgage-Money ought to be paid, or other Conditions performed as aforesaid, to sue forth a Writ or Writs of *Scire facias*, which the Clerk of the Court of Common Pleas for the County where the said mortgaged Lands or Hereditaments lie or be, is hereby required and impowered to make out and dispatch, directed to the proper Officer, requiring him by honest and lawful Men of the Neighbourhood, to make known to the Mortgagor or Mortgagors, his, her or their Heirs, Executors or Administrators, That he or they be and appear before the said Court or Courts, to shew, if any thing he, she or they have to say wherefore the said mortgaged Premisses ought not to be seized and taken in Execution for Payment of the said Mortgage-

Money

Mortgagee in Default of Payment, may after one Year sue forth a Writ of Scire facias, &c.

Money with Interest, or to satisfy the Damages which the Plaintiff in such *Scire facias* shall upon the Record suggest for the Breach or Non-performance of the said Conditions; and if the Defendant in such *Scire facias* appears, he or they may plead Satisfaction or Payment of Part or all the Mortgage-Money, or any other lawful Plea, in Avoidance of the Deed or Deeds, as the Case may require. But if the Defendants in such *Scire facias* will not appear at the Day whereon the said Writ shall be made returnable, then definitive Judgment therein, as well as all other Judgments to be given upon such *Scire facias*, shall be entered, that the Plaintiff in such *Scire facias* shall have Execution by *Levari facias*, directed to the proper Officer, by Virtue whereof the said mortgaged Premisses shall be taken in Execution, and exposed to Sale, and upon Sale conveyed to the Buyer or Buyers thereof, and the principal Money and Interest, with all Costs and Charges, rendered to the Mortgagee or Creditor; but for want of Buyers, to be delivered to the Mortgagee or Creditor, in Manner and Form as is herein before directed concerning other Lands and Hereditaments to be sold and delivered upon Executions for other Debts or Damages. And when the said Lands and Hereditaments shall be so sold or delivered, as aforesaid, the Person or Persons to whom they shall be so sold or delivered, shall and may hold and enjoy the same, with their Appurtenances, for such Estate or Estates as they were sold or delivered, clearly, discharged and freed from all Equity and Benefit of Redemption, and all other Incumbrances made and suffered by the Mortgagors, their Heirs or Assigns; and such Sales shall be available in Law, and the respective Vendees, Mortgagees or Creditors, their Heirs and Assigns, shall hold and enjoy the same, freed and discharged as aforesaid. But before such Sales shall be made, Notice shall be given in Writing in Manner and Form as is herein above directed concerning the Sales of Lands upon Executions, any Law or Usage to the contrary notwithstanding.

And take out Execution, and expose the mortgaged Premisses to Sale, &c.

If such Sales shall be available in Law, &c.

PROVIDED ALSO, AND BE IT FURTHER ENACTED by the Authority aforesaid, That when any of the said Lands, Tenements or Hereditaments, which by the Direction and Authority of this Act are to be sold for Payment of Debts and Damages in Manner aforesaid, shall be sold for more than will satisfy the same Debts or Damages, and reasonable Costs; then the Sheriff, or other Officer who shall make the Sale, must render the Overplus to the Debtor or Defendants; and then

Overplus of the Money arising on Sale of Lands &c. to be rendered to the Defendant.

and

and not before the said Officers shall be discharged thereof upon Record in the same Court where he shall make Return of his Proceedings concerning the said Sales.

Such Sale not to create any farther Estate than, &c. **PROVIDED ALSO,** That no Sale or Delivery which shall be make by Virtue of this Act, shall be extended to create any further Term or Estate to the Vendees, Mortgagees or Creditors, than the Lands or Hereditaments so sold or delivered shall appear to be mortgaged for by the said respective Mortgages or defeazable **Deeds.**

Lands, &c. so sold, not to be restored on Reversion of Judgment, &c. **PROVIDED ALSO,** That if any of the said Judgments which do or shall warrant the awarding of the said Writs of Execution, whereupon any Lands, Tenements or Hereditaments have been or shall be sold, shall at any Time hereafter be reversed for any Error or Errors, then, and in every such Case, none of the said Lands, Tenements or Hereditaments, so as aforesaid taken or sold or to be taken or sold upon Executions, nor any Part thereof, shall be restored, nor the Sheriff's Sale or Delivery thereof avoided, but Restitution in such Cases only of the Money or Price for which such Lands were or shall be sold.

Proceeding in Case the Sheriff die or be removed before a Title is made. **AND BE IT FURTHER ENACTED** by the Authority aforesaid, That if any Sheriff or other Officer who have sold, or hereafter shall, by Virtue of any Writ or Writs of *Execution, Venditioni Exponas* or *Liberari facias,* sell or deliver any Lands, Tenements or Hereditaments within this Government to any Person, and shall happen to die or be removed from his Office, before he executes a Deed or Deeds for perfecting and compleating the Title of the Purchaser to the Lands or Tenements by him sold, that then it shall and may be lawful, as well for the Purchaser as the Creditor, at whose Suit such Lands and Tenements were taken in Execution, to represent the Truth of the Case to the Justices of the Court of Common-Pleas, to be held for the County where the Lands lie: And if it shall appear to the said Courts, by the Records and Proceedings of the said Courts, that the Lands and Tenements have been taken and sold in manner directed by the Laws of this Government, and that the Officer who sold the same, is dead or removed from his Office, and no lawful Deed executed for conveying the same to the Purchaser, it shall and may be lawful for the Justices of the said

said Courts, and they are hereby required, in such Cases, to cause an Order of Court to be made, thereby commanding and authorising the present Sheriff or Coroner, upon payment of the Confideration Money for which such Lands and Tenements were sold by the former Officer, to execute such lawful Deed or Deeds, and to do all other lawful Acts for the conveying or delivering over the said Lands and Tenements to the Purchafer or Creditor, as the Officer who sold the fame could or ought to have done by Virtue of the faid Writ or Writs, or by any Law of this Government ; and fuch Sale or Sales, fo made by Virtue of any fuch Order of Court, shall be available in Law, and the refpective Vendees, Mortgagees or Creditors, their Heirs and Affigns, shall hold and enjoy the fame, freed and difcharged as aforefaid.

Signed by Order of the House,

A. HAMILTON, *Speaker.*

An ACT *againft* Adultery *and* Fornication.

FOR the Prefervation of Virtue and Chaftity among the People of this Government, and to prevent the heinous Sins of Adultery and Fornication, BE IT ENACTED by the Honourable *PA-TRICK GORDON,* Efq; Lieutenant Governor of the Counties of *New-Caftle, Kent* and *Suffex* upon *Delaware,* and Province of *Pennfylvania,* by and with the Advice and Confent of the Reprefentatives of the Freemen of the faid Counties in General Affembly met, and by the Authority of the fame ; That whofoever shall commit Adultery, and be thereof legally convicted, shall forfeit and pay the Sum of *Fifty Pounds,* one Moiety thereof to the Ufe of the Governor for the Support of Government, and the other Moiety to the Ufe of the Poor of the County where the fame is committed, or otherwife to be publickly whipt with *Twenty-one* Lashes on his or her Back, well laid on at the common Whiping-Poft, at the Election of the Party convicted.

Penalty on Committing Adultery.

Q

PRO-

PROVIDED ALWAYS, That the Testimony of either the Parties concerned in committing the Adultery, shall not be sufficient to convict the other, without further Evidence, that shall at least amount to violent Presumption.

Penalties on Fornicators.

AND BE IT FURTHER ENACTED by the Authority aforesaid, That if any Person shall commit Fornication and be thereof legally convict, such Person or Persons shall receive *Twenty-one* Lashes on his or her bare Back well laid on, at the common Whipping-Post, or otherwise shall pay to the Proprietor or Governor towards the Support of Government, the Sum of *Three Pounds*, at the Election of the Party so committed as aforesaid.

What shall be Proof.

And any single or unmarried Woman having a Child born of her Body, the same shall be sufficient Proof to convict her of Fornication, without the Charges of Presentment or Indictment; and the Man charged by such Woman to be the Father of such Child, shall be the reputed Father, and she persisting in her said Charge in the Time of her Extremity and Labour, and afterwards in open Court upon the Tryal of such Person so charged, the same shall be given in Evidence in order to convict such Person of Fornication.

Any Woman bearing a Bastard Child, to be punished in the County where the Child is born, &c.

AND BE IT FURTHER ENACTED by the Authority aforesaid, That if any unmarried Woman, or any Woman who cannot make Proof of her having a Husband, absenting herself from the Place where she usually lived, shall come into any County within this Government, and there bear a Child, she shall be liable to be punished in the County where the said Child shall be born, as she should or ought to have been had the Child been there begotten; and if any such unmarried Woman shall be with Child in any County within this Government, and shall go out of the same and bear such Bastard Child in any other Place, and afterwards return into the County from whence she went with the said Child within one Year, without receiving any Punishment for her Fornication, she shall be punished as if such Bastard Child had been begotten and born in such County into which she shall return as aforesaid.

Penalty on Persons entertaining unmarried Women with Child.

And if any Person or Persons within this Government, shall knowingly entertain or shelter any such unmarried Woman being with Child coming into this Government, without giving Notice thereof unto some Justice of the Peace with *three* Days after her coming into

into his or her House; such Person or Persons being legally convicted thereof, shall forfeit *Five Pounds* for every such Offence, to the Use of the Government, as aforesaid.

AND BE IT FURTHER ENACTED by the Authority aforesaid, That if any Woman-Servant shall bear a Bastard Child within the Time of her Servitude, in regard of the Loss and Trouble her Master and Mistress must sustain thereby, and of the Maintenance of the Child until it shall be Nine Months old, in case no Father can be found of Ability sufficient to maintain such Child, she shall serve One whole Year after her Time by Indenture or Covenant is expired, and pay all such Costs and Charges as shall happen or arise by reason of any Prosecution to be had against her for such Offence. *Woman-Servant having a Bastard Child shall Serve, &c.*

AND whereas sundry vagrant Persons do frequently come into this Government, and pretending to be Man and Wife, without a legal Certification of their being married Persons, and as such cohabit together; BE IT ENACTED by the Authority aforesaid, That all Persons coming into this Government as Man and Wife, without giving some sufficient Satisfaction within Ten Days after such their coming, to some Justice of the Peace for the County into which they come, if thereto required, of their being married, they shall be deemed and taken to be Fornicators, and shall forfeit or be punished accordingly. *Vagrant Persons pretending to be Man and Wife, how to be proceeded with.*

AND BE IT FURTHER ENACTED, That whosoever shall after the End of this Sessions of Assembly, directly or indirectly entertain, provide for, or cause to be entertained or provided for, any lewd Woman or Women, or that shall frequent her or their Company, after that Admonition be given by the Justices of the Court of Quarter-Sessions, or any two of them, of the said County where such Persons shall inhabit, shall be judged a Fornicator or Adulterer, as the Case shall require, and shall suffer such Penalties as by the Laws of this Government is appointed for such Offence. *Persons providing for, or entertaining Lewd Women, to be deemed Fornicators, &c.*

AND for the Ascertaining what shall be accounted a lewd Woman, BE IT ENACTED by the Authority aforesaid, That the Justices of the Peace aforesaid, or any two of them, before any Admonition by them or any of them given in Manner aforesaid, shall give or cause Notice to be given to any Person or Persons by them, or any *Notice to be given before Admonition, &c.*

71

any two of them, fufpected of Lewdnefs or Incontinency, and being or refiding within their refpective Counties, to appear at the next Court of Quarter-Seffions to be held for the faid County, and on the Appearance of fuch Perfon or Perfons to acquaint them of the Sufpicion that is had of them, and to hear what reafonable Excufe fuch Perfons fhall offer why they ought not to be proceeded againft as Fornicators or Adulterers, as the Cafe may be : And in cafe the Perfon or Perfons having fuch Notice given them, and the fame proved by *Affidavit*, do not appear, or if appearing do not acquit themfelves of the Caufe of fuch Sufpicion, in fuch Manner as the Juftices of the faid Quarter-Seffions fhall approve ; then it fhall and may be lawful for fuch Juftices, or any two of them, and they are hereby required to admonifh fuch Perfon or Perfons according to the Direction afore-mentioned ; which Admonition, together with Proof of the Cohabitation of the Parties fo admonifhed, or their frequenting each other's Company after Admonition given, fhall be fufficient in any Court of Record within this Government, to convict the Perfons fo cohabiting or frequenting each other's Company after Admonition given, as aforefaid, of Fornication or Adultery, as the Cafe may happen, and fubject them to the Penalties afore-mentioned; any Law of this Government to the contrary notwithftanding.

Penalty on White Women that fhall have Mulatto Children, &c:

A N D   B E   I T   F U R T H E R   E N A C T E D by the Authority aforefaid, That if any White Woman within this Government fhall bear a Baftard Child begotten by a Negro or Mullatto Man, fuch Child fhall be put out to Servitude, and fhall ferve fuch Perfon or Perfons as the County-Court fhall fee fit, or order and appoint, to and for the Ufe, Benefit and Advantage of the County wherein fuch Child fhall happen to be born, as aforefaid, until he or fhe attain to the Age of Thirty-one Years : And that the Mother of fuch Child fhall forfeit and pay the Sum of *Ten Pounds* to the Governor for the Support of Government, and be publickly whipt with Thirty-nine Stripes on her bare Back well laid on at the common Whipping-Poft, and ftand in the Pillory the fpace of Two Hours ; and if a Servant, and uncapable of paying the faid Fine of *Ten Pounds*, fhe fhall in Lieu of and Satisfaction of the faid Fine be adjudged to ferve her faid Mafter, Miftrefs, or fuch other Perfon, after her Servitude and the Time allowed by the Court to her Mafter or Miftrefs for their Lofs and Trouble is expired, as the Juftices before whom fhe is or fhall be convict

convict or convicted, shall think fit, for any Term not exceeding *Five* Years; and that the Negroe or Mulatto Man, after Conviction thereof, shall be publickly whipt with *Thirty-nine* Lashes on his bare Back, and stand in the Pillory for the Space of two Hours, with one Ear nailed thereunto, and cropp'd off.

Punishment of the Negro, &c.

A N D   B E   I T   F U R T H E R   E N A C T E D by the Authority aforesaid, That if any white Man shall be legally convicted of committing Fornication with a Negroe or Mulatto Woman, such white Man shall forfeit and pay the Sum of *Twenty* Pounds, and be publickly whipt with *Twenty-one* Lashes, well laid on, at the common Whipping-Post.

Penalty on white Men committing Fornication with Negroe Women, &c.

Signed by Order of the House

A. HAMILTON, *Speaker.*

An ACT *for the Tryal of Negroes.*

B E   I T   E N A C T E D by the Honourable *PATRICK GORDON*, Esq; Lieutenant Governor of the Counties of *New-Castle, Kent* and *Suffex* upon *Delaware,* and Province of *Pennsylvania,* by and with the Advice and Consent of the Representatives of the Freemen of the said Counties in General Assembly met, and by the Authority of the same, That from and after the Publication of this Act, it shall and may be lawful for two Justices of the Peace of this Government, who shall be particularly commissionated by the Governor for that Service within the respective Counties thereof, and six of the most substantial Freeholders of the Neighbourhood, to hear, examine, try and determine all such Offences committed by any Negro or Mullato Slaves within this Government, which said Freeholders shall be by Warrant under the Hands and Seals of the respective Justices commissionated as aforesaid, directed to some Constable of the said County, be summoned to appear at

Two Justices and six Freeholders impowered to try all Offences committed by Negroes, &c.

R

such

such Time and Place as the said Justices shall appoint, which said Freeholders the said Justices shall solemnly swear or attest well and truly to give their Assistance and Judgment together with the said Justices, upon the Tryal of such Negroes or Mulattoes ; which Freeholders, or any four of them, being qualified as aforesaid, shall hold a Court at the Court-House in the said respective Counties where the Crime is committed, for the Hearing, Trying, Determining and Convicting of such Negro or Negroes or Mulato Slaves, as shall be before them charged or accused of committing any Murder, Man-Slaughter, Buggery, Burglary, Robbery, Rape, Attempts of Rape, or any other high and heinous Offences, committed, acted or done in any the respective Counties within this Government as aforesaid.

AND BE IT FURTHER ENACTED by the Authority aforesaid, That it shall and may be lawful for the said Court of Justices and Freeholders as aforesaid, to examine, try, hear, judge, determine, convict, acquit or condemn according to their Evidence, any Negro or Negroes or Mulatto Slaves for any the Crimes or Offences aforesaid, or any other High or Capital Offences, upon due Proof to them made, to pronounce such Judgment or Sentence as is agreeable to Law and the Nature of the Offence, and to order Execution of the said Judgment or Sentence accordingly, or otherwise to acquit, free and discharge such Negro or Negroes or Mulatto Slaves, in Case the Evidence shall not be sufficient for a Conviction therein.

Who may acquit or condemn, according to their Evidence, and order Execution, &c.

AND BE IT FURTHER ENACTED, That upon the Conviction of any Negro or Mulatto Slave belonging to any of the Inhabitants of this Government, for any Capital Cause for which the Party convicted shall suffer Death, the said Justices and Freeholders before whom they were convicted, shall immediately value the said Slave or Slaves, and in Case the Negro or Mulatto Slave shall be put to Death, that the two Thirds of the appraised Value of such Slave so executed, shall be paid to the Master or Owner of such Slave by the County Treasurer out of the publick Levy, to be raised in the same manner as the County Levies.

Slaves condemned to Death, to be valued, and two Thirds of the Value paid to the Master, &c.

AND BE IT FURTHER ENACTED by the Authority aforesaid, That where such Negro or Negroes grocs or Mulatto Slaves shall be convict, and such Judgment or Sentence shall be pronounced by the respective Justices and Freeholders as aforesaid, and a Warrant by them, or any four of them, one of which to be one that sat upon the Tryal, signed, sealed and delivered to the High Sheriff of the County where the Fact was committed, for the Execution of such Negro or Mulatto, the same shall be duly executed or caused to be duly executed *Sheriff to cause* by the said Sheriff, according to the Directions of such *the Sentence to* Warrant, on Pain of being disabled to act any longer in *be executed.* that Post or Office; and if any of the said Justices or Freeholders neglect or refuse to do their Duty herein, they shall be liable to be fined by the Justices at their next Court of General Quarter-Sessions of the same to be held for the said County, in any Sum not exceeding *five Pounds,* *Penalty on Jus-* for the Use of the Governor towards the Support of Go- *tices or Free-* vernment, to be levied by Distress and Sale of the Goods *holders neglec-* and Chattels of such Justices or Freeholders so refusing *herein.* as aforesaid.

AND BE IT FURTHER ENACTED by the Authority aforesaid, That if any Negro or Mulatto *Punishment of* Slave within this Government, shall attempt to commit *Slaves attemp-* a Rape on any White Woman or Maid, they shall be tryed *ting to commit* in manner aforesaid, and shall be punished by standing four *Rapes;* Hours in the Pillory at the Court-House on some Court Day, with both his Ears nailed to the Pillory, and before he be taken down from the same shall have both his Ears cut off close to his Head. And if any Negro or Mulatto Slave shall be convict before two Justices of the Peace in *Or convicted of* this Government, of stealing or fraudulently taking or car- *Stealing, &c.* rying away any Goods living or dead, the Master or Owner of such Negro or Mulatto Slave, if such Goods shall not be found, shall make Satisfaction to the Party wronged, and pay all Costs, to be levied by Distress and Sale of the said Master's or Owner's Goods and Chattles, and the Negro or Mulatto, so offending, to be whipped as the said Justices shall adjudge and appoint.

AND BE IT FURTHER ENACTED by the Authority aforesaid, That if any Negro or Mulatto *Punishment of* Slave shall presume to carry any Guns, Swords, Pistols, *of Slaves pre-* Fowling-Pieces, Clubs, or other Arms, and Weapons what- *suming to carry* ever, without his Master's special Licence for the same, *Arms, &c.* and be convicted thereof before a Magistrate, he shall be whipt with *Twenty-one* Lashes upon his bare Back.

AND

Punishment of Negroes meeting in Companies.

AND BE IT FURTHER ENACTED by the Authority aforesaid, That if any Negroes above the Number of Six in one Company, not belonging to one Owner, shall meet together, and upon no lawful Business of their Masters or Owners, and being convicted thereof, by the View of one Justice of the Peace, or the Testimony of one credible Witness, such Negro or Negroes so offending shall be publickly whipped at the Discretion of one Justice of the Peace, not exceeding *Twenty-one* Lashes, each Negro.

Signed by Order of the House,

A. HAMILTON, *Speaker.*

An ACT against Wears across Creeks and Rivers.

TO the End that all Persons inhabiting in or near any Creek or River in this Government, may enjoy all Privileges and Advantages that from them are to be reaped; BE IT ENACTED by the Honourable *PATRICK GORDON*, Esq, Lieutenant Governor of the Counties of *New-Castle*, *Kent* and *Sussex* upon *Delaware*, and of the Province of *Pennsylvania*, by and with the Advice and Consent of the Representatives of the Freemen of the said Counties, and by the Authority of the same, *Penalty on making Wears, &c.* That whosoever shall make any Wear or Wears, or set any Nets from one Side to the other of the Channel of any Creek or River within this Government, being thereof convicted, by the View of one Justice of the Peace, or by the Testimony of one credible Witness, shall for every such Offence pay *Ten Shillings*, and the Wear or Wears shall be destroyed by Order of the Justice before whom the Complaint shall be heard.

PROVIDED, That nothing in this Act extend to restrain the Making of Wares over Mill-Dams or Races, nor to such as make Wears on their own Lands so as that they

they in either of these Cases shall not be injurious to others.

AND BE IT FURTHER ENACTED, That no Wear or Wears shall be made on the South-side of *Lewes* Creek, in *Sussex* County, under the Penalty of *Ten Shillings*, and the Wear to be destroyed by the Order of any Justice of the said County.

Signed by Order of the House,

A. HAMILTON, *Speaker.*

An ACT *against removing Land-Marks.*

FOR the greater Security and Certainty of Boundaries of Lands, BE IT ENACTED by the Honourable *PATRICK GORDON*, Esq; Lieutenant Governor of the Counties of *New-Castle, Kent* and *Sussex* upon *Delaware*, and of the Province of *Pennsylvania*, by and with the Advice and Consent of the Representatives of the Freemen of the said Counties in General Assembly met, and by the Authority of the same, That no Person or Persons whatsoever within this Government shall cut, fall, alter or remove any certain bounded Tree, or other allowed Land-Mark, or shall survey any Land, or mark any Tree as a Corner-Tree, or a Line-Tree, upon any Land not belonging to the Party so doing, without lawful Authority, under the Penalty of any Sum, not exceeding *Fifty* Pounds, and not less than *Ten* Pounds, to the Use of the Party wronged, to be recovered in any Court of Judicature within this Government, by Bill, Plaint or Information, wherein no Essoign, Protection or Wager of Law shall be allowed, nor any more than one Imparlance.

Signed by Order of the House,

A. HAMILTON, *Speaker.*

S   A

A Supplement to an Act of this Government, entituled, An ACT for the better Confirmation of the Owners of Lands, &c. in their just Rights and Possessions.

Preamble. WHEREAS by the Laws of this Government formerly made for confirming the Owners of Lands in their just Rights, and for Quieting the Possession of such as were *bona fide* Purchasers of Lands within this Government for a valuable Consideration, are found not to be sufficient to answer the good Ends proposed in the said Laws : And forasmuch as at the first Settlement of these Counties, and for a long time after, the Inhabitants were very unskilful in Making Deeds and Wills, or Conveying and Devising of Lands, which heretofore were but of very small Value in these Counties, and by the Laws of this Government were always subject to be taken in Execution, and sold for the Payment of Debts, as well as to be sold by Executors and Administrators for the Payment of the Debts of their Intestates and Testators, and for Maintainance of their Children, &c.

AND WHEREAS through the Negligence of some Persons who have been intrusted with the Offices of Clerks and Registers of this Government, not only many of the Records of the several Courts of Judicature, Orphans Courts, &c. within this Government, are burned, or otherwise lost and destroyed ; but even some of the former Laws are imbezelled, so that except where it appears by the Recitals of such Deeds as are yet in being, there is no legal Proof can be made of the Judgments, Orders or Decrees, by Vertue whereof many Lands within these Counties have been sold, and many Wills, Powers of Agency, and Letters of Attorney are not now to be found, to warrant the Sales and Conveyances of Lands made by Executors or other Persons, who are said to have had Authotity to sell by Vertue of the Powers contained in the said Wills, Powers of Agency, or Letters of Attorney.

AND

AND WHEREAS through the Unskilfulness which so generally prevailed formerly in this Government among Persons pretending to be Scriveners, or to have some Understanding in the Law, sundry Lands have been devised to the Children of the Testators without the Addition of the Word *Heirs*, or any other Word by which, in Construction of Law, such Devises could be understood to be any other than Estates for Life, tho' it has been well known that the Intention of the Testator has been otherwise; and therefore, by constant Usage, the Children of such Testators, claiming under such Devises, have held the Lands as Estates of Inheritance, and have sold, and devised the same accordingly: And other Testators, and Scriveners, for want of a due Understanding and Knowledge of the Nature of Devises, and Distinction between Words which make an Estate in Fee-simple, and Fee-tail, have devised Lands to their Children, and their Issue, or their Heirs or Issue of their Bodies, or to them and their Children; when it has been known that all that was intended by the Testator was no more, than that the Lands should go to his Child or Children, and their Heirs; and yet the Devisees for want of being truely informed of the legal Construction of such Devises, have, as soon as they had Children, conceived themselves to have a good Right to devise or sell the Lands so devised to them, and have disposed of the same accordingly; and oftentimes when it hath happened that such Devisees have died, but have not sold such Lands in their Life-time, and have left Issue, who in Construction of Law were really the Heirs or Issue in Tail, such Issue, from a Belief of their having an Estate of Inheritance in the Lands so devised to them, have devised, or for a valuable Consideration, sold or mortgaged the said Lands.

AND WHEREAS the former Assemblies of this Government considering that rough and unimproved Lands were of very little Value, and that if Persons having any Right or Title to Lands within this Government should neglect to take Possession, or claim the same in a reasonable time, and by that Means, Persons being ignorant of the Claim of such Owners, should purchase the same Lands for a valuable Consideration of other Persons who have had the same surveyed to them, or of Persons pretending to be the true Heir or Heirs of the first Owners of such Lands, and such Purchaser should afterwards, at a great Expence of Labour and Money, render the same Lands of

considerable

confiderable Value by their Improvements, and die, and leave the faid Lands to their Children: It was therefore provided by a Law of this Government, above *Thirty* Years ago, that *Seven* Years quiet Poffeffion of Lands within thefe Counties, which were firft entered on upon an equitable Right, fhould give an unqueftionable Title to the fame, excepting as in the fame Act is excepted: And the People of this Government generally trufting to the Equity of that Law, and the Provifion therein made for quieting Men's Poffeffions, many honeft Perfons, ignorant of the Titles of Lands, have purchafed Lands and Tenements within this Government under the Circumftances before in this Act mentioned, which Purchafes have been made *bona fide*, and for a valuable Confideration, and the Purchafers, and thofe claiming under them, have hitherto continued in the peaceable and quiet Poffeffion of the faid Lands, without any Claim made by any Perfons pretending Right or claiming the fame as Heirs or Owners, or Heirs in Tail, Remainder or Reverfion; and many of the faid Lands fo devifed and fold as aforefaid, have been taken afterwards in Execution, and fold for the Payment of the Debts of the Perfons to whom they have afterwards been fold, and others of the faid Lands have been taken into the refpective Loan-Offices of this Government for fecuring the Payment of the Monies borrowed on the Credit of the faid Lands:

WHEREFORE to avoid the great Inconveniencies, and the Ruin of great Number of Families which might happen if the Per ˙ who heretofore, without Fraud and for a valuable Confideration, merely for want of Knowledge and Skill in the Laws, and for want of Opportunities of being better informed, have *bona fide* and for a valuable Confideration purchafed Lands under any of the aforefaid Circumftances, or if the Perfons claiming under fuch Purchafers, who have fpent their Strength and Subftance in improving the faid Lands which formerly were but of fmall Value, fhould now be turned out of their Poffeffions by Perfons pretending to claim the fame, as Owners or as Heirs in Tail, Reverfion or Remainder, or for want of being able to produce the Records of the Judgments, Decrees or Orders of the Courts where the fame were entered, or the laft Wills and Teftaments, or Powers of Attorney, by Virtue of which the faid Lands were fold; it is prayed that it may be Enacted, AND BE IT THEREFORE ENACTED by the Honourable *PATRICK GORDON* Efq; Lieutenant Governor of the Counties of

of *New-Caftle*, *Kent* and *Suffex* on *Delaware*, and **Province**
of *Pennfylvania*, by and with the Advice and Confent of
the Reprefentatives of the Freemen of the faid Counties in
General Affembly met, and by the Authority of the fame,
That where any Lands or Tenements within thefe Counties,
which have been devifed to any Perfon or Perfons (where
the Words of the Will in which the fame are devifed may
be conftrued to be an Eftate in Tail) have at any Time
before the *Thirty-firft* Day of *December*, in the Year of our
Lord *One Thoufand Seven Hundred and Fifteen*, been fold
by the Tenant for Life, or by the Tenant or Iffue in Tail,
who, in ftrictnefs of Law, had not a good Right to fell
the fame; neverthelefs, the Purchafer of fuch Lands and
Tenements having hitherto continued in the peaceable and
quiet Poffeffion of the fame, and for the Recovery of which
no Suit in Law or Equity hath hitherto been brought
againft fuch Purchafer or Purchafers, or thofe claiming under him, her or them; then fuch Purchafer or
Purchafers, upon Payment to the Heir in Tail, Remainder
or Reverfion, claiming Right under fuch Will, the Sum of
Money or Price for which the faid Lands or Tenements
were at firft fold, fhall hold the faid Lands and Tenements,
with their Appurtenances, unto the faid Purchafer or Purchafers, his or their Heirs and Affigns forever, againft the
Claim of any Heir in Tail, Remainder or Reverfion, and
againft all and every other Perfon or Perfons whomfoever,
claiming by, from or under any fuch Devife as aforefaid;
the faid Will, or any Thing therein contained, to the contrary in any wife notwithftanding.

Purchafers of Lands from Tenants for Life, &c how to be quieted in their Poffeffions.

PROVIDED, That fuch Heir in Tail, Reverfion or
Remainder, or other Perfon claiming under fuch Devifes as
aforefaid, do profecute his or her Right within three Years
after the *Firft* Day of *May*, in the Year *One Thoufand Seven
Hundred and Thirty-four*.

AND BE IT FURTHER ENACTED
by the Authority aforefaid, That where any Lands have
been fold by any of the Sheriffs within this Government,
and it appears by the Recitals in fuch Sheriffs Deeds, that
fuch Sale was made by Vertue of fome Execution or
Judgment of Court, for the Payment of the Debts of the
Owners of fuch Lands, altho' the Judgment, Order or
Decree of the Court cannot be found; or where it appears
by the Recitals in the Grants or Conveyances made by Executors of the Lands of their Teftators, that fuch Sale or

Lands taken in Execution for Payment of Debts, &c and fold by Sherffs; or Lands fold by Vertue of fome Will, Order of Court, Power of Attorney, &c. How the Poffef-

T

Grant

Grant was made by an Authority in the said Will, given to the Executor or other Person granting such Lands, to sell the same ; or it be recited that the Lands granted were sold by Vertue of some Power of Attorney from the Person having Right to the same, altho' such Will or Power of Attorney recited in the said Deeds cannot be found ; or if it be recited in the Grant made by any Executor or Administrator, that the same was made by some Judgment, Order or Decree of some Court within this Government, altho' the Record of such Judgment or Decree cannot be found ; that the Sales of Lands and Tenements made by Sheriffs, Executors, Administrators or Attornies, at any Time before the *Thirty-first* Day of *December*, in the Year *One Thousand Seven Hundred and Twenty*, and for the Recovery of which Lands and Tenements, no Suit in Law or Equity hath hitherto been brought or prosecuted by the Persons pretending Right to the same, shall and are hereby adjudged and allowed to be good and available to the Purchasers and their Heirs forever ; the want of the Record of the Judgment, Orders or Decrees of Court, or the want of any last Will and Testament, or Power of Attorney, or any of them, notwithstanding.

AND WHEREAS it has formerly been a Practice within this Government, for Executors and Administrators to have the Lands of their Testators or Intestates appraised with the personal Estate, and have usually accounted for the appraised Value of such Lands, either by paying the Value for which such Lands have been appraised, in Payment of the Testators or Intestates Debts, or in Maintenance of their Children, or to the Children of such Testators or Intestates themselves, or to their Use. BE IT THEREFORE ENACTED by the Authority aforesaid, That all Sales and Grants of Lands within these Counties, made before the Year *One Thousand Seven Hundred and Twenty*, by any Executors or Administrators, where it appears the Executors or Administrators who sold the same, have accounted for and paid the appraised Value of such Lands for the Use of their Testators and Intestates, and for the Recovery of which no Suit in Law or Equity hath hitherto been brought, altho' it does not appear that the said Lands were sold by any Judgment, Order or Decree of any Court, or by any Authority from the Will or Wills of the Testators, shall and are hereby judged and allowed to be good and

and effectual for conveying such Lands for the Uses aforesaid in the said Deeds mentioned.

AND WHEREAS ever since the Settlement of these Counties, Women under covert have been used to join with their Husbands in selling and conveying the Lands of such *Feme Coverts*, and the same hath been constantly hitherto deemed and adjudged a good Conveyance of the Lands of the Wife; and no *Feme Covert* who jointly with her Husband hath made any such Grant or Conveyance of her Lands within these three Counties, have ever after the Death of their Husbands, or any of the Heirs of such *Feme Coverts* after their Decease, sued for or laid any Claim to any of the Lands sold by such *Feme Coverts* as aforesaid: Therefore in order to confirm the Rights and quiet the Possessions of such Persons as have (*bona fide*) purchased Lands within these three Counties, of *Feme Coverts* with their Husbands, and to declare for the future, what Method of Conveyance shall be good and effectual to pass the Lands of *Feme Coverts* within this Government: BE IT ENACTED by the Authority aforesaid, That all Grants, Bargains, Sales and Alienations of any Lands within this Government, made by Husband and Wife, of the Lands belonging to the Wife in her own Right, where the same does not appear to have been done by such *Feme Covert* by Compulsion of her Husband and against her Will, declared by her at the Time of her executing the Deeds or other Writings for selling or alienating such Lands, all and every such Grant, Bargain and Sale or Conveyance by such *Feme Covert*, made before the *Twenty-fifth* Day of *March*, in the Year *One Thousand Seven Hundred and Thirty-four*, shall be and is hereby adjudged and deemed to be good and available in Law, to convey the said Lands so sold to the Purchaser and his Heirs; and that such Sale shall be as effectual a Bar against such *Feme Covert* and her Heirs, as if the same had been done by Fine and Recovery or otherwise howsoever. And that for the future no Grant, Bargain or Sale of any Lands of any *Feme-Covert* within this Government, to be made by such *Feme* during her Coverture, shall be good to pass away the Estate or Right of such *Feme Covert*, unless the said *Feme Covert*, granting the same, be examined apart from her Husband, by some Judge or Justice of the Court where such Deed shall be acknowledged, and the same be indorsed on such Deed by the Judge or Justice who takes such Examination, and the Time when the same

Sales of Lands formerly made by Feme Coverts with their Husbands, shall be good.

But for the future shall not be good, unless the Feme Covert be examined apart by some Judge, &c.

was

was taken; any former Custom, Law or Usage of this Government to the contrary in any wise notwithstanding.

PROVIDED ALWAYS, That nothing herein contained, shall be deemed or understood to make good or valid any Deed, Grant or Conveyance made of Lands within this Government, of which the Person selling the same, or his or their Under-Tenants, or some Person for him, her or them, have not been in Possession at least within three Years next before such Sale; or shall be deemed, taken or understood to make good and effectual any Grant, Bargain or Sale, where it shall appear any Fraud or Forgery hath been made or used about any Deeds or Conveyances of any Lands, or of any Powers of Agency, Letters of Attorney, last Wills and Testaments, or other Deeds, Writings or Conveyances of any Lands, grounded upon such fraudulent or forged Powers of Agency, Letters of Attorney or last Wills and Testaments, or to make good the Sale of any Lands and Tenements which have been taken in Execution or sold for any Debt, or by any Person other than the lawful Owner of the said Lands at the Time they were sold, or where any Suit either in Law or Equity hath been commenced before the Publication of this Act, for the Recovery of such Lands, but that the same shall be and continue as before the making of this Act; any thing herein contained to the contrary notwithstanding.

Nothing herein contained shall make good any fraudulent Grant, Bargain, &c.

Signed by Order of the House,

A. HAMILTON, *Speaker.*

An ACT *for Regulating Elections, and Ascertaining the Number of the Members of Assembly.*

WHEREAS the several Laws of this Government now in force for regulating Elections and ascertaining the Number of Members of Assembly, are found upon Experience in some Things to be uncertain **and**

and deficient, in making due Provision for the Freedom and Impartiality of such Elections, and the Maintenance of those Priviledges which the Assembly of this Government ought to enjoy, according to the true Intent and Meaning of the Charter granted to the People of of the Province of *Pennsylvania*, and the Counties of *New-Castle, Kent* and *Sussex* on *Delaware* : For remedying whereof, BE IT ENACTED by the Honourable *PATRICK GORDON*, Esq; Lieutenant Governor of the Counties of *New-Castle, Kent* and *Sussex* on *Delaware*, and Province of *Pennsylvania*, by and with the Advice and Consent of the Representatives of the Freemen of the said Counties in General Assembly met, and by the Authority of the same, That for the well Governing of the said Counties, there shall be an Assembly yearly chosen ; and *An Assembly to be chosen yearly.* for that End, it shall and may be lawful to and for the Freemen and Inhabitants of the respective Counties of this Government, without any Writ or Summons, to meet on the first Day of *October* yearly forever, at the most usual *The Freemen, &c. to meet on the first of October, &c.* Place of Elections in the said respective Counties, that is to say, for the County of *New-Castle*, at the Court-House in the Town of *New-Castle* : For the County of *Kent*, at the Court-House in the Town of *Dover* : And for the County of *Sussex*, at the Court-House in the Town of *Lewes* : And then and there choose their Representatives or Delegates to serve them in Assembly, which shall con- *Not less than six Representatives to be chosen for each County.* sist of not less than six Persons for each County of this Government, or a greater Number as the Governor and Assembly shall at any Time hereafter agree. And that every Person within this Government, qualified to elect according to the Directions of this Act, refusing or neglecting (not being hindred by Sickness or other unavoidable Accident) to attend at the Election and to give in his Vote, and being thereof legally convicted by the Oath or Affirmation *Penalty on Persons not attending, who are qualified to elect.* of one credible Witness, before the Justices at their next Court of General Quarter Sessions of the Peace, to be held for the County to which he belongs, shall be fined the Sum of *Twenty Shillings*, one half thereof to be paid to the Treasurer for the Use of the County, and the other half to any Person who will sue for the same. And that the Members so to be chosen, shall meet and sit in Assembly on the *Twentieth* Day of *October* yearly for- *The Assembly shall sit on the 20th of October yearly, &c.* ever at *New-Castle*, unless the Governor for the time being, in Case of some foreign Invasion, or raging Sickness prevailing in the Place to which the Assembly shall stand

V adjourned

adjourned, fhall fee caufe to appoint another Place within this Government to meet at: But when any of the faid Days of Elections or Meeting of Affembly, fhall happen to fall on the firft Day of the Week called *Sunday*, then fuch Election and Meeting fhall be the next Day following.

PROVIDED ALWAYS, That no Inhabitants of this Government, fhall have Right of electing or being elected as aforefaid, unlefs he or they be natural-born Subjects of *Great-Britain*, or be naturalized in *England*, or in this Government, or in the Province of *Pennfylvania*, and unlefs fuch Perfon or Perfons be of the Age of *Twenty-one* Years or upwards, and be a Freeholder or Freeholders in this Government, and have Fifty Acres of Land or more well fettled, and twelve Acres thereof cleared and improved, or be otherwife worth *Forty Pounds* lawful Money of this Government clear Eftate, and have been refident therein for the Space of two Years before fuch Election : And that every Man who fhall give his Vote without being qualified as aforefaid, or that fhall receive any Reward or Gift for his Vote, or that fhall give, offer or promife any Reward to be elected, or fhall offer to ferve for nothing or lefs Allowance than the Law prefcribes, fhall forfeit *Five Pounds*, the one half thereof to the Governor, and the other to him or them who will fue for the fame in any Court of Record within this Government ; and the Perfon fo elected fhall be incapable to ferve for that Year.

Who are qualified to elect or be elected.

Penalty on bribing or being brib'd to vote.

AND BE IT FURTHER ENACTED by the Authority aforefaid, That every Sheriff, or in his Abfence his Under-Sheriff, or fuch as he fhall depute, or for want of fuch Deputation, the Coroner or fuch as he fhall appoint ; or for want of fuch Appointment, any two of the Freeholders, who by the major Part of the Electors then and there prefent, fhall be nominated and appointed Judges of the faid Elections in the Abfence of the faid Sheriff or Coroner, fhall attend at the faid Elections ; and the Electors fhall then proceed to the Choice of Infpectors of the faid Elections, who fhall be Freeholders, and be nominated one out of each Hundred by the free Electors thereof, and when fo chofen fhall be qualified by Oath or Affirmation, by the Sheriff of the proper County or other Judges of the Elections, who are hereby impowered and required to adminifter the fame, That they will duly attend the enfuing Election during the Continuance thereof, and will truly and faithfully

The Method of making and carrying on of Elections.

Qualification of Infpectors.

faithfully affift the Sheriff, Coroner or other Perfons who fhall by Vertue of this Act officiate as Judges of the faid Elections, to prevent all Frauds and Deceits whatfoever of Electors or others, in the Management and carrying on the fame, and in caufing the Poll or Votes at fuch Elections to be taken and caft up according to the Directions of this Act ; and being fo qualified fhall appoint Clerks, who fhall take the faid Poll or Names of the Electors in the Prefence of the faid Sheriff, Coroner or other Judges as aforefaid, or fuch as any of them fhall depute or appoint, and fhall make as many diftinct Columns on fair Paper as there fhall be Candidates voted for, as is herein after ex- *Vide 13 of K.* preffed; but before they begin, every Clerk fo appointed, *George I.* fhall, by the faid Sheriff or Coroner, or by fome Magiftrate then prefent, be attefted or charged on his Oath or folemn Af- *Qualifications* firmation, truly and indifferently to take the faid Poll and *of Clerks.* fet down the Names of each Freeholder and Elector, and the Place of his Freehold or Eftate, and to Poll no Elector who is not attefted, if fo required by the Infpectors of fuch Elections. And every Perfon coming to elect Mem- *Names of Per-* bers for the faid refpective Counties, fhall deliver in Writing *fons voted for to* the Names of thofe Perfons for whom they vote, to the Sheriff *be delivered in* or fome other of the faid Perfons fo as aforefaid appointed *Writing, &c.* Judges of the faid Elections, who fhall open the Paper, if the Perfon be illiterate, and read the Perfons Names contained therein, and afk fuch Elector whether thefe are the Per- fons for whom he votes, which Paper, upon his anfwering in the Affirmative, fhall be received and put with the reft of the Electors Papers in a Box, which every Sheriff is hereby required to provide for that Purpofe : But if the Elector brings no fuch Paper or Ticket, or if the illite- rate Elector will not vote for the Perfons contained in his Paper, then, and in all fuch Cafes, the Elector fhall verbally give in the Names of the Perfons he moftly de- fires fhould be chofen, which Names fhall be entered down by the faid Clerks.

PROVIDED ALWAYS, That every Elector before he be admitted to poll (if required by any of the faid Infpectors) fhall upon his Oath or folemn Affirmation, *The Qualifica-* declare, That he is *Twenty-one* Years of Age, and a Free- *tion of Electors,* holder of the County of   and has *Fifty* Acres *&c.* of Land or more well feated, and *Twelve* Acres or more thereof cleared, or that he is otherwife worth *Forty Pounds* Money of this Government clear Eftate, and hath been re- fident

fident therein for the Space of two Years, and that he has not been before polled at that Election. And in Case any Person taking the said Oath or Affirmation, shall be lawfully convicted of wilfully and corruptly making a false Oath or Affirmation therein, or if any shall suborn any Person to take such false Oath or Affirmation, he or they shall incur the same Penalties and Forfeitures as by the Laws and Statutes of *England*, are provided against Persons convicted of wilful and corrupt Perjury and Subornation of Perjury respectively : And that the said Poll shall not be delayed, nor the Election adjourned to another Place or Part of the County other than where the same begins, but shall continue from Day to Day till the Freeholders and Electors then and there present shall be polled, and no longer : And when all the Electors then appearing shall have delivered in all their Papers or Names, the said Box shall be opened by the Sheriff or some other of the Persons appointed by this Act to officiate as Judges of the said Elections, and the said Papers taken out in the Presence of the said Inspectors, and delivered one by one to the said Clerk or Clerks, to enter the Names therein exprest in fair Columns or otherwise, so that they shall cast up how many times such Persons Name is repeated in the same, and set it down, and shall then pronounce publickly to the People, him whose Name is oftenest mentioned in the said Papers, to be first elected, and so the next highest Number successively, until the whole six Persons for the County be pronounced elected by Majority as aforesaid. But if when the said Papers are opened, there appear fewer or more Names in any one of them, or more than one Paper deceitfully folded together, containing more Names than by this Act is allowed any one Elector to vote for, such Papers shall be rejected and not accounted amongst the Votes.

Penalty on false Oath or Affirmation.

The Poll not to be delayed or adjourned, &c.

Votes to be cast up, and the Election proclaimed.

Any Deceit in a Ticket makes it void.

A N D after the said Representatives are so chosen as aforesaid, their Names (be they present or absent) shall be written in a pair of Indentures sealed between the said Sheriff, or other Persons officiating as Judges of the said Election, and six or more of the said Electors ; and every Sheriff or other Person officiating as Judges of the said Elections, shall, on the first Day of the Meeting of every Assembly, in Person or by Deputy, present one Part of the said Indentures to the Governor for the time being, and the other Part thereof to the House of Representatives ; which said Indentures shall be deemed and taken to be the

The Names of the Representatives to be written in Indentures ; one of which to be delivered to the Governor, and the other to the House, &c.

Sheriffs

Sheriffs Return of the Representatives or Delegates of the Freemen of this Government, to serve and act in the Legislative or General Assemblies of the same Government from time to time, and the Representatives so as aforesaid chosen, shall yield their Attendance accordingly.

AND if any Person or Persons so chosen and returned to serve as aforesaid, shall be absent from the Service for which he or they shall be so elected, he or they shall forfeit any Sum not exceeding *Ten Pounds* current Money of this Government, the one half thereof to the Governor and the other half to him or them that shall sue for the same in manner aforesaid, unless his or their Excuse for such Absence be allowed of by the Assembly. *Penalty on Persons chosen refusing to serve.*

AND if any Person so chosen and returned as aforesaid, shall happen to die or be wilfully absent, or by Vote of the House be disabled to sit or serve in Assembly, that then, and in every such Case, the Speaker of the Assembly for the time being, by Direction of the House, shall signify to the Governor for the Time being, the Order of the House for electing a new Member in the Room of the Person deceased, wilfully absent, or disabled by Vote of the House to serve in Assembly; and in Case the Governor shall not within two Days after such Application to him made as aforesaid, issue out Writs to the Sheriff of the respective Counties where there shall be Occasion for electing such new Member, and cause Notice of his having so done to be given to the Assembly within the Time aforesaid, it shall and may be lawful for the Speaker of the Assembly for the time being, by Order of the House, to issue forth the said Writs, which shall be made in the Governor's Name, under the Hand and Seal of the Speaker, whereupon every Sheriff or other Officer to whom such Writ or Writs are directed, shall indorse the Receipt thereof on the Back, and with all convenient speed, after he receives such Writ, shall cause publick Notice to be given of the Time and Place of Election, and proceed to elect thereupon in manner aforesaid, within the Space of five Days after the Receipt of the said Writ, and give three Days Notice at least of the Day appointed for the Election; which Notice shall be given in Writing, and shall be proclaimed in the most publick Places of the capital Town or Place where such Election is to be; and the said Sheriff or other Officer shall cause Copies of such Notice or Advertisement *How Vacancies in the House are to be filled.*

X

tisement

tifement to be pofted on fome Tree or Houfe in the Way leading from every Hundred, Townfhip or Precinct to the Town or Place where the faid Election is to be, as alfo upon the Court-Houfes and publick fixed Meeting-Houfes for Religious Worfhip in the faid refpective Counties: And when thofe Elections are made by Virtue of the faid Writs in manner aforefaid, the Sheriff or other Officer who fhall officiate as Judges of the faid Elections, fhall write down the Names of the Perfons fo elected in a pair of Indentures fealed, and prefent one Part thereof to the Governor, and the other Part to the Affembly on the Day of the Return of fuch Writs; which faid Indentures fhall be deemed to be the Sheriff's Return of fuch Reprefentatives; all which faid Elections fhall begin between the Hours of *Ten* in the Morning and *Two* in the Afternoon; and that no Perfon or Perfons whatfoever, by Force of Arms or Menacing, fhall difturb the Freemen of this Government in the free Election of their Reprefentatives, but that the fame Election fhall be freely and indifferently made.

AND BE IT FURTHER ENACTED by the Authority aforefaid, That if any Sheriff fhall refufe or neglect to give Notice of the faid Election by Writs, then the Coroner of the refpective County where the fame fhall happen, is hereby required by himfelf or his Deputy, to officiate and perform all that the faid Sheriff or his Deputy ought to have done and performed at the faid Elections, according to the Tenour and Directions of this Act. And every Sheriff or other Officer not making good and true Returns of the faid Elections of Reprefentatives or Members of Affembly, according to the Direction of this Act, or refufing or wilfully neglecting to do and perform all or any of the Matters and Things in this Act required to be done by fuch Sheriff or Coroner at and after the faid Elections, fhall forfeit for every fuch Offence, the Sum of *One Hundred Pounds* Money aforefaid, the one half thereof to the Governor, and the other Moiety thereof to him who will fue for the fame in manner aforefaid.

Penalty on Sheriffs, &c. not performing the Duty required of them by this Act.

AND BE IT FURTHER ENACTED by the Authority aforefaid, That the Reprefentatives fo chofen and met according to the Directions of this Act, fhall be and continue the Affembly of this Government for the enfuing Year, and fhall have Power to choofe a Speaker and other their Officers, and fhall be Judges of the Qualifications and Elections of their own Members,

The Powers & Privileges of an Affembly.

fit

sit upon their own Adjournments, appoint Committees, prepare Bills in Order to pass into Laws, impeach Criminals, and redress Grievances, and shall have all other Powers and Priviledges of an Assembly according to the Rights of the free-born Subjects of *England*, and as is usual in any of His Majesty's Plantations in *America*. And if any County or Part of this Government shall refuse or neglect to choose their respective Representatives as aforesaid, or if chosen do not meet to serve in Assembly, those who are so chosen and met, shall have the full Power of an Assembly, in as ample manner as if all the Representatives had been chosen and met, provided they are not less than two Thirds of the whole that ought to meet.

Two Thirds of of the whole Number may act.

AND BE IT FURTHER ENACTED by the Authority aforesaid, That no Person who shall be hereafter a Member of the Assembly or House of Representatives of this Government, shall be capable to vote in the said House, or sit there during any Debate after their Speaker is chosen, until he shall make and subscribe the following Declarations and Profession of his Christian Belief, *viz.*

No Member to vote in the House till qualified.

I A. B. *do sincerely promise and solemnly declare before God and the World, That I will be faithful and bear true Allegiance to King* GEORGE *the Second. And I do solemnly profess and declare, that I do from my Heart abhor, detest and renounce as impious and heretical, that damnable Doctrine and Position, that Princes, excommunicated or deprived by the* Pope, *or any Authority of the See of* Rome, *may be deposed or murthered by their Subjects, or any other whatsoever.*

The Qualification of every Member of Assembly.

AND I do declare that no foreign Prince, Person, Prelate, State or Potentate, hath, or ought to have, any Power, Jurisdiction, Superiority, Preeminence or Authority, Ecclesiastical or Spiritual, within the Realm of Great-Britain *or the Dominions thereunto belonging.*

AND I the said A. B. do solemnly and sincerely in the Presence of God, profess, testify and declare, that I do believe that in the Sacrament of the Lord's-Supper *there is not any Transubstantiation of the Elements of the Bread and Wine into the Body and Blood of* CHRIST, *at or after the Consecration thereof by any Person whatsoever; and that the Invocation or*
Adoration

Adoration of the Virgin Mary, *or any other Saint, and the Sacrifice of the Mass, as they are now used in the Church of* Rome, *are superstitious and idolatrous.*

AND I do solemnly, in the Presence of Almighty God, profess, testify and declare, that I do make this Declaration, and every Part thereof, in the plain and ordinary Sense of the Words read unto me, as they are commonly understood by English *Protestants, without any Evasion, Equivocation or mental Reservation whatsoever, and without any Dispensation already granted me for this Purpose by the Pope or any other Authority or Person whatsoever, or without any hope of any such Dispensation from any Person or Authority whatsoever, or without thinking I am or may be acquitted before God or Man, or absolved of this Declaration or any Part thereof, altho' the Pope or any other Person or Persons or Power whatsoever, should dispence with or annul the same, or declare that it was null or void from the Beginning.*

AND I A. B. profess Faith in GOD *the Father, and in* JESUS CHRIST *his eternal Son, and in the* HOLY-SPIRIT, *one God blessed for evermore ; and I do acknowledge the Holy Scriptures of the Old and New Testament to be given by divine Inspiration.*

Time of taking the Qualification.

WHICH said Declarations and Profession of Faith shall be in the next and every succeeding Assembly to be held in this Government, solemnly and publickly made and subscribed in their House, between the Hours of *Nine* in the Morning and *Four* in the Afternoon, by every such Member of the House of Representatives at the Table, and while a full House of Representatives is there sitting with their Speaker in his Chair ; and during the making and subscribing thereof, all Business and Debates in the said House shall cease.

Qualification to be recorded, &c.

Manner of making the Declaration, &c

AND the Clerk of the Assembly is hereby required to Record the same in Rolls or Books prepared for that Purpose, and every Member of Assembly shall pay the Clerk for recording thereof *Six Pence* and no more : And that the Manner and Method of making the said Declarations shall be as followeth (*to wit*) The Speaker shall first read and and subscribe the same, and after him every Member as he is called over shall either read and subscribe the said Declarations in Manner and Form aforesaid, or else subscribe them

them as they shall be read unto him by the Clerk of the Assembly.

AND BE IT ENACTED, by the Authority aforesaid, That no Person whatsoever who at any Time shall be elected Member of Assembly in this Government, and who shall make, and be willing and offer to make and subscribe the said Declarations in Manner and Form aforesaid, shall be rejected or denied to sit, debate and act in the House of Representatives or General Assembly of this Government, he being otherwise qualified as this Law directs.

No Person chosen, that makes and subscribes the same shall be denied his Seat in the House.

PROVIDED NEVERTHELESS, That nothing herein contained, shall extend to debar or hinder the House of Representatives to reject such Persons as are or shall be unduly elected Members to serve in Assembly, or such as the Assembly, or major Part of them, shall see cause from time to time by Vote to expel or disable to sit or serve there, by reason of ill Practice in Elections or Misbehaviour in the House.

Except unduly elected, &c.

AND BE IT FURTHER ENACTED by the Authority aforesaid, That every Member chosen to serve in Assembly as aforesaid, shall be allowed the Sum of *Six Shillings* per Day, and the Speaker *Ten Shillings* per Day during his or their Attendance, by the Counties they respectively represent ; and that every Member of Assembly shall be allowed towards his travelling Charges after the Rate of *Three Pence* per Mile, coming to and going from the Place where the Assembly is or shall be held.

Members Allowance per Diem.

Signed by Order of the House

A. HAMILTON, *Speaker.*

Y   *An*

An ACT *for the further securing the Administration of the Government.*

Preamble. WHEREAS the Prosperity of a Country very much depends upon a full and regular Administration of Government, and considering the uncertainty of Human Life, and that hitherto there hath not been made any effectual Provision for the due executing the Powers of Government in these Counties, in Case of the Death, Absence or Removal of the Deputy or Lieutenant Governor, it is therefore highly necessary to make such Provision against the Inconveniencies that may happen upon such an Emergency, as may effectually preserve the Peace, and maintain the regular Administration of Justice within this Government.

BE IT THEREFORE ENACTED by the Honourable *PATRICK GORDON*, Esq; Lieutenant Governor, with the Royal Approbation, under the Honourable *JOHN PENN, THOMAS PENN* and *RICHARD PENN*, Esquires, absolute Proprietaries and Governors in Chief of the Counties of *New-Castle, Kent* and *Sussex* on *Delaware*, and the Province of *Pennsylvania*, by and with the Advice and Consent of the Representatives of the Freemen of the said Counties in General Assembly met, and by the Authority of the same, That in Case of the *In Case of Death, Absence, &c. of the Lieutenant Governor, on whom the Administration shall devolve, &c.* Death, Absence or Removal of the Deputy or Lieutenant Governor of the said three Counties, and no sufficient Provision being made by the Governors or Governor in Chief for the full Administration of the said Government, That then the President, or the first Person named of the Governor's Council of the said Province of *Pennsylvania*, shall immediately take upon him the Administration of this Government, and with the Advice and Consent of the Speaker of the House of Representatives of the said three Counties for the time being, and the three Magistrates that shall then happen to preside or be first nominated in the Commissions of the Peace for the said three Counties of *New-Castle, Kent* and *Sussex*, or any three of them, the the said Speaker and Magistrates shall have the full Power and Authority of a Lieutenant Governor of these Counties,

as

as effectually as any Deputy or Lieutenant Governor commissionated by the Governors or Governor in Chief, and approved by His Majesty, may or ought to have.

AND the said President, with the Advice and Consent of the said Speaker and Magistrates aforesaid, or of any three of them, shall accordingly act and exercise all the Powers of Government, as fully and amply as any Deputy or Lieutenant Governor can or ought to do, Legislation excepted, until the said Lieutenant Governor return again, or until another Person shall be duly commissionated and empowered by the Governors or Governor in Chief, with His Majesty's Approbation, to act in his stead, or until His Majesty's Pleasure shall be known therein. *Until the Vacancy be supplied, &c.*

AND to the End that no Confusion or Disorder may happen in Case of such Death, Absence or Removal of the Deputy Governor as aforesaid, before the said President and the other Persons, by whose Advice and Consent he is herein directed to act, can meet and consider of the Affairs of Government; BE IT FURTHER ENACTED by the Authority aforesaid, That all Magistrates and other Officers within this Government, shall continue to execute all the Powers and Authorities to them given by Law and their respective Commissions, as fully and amply as they might or could do before the Death, Absence or Removal of the said Deputy or Lieutenant Governor, for and during the Space of six Months next after the Death, Absence or Removal of such Deputy or Lieutenant Governor, unless such Magistrates or Officers shall be removed by the Persons having Authority so to do, or the Time of the continuance of their respective Commissions shall determine by the Laws of this Government. *All Magistrates &c. to continue in Place, &c.*

AND BE IT FURTHER ENACTED by the Authority aforesaid, That an Act of Assembly of this Government, entitled, *An Act for Providing for the Security of this Government in Case of the Demise of the Lieutenant Governor for the time being*, and every Article, Clause or Thing therein contained, shall be and are hereby repealed. *Repeal of the former Act.*

Signed by Order of the House,

A. HAMILTON, *Speaker.*

An

An ACT *for the striking and making Current* Six Thousand Pounds *in new Bills of Credit, to exchange such of the Bills of Credit of this Government emitted Anno* Domini One Thousand Seven Hundred and Thirty-four, *as are worn and defaced.*

Preamble.　WHEREAS many of the Bills of Credit of this Government made Current by one Act of General Assembly of the same, in the *Eighth* Year of His present Majesty's Reign, are very much worn and defaced, more especially those of the lesser Denominations, and are scarce fit to pass : For Prevention therefore of the Inconveniencies and Difficulties arising thereby, may it please the Governor that it may be Enacted, And

BE IT ENACTED by the Honourable *GEORGE THOMAS*, Esq; by and with His Majesty's Royal Approbation, Lieutenant Governor and Commander in Chief of the Counties of *New-Castle*, *Kent* and *Sussex* upon *Delaware*, and Province of *Pennsylvania*, by and with the Advice and Consent of the Representatives of the Freemen of the said Counties in General Assembly met, and by the Authority of the same, That for the Exchanging of the worn and defaced Bills of Credit of this Government, emitted and made Current by Vertue of the said Act, entitled, *An* ACT *for emitting and making Current* Twelve Thousand *Pounds in Bills of Credit*, other Bills of *6000 l. in new Bills to be struck for exchanging the worn and defaced.* Credit to the Value of *Six Thousand Pounds* Current Money of *America*, with the same Arms and of the like Tenor and Form, the Signers Names excepted, with those above mentioned, shall be made and prepared with all convenient speed ; which Bills shall severally contain therein the Sums hereafter respectively mentioned, and no other, (that is to *Quantity of each sort.* say) *Two Thousand two Hundred* of the said Bills the Sum of *Ten Shillings* in each of them : *Four Thousand eight Hundred* of the said Bills, the Sum of *Five Shillings* in each of them: *Twelve Thousand four Hundred* of the said Bills, the

Sum

Sum of *Two Shillings and Six Pence* in each of them : *Eight Thousand* of the said Bills, the Sum of *Two Shillings* in each of them : *Ten Thousand* of the said Bills the Sum of *Eighteen Pence* in each of them : And *Twelve Thousand* of the said Bills the Sum of *One Shilling* in each of them.

AND that all the said Bills shall bear Date the *First* Day of *December*, Anno Domini *One Thousand Seven Hundred and Thirty-nine* : And that *Jehu Curtis* and *William Till*, Gentlemen, shall, at the Charge of this Government, to be paid and defrayed in Bills of Credit, cause and procure the said Bills of Credit to be printed on good Paper.

ALL which Bills shall be numbred and signed by *Thomas Noxon*, of *New-Castle* County, Gent. *John Holiday*, of *Kent* County, Gent. and *Jabez Maud Fisher*, of *Sussex* County, Gent. *Signers Names.*

AND the said Signers shall also deliver to the Trustees, hereafter named, at the respective Offices, all the Bills so made forth, numbred and signed as aforesaid, not exceeding the Numbers herein before respectively limited and appointed (taking the said Trustees Receipt for the same, and charging them respectively with the Monies contained in the Bills so delivered) in order to be exchanged for worn and defaced Bills, as herein after is directed. *Bills Signed, to be delivered to the Trustees.*

AND the said Signers shall cause to be kept a true Account of all the said Bills by them numbred, signed and delivered to the said Trustees, which Account shall by the said Signers be delivered to the General Assembly of this Government at their first Meeting next after the signing the said Bills : And for their Trouble, Care and Diligence in doing what is required of them by this Act, they shall receive each of them *Twelve Shillings* for every Thousand Bills by them so numbred and signed, to be paid to each of them, his Executors, Administrators or Assigns in Bills of Credit, to be delivered by the Trustees out of the Interest Money of the General Loan-Offices for this Government, appointed by Vertue of the said recited Act, within six Days after they deliver the said Bills into the Loan-Offices as aforesaid. *Signers to keep an Account of the Bills, &c.* *Their Reward.*

BUT before the said Persons hereby appointed, or hereafter to be appointed by Vertue of this Act, to be

Z

Signers

Signers of the said Bills of Credit, presume to act therein, they shall take an Oath or Affirmation before any one Justice of the Peace for the respective County where such Signer lives, who is hereby empowered and required to administer the same, That they, and each of them, will *Signers Qualification.* well and truly sign, number and deliver all the said Bills of Credit, and keep a true Account of what Bills they sign and deliver according to the Directions of this Act.

Manner of appointing a new Signer in Case of vacancy. AND in Case any of the said Signers die, or be rendered uncapable of executing the said Trust, it shall and may be lawful for the Members of the County of *New-Castle*, or the Majority of them, with the Consent of the Governor, to appoint another in the stead of such Person so dying or being rendered uncapable as aforesaid, which Person or Persons so to be appointed, shall, before his or their Entry upon the said Trust, take the same Oath or Affirmation as the Signers in this Act appointed are required to take.

How the Bills are to be divided. AND BE IT FURTHER ENACTED by the Authority aforesaid, That the Sum of *Two Thousand four Hundred* Pounds of the said Bills of Credit, being numbred and signed as aforesaid, shall be put into the Hands of *David French* and *Andrew Peterson*, of the said County of *New-Castle*, Gentlemen, Trustees of the General Loan-Office for the said County of *New-Castle*, or into the Hands of the Trustees of the said Office for the time being.

AND the Sum of *Two Thousand* Pounds of the said Bills of Credit, shall be put into the Hands of *Mark Manlove* and *John Tilton*, of *Kent* County, Gentlemen, Trustees of the General Loan-Office for the said County of *Kent*, or into the Hands of the Trustees of the said Office for the time being.

AND the Sum of *One Thousand Six Hundred* Pounds of the said Bills of Credit, shall be put into the Hands of *William Till*, of *Sussex* County, Gentleman, Trustee of the General Loan-Office for the said County of *Sussex*, or into the Hands of the Trustee or Trustees of the said Office for the time being.

AND that all and singular the said Bills of Credit which shall be made and issued in pursuance of this Act, shall

shall have the same Currency, and be of the same Effect in Law and Equity, with Respect of Payments, Tenders, or bringing the same into Court for Performance of any Contract, Bargain or Promise whatsoever, and to all Intents and Purposes whatsoever, as any Bills of Credit emitted and made Current by any former Act or Acts of General Assembly of this Government.

The New Bills shall be a lawful Tender, &c.

AND that the said Trustees for the time being, or some other Person or Persons under their and his Direction respectively, and for whom they or he shall be accountable, shall duly attend at their respective Loan-Offices the first *Tuesday* in each Month, at *New-Castle* in the County of *New-Castle*; at *Dover*, in the County of *Kent*; and at *Lewes*, in the County of *Sussex*; then and there to deliver out new Bills of Credit by Virtue of this Act directed to be made, to such Persons as demand the same in exchange and lieu of such Bills of Credit of this Government, emitted and made current by the afore-recited Act, as are worn or defaced, yet by the said Trustee or Trustees shall be judged to be genuine Bills and of equal Value with those so to be given in exchange, until the whole *Six Thousand* Pounds aforesaid, be wholly exchanged; which worn and defaced Bills being kept by the said Trustee and Trustees respectively, shall from time to time by him and them be produced as Vouchers, to discharge him and them of the said *Six Thousand* Pounds Value, before the Committees of the General Assemblies of this Government, to be appointed Auditors of the said Trustees Accounts; which said Committees shall thereupon cause the said worn and defaced Bills to be sunk and destroyed.

Attendance to be given for exchanging old Bills &c.

AND the said Trustee and Trustees respectively, for his and their Trouble and Charge in exchanging the said Bills of Credit, during the residue of the Term or Time he and they shall remain and be Trustees for the said General Loan-Offices by Virtue of the said recited Act, shall be allowed as follows, that is to say, to the Trustees for the County of *New-Castle*, shall be allowed the Sum of *Ten Pounds* per Annum each: To the Trustees for the County of *Kent*, shall be allowed the Sum of *Eight Pounds* per Annum each: and to the Trustee or Trustees for the County of *Sussex*, shall be allowed the Sum of *Seven Pounds* per Annum each, payable to each of them, his Executors, Administrators and Assigns, out of the Interest Money arising

Trustees Reward for Exchanging.

in

in the respective Loan-Offices by Vertue of the said re-cited Act.

BUT the said Trustees, before they shall take into their Hands the Sums of Money in Bills of Credit to them re-spectively directed to be delivered by Vertue of this Act, *Trustees to give Bond,* shall each of them enter into a Bond to the Governor for the time being, in the Penalty of the Sum to each of them to be delivered by Vertue of this Act, conditioned for the true Observance of all Things required of them by this Act, and true Performance of the Trust reposed in them; which said Bonds shall be duly acknowledged by the Trustees in the respective Courts of Common-Pleas for the Counties of *New-Castle, Kent* and *Sussex* upon *Delaware,* where the said Trustees dwell, and recorded in the said re-spective Courts, and the Originals shall be safely kept in the Rolls Offices of the said respective Counties; and shall *And take an Oath or Affir-mation, &c.* also take an Oath or Affirmation before any one Justice of the Peace for the respective County where they dwell, who is hereby empowered and required to administer the same, in these Words, *viz.*

I A. B. will, according to the best of my Skill and Know-ledge, faithfully, impartially and truly demean myself in discharge of the Trust committed to me by an Act of General Assembly of this Government, entitled, An Act for the strik-ing and making Current Six Thousand Pounds in new Bills of Credit, to exchange such of the Bills of Credit of this Government, emitted Anno Domini One Thousand Seven Hundred and Thirty-four, as are worn and defaced, according to the Tenour and Purport of the said Act, so as none may be prejudiced by my Consent, Privity or Procurement.

AND BE IT FURTHER ENACTED *Farther Duty of the Trustees.* by the Authority aforesaid, That the said Trustees, after they are so qualified, shall well and truly keep in their Hands and Custody all worn and defaced Bills of Credit by them to be taken in Exchange for new Bills by Vertue of this Act; and that the same worn and defaced Bills, together with the said new Bills of Credit which shall remain in the said Offices unexchanged, shall as often as required be produced by the said Trustees respectively, to the Committees from time to time hereafter to be appointed by the Assemblies of this Government, to audit the said Trustees Accounts; and that the same worn and defaced Bills, taken into the said respective Loan-Offices in ex-change

change, shall from time to time be delivered to the said Committees, and by them, in the Presence of the said Trustees, respectively be burnt and destroyed.

AND BE IT FURTHER ENACTED by the Authority aforesaid, That if any Person or Persons *Punishment of* whatsoever, shall presume to forge or counterfeit, or be *Counterfeiting,* aiding or assisting in forging or counterfeiting any of the *&c.* said Bills of Credit to be made current by this Act, or shall presume to forge or counterfeit or be aiding or assisting in the forging or counterfeiting any of the Bills of Credit of this Government, made current by any former Act or Acts of Assembly, or change the Values of any of the said Bills, or utter or cause to be uttered or offered in Payment any of the said Bills knowing the same to be actually forged, counterfeited or changed in their Value, with an Intent to defraud any other Person, and be thereof legally convicted, he or she so offending shall suffer Death without Benefit of Clergy.

AND all Magistrates and others into whose Hands any *How counterfeit* counterfeited Bills may happen to come, shall forthwith *Bills are to be* deliver the same to one of the Trustees of the respective *disposed of.* Loan-Offices, who shall cause the Names of those that deliver them, and of the Persons from whom they shall be taken, to be endorsed thereon, which Bills shall be safely kept in the said Offices, and be forth-coming when there may be Occasion to make use of the same, and afterwards delivered to a Committee as aforesaid, to be destroyed.

AND IT IS HEREBY DECLARED AND ENACTED by the Authority aforesaid, That this present Act shall be taken and allowed in all *This Act de-* Courts within this Government as a publick Act, and all *clared to be a* Judges, Justices and other Persons concerned therein, are *publick Act,* hereby required to take Notice thereof as such without *&c.* pleading the same specially.

AND BE IT FURTHER ENACTED by the Authority aforesaid, That all the said Bills of *How the Bills* Credit to be made current by Vertue of this Act, shall be *made current by* sunk and destroyed, in like manner, and at such time and *this Act, are* times as the Bills of Credit emitted and made current by *to be sunk.* the afore-recited Act, are by the same Act directed to be sunk and destroyed. A a AND

AND BE IT FURTHER ENACTED, by the Authority aforefaid, That *Jacob Kollock,* of *Suffex* County, Gent. is hereby conftituted and appointed one of the Truftees of the feveral General Loan-Offices of the County of *Suffex,* together with *William Till* the former Truftee ; and that he the faid *Jacob Kollock* fhall have the fame Power and Authority to all Intents and Purpofes whatfoever, as if he had been nominated, conftituted and appointed by the former Acts of Affembly of this Government for the emitting of Paper Money or Bills of Credit.

Another Truf-
tee appointed for
Suffex County;

AND that the faid *Jacob Kollock* fhall be ftiled one of the Truftees of the General Loan-Offices for the County of *Suffex,* and fhall have all the Powers which to any of the Truftees of this Government by Vertue of any of the Acts of Affembly of this Government are given and granted, and may do and execute all Matters and Things purfuant to the faid Acts and this prefent Act, as if his Name had been therein particularly mentioned and inferted, fubject to the Provifoes, Limitations and Reftrictions in the feveral Acts mentioned and expreffed.

Who fhall have
all the Powers
of other Truf-
tees;

AND that the faid *Jacob Kollock,* before he fhall enter upon the Execution of the faid Truft, fhall enter into Bond to the Governor, in the Penalty of *One Thoufand Pounds,* Conditioned for the due Obfervance of all Things required of him by this prefent and the aforefaid Acts of Affembly, and for the true Performance of the Truft hereby repofed in him, which faid Bond fhall be acknowledged and recorded as by this Act before is directed, and fhall alfo take fuch an Oath as is herein before mentioned and directed to be taken by the other Truftees of the General Loan-Offices of this Government.

And fhall give
Bond, &c.

Signed by Order of the Houfe,

DAVID FRENCH, *Speaker.*

A

A Supplementary ACT *to to the Act entitled,* An Act for the striking and making Current *Six Thousand* Pounds in new Bills of Credit, to exchange such of the Bills of Credit of this Government, emitted Anno Domini *One Thousand Seven Hundred and Thirty-four* as are worn and defaced.

WHEREAS the Act of Assembly entitled, *An Act for the striking and making Current* Six Thousand Pounds *in new Bills of Credit, to exchange such of the Bills of Credit of this Government emitted Anno Domini* One Thousand Seven Hundred and Thirty-four *as are worn and defaced*, is found to be defective and insufficient to answer all the Ends and Purposes for which the same was made; AND WHEREAS several Frauds have been committed in counterfeiting the Bills of Credit of this Government : THEREFORE for the remedying thereof, and for preventing such ill Practices for the future ;

Preamble.

BE IT ENACTED by the Honourable *GEORGE THOMAS*, Esq; by and with His Majesty's Royal Approbation, Lieutenant Governor and Commander in Chief of the Counties of *New-Castle, Kent* and *Suffex* on *Delaware*, and Province of *Pennsylvania*, by and with the Advice and Consent of the Representatives of the Freemen of the said Counties, in General Assembly met, and by the Authority of the same, That if any Person or Persons whatsoever within this Government or elsewhere, except such Person or Persons only as by the Government shall be employed for that Purpose, shall presume to print or make or cause to be printed or made, or shall import or cause to be imported into this Government, or shall in anywise be aiding or assisting in the Printing or Making or such Importation of any Bill or Bills, in Imitation of any of the Bills of Credit of this Government made current by the above mentioned Act, or which are now current by Virtue of any former Act or Acts of Assembly

Punishment of counterfeiting, &c.

fembly of this Government, or fhall fign or caufe to be
figned any fuch Bill or Bills printed or made in Imitation
of any of the Bills of Credit of this Government now
current as aforefaid, with an Intent to defraud any other
Perfon, and be thereof, or of any one or more of the
Offences aforefaid, legally convicted, he, fhe or they fo
offending, fhall fuffer Death without Benefit of Clergy.

Signed by Order of the Houfe,

DAVID FRENCH, *Speaker.*

An ACT *for the Relief of Infolvent Debtors within this Government.*

Preamble. WHEREAS the Act of Affembly of this Government, entitled, *An Act for the Relief of Infolvent
Debtors*, made in the *Seventh* Year of His prefent Majefty's
Reign, is found by Experience not to anfwer the Ends and
Purpofes for which the fame was intended: AND
WHEREAS no Perfon whatfoever can take any Benefit by the faid Act, who hath not refided within this
Government two Years next before his or her Imprifonment, by Means whereof many Perfons cannot be relieved, who are equally entitled to Compaffion with fuch
as have refided a longer Time within the fame; For remedy
whereof, BE IT ENACTED by the Honourable
GEORGE THOMAS, Efq; by and with His Majefty's
Royal Approbation, Lieutenant Governor and Commander in Chief of the Counties of *New-Caftle*, *Kent* and *Suffex*
upon *Delaware*, and Province of *Pennfilvania*, by and with
the Advice and Confent of the Reprefentatives of the
Freemen of the faid Counties in General Affembly met, and
by the Authority of the fame, That if any Perfon or
Perfons, having a Charge of fmall Children not of fufficient Age to be bound out as Apprentices, or if any Perfon or Perfons above the Age of *Forty* Years, fhall be imprifoned within this Government for any Sum or Sums of
Money or other Debts above the Value of *Forty Shillings,*
and

and from and after the Publication of this Act, be willing
to deliver up to his, her or their Creditors, all his, her or
their Effects, towards Satisfaction of the Debts wherewith
he, she or they stand charg'd, it shall and may be lawful for
every such Prisoner to exhibit a Petition to any of the Courts *Prisoner to ex-*
of Law within this Government from whence the Process *hibit a Petition,*
issued, upon which he or she was taken or arested, certify- *&c.*
ing the Cause or Causes of his or her Imprisonment, and an
Account of his or her whole real and personal Estate, with
the Dates of the Securities wherein any Part of it consists,
and the Deeds or Notes relating thereunto, and the Names
of the Witnesses to the same, as far as his or her Knowledge
extends thereunto. And upon such Petition the Court
may and is hereby required, by Order or Rule of Court,
to cause the Prisoner to be brought up, and the several
Creditors at whose Suit he or she stands charged as afore- *Creditors to be*
said, and all his or her Creditors that are or can be known *summoned to*
to the Court, to be summoned to appear personally or by *appear, &c.*
their Attorney in Court, at a Day to be appointed for that
Purpose; and upon the Day of such Appearance, if any
of the Creditors summoned refuse or neglect to appear,
upon Affidavit made of Notice given to the Creditor or
Creditors, or that the Creditor or Creditors are not to be
found, the Court shall in a summary Way examine into
the Matter of such Petition, and hear what shall be alledged
on either side for or against the Discharge of such Prisoner;
and if upon Examination the Court shall be of Opinion
that the Prisoner ought to be discharged, the Court may
and are hereby required to administer or tender to the
Prisoner an Oath or Affirmation to the Effect following;

I A. B. *do* [*solemnly swear, in the Presence of Almighty God*]   *The* OATH.
[*or, sincerely and truly declare and affirm*] *that the Account
by me delivered in to this Honourable Court, in my Petition
to this Court, doth contain a full and true Account of all my
real and personal Estate, Debts, Credits and Effects whatsoever,
which I, or any in trust for me, have, or at the time of my
Imprisonment had, or am or was in any respect entitled to, in
Possession, Remainder or Reversion; and that I have not at
any Time since my Imprisonment, or before, directly or indirectly
sold, leased, assigned or otherwise disposed or made over in Trust,
for myself or otherwise, other than as mentioned in such Account, any Part of my Lands, Estate, Goods, Stock, Money, Debts
or other real or personal Estate, whereby to expect to have any
Benefit or Profit to myself, or to defraud any of my Creditors to
whom I am indebted.*

B b   **AND**

AND in Case the Prisoner shall in open Court take the said Oath or Affirmation, and the Creditor or Creditors shall be satisfied with the Truth thereof, the Court may immediately order the Lands, Goods and Effects contained in such Account (except the wearing Apparel and Bedding for such Debtor and his or her Family, and the Tools or Instruments of such Debtor's Trade or Calling, not exceeding *Five Pounds* in Value for the whole, as the same shall be appraised by two credible Persons duly qualified for that Purpose) or so much of them as may be sufficient to satisfy the Debt or Debts wherewith he or she is or shall be charged, together with Costs of Suit, and the Fees due to the Keeper of the Goal or Prison from which the Prisoner was brought, to be by a short Indorsement on the back of such Petition, signed by the Prisoner, assigned to

Prisoner to af sign his Effects to the Creditors, &c.

the said Creditors, or to one or more of them in Trust for themselves and the rest of them, or to some proper Person or Persons to be by the said Court appointed in Trust for all the Creditors: And by such Assignment the Estate, Interest and Property of the Lands, Goods, Debts and Effects so assigned shall be vested in the Person or Persons to whom such Assignment is or shall be made, who may take Possession of or sue for the same, in his or their own Name or Names, in like Manner as Assignees of Commissioners of Bankrupts, to which Suit no Release of the Prisoner, his or her Executors or Administrators, or any Trustee for him or her subsequent to such Assignment, shall be any Barr. And immediately upon such Assign-

And upon such assignment to be discharged;

ment executed, the said Prisoner shall be discharged out of Custody by Order of Court, and such Order shall be a sufficient Warrant to the Sheriff, Goaler or Keeper of such Goal or Prison, to discharge the said Prisoner, if detained for the Causes mentioned in such Petition and no other, and he is hereby required to discharge and set him or her at Liberty forthwith without Fee, nor shall such Sheriff or Goaler be liable to any Action of Escape or other Suit or Information upon that Account; and the Person or Persons to whom the said Effects shall be assigned, paying the Fees to the Goaler or Keeper of the Prison in whose Custody the Party discharged was, shall and is and are

Effects to be appraised and divided, &c.

hereby required to procure the said Effects so assigned to be appraised by Men lawfully qualified, and after such Appraisment to be divided among all the Creditors and other Persons for whom he or they shall be intrusted, in Proportion to their respective Debts: But in Case any of the

In what Cases the Prisoner may be remanded.

Creditors of the Prisoner shall not be satisfied with the Truth of

of such Oath or Affirmation, but shall desire further time
to inform him or herself of the Matters contained therein,
the said Court may and shall remand the said Prisoner, and
direct the said Prisoner and the Person or Persons dissatisfied
with such Oath or Affirmation, to appear at another Day
to be appointed by the said Court, some time within the
Term next following the time of such Examination; and
if at such second Day so to be appointed, the Creditor or
Creditors dissatisfied with such Oath or Affirmation shall
make Default in appearing, or in Case he or they shall
appear but shall not be able to discover any Estate or
Effects of the Prisoner omitted in such his or her Petition,
or to shew any Probability of his or her having been for-
sworn or to have declared falsely in the said Oath or Affirmation, then the said Court shall immediately cause the
said Prisoner to be discharged, upon such Assignment of
his or her Effects in Manner aforesaid, unless such Creditor
or Creditors do insist upon his or her being detained in *Creditors insist-*
Prison, and do immediately give sufficient Security within *on the Prisoner's*
this Government, to the Treasurer of the County wherein *being remanded,*
the Debtor is imprisoned for the time being, that the said *must maintain*
Prisoner, or any of his or her small Children, shall not by *him, &c.*
Sickness or otherwise become a Charge to the said County
or any of the Hundreds thereof, and to allow and pay
unto such Person or Persons as the Court shall appoint,
such Sum of Money as the said Court shall judge reasonable for the Maintenance of the said Prisoner and his or
her small Children, to be paid on the second Day of every
Week, so long as he or she shall continue in Prison at his,
her or their Suits: But in Case the said Prisoner shall refuse to take the said Oath or Affirmation, or having taken
the same shall be detected of Falsity therein, he or she shall
be presently remanded.

AND BE IT FURTHER ENACTED
by the Authority aforesaid, That no Person to be dis- *No Person dis-*
charged by this Act, shall at any time hereafter be impri- *charged by this*
soned by Reason of any Judgment or Decree obtained for *Act, to be here-*
Payment of Money only, or for any Debt, Damages, *after imprison-*
Contempts, Costs, Sum or Sums of Money, contracted, *ed, &c.*
occurred, occasioned, owing or growing due before the
time of his or her Discharge, but that upon every Arrest
upon every such Judgment or Decree, or for such Debts,
Damages or Contempts, Costs, Sum and Sums of Money,
it shall and may be lawful for any Judge of the Court
whence the Process issued, upon shewing the Duplicate of
such

such Prisoner's Discharge, to release and discharge out of Custody such Prisoner or Prisoners as aforesaid, and the Judge of the Court is hereby impowered so to do, so as every such Prisoner or Prisoners, arrested or detained as aforesaid, do give a Warrant of Attorney to appear to every such Action and to plead thereunto.

Justices, Sheriff, &c. may plead the General Issue, &c. AND BE IT FURTHER ENACTED by the Authority aforesaid, That if any Action of Escape, or any Suit or Action be brought against any Justice or Justices of the Peace, Sheriff, Goaler or Keeper of any Prison, for performing their Office in pursuance of this Act, they may plead the General Issue and give this Act in Evidence ; and if the Plaintiff be nonsuited, or discontinue his Action, or Verdict pass against him, or Judgment upon Demurrer, the Defendant shall have treble Costs.

PROVIDED, That the Discharge of any Person by Vertue of this Act shall not acquit any other Person from such Debt, Sum or Sums of Money, for which such other Person became liable or answerable, or any Part thereof, but that all others shall be answerable for the same in such Manner as if no Suit had been brought against the said Person so discharged.

AND PROVIDED, That this Act shall not extend to discharge any Person out of Prison who shall stand chargeable at the Suit of the Crown only.

Judgment to stand good against what the Prisoner may hereafter possess, &c. PROVIDED ALWAYS, AND BE IT FURTHER ENACTED by the Authority aforesaid, That notwithstanding the Discharge of the Person of the Prisoner or Prisoners as aforesaid, all and every Debt and Debts, due or owing from the said Prisoner or Prisoners, and all and every Judgment or Judgments had and taken, and Decree obtained against him or her, shall stand and be good and effectual in Law to all Intents and Purposes, against the Lands, Tenements, Hereditaments, Goods and Chattles of the said Prisoner so discharged as aforesaid, which he or she or any other Person or Persons in Trust for him or her at the Time of such Discharge hath or have, or at any Time hereafter shall or may be any ways seized or possessed of, interested in or intitled to, either in Law or Equity, except his or her Wearing Apparel, Bedding for his or her Family, and Working Tools and Implements necessary for his or her Occupation, not exceeding the Value of *Five Pounds*
in

in the Whole as aforesaid ; and altho' such Prisoner were actually in Execution at the Time of his or her Discharge as aforesaid, it shall and may be lawful for the Creditor or Creditors of such Prisoner so discharged as aforesaid, his her or their Executors or Administrators, to take out a new Execution against the Lands, Tenements, Hereditaments, Goods and Chattels of such Prisoner (except as before excepted) for the Satisfaction of his, her or their Debts, in such Manner and Form, as he, she or they might have done if the Person of the Prisoner so discharged as aforesaid, had not been taken in Execution ; any Act, Statute, Law or Custom to the contrary in any wise notwithstanding.

And the Creditors may take out a new Execution, &c.

PROVIDED ALSO AND BE IT FURTHER ENACTED by the Authority aforesaid, That if the Effects so assigned shall not extend to satisfy the whole Debts due to the Creditors of the Person so discharged, and Costs of Suit or Suits, then there shall be an Abatement in Proportion, and all the Officers concerned in the Prosecution of the Suit or Suits against such Prisoner, shall come in as Creditors for what shall be due to them for their Fees, in Proportion with the other Creditors.

The Debtor's Effects not being sufficient, are to be divided in proportion, &c.

PROVIDED That where any Rent shall be due from any Prisoner at the time of his or her Discharge, no Goods or Chattels then lying, or being in or upon the Tenement or Lands in Lease, or liable to be distrained, shall be removed or disposed of without the Consent of the Landlord or Person to whom the Rent is due, until the same, not exceeding one Years Rent, be paid or satisfied; and that the Landlord may use all lawful Ways for the having and recovering his Rent, so as the same exceed not one Years Rent, by Distress or otherwise, as he might have, had or could have done before the making of this Act; any Thing herein contained to the contrary in any wise notwithstanding.

Landlords may recover one Year's Rent as before this Act.

AND PROVIDED ALSO, That this Act shall not bar any absent or distant Creditor, who had not Notice of the Prisoner's Application to the Court as aforesaid.

No absent Creditor barred by this Act.

AND BE IT FURTHER ENACTED by the Authority aforesaid, That were any Person what-

C c

soever

How Prisoners for Debt under 40 s. are to be relieved. foever, fhall be arrefted or taken by Warrant from any Juftice of the Peace for a Debt under *Forty Shillings*, if the Plaintiff cannot make appear that the Defendant hath Goods, Chattels or other Effects wherewith to fatisfy the faid Debt and Cofts, and the Defendant offering to make Oath or Affirmation that he or fhe hath not any Goods, Chattels or Effects wherewith to make Satisfaction for the fame (except his or her wearing Apparel, Bedding for his or her Family, and the working Tools or Inftruments neceffary for his or her Trade or Calling, not exceeding the Value of *Five Pounds* in the Whole, as aforefaid) and withal fignifying his or her Willingnefs to fatisfy the Plaintiff by Servitude, it fhall and may be lawful to and for the faid Juftice, and he is hereby required to adminifter to the Defendant fuch Oath or Affirmation, and thereupon to order Satisfaction to be made to the Plaintiff for his Debt and Cofts, by adjudging the Defendant to ferve the Plaintiff or his or her Affigns, fo long as the faid Juftice fhall judge reafonable for the fatisfying the faid Debt and Cofts, fo as the time of fuch Service do not exceed the Term of Six Months : And if the Plaintiff refufe to accept of fuch Service, it fhall and may be lawful for fuch Juftice before whom the Action is brought, and he is hereby required to difcharge fuch Defendant, and to oblige the Plaintiff to pay all the Cofts of the faid Action.

Prisoner convicted of Perjury, fhall fuffer, &c. PROVIDED ALWAYS, AND BE IT FURTHER ENACTED by the Authority aforefaid, That if any Perfon who fhall take any Oath or Affirmation, as by this Act before is directed, fhall upon any Indictment for Perjury or falfe Affirming in any Matter or Particular contained in the faid Oath or Affirmation, be convicted by his or her own Confeffion, or by Verdict of twelve Men; the Perfon fo convicted fhall fuffer all the Pains and Forfeitures which may by Law be inflicted on any Perfon convicted of wilful Perjury, and fhall likewife be liable to be taken on any Procefs *de novo*, and charged in Execution for Debt, in the fame Manner as if he or fhe had never been taken in Execution before or difcharged, and fhall never after have the Benefit of this Act.

AND WHEREAS many Perfons may fuffer by the Oppreffion and Exaction of Goalers, and other inferior Officers, in the Execution of Procefs for Debt : For Prevention whereof, BE IT FURTHER ENACTED by the Authority aforefaid, That no Sheriff, Under-Sheriff, Bailiff, or other Officer or Minifter whatfoever, fhall at any

Time

Time or Times hereafter convey or carry, or cause to be conveyed or carried, any Person or Persons by him or them arrested, or being in his or their Custody, by Virtue or Colour of any Writ, Process, or Warrant, to any Tavern, Ale-house, or other publick Victualing or Drinking-House, or to the private House of any such Officer, without the voluntary Consent of the Person so taken or arrested; or charge, demand, take or receive, or cause to be demanded, taken or received, directly or indirectly, any other or greater Sum or Sums of Money than is or shall by Law be allowed to be taken or demanded for such Arrest, Taking, Detaining or Waiting till the Person or Persons so arrested or in Custody shall have given in an Appearance or Bail, as the Case shall require, or agree with the Person or Persons at whose Suit or Prosecution he, she or they shall be taken or arrested, or until he, she or they shall be sent to the proper Goal belonging to the County, Town or Place where such Arrest or Taking shall be; nor shall keep the Person or Persons so taken or arrested, in any Tavern, Alehouse, or other publick Victualing-House or private House of any Officer, with or without the Content of the Person or Persons so arrested, above the Space of Twenty Days; nor shall exact or take any Reward, Gratuity or Money for keeping the Person or Persons so arrested or in Custody out of Goal or Prison; nor shall take or receive any other or greater Sum or Sums of Money for one or more Night's-Lodging, or for a Day's Diet, or other Expences, than what shall be allowed as reasonable in such Cases, by some Order or Orders, to be made by the Justices of the respective Courts of Common-Pleas within this Government, at some Court to be held for such County, Town or Place where such Arrest or Taking shall be, who are hereby authorized and required, with all convenient Expedition, to make some standing Order or Orders, for ascertaining such Expences within their respective Counties.

Prisoners not to be carried to Taverns, &c. without their Consent, &c.

Extravagant Fees, &c. not to be demanded.

Justices to make Orders for regulating Expences of Prisoners, &c.

AND BE IT FURTHER ENACTED by the Authority aforesaid, That every Sheriff, Under-Sheriff, Goaler, Keeper of any Prison or Goal, or other Person or Persons whatsoever, to whose Custody or Keeping any one so arrested or taken shall be committed on any Pretence, shall permit or suffer him or her so arrested or taken, at his or her Will and Pleasure, to send for and have any Beer, Ale, Victuals, or other necessary Food from what Place he or she doth please; and also to have and use such Bedding, Linnen, and other Things, as he or she shall think fit, without

Officers shall permit Prisoners to send for Necessaries to where they please.

without Purloining or Detaining the same, or any Part thereof, or enforcing or requiring him or her to pay for the Having or Using thereof, or putting any Manner of Restraint or Difficulty upon him or her in the Using thereof or relating **thereto.**

AND BE IT FURTHER ENACTED by the Authority aforesaid, That no Fees shall be taken by any Goaler, or Keeper of any Goal or Prison within this Government, for any Prisoner or Prisoners Commitment or Coming into Goal, or Chamber-Rent there, or Discharge from thence, or other Expences, than what shall be allowed by Law, until such Fees shall be settled and established by the Justices or Judges of the respective County-Courts, and other Courts of Record within this Government, for and in respect of the Counties and Courts to which they belong, who are hereby directed, impowered and required to settle *Judges shall set-* and establish the same as soon as conveniently may be ; *tle Tables of* and Tables shall be made of the respective Orders, Rules *Fees, &c.* and Fees so settled and established, and signed by the Justices or Judges of the respective County-Courts, Courts of General Quarter-Sessions of the Peace, and other Courts of Record, for their respective Goals within their respective Jurisdictions ; which Rules, Orders and Fees may from time to time, be enlarged, reformed, altered and amended, as Occasion shall require, by the Judges of the Supreme-Court, by Rules and Orders of the said Court, to be signed by the Judges of the same, and Duplicates shall be transmited to the respective County Courts, and other Courts of Record, for which they are made, to be entered of Record, and inrolled, without any Fee to be taken for the Enrollment thereof.

AND BE IT FURTHER ENACTED *Courts shall en-* by the Authority aforesaid, That the several Courts of *quire concerning* Common-Pleas, and other Courts of Record within the se- *the Tables of* veral Counties of this Government, shall at every time of *Fees, &c.* the Sitting of such Court or Courts enquire whether such Tables of Fees, and such Rules as aforesaid, be hung up and remain Publick, and easy to be resorted to in the several Prisons to the Courts respectively belonging, and whether the same be duly complied with and observed, and cause eight Days Notice to be given to the Prisoners in the said Prison of the time appointed for such Enquiry, and shall inform themselves touching the same in the best Manner they can, and supply and redress whatever they find

find neglected or transgressed: And that the Judges of the Court of Oyer and Terminer and General Goal-Delivery shall likewise make Enquiry of the Matters aforesaid, at such Courts and Sessions of Goal-Delivery within this Government, for and in respect of the Goals and Prisons within their respective Jurisdictions, and shall expresly give it in Charge to the Grand-Jury to enquire concerning the same.

AND for the more speedy Punishing Goalers, Bailiffs and others imployed in the Execution of Process, for Extortions, or other Abuses in their respective Offices and Places; BE IT FURTHER ENACTED by the Authority aforesaid, That upon Petition of any Prisoner or Person being or having being under Arrest or in Custody, complaining of any Exaction or Extortion by any Goaler, Bailiff, or other Officer or Person imployed in the keeping or taking Care of any Goal or Prison, or the Arresting or Apprehending of any Person or Persons by Virtue of any Process or Warrant, or any other Abuse whatsoever committed or done in their respective Offices or Places, unto any of his Majesty's Courts of Record within this Government from whence such Process issued, or under whose Power such Goal or Prison is, or to any two Justices of such Court in the time of the Vacation, or to the Judges of the Supreme Court, or any of them in their respective Sessions of Oyer and Terminer or General Goal Delivery, it shall and may be lawful for the same Court, Justices or Judges to hear and determine the same in a summary Way, and to make such Order thereupon for Redressing such Abuse, and Punishing such Officer or Person complained of, and making Reparation to the Party or Parties injured as they shall think just, together with the full Costs of such Complaint: And all Orders and Determinations which shall be made by the said Courts, or of the said Justices or Judges respectively, in such summary Way as herein prescribed, shall have the same Effect, Force and Virtue to all Intents and Purposes as any other Orders of the said respective Courts, and Obedience thereto may be inforced either by Attachments ordered by the said respective Courts, or by Attachments to be issued under the Seal of the said Courts, by Direction of the Justices or Judges making such Order.

How Goalers, &c. guilty of Extortion, shall be punished.

AND for the preventing Prisoners being imposed upon by being under a Necessity of Spending their Money in Prisons where strong Liquors are sold, BE IT ENACTED

No Sheriff, &c. to keep any Tavern, &c.

D d   by

by the Authority aforesaid, That no Goaler or Keeper of any Goal, or any Sheriff, or Under-Sheriff having the Care or Keeping of any Goal or Prison within this Government, shall keep or suffer to be kept any Tavern, Publick-House or Ale-house, or shall utter or sell to any Person or Persons 'under Arrest or in Prison any Wine, Rum, Beer, Ale, Cyder, Punch, or any other strong Liquors, other than what shall be allowed by the Justices as aforesaid for a Day's Diet or Expences by such Order to be made as aforesaid, on Pain of being removed from his or their Office or Offices of Sheriff, Under-Sheriff or Goaler, upon Complaint made, to be heard and determined upon Petition in a summary Way as aforesaid, before the Justices in their respective Courts of Common-Pleas for the County to which such Goaler, Sheriff or Under-Sheriff, having the Keeping of any Goal does belong.

AND BE IT FURTHER ENACTED by the Authority aforesaid, That any Person or Persons being imprisoned within any of the Counties of this Government for any Debt, Sum or Sums of Money above *Forty Shillings*, and not being above the Age of Forty Years, or not having a Charge of such small Children as aforesaid, may at any succeeding Court, to be held for the County where he or she is imprisoned, next after his or her Imprisonment, exhibit to the Justices of the said Court, upon Oath or Affirmation, an Account of all their Effects (if any they have) and to which they have any Right in Law or Equity, and the Names of their Creditors at whose Suit such Person or Persons are imprisoned, and the Sums of Money which they owe, and when the same became due, as far as their Knowledge does extend, and shall by Petition shew to the Court their Inability to pay the Debts for which such Person or Persons are imprisoned, and shall make an Assignment of their Effects (if any they have) to any Person or Persons that shall be appointed by the Court in Trust for all his or her Creditors, or for such of them as the said Court shall direct, and shall signify his or her Willingness to make Satisfaction by Servitude for the Debt or Residue of his or her Debts according to the Judgment of the Court where such Cause is depending or Judgment given, in Order as the Judgments shall be entered against him or her, and Dignity of the Debts, if the Plaintiff or Plaintiffs will accept of the same; and the said Court may and is hereby impowered and required to adjudge the said Debtor

Persons under Forty Years of Age, having no Charge of Children, and whose Debts exceed 40 s. may be adjudged (if willing) to serve their Creditors.

to

to serve his or her Creditors, their Executors, Administrators and Assigns accordingly.

PROVIDED ALWAYS, That the Time the Defendant shall be adjudged to serve all his or her Creditors shall not exceed Seven Years in the Whole.

The Time not to exceed seven Years.

BUT if any of the Plaintiffs or Creditors will not accept of such Manner of Satisfaction as aforesaid, then and in such Case the Defendant shall be discharged from the Judgment, Suit, Debt or Demand of every such Plaintiff or Creditor so Refusing.

Creditors not accepting such Satisfaction, his Debt is discharged.

AND WHEREAS it often happens that many poor Persons are arrested and imprisoned within the Counties of this Government, and are so poor that they immediately become a Charge to the County where they are imprisoned: For Remedy whereof, BE IT ENACTED by the Authority aforesaid, That every Person and Persons who shall make Application by him or themselves, or any other Person, for any Writ or Warrant for the Taking or Arresting any such poor Person within this Government, for any Debt or Demand whatsoever, shall before the Granting of any such Writ or Warrant be required by the Officer or Justice who grants the same to give sufficient Security within the same County, to be taken in the Name of the Treasurer of the said County, or of the Overseers of the Poor of the Town or Hundred where the Party shall be likely to be imprisoned for the Time being, and his and their Successors, to indemnify the said County, Town or Hundred from all Charges that may arise either by the Maintenance or Sickness of the Person so to be imprisoned; and that until such Security be given as aforesaid, the Officer or Justice, to whom such Application shall be made, shall not grant any such Writ or Warrant, on Penalty of being answerable for all such Charges as may arise by means of such Imprisoning the Party by Virtue of such Writ or Warrant as aforesaid.

Those who take Writs, &c. against poor Persons, shall give Security that they do not become chargeable.

They who grant such Writs, &c. without taking such Security, shall be answerable themselves.

AND BE IT FURTHER ENACTED by the Authority aforesaid, That no Person or Persons who have not resided within this Government for the Space of one Year, next before his, her or their Arrest or Imprisonment, shall have any Benefit of this Act, saving that Persons arrested for any Debt or Demand under *Forty Shillings*, and having no Effects wherewith to make Satisfaction for the

No Person to have the Benefit of this Act, that has not resided one Year in the Government; except, &c.

the Debt and Costs, shall be liable to make Satisfaction to the Plaintiff or Plaintiffs by Servitude as aforesaid.

AND BE IT FURTHER ENACTED by the Authority aforesaid, That one Act of General Assembly of this Government, made in the Seventh Year of his Majesty's Reign, entituled, *An Act for the Relief of insolvent Debtors*, is hereby repealed and made void.

Repeal of a former Act.

Signed by Order of the House,

DAVID FRENCH, *Speaker.*

An ACT Limiting the Time of the Sheriffs within this Government Holding their Offices, and preventing Bribery and Corruption in the Election of the said Sheriffs.

Preamble.

WHEREAS it is found by Experience that many Evils have arisen by Persons holding the Office of Sheriff within the several Counties of this Government so often as they could procure themselves to be elected and appointed to that Office: AND WHEREAS such Persons as stand Candidates, or make Interest for being elected and returned for the Office of Sheriff within this Government, make it their frequent Practice to engage Persons to vote for them, by giving them strong Drink, and Using other Means, inconsistent with the Design of free Voting at Elections; by Means whereof many unguarded Persons are drunk and disorderly more particularly at the Time of Elections; whereby great Confusions and Mischiefs arise:

FOR Prevention whereof, BE IT ENACTED by the Honourable *GEORGE THOMAS*, Esq; with his Majesty's Royal Approbation, Lieutenant Governor and Commander in Chief of the Counties of *New-Castle*, *Kent* and *Sussex* upon *Delaware*, and Province of *Pennsylvania*, by and with the Advice

Advice and Confent of the Reprefentatives of the Freemen of the faid Counties in General Affembly met, and by the Authority of the fame, That no Perfon or Perfons within this Government, who hath been elected or ferved in the Office of Sheriff in any County of this Government for the Space of three Years fucceffively, or at any one time, fhall again be elected, or be capable to ferve as Sheriff of the fame County within the Space of three Years next after his being Sheriff as aforefaid: And that of the two Perfons elected to be Sheriff, the one being commiffionated by the Governor for the time being, the other fhall not act as Under-Sheriff in the faid County during that Year for which he was elected. AND that no Perfon or Perfons who hath ferved in the Office of Sheriff as aforefaid for the Space of three Years fhall be capable of being appointed, or ferve in the Office of Under-Sheriff within the Space of three Years next after his Serving in the Office of Sheriff as aforefaid: And that, in like Manner, no Perfon or Perfons who fhall have ferved in the Office of Under-Sheriff for the Space of three Years fucceffively, in Manner aforefaid, or at any one time, fhall again be elected or capable to ferve as Sheriff of the faid County wherein he hath fo ferved, within the Space of three Years next after his having ferved as Under-Sheriff as aforefaid. AND if any Sheriff or Under-Sheriff within this Government fhall be elected, or appointed contrary to this Act, fuch Election and Appointment fhall be void. AND if any Sheriff or Under-Sheriff fhall again enter upon and execute the Office of Sheriff or Under-Sheriff contrary to the Directions of this Act, he fhall forfeit the Sum of *Two Hundred Pounds*, one Moiety thereof to the Governor for the time being, the other Moiety to fuch Perfon or Perfons as will fue for the fame, to be recovered by Action of Debt, Bill, Plaint or Information, in any Court of Record within this Government.

Sheriffs having ferved 3 Years fucceffively, may not be chofen again within 3 Years

The Under-Sheriff may not be one of the Perfons chofen to be Sheriff.

Sheriffs having ferved 3 Years, may not be Under-Sheriffs, within 3 Years; nor Under-Sheriffs, Sheriffs.

Elections, &c. contrary to this Act, are void.

Penalty on Sheriffs, &c. acting contrary to this Act.

AND BE IT FURTHER ENACTED

by the Authority aforefaid, That if any Perfon or Perfons within this Government, after the Publication of this Act, who fhall ftand as Candidate, or make Intereft by himfelf or others, to be elected and returned for the Office of Sheriff, fhall prefume, by himfelf, or any other Perfon or Perfons whatfoever, to procure him or themfelves to be voted for or elected for the Office of Sheriff as aforefaid, by giving to any Perfon or Perfons, either by themfelves, or others in their Behalf, or for their Ufe or Purpofe, any Gratuity,

Penalty on Candidates, bribing or treating Electors.

E e

Wages,

Wages, Gift, Bribe, ftrong Drink of any Kind, Treats, Entertainments, or any other Reward whatfoever, or fhall covenant, engage, promife or procure fo to be done by himfelf or any other Perfon or Perfons, every Perfon or Perfons fo offending, fhall, for every fuch Offence, forfeit and pay the Sum of *Ten Pounds* current Money of this Government, to be, with Cofts, recovered and applied in Manner aforefaid.

Penalty on E-lectors who accept any Bribe, &c.

AND every Perfon and Perfons whatfoever, who fhall by himfelf, or any other Perfon or Perfons for his or their Ufe, or by his or their Means or Procurement, prefume to take, accept or receive any fuch Gratuity, Gift, Bribe, ftrong Drink, Treats, Entertainments, or other Reward whatfoever as aforefaid, for giving any Vote or Votes, or Caufing or Procuring any Vote or Votes to be given to any fuch Candidate, or Perfon or Perfons making Intereft by himfelf or others as aforefaid, to be elected and returned to ferve in the Office of Sheriff as aforefaid; every Perfon or Perfons fo offending fhall, for every fuch Offence, forfeit and pay the Sum of *Five Pounds*, current Money aforefaid, to be recovered and applied in Manner aforefaid.

Signed by Order of the Houfe,

DAVID FRENCH, *Speaker.*

An ACT *for Regulating Fences within this Government.*

BE IT ENACTED by the Honourable *GEORGE THOMAS*, Efq; by and with his Majefty's Royal Approbation Lieutenant Governor and Commander in Chief of the Counties of *New-Caftle, Kent* and *Suffex* upon *Delaware*, and Province of *Pennfylvania*, by and with the Advice and Confent of the Reprefentatives of the Freemen of the faid Counties, in General Affembly met, and by the Authority of the fame, That Corn-Fields and

and Ground kept for Enclofures fhall be fenced with a Poft- and Rail-Fence or Worm-Fence well ftak'd and rider'd, at leaft four Feet and an half high from the Top of the Upper-Rail or Rider to the Ground; and all Worm-Fences not ftak'd and rider'd fhall be at leaft five Feet high from the Top of the Upper-Rail to the Ground : A N D if any Horfes, Kine, Sheep, Hogs or Goats, or any kind of Cattle, fhall break into any Perfon's Inclofure, the fame being found by the Perfons to be appointed Viewers, according to the Direction of this Act, to be of the Height and Sufficiency aforefaid, then the Owner of fuch Horfes, Sheep, Goats or Cattle fhall be liable to make good all fuch Damages to the Owner of fuch Inclofure, as fhall be found and awarded by the faid Viewers, upon their Oath or Affirmation made before fome Juftice of the Peace of the County where the Trefpafs is committed, to be levied, together with Cofts, by Warrant under the Hand and Seal of the Juftice before whom fuch Oath or Affirmation fhall be made, on the Goods and Chattels of the Owners of fuch Cattle fo Trefpaffing.

Poft- and Rail Fences to be four Foot and half high; Worm Fences five Feet.

If Horfes, &c. break through fuch Fences, the Owner of the Creatures to make good the Damage.

AND BE IT FURTHER ENACTED by the Authority aforefaid, That all Perfons having any unruly Horfes, Sheep, Goats or Cattle as aforefaid, not to be kept off by fuch Fences as aforefaid, and Notice being firft given to him, her or them of fuch Creatures being unruly, are ordered and fhall be obliged to take effectual Care to reftrain the fame from Trefpaffing on any Perfon's Inclofures, upon Penalty of *Five Shillings*, or double Damages for every fuch Trefpafs, at the Election of the Party injured, to be levied, together with Cofts, in Manner aforefaid.

Penalty on Perfons owning unruly Cattle, not taking Care to reftrain them.

AND BE IT FURTHER ENACTED by the Authority aforefaid, That where any Perfon or Perfons fhall enclofe any Land adjoining to another's Land already inclos'd with a Fence, fo that any Part of the Fence firft made become the Partition between them, in fuch Cafe the Charge of fuch Divifion-Fence, fo far as is inclos'd on both Sides, fhall be equally borne and maintained by both Parties ; to which End, and the others mentioned in this Act, each County-Court within this Government fhall nominate, and are hereby impowered and required, at their refpective Courts of Quarter-Seffions, to be held in the Month of *May* every Year, to nominate and appoint fo many proper Perfons as they fhall think fit for each Hundred, in each County refpectively, to view all fuch Fence

Divifion Fences to be made and maintain'd equally by both Parties.

Viewers to be appointed.

and

and Fences about which any Difference may happen to
Who shall be arise: And that the aforesaid Persons in each Hundred re-
sole Judges; spectively, shall be the sole Judges of the Charge to be born
by both or either of the said Parties, and of the Sufficiency
of all Fences, whether Partition or other Fences, and of the
Damages sustain'd by means of any Creature's Trespassing
within the true Intent and Meaning of this Act; and where
they judge any Fence to be insufficient, they shall give Notice thereof to the Owners or Possessors; and if one
of the said Owners and Possessors, upon the Request
of the other, and due Notice given by the said Viewers,
shall refuse to make or repair the said Fence or Fences or
pay the Moiety of any Fence before made, being a Divi-
sion-Fence, within five Days after Notice given, that then,
upon Proof thereof before two Justices of the Peace of the
respective County, it shall be lawful for the said Justices to
order the Person agrieved and suffering thereby to repair the
said Fence or Fences, who shall be reimbursed double his
Costs and Charges from the Person so Refusing to make
good the said Partition-Fence; and that the said Costs and
Charges, together with the Damages in respect of Partition-
Fences as aforesaid, to be assessed by Virtue of this Act,
shall be levied by Distress and Sale of the Offender's Goods
and Chattels, by Warrant from the said Justices, and the
Overplus, if any be, to be returned to the Owner thereof;
Their Allow- and the said Viewers to be allowed *Two Shillings* each for
ance. Viewing such Fence so complained against, and Assessing
the Damages sustained by Trespass, and *Two Pence* per
Mile each, for Travelling-Charges.

PROVIDED ALWAYS, AND BE IT
FURTHER ENACTED by the Authority
aforesaid, That nothing in this Act contained shall be construed, deemed or taken to repeal or make null or void an
Act of General Assembly of this Government, entituled,
An Act for erecting a Pound in the Town of New-Castle, or
any Part thereof; but that the same shall continue and be
in full Force, any thing herein contained to the contrary
in anywise notwithstanding.

Signed by Order of the House,

DAVID FRENCH, *Speaker.*

An ACT *to prevent the un-seasonable Killing of Deer within this Government.*

BE IT ENACTED by the Honourable *GEORGE THOMAS*, Esq; by and with His Majesty's royal Approbation, Lieutenant Governor and Commander in Chief of the Counties of *New-Castle, Kent* and *Sussex* upon *Delaware*, and Province of *Pennsylvania*, by and with the Advice and Consent of the Representatives of the Freemen of the said Counties, in General Assembly met, and by the Authority of the same, That if any Freeman within this Government (*Indians* excepted) shall kill or destroy, by Guns or otherwise, any Deer or Fawns, within any of the Counties of this Government, between the first Day of *January* and the first Day of *August* in every Year, and be thereof duly convicted, by the Testimony of one or more credible Witnesses, or otherwise, before any Justice of the Peace of the County where such Offence shall be committed, the Offender, for every such Offence, shall forfeit and pay the Sum of *Forty Shillings* for every Deer or Fawn so killed or destroyed, contrary to the Directions of this Act, to be levied upon the Offender's Goods and Chattles, by Distress and Sale thereof, by Warrant under the Hand and Seal of the Justice before whom the Offender shall be convicted, and paid, the one Moiety thereof to the Use of the Poor of the Hundred where the Conviction is, the other Moiety to the Informer.

Forty Shillings Penalty on killing Deer out of Season.

AND if no such Goods and Chattles shall be found, then it shall and may be lawful to and for such Justice, before whom the said Conviction is made, to judge such Offender to make Satisfaction by Servitude, for any Time not exceeding *Six Months*.

Or 6 months Servitude.

AND BE IT FURTHER ENACTED by the Authority aforesaid, That if any white Servant, Mulatto or Negro Slave, shall kill or destroy any Deer or Fawns within any of the Counties aforesaid, contrary to the Intent and Meaning of this Act, such Servant, Mulatto or Negro so offending, being thereof duly convicted, shall, for every such Offence, be publickly whipt on his or her

Servants or Slaves so offending, to be whipt.

F f

bare

bare Back, with any Number of Stripes not exceeding *Twenty-one.*

Fresh Venison, &c. in Possession of any Person, shall be good Evidence.

AND BE IT FURTHER ENACTED by the Authority aforesaid, That the Finding of any Venison or Skins of Deer or Fawns newly killed, in the Possession of any Person or Persons, shall be good Evidence to convict such Person, in whose Custody the same shall be found, unless such Person or Persons shall bring good Evidence to acquit him or themselves of such Charge.

Any Person purchasing such Venison or Skins, &c. of Indians, shall suffer, &c.

AND BE IT FURTHER ENACTED by the Authority aforesaid, That if any Person or Persons (*Indians* excepted) between the first Day of *January* and the first Day of *August* in every Year, shall have in his or her House or Custody any Venison, or Deer or Fawn Skin or Skins, by him or them purchased of or killed, within the said Term, by any *Indian* or *Indians* within this Government, the said Person or Persons, in whose Possession the same shall be found, being duly convicted thereof, shall be subject to the like Pains and Forfeitures, as if he or they had been convicted of killing or destroying the same.

Signed by Order of the House,

DAVID FRENCH, *Speaker.*

An ACT against unseasonable Firing the Woodlands and Marshes within this Government.

FOR Prevention of Damages and Dangers that may ensue upon Firing the Woodlands or Marshes within this Government, at unseasonable Times of the Year, **BE IT ENACTED** by the Honourable *GEORGE THOMAS*, Esq; by and with his Majesty's Royal Approbation, Lieutenant Governor and Commander in Chief of the Counties of *New-Castle*, *Kent* and *Sussex* upon *Delaware*, and Province of *Pennsylvania*, by and with the
Advice

Advice and Confent of the Reprefentatives of the Freemen of the faid Counties in General Affembly met, and by the Authority of the fame, That whofoever fhall prefume to fet or caufe to be fet on Fire any Woodlands or Marfhes, within this Government, before the *Tenth* Day of *March* or after the *Firſt* Day of *May* yearly, and be duly convicted thereof, by the Teſtimony of one or more credible Witneffes, before any two Juſtices of the Peace of the County where fuch Offence is committed, fhall, for every fuch Offence, forfeit any Sum not exceeding *Five Pounds*, to be levied, together with Cofts, by Warrant under the Hands and Seals of the Juſtices before whom the Conviction is had, on the Offender's Goods and Chattels; and paid, the one Moiety thereof to the Overfeers of the Poor of the Hundred for the Ufe of the Poor where the Offence is committed, the other Moiety to the Ufe of the Informer; and for Want of Goods and Chattels the Offender fhall be adjudged, by the faid Juſtices, to make Satisfaction by Servitude; and fhall alfo make good all Damages that fhall thereby happen to any of the Inhabitants of this Government, to be recovered by Bill, Plaint or Information in any of His Majeſty's Courts of Record within this Government. And if any Negro or Mulatto Slave or Slaves fhall be duly convicted of fuch Offence as aforefaid, the faid Juſtices fhall order him, her or them to be publickly whipt with any Number of Lafhes not exceeding *Thirty-one*.

Woodlands or Marſhes to be fired only between the 10th of March and 1ſt of May; on Penalty of 5 l.

Offender to make good all Damages.

Slaves fo offending to be whipt.

Signed by Order of the Houfe,

DAVID FRENCH, *Speaker.*

An ACT for Regulating Innholders, Tavern-keepers, and other Publick Houfe-keepers within this Government, and impowering the Juſtices to fettle the Rates of Liquors.

FOR regulating Inn-holders, Tavern-keepers, and other Publick Houfe-keepers within this Government, BE IT ENACTED by the Honourable *GEORGE THOMAS*, Efq; by and with his Majeſty's Royal Approbation Lieutenant Governor and

Commander

Commander in Chief of the Counties of *New-Castle*, *Kent* and *Suffex* upon *Delaware*, and Province of *Pennsylvania*, by and with the Advice and Consent of the Representatives of the Freemen of the said Counties, in General Assembly met, and by the Authority of the same, That no Person or Persons within this Government shall presume to keep any Publick House of Entertainment, Tavern, Inn, Ale-house, Ordinary or Victualing-House, without obtaining, by Petition, a Recommendation from the Justices of the Court of Quarter-Sessions, to be held in *August*-Term in each County within this Government, to his Honour the Governor for the time being, for a Licence for keeping the same, setting forth that the Person so petitioning is a fit Person and well qualified for keeping a Tavern or House of Entertainment.

No Person may keep Tavern, &c. until recommended and licenced.

AND BE IT FURTHER ENACTED

by the Authority aforesaid, That it shall and may be lawful for the Governor for the Time being, and his Secretary, to take and receive for all Licences to be granted, the same Fees and Perquisites as were usually paid before the Making of this Act.

Fees, &c. for granting Licences.

AND BE IT ENACTED by the

Authority aforesaid, That no Person or Persons within this Government, shall be recommended to the Governor by such Justices as aforesaid, for a Licence for keeping such Publick-House, Tavern, Inn or Ordinary, without making first appear, to the Satisfaction of the said Justices, that such Petitioner is well qualified for keeping the same, and hath Necessaries fit and suitable for the Entertainment of Travellers, and that the Place or Habitation of such Petitioner is situate in a proper and convenient Place and Stage for the Entertainment of Travellers as aforesaid.

None but fit Persons may be recommended by the Justices.

AND BE IT ENACTED by the

Authority aforesaid, That if any Master or Keeper of any such House of Entertainment, Tavern, Ale-house or Victualing-House, shall suffer any Person or Person whatsoever to continue Drinking and Tipling in his or her House at any unseasonable Hours of the Night, or suffer Drunkenness, corrupt or unlawful Gaming with Cards, Dice or at other Games within his or her House, Out-house, Office or any other Place thereto belonging, every such Master or Owner of such House, upon Complaint, and due Proof thereof made before any one Justice of the Peace of the

Penalty on Tavern-keepers, &c. suffering Gaming, Drunkenness, &c. in their Houses.

the County where the Offence shall be committed, or by the View of the said Justice, shall, for the first Offence forfeit *First Offence.* the Sum of *Twenty Shillings*, to be levied, together with Costs, on the Offender's Goods and Chattels, by Distress and Sale thereof, by Warrant under the Hand and Seal of such Justice, to be paid the one Moiety thereof to the Use of the Poor of the Hundred where such Offence shall be committed, the other Moiety to the Informer; and for the second Offence, *Second Offence.* upon Complaint and due Proof thereof made before any two Justices of the said County, the Offender shall forfeit any Sum not exceeding *Five Pounds*, nor less than *Forty Shillings*, to be recovered as aforesaid by Warrant under the Hands and Seals of the said Justices, and applied and paid in like Manner as aforesaid: And for the third Offence, *Third Offence.* upon due Proof thereof made before any two Justices as aforesaid, the Offender shall have his or her House suppress'd by Order of the said two Justices, and be disabled from keeping any such Publick-House as aforesaid, for the Space of three Years next after such Offence committed as aforesaid.

AND BE IT ENACTED by the Authority aforesaid, That if any Person or Persons within *Penalty on* this Government shall presume, after the Publication of *keeping Publick* this Act, to keep any Tipling-House or sell or retail any *House without* Wine by any less Measure than half a Gallon; Rum, Brandy, or any spirituous Liquors, by any Measure less than a Quart; Beer, Ale, Metheglin, Perry or Cyder, by any Measure less than one Gallon; Punch, or any other mix'd Liquor, by any Measure whatsoever, without Licence as aforesaid; the Person or Persons so offending shall, for every such Offence, forfeit and pay *Five Pounds*, to be recover'd, together with Costs, by the Order of any Court of Quarter-Sessions within this Government where the Offence is committed, upon Conviction of the Offender, by Presentment, Bill, Plaint, Information, or Confession of the Party offending, to be paid to the Governor for the time being, towards the Support of Government.

AND BE IT FURTHER ENACTED by the Authority aforesaid, That if any Master or Keeper *Publick House-* of any such Publick-House or Houses, or Tavern as afore-*keepers giving* said, shall, after the Publication of Act, presume to trust or *Credit to Minors* give any Credit to any Minor or Minors, every such Mas-*shall lose the* ter or Keeper of such House or Houses shall lose the whole *Debt.* Sum or Sums so trusted and credited, and is hereby precluded

G g   cluded

cluded and debarr'd from Suing for the same before any Magistrate, or in any Court within this Government.

AND BE IT FURTHER ENACTED

Penalty on continuing a Publick House after Suppression.

by the Authority aforesaid, That if any Person or Persons who shall have been Masters or Keepers of any such Publick-House or Houses as aforesaid, and shall have his, her or their Houses suppressed for offending against this Act in Manner aforesaid, and after such Suppression shall presume to retail any kind of strong or mix'd Liquors contrary to the Intent and Meaning of this Act, and shall be thereof convicted in Manner of other Convictions, by Virtue of this Act, the Person or Persons so offending shall, for every such Offence, forfeit and pay the Sum of *Five Pounds*, to be recovered, together with Costs of Prosecution, by Presentment, Bill, Plaint, Information or Confession of the Party offending, in any Court of Quarter-Sessions for any County of this Government where the Offence shall be committed, and paid to the Governor for the time being, for the Support of Government.

AND BE IT FURTHER ENACTED

Justices impowered to settle Rates, Prices, Orders, &c. for Publick Houses;

by the Authority aforesaid, That the Justices of the Peace in the respective Counties within this Government, during the Sitting of the *Quarter-Sessions* in the Month of *November* in each Year, are hereby impowered and required to make and settle such Rates, Prices and Orders, on and for all Sorts of Liquors retail'd by all Masters and Keepers of Publick Houses of Entertainment, as aforesaid, within the respective Counties of this Government, as to them shall appear to be just, meet and convenient; and that Copies of all such Rates, Prices and Orders shall, by such Masters

Which shall be set up in the most publick Room; on Penalty of Twenty Shillings.

and Keepers of Publick Houses, be set up in the most publick Room or Rooms of his, her or their Houses, within *Ten* Days next after the same shall be made and settled; and be truly complied with and conform'd unto, by all such Masters or Keepers of such licensed Publick Houses, on the Penalty of Forfeiting the Sum of *Twenty Shillings* for every such Default made by such Master or Keeper of such Licensed Publick Houses, upon Complaint and Proof made as in this Act before is directed, to be applied and paid, the one Moiety thereof to the Overseers of the Poor of the Town or Hundred where the Offender dwells, the other Moiety to the Informer.

AND

AND BE IT FURTHER ENACTED by the Authority aforesaid, That no Justice of the Peace, being himself an Inn-holder, shall judge or determine concerning any Matter or Thing contained in this Act, any Thing herein contained to the contrary notwithstanding.

No Justice being an Innholder, shall judge in any Matter contained in this Act.

AND BE IT FURTHER ENACTED by the Authority aforesaid, That all other Acts of General Assembly of this Government, heretofore made, for regulating of Publick Houses, and for settling the Rates and Prices of Liquors retail'd therein, be and are hereby repealed, made null and void, any Thing in the said Acts contained to the contrary in any wise notwithstanding.

Repeal of former Acts.

Signed by Order of the House,

DAVID FRENCH, *Speaker.*

An ACT *against Drunkenness, Blasphemy; and to prevent the grievous Sins of prophane Cursing, Swearing and Blasphemy.*

WHEREAS many Persons of vicious Lives and Morals, make a common Practice of getting Drunk, and prophane Cursing and Swearing, and Blasphemy, to the great Dishonour of Almighty God, the Scandal of our Christian Profession and civil Society, and the evil Example of others.

Preamble.

FOR the Discouragement and just Punishment whereof, BE IT ENACTED by the Honourable *GEORGE THOMAS*, Esq; by and with his Majesty's Royal Approbation, Lieutenant Governor and Commander in Chief of the Counties of *New-Castle*, *Kent* and *Sussex* on *Delaware*, and Province of *Pennsylvania*, by and with the Advice and Consent

Penalty on Drunkenness.

Consent of the Representatives of the Freemen of the said Counties, in General Assembly met, and by the Authority of the same, That all and every Person and Persons being Drunk, and being thereof convicted, by View of one Justice of the Peace, the Testimony of one lawful Witness, or Confession of the Party before any one Justice of the Peace within this Government, shall forfeit or pay the Sum of *Five Shillings* for every such Offence, to be levied by a Warrant, under the Hand and Seal of such Justice before whom the Party shall be convicted, upon the Goods and Chattels of the Offender, to be applied to the Relief of the Poor of the Town or Hundred where the Offence is committed; and if no such Goods can be found, the Party offending shall be set in the Stocks, there to remain for the Space of Two Hours.

Penalty on abusing or threatning Courts or Justices, &c.

AND in Case any Offender or Offenders against this Act, or any other Person or Persons, taken or arrested by the Warrant, Order or Command of any Court or Justice of the Peace within this Government, shall use any abusive, reviling or threatning Speeches against such Court or Justice, or resist or assault the Person or Persons executing such Warrant or Order, and be thereof convicted, shall be deemed a Breaker of the Peace, and shall be fined in any Sum not exceeding *Five Pounds*, to be paid to the Governor, for the Support of Government. AND in Case the Party aggrieved, resisted or assaulted, shall sue such Offender, for such Resistance or Assault, he shall recover treble Damages; and the Party offending shall be bound to his or her good Behaviour.

Penalty on prophane Cursing & Swearing.

AND BE IT FURTHER ENACTED by the Authority aforesaid, That if any Person within this Government, shall, in the Hearing of any one Justice of the Peace, in his or her common Conversation, prophanely swear, by the Name of God, Christ Jesus, or the Holy Spirit, or curse himself or any other Person, and be duly convicted thereof, by one or more credible Witnesses, before any one Justice of the Peace of the Town or County where such Offence is committed, the Person so offending shall, for every such Offence, forfeit and pay the Sum of *Five Shillings*, to be levied on his or her Goods and Chatties, by Warrant under the Hand and Seal of the Justice before whom the Offence is committed or Conviction made, for the Use of the Poor of the Town or Hundred where the Offence is committed, or the Party offending shall be

set

set in the Stocks, there to remain any Time not exceeding Three Hours.

AND BE IT FURTHER ENACTED by the Authority aforesaid, That if any Person shall wilfully or premeditately be guilty of Blasphemy, and shall thereof be legally convicted, the Person so offending shall, for every such Offence, be set in the Pillory for the Space of Two Hours, and be branded in his or her Forehead with the Letter B, and be publickly whipt, on his or her bare Back, with *Thirty-nine* Lashes well laid on.

Punishment Blasphemy.

Signed by Order of the House,

DAVID FRENCH, *Speaker.*

An ACT *to prevent the Breach of the* Lord's Day *commonly called* Sunday.

WHEREAS many loose and disorderly Persons do make a frequent Practice of Prophaning the Lord's Day, commonly called Sunday, to the great Reproach of the Christian Religion. For Prevention whereof, BE IT ENACTED by the Honourable *GEORGE THOMAS*, Esq; by and with His Majesty's Royal Approbation, Lieutenant Governor and Commander in Chief of the Counties of *New-Castle*, *Kent* and *Sussex* upon *Delaware*, and Province of *Pennsylvania*, by and with the Advice and Consent of the Representatives of the Freemen of the said Counties in General Assembly met, and by the Authority of the same, That if any Person or Persons within this Government, shall, after the Publication of this Act, do any servile Work, Labour or Business, upon the Lord's Day, commonly called Sunday (excepting Works of Necessity, Charity and Mercy) and be duly convicted thereof, by his or her own Confession, the Testimony of one or more credible Witnesses, before any one Justice of the Peace, or by the View of

Preamble.

Penalty for Working on Sundays.

Hh   such

such Justice, such Person or Persons so offending shall, for every such Offence, forfeit the Sum of *Ten Shillings*; or, upon Refusal to pay the said Fine, be set in the Stocks, for any Space of Time not exceeding Four Hours.

Penalty on Carriers, Pedlars, &c. travelling on Sundays; and on Persons selling Goods, &c. on that Day.

A N D B E I T E N A C T E D by the Authority aforesaid, That if any Carrier, Pedlar, Waggoner, Carter, Butcher or Drover, with Horse, Pack or Drove shall travel upon the Lord's-Day, or if any Person or Persons within this Government shall expose any Goods, Wares or Merchandizes to Sale on the said Day, and shall thereof be duly convicted, the Person or Persons so offending, shall, for every such Offence, forfeit the Sum of *Twenty Shillings.*

Penalty on Fishing, Fowling, &c. on Sundays.

A N D B E I T F U R T H E R E N A C T E D by the Authority aforesaid, That if any Person shall be duly convicted of Fishing, Fowling, Oystering, Horse-hunting or Horse-racing on the Lord's-Day, the Person so offending, shall, for every such Offence, forfeit the Sum of *Ten Shillings,* or upon Refusal to pay the said Fine, be set in the Stocks, there to remain the Space of four Hours.

Penalty on Gaming, Dancing, &c. on Sundays.

A N D B E I T F U R T H E R E N A C T E D by the Authority aforesaid, That if any Number of Persons shall meet to game, play or dance on the Lord's-Day, every Person so offending shall forfeit the Sum of *Five Shillings,* or upon Refusal to pay the said Fine, be set in the Stocks, there to remain for the Space of four Hours.

Penalty on Innholders, &c. suffering Persons to sit Tipling, during Divine Service.

A N D B E I T F U R T H E R E N A C T E D by the Authority aforesaid, That if any Innholder, Ordinary or Tavern-keeper shall suffer any Person or Persons to sit Tipling or Drinking in his or her House on the said Day during the Time of Divine Service, and be thereof duly convicted before any two Justices of the Peace of the County where such Offence is committed, the Person or Persons so offending, shall, for every such Offence, forfeit the Sum of *Forty Shillings.*

How the Forfeitures on this Act shall be recovered and disposed of.

A N D B E I T F U R T H E R E N A C T E D by the Authority aforesaid, That all the Fines and Forfeitures mentioned in this Act, shall be levied by Distress and Sale of the Offender's Goods and Chattels respectively, by Warrant under the Hand and Seal of such Justice or Justices before whom such Conviction shall be made, returning the

the Overplus, if any be, to the Owner or Owners thereof, and shall be applied to the Use of the Poor of the Town or Hundred where such Offence is committed, any Law, Usage or Custom to the contrary in anywise notwithstanding.

Signed by Order of the House,

DAVID FRENCH, *Speaker.*

An ACT *for determining Debts under* Forty Shillings.

FOR the Recovery of Debts under *Forty Shillings*, BE IT ENACTED by the Honourable GEORGE THOMAS, Esq; by and with his Majesty's Royal Approbation Lieutenant Governor and Commander in Chief of the Counties of *New-Castle, Kent* and *Suffex* upon *Delaware*, and Province of *Pennsylvania*, by and with the Advice and Consent of the Representatives of the Freemen of the said Counties, in General Assembly met, and by the Authority of the same, That upon Complaint made to any Justice of the Peace within this Government against any Person or Persons for any Debt under *Forty Shillings*, it shall and may be lawful to and for such Justice, and he is hereby impowered and required to issue out his Warrant, in the Nature of a Summons or Capias, as the Case may require, directed to some Constable of the Hundred or County, commanding to bring, or cause such Defendant to come before him or some other Justice of the Peace of the same County ; and when such Justice shall have heard the Proofs and Allegations of both Parties, or such of them as shall be present at such Time and Place as he shall appoint, he shall give his Judgment in the Matter according to the very Right of the Cause, which Judgment shall be final and conclusive to both Plaintiff and Defendant without further Appeal, and Execution, if required, shall be awarded by him against the Person refusing to comply with such Judgment, directed to some Constable to levy the same upon the Goods and Chattels of the Party so refusing, and for want of such Goods and Chattels, to take the Body of the said non-complying Party, and him or her to commit to the Goal of the County, until the Debt and Costs be satisfied. AND

Justices impowered to issue Warrants, &c. in Debts under 40 s. commanding, &c.

And to give Judgment and award Execution, &c.

Justices shall keep fair Entries, &c.

AND the Justice who gives such Judgment, shall keep fair Entries of the Names of the Complainants and Defendants, and of the Debt or Sum contained in such Judgment, with the Day and Year when such Judgment was given.

Justices may grant Attachments, &c.

AND BE IT FURTHER ENACTED by the Authority aforesaid, That if any Person shall absent him or her self out of this Government, or conceal him or her self, so that he or she cannot be taken to answer his or her just Debts, it shall and may be lawful for any Justice of the Peace of the County where such Person's Goods or Effects are, upon Oath or Affirmation made of the Truth of the Debt, and that the Defendant is gone out of the Government, as is believed, or doth conceal him or her self so that he or she cannot be taken, and that the Complainant is in Danger of losing his or her Debt, to grant a Warrant of Attachment for any Debt under *Forty Shillings*, directed to some Constable of the County, to attach the Goods and Chattels or other Effects of such Person, in whose Hands soever the same be found, within the said County, to answer the said Creditor, to the Value of the Debt and Costs; and the Person or Persons, in whose Hands any Goods or other Effects are attached, shall be oblig'd to appear before the said Justice, and declare, upon Oath or Affirmation, what Effects of the Defendant he or they have in his or their Hands, and pay the same to the Use of the Plaintiff, when so required by the said Justice: And upon Proof being made, to the Satisfaction of the Justice, of the Truth of the Debt or Demand, the same Justice shall award Execution for the Debt and Costs, to be executed by the Constable, who shall have *Two Shillings* for serving the said Warrant of Attachment, and *Three Shillings* for serving the Execution; which said Goods or other Effects, not being ready Money, shall be brought to an Appraisment, but not sold until the Expiration of one Month next after such Attachment and Appraisement, to the End that the Debtor may have Time to redeem them, if he or she shall see Cause so to do; but in Case such Goods be living or perishable Goods, the Constable or Constables so attaching, shall and may, by Virtue of an Order of the Justice or Justices granting such Attachment, after Appraisment, make lawful Sale thereof, and deliver the Money arising thereby into the Hands of the same Justice, who shall keep the same, and at the Expiration of one Month, as aforesaid, shall satisfy to the Plaintiff his Debt and Costs, and the Overplus,

And award Execution for Debt and Costs, &c.

Fees.

verplus, if any be, fhall be returned to the Defendant, or any other Perfon lawfully reprefenting him or her, any Law, Cuftom or Ufage to the contrary thereof in any wife notwithftanding.

PROVIDED ALWAYS, That no Lands or Tenements within this Government, fhall be fubject to be attached or taken in Execution, by Virtue of this Act; and that no Warrant of Attachment, or other Warrant, fhall be granted or iffue, for any Sum or Sums of Money, due or to become due, for the Rent of any Lands or Tenements within this Government, or for any Trefpafs, or Damage done to any Perfon in the Nature of a Trefpafs.

Lands and Tenements not to be attached by Virtue of this Act; nor fhall Attachments iffue for Rent or Damages, &c.

Signed by Order of the Houfe,

DAVID FRENCH, *Speaker.*

An ACT *for preventing Accidents that may happen by Fire in any of the Towns or Villages within this Government.*

BE IT ENACTED by the Honourable *GEORGE THOMAS*, Efq; by and with His Majefty's Royal Approbation, Lieutenant Governor and Commander in Chief of the Counties of *New-Caftle*, *Kent* and *Suffex* upon *Delaware*, and Province of *Pennfylvania*, by and with the Advice and Confent of the Reprefentatives of the Freemen of the faid Counties in General Affembly met, and by the Authority of the fame, That if within Ten Days after the Publication of this Act any Perfon or Perfons, within any Town or Village of this Government, fhall fet on Fire any Chimney or Chimnies of the Houfe or Houfes wherein he or fhe dwells, to cleanfe the fame, or by Neglect fhall fuffer his or her Chimney to take Fire, and blaze out at the Top thereof, every fuch Perfon being thereof duly convicted, by the Oath or Affirmation

Penalty on Firing Chimneys, &c.

I i

mation of one credible Witnefs, or the Confeffion of the Party, before any one Juftice of the Peace of the Town or Hundred wherein fuch Chimney fhall take Fire, fhall, for every fuch Offence or Neglect, forfeit the Sum of *Twenty Shillings*, to be levied, together with Cofts of Profecution, on his or her Goods and Chattels, by Diftrefs and Sale thereof made by Warrant under the Hand and Seal of fuch Juftice; which faid Forfeiture fhall be paid to the Treafurer of the refpective County, for the Time being, for the Ufe of the Poor of the Town or Hundred wherein fuch Chimney fhall take Fire.

Signed by Order of the Houfe,

DAVID FRENCH, *Speaker.*

An ACT *about Departers out of this Government.*

BE IT ENACTED by the Honourable GEORGE THOMAS, Efq; by and with His Majefty's Royal Approbation, Lieutenant Governor and Commander in Chief of the Counties of *New-Caftle*, *Kent* and *Suffex* upon *Delaware*, and Province of *Pennfylvania*, by and with the Advice and Confent of the Reprefentatives of the Freemen of the faid Counties, in General Affembly met, and by the Authority of the fame, That no Perfon or Perfons whatfoever fhall prefume to depart this his Majefty's Government, who hath refided three Months, next before his Departure, in any of the Counties of this Government, but fhall firft fignify the fame in Writing under his Hand, affixed upon the Court-Houfe-Door, in the County wherein he fhall refide, at leaft thirty Days before his Departure, or fnall have a Certificate under the Hands and Seals of two Juftices of the Peace of the County.

Departers fhall publifh their Defigns 30 Days before they leave the Government, &c.

AND if any Perfon or Perfons fhall prefume to tranfport or convey, or be Aiding or Affifting to the Tranfporting or Conveying any Perfon or Perfons out of this Government, either by Land or Water, that hath not complied

Otherwife, thofe who tranfport them, &c. are liable to pay all Damages.

plied with this Act, he or they shall make good and pay to the Party or Parties aggrieved all Damages that shall accrue by reason of his or their Aiding, Assisting, Transporting or Carrying away any such Person or Persons as aforesaid, to be recovered by Bill, Plaint or Information in any of his Majesty's Courts of Record within this Government.

AND BE IT FURTHER ENACTED by the Authority aforesaid, That all Deeds and Bills of Sale privately and clandestinely given for Lands or Goods by such Departers, shall be void, in respect of the Creditors of such Person or Persons so departing this Government without such Notice or Certificate as aforesaid.

Deeds, &c. given by Departers, void in respect of their Creditors.

Signed by Order of the House,

DAVID FRENCH, *Speaker.*

An ACT *about Boats and Canoes.*

BE IT ENACTED by the Honourable *GEORGE THOMAS,* Esq; by and with his Majesty's Royal Approbation, Lieutenant Governor and Commander in Chief of the Counties of *New-Castle, Kent* and *Suffex* upon *Delaware,* and Province of *Pennsylvania,* by and with the Advice and Consent of the Representatives of the Freemen of the said Counties in General Assembly met, and by the Authority of the same, That if any Person or Persons within this Government shall take up any Boat or Canoe, being adrift, and secure the same, the Taker-up of such Boat or Canoe shall forthwith, at the reasonable Charge of the Owner, if known, send him or her Notice thereof; if not known, shall advertise the same in three of the most publick Places of the Town or Hundred where the same are taken up, on Penalty of making good to the Owner all the Damages he or she shall sustain by the Want of such Boat or Canoe after being taken up.

The Taker-up of Boats or Canoes shall give Notice, &c.

AND

A N D that the Taker-up of a Boat or Canoe shall receive,

His Reward. as a Reward from the Owner thereof, the Sum of *Five Shillings* for a Boat, and *Two Shillings and Six-pence* for a Canoe.

Penalty on carrying away or setting adrift, Boats, &c.   A N D if any Person or Persons shall at any time, after the Publication of this Act, take, carry away, or set adrift any Boat or Canoe from any Landing or other Place within the said Counties, or within one hundred Yards of any Shore or Landing-Place within this Government, without the Leave or Consent of the Owner or Possessor of such Boat or Canoe, and be thereof convicted before any one Justice of the Peace of this Government, he or she shall pay to the Party aggrieved, all such Damages, Costs and Charges as shall be awarded by the Justice before whom the Complaint shall be brought, so as the Costs and Damages do not in the whole amount to above *Forty Shillings.*

Signed by Order of the House,

D A V I D   F R E N C H, *Speaker.*

An ACT *for the Amendment of an Act of General Assembly of this Government, entituled,* An Act for regulating Attachments within this Government.

Preamble.   W HEREAS the said Act has been found imperfect and insufficient, in Regard that Persons becoming Securities for others, who shall abscond or absent themselves out of this Government, in order to defraud their Creditors of their just Debts; and that the Creditors of Persons living out of this Government have not a suitable Remedy provided by the said Act:

F O R Remedy whereof, **B E I T E N A C T E D** by the Honourable *G E O R G E   T H O M A S,* Esq; by and with his Majesty's Royal Approbation Lieutenant Governor and Commander in Chief of the Counties of *New-Castle, Kent* and *Sussex* upon *Delaware,* and Province of *Pennsylvania,* by and with the Advice and Consent of the Representatives

sentatives of the Freemen of the said Counties, in General Assembly met, and by the Authority of the same, That upon any Person's absconding or absenting from his or her usual Place of Abode, or absenting him or herself out of this Government, and being indebted any Sum or Sums of Money, or other Effects, for which any other Person or Persons are or stand his or her Surety by Recognizance, Bond, Bill, Assumption, or otherwise, it shall and may be lawful to and for such Surety or Sureties, or any other credible Person, in his, her or their Behalf, to make an Oath or Affirmation, that such Person is indebted, and doth abscond or absent from his or her usual Place of Abode, or doth absent him or her self out of this Government, and that by Means thereof such Surety or Sureties is or are liable to suffer Damage; which Oath or Affirmation being administred by the Justice or Officer who grants the Warrant or Writ of Attachment, and sufficient Security within the County where the Warrant or Writ shall be granted being given for Costs, if required, and that the Effects by the said Attachment to be recovered, shall, after Deduction of Costs, be applied to the Discharge of such Debt or Debts for which the said Plaintiff or Plaintiffs become bound or were Surety or Sureties, as aforesaid, such Surety or Sureties shall have Remedy and be entituled to such Warrant or Writ of Attachment, in like Manner as is provided for Creditors by the afore-recited Act, entitled, *An Act for regulating Attachments within this Government.*

The Sureties of Persons absconding, shall have Remedy by Writ of Attachment, &c.

AND BE IT FURTHER ENACTED by the Authority aforesaid, That where any Person or Persons who do not reside within this Government, stand or are justly indebted to any of the Inhabitants of the same, in any Sum or Sums of Money, Goods, Wares, or other Effects, and shall keep out of this Government in such a Manner that he, she or they cannot be taken to answer such their just Debt or Debts, as aforesaid; in such Case, upon Oath or Affirmation made, as aforesaid, of the Truth of such Debt or Debts, and that the said Debtor or Debtors, as it is believed, doth avoid coming into this Government, lest he, she or they be taken, to answer his, her or their just Debts, the Creditor or Creditors shall be entituled to such Warrant or Writ of Attachment, in like Manner, as aforesaid.

And the Creditors of Non-Residents in like Manner.

Signed by Order of the House,
DAVID FRENCH, *Speaker.*

An ACT *impowering* John Holliday, James Gorrel *and* Thomas Skidmore, *jun. of* Kent *County, Gentlemen, to sell and dispose of all such of the Lots of Ground within the Town of* Dover, *in the said County, as have not hitherto been sold and disposed of ; and also to confirm to the present Possessors all such Lots as have been heretofore purchased within the said Town from the former Trustees, and which have not been duly conveyed to them.*

Preamble.   WHEREAS by an Act of General Assembly of this Government, entituled, *An Act appointing Persons to lay out* Two Hundred *Acres of Land in Lots adjoining to the Court-House of the County of* Kent, *and to dispose of the same to the Use of the Publick ;* Benjamin Shurmer, William Brinkloe *and* Richard Richardson, of the said County, Gentlemen, or any two of them, were impowered and appointed to survey and lay out into Lots a certain Tract of Land in the said County, adjoining to the Court-House of the said County, and purchased by the People thereof, and commonly called the Town of *Dover*, in such Measures and Proportions as to them should seem meet and convenient ; and the said Lots, so surveyed and laid out, to dispose of and sell, to such Persons as should be willing to purchase the same ; and further, to execute all such Deeds and Conveyances for the same as should be necessary and requisite, as by the said recited Act may appear.

AND WHEREAS the aforesaid *Benjamin Shurmer*, *William Brinkloe* and *Richard Richardson*, are since deceased, and many of the Lots of Ground within the said Town remain unsold, to the great Detriment of the Publick.

AND WHEREAS, also after the Decease of *William Brinkloe* and *Richard Richardson*, two of the said Trustees, many Persons did actually and *bona fide* purchase of *Benjamin Shurmer*, the Survivor, several Lots of Ground within the said Town ; but because the Trust did not survive to the said *Benjamin Shurmer* by Virtue of any Words of the Act aforesaid, such Persons could not have sufficient
Titles

Titles for such Lots from the said *Benjamin Shurmer*, but are in Danger of being dispossessed of the same: For the Remedying and Preventing therefore of such Inconveniencies both to the Publick and such Persons as have been *bona fide* Purchasers as aforesaid, and in order that the Intention of the said Act may be fully complied with;

BE IT ENACTED by the Honourable *GEORGE THOMAS*, Esq; Lieutenant Governor and Commander in Chief of the Counties of *New-Castle*, *Kent* and *Sussex* upon *Delaware*, and Province of *Pennsylvania*, by and with the Advice and Consent of the Representatives of the Freemen of the said Counties, in General Assembly met, and by the Authority of the same, That *John Holliday*, *James Gorrel* and *Thomas Skidmore*, jun. of the County of *Kent*, Gentlemen, or any two of them, and the Survivors and Survivor of them, shall, and are hereby impowered to grant, bargain, sell and confirm all such Lots of Ground within the Town of *Dover* aforesaid, as have not hitherto been sold or disposed of by the Trustees in the aforesaid Act named, to such Person and Persons as shall be willing to purchase the same, for such Value and Consideration as shall be agreed upon between them and the Purchasers.

John Holliday, and others, impowered to sell Lots within the Town of Dover.

AND BE IT FURTHER ENACTED by the Authority aforesaid, That the said *John Holliday*, *James Gorrel* and *Thomas Skidmore*, jun. or any two of them, and the Survivors and Survivor of them are hereby impowered and required to make, execute and acknowledge all such Conveyances and Assurances as shall be reasonably required, and are necessary for the Confirming all such Persons in their Rights and Possessions, who shall appear to them the said Trustees actually and *bona fide* to have purchased any Lots within the said Town of *Dover*, of the aforesaid *Benjamin Shurmer*, since the Decease of the aforesaid *William Brinkloe* and *Richard Richardson*, at the proper Costs and Charges of the said Purchasers, their Heirs and Assigns, to be had, made and executed.

And to make Assurances to such as purchased of B. Shurmer,

PROVIDED ALWAYS, That such Person or Persons shall pay, or secure to be paid to the said Trustees, for the Use of the Publick, such Sum and Sums of Money as the said Lots were originally contracted for; all which Conveyances and Assurances shall be good and valid to all such Purchaser and Purchasers, their Heirs and Assigns forever.   AND

The Purchasers paying the Sum originally contracted for to the Use of the Publick.

The Truftees to account yearly with the Juftices & Grand-Jury.

AND BE IT FURTHER ENACTED by the Authority aforefaid, That the faid Truftees fhall, once in every Year, render an Account to the Juftices of the Peace of the faid County and fuch of the Grand-Jury as fhall be prefent, of all the Lots fo by them fold or difpofed of, and the Confideration for which the fame have been purchafed and bought; and fhall alfo pay to the Treafurer of the faid County, for the Time being, all fuch Sums of Money as they have received for Lots fold as aforefaid; all which Sums of Money fhall be difpofed of, and applied to fuch Ufes and Purpofes as the faid Juftices and Grand-Jury, at the Time of the laying of the Levies for the faid County, fhall direct and appoint. AND that the Juftices together with the Grand-Jury, or fuch of them as will be prefent, fhall and may, at the Time aforefaid, yearly allow to the faid Truftees fuch Reward, for their Care and Pains in executing the Truft repofed in them by this Act, as they the faid Juftices and Grand-Jury fhall think fit and reafonable.

Whofo fhall allow them a Reward for their Trouble.

Signed by Order of the Houfe,

DAVID FRENCH, *Speaker.*

An ACT *for the better Regulation of Servants and Slaves within this Government.*

Preamble.

FOR the due Encouragement of Servants in the Difcharge of their Duty, and preventing of their Defertion from their Mafters or Owners Service; and for the Difcouraging of fuch who corrupt, entertain, traffick or deal with any Servant or Slave: BE IT ENACTED by the Honourable *GEORGE THOMAS,* Efq; by and with his Majefty's Royal Approbation, Lieutenant Governor and Commander in Chief of the Counties of *New-Caftle, Kent* and *Suffex* upon *Delaware,* and Province of *Pennfylvania,* by and with the Advice and Confent of the Reprefentatives of the Freemen

Freemen of the said Counties in General Affembly met, and by the Authority of the fame, That no indentured Servant or Perfon, bound to ferve his or her Time in this Government, fhall have the Term of his or her Servitude, or any Part thereof, affigned, transferred or fold to any Perfon refiding in any other Province or Government, without the Confent of fuch Servant, and the Approbation of at leaft one Juftice of the Peace of the County, whereof the Mafter or Owner of fuch Servant is a Refidenter, under Penalty of *Ten Pounds*, and the faid Affignment and Sale fhall be void.

No Servant to be fold into another Government, without the Approbation of at leaft one Juftice, &c.

AND BE IT FURTHER ENACTED by the Authority aforefaid, That no indentured Servant within this Government, fhall have the Time of his or her Servitude, or any Part thereof, affigned, transferred or fold to any other Perfon within this Government, but in the Prefence and with the Approbation of one Juftice of the Peace of the County, whereof the Mafter or Owner of fuch Servant is a Refidenter, under the Penalty of *Five Pounds*, and the Affignment and Sale fhall be void.

Nor affigned over, but in the Prefence of one Juftice.

AND BE IT FURTHER ENACTED by the Authority aforefaid, That no Perfon or Perfons whatfoever, fhall, upon any Pretence or Confideration whatfoever, take or receive any Indenture of Servitude or Apprenticefhip from any Perfon or Perfons whatfoever within this Government, but in the Prefence and with the Approbation of one Juftice of the Peace of the County where the Party taking fuch Indenture dwells, under the Penalty of *Five Pounds*, together with Cofts of Profecution, to be paid by the faid Party, and every fuch Indenture fhall be void.

Nor Indentures taken, &c.

AND BE IT FURTHER ENACTED by the Authority aforefaid, That fuch Servants as fhall be imported into this Government, and truely ferve his or her Time mentioned in his or her Indenture, fhall, at the Expiration of the Term of his or her Servitude, have a Difcharge from his or her Mafter or Miftrifs, and by them be cloathed with two Suits of Apparel, whereof one fhall be new, to be approved by at leaft one Juftice of the Peace upon Complaint to him by fuch Servant becoming free.

The Allowance to Servants, at the Expiration of their Servitude.

AND for the Prevention of Servants abfenting themfelves from their Mafter's or Miftrefs's Service, **BE IT ENAC-**

L l

*Servants ab-
senting them-
selves, shall
make Satisfac-
tion; &c.*
ENACTED by the Authority aforesaid, That from
such Time as any Servant shall absent him or her self from
his or her Master or Mistress's Service, without Leave first
obtained for the same, every such Servant, for such Absence, and Expences of taking up, securing, and other necessary Charges, shall, at the Expiration of the Time of his
or her Servitude, make Satisfaction by Servitude, according
to the Judgment of any Court of Quarter-Sessions within
this Government, before which the said Servant shall be
brought for that Purpose.

AND BE IT FURTHER ENACTED

*Notice to be gi-
ven of the Ta-
king up of Run-
away Servants,
&c.*
by the Authority aforesaid, That if any Person shall apprehend or take up any Run-away Servant, and carry him
or her before the next Justice of the Peace of the County
where such Servant shall be so taken up, in order to be
sent to and secured in the Goal of the said County, for his
or her Master or Mistress's Service (whom the Sheriff of the
said County, or the Goaler, is hereby commanded to receive,
and immediately to send Notice thereof to the said Servant's
Master or Mistress, if the same can be known, and if not
known, the said Servant to be advertized in some publick
News-paper of the City of *Philadelphia*, for the Space of
one Month next after such Servant's Commitment) At
the Discharge of such Servant the said Sheriff or Goaler
shall pay to the Taker-up of such Servant or his Order, as
*Rewards for Ta-
king up Run-
away Servants,
&c.*
follows, *That is to say*, If the Place of the Taking-up the
said Servant be Ten Miles distant from the Place of the
said Servant's last Abode or under, the Sum of *Ten Shillings*,
and if upwards of Ten Miles the Sum of *Twenty Shillings*,
and to all others concerned in the carrying to Prison or
securing the said Servant, such Sum or Sums of Money,
as by the said Justice or any other Justice shall be allowed
reasonable. AND the said Sheriff or Goaler shall detain
the said Servant in Prison, until the Master or Mistress of
such Servant shall pay unto him for the Taking-up, together with the Charges of Committing, Securing, Maintaining, and all other necessary Expences arising upon such
Servant. AND if the Master or Owner of such Servant
so imprisoned as aforesaid, shall, for the Space of Six
Weeks next after Notice had of his or her Servant's Imprisonment, neglect or refuse to release such Servant, it
shall and may be lawful for the said Sheriff, and he is hereby required and commanded, upon Affidavit made of the
due Service of such Notice, to expose every such Servant
to sale at Publick Vendue, and him or her to sell to the
highest

higheft Bidder, for fuch Term and Sum as fhall be fufficient for the defraying the Cofts and Charges arifing upon the Apprehending and Imprifoning the faid Servant.

AND BE IT FURTHER ENACTED by the Authority aforefaid, That if any fufpicious Perfon fhall be taken up, travelling in or through this Government, without having a fufficient Pafs, figned by fome Juftice or proper Officer of the Place from whence he or fhe came, approved and renewed by fome Juftices of the Peace in the Parts through which fuch Perfon hath travelled, or fhall not otherwife be able to give a good and fatisfactory Account of him or her felf to the Juftice before whom he or fhe fhall be brought, fuch Perfon fhall, by the faid Juftice, be committed to the Goal of the County where he or fhe fhall be taken up, and be deemed to be, and dealt withal as a Run-away Servant.

Sufpicious Perfons travelling without a Pafs fhall be deemed Run-away Servants.

AND that no Sheriff or Goaler, within this Government, fhall allow or receive, for the Maintenance or Victualling of any Servant, Slave, or other Perfon committed to Goal as a Servant, any more than at the Rate of Twopence per Day for fuch Maintenance.

Allowance to the Goaler for the Maintenance of Servants, &c.

AND BE IT FURTHER ENACTED by the Authority aforefaid, That if any Perfon or Perfons, from and after the Publication of this Act, fhall prefume to deal, trade or barter with any indentured Servant, or Negro or Mullatto Slave, belonging to any Perfon within this Government, without the Confent, Approbation or Allowance of the Mafter or Owner of fuch Servant or Slave, from time to time, firft had and obtained, fpecifying and limiting the particular Sum for which fuch Servant or Slave, at every fuch Time, are permitted or allowed to deal, trade or barter for, as aforefaid, and be thereof duly convicted, by the Teftimony of one or more credible Witneffes, or otherwife, before any three Juftices of the County where any fuch Offence fhall be committed, to be heard in any Time of the Vacation, the Offender, for fuch his or her firft Offence, fhall be fined, in any Sum not exceeding *Five Pounds*, and for the fecond, in any Sum not exceeding the Sum of *Ten Pounds*, together with Cofts, and be obliged to enter into a Recognizance with fufficient Sureties for his or her good Behaviour. **AND** in Cafe any Mafter or Miftrefs fhall complain to any two Juftices of the Peace of any County within this Government, againft any Perfon inhabiting

Penalty on Perfons dealing with Servants or Slaves.

inhabiting the fame, that he or fhe hath juft Reason to fufpect and believe, that the faid Person doth deal, trade or barter with his or her Servant or Slave, contrary to the Intent and Meaning of this Act, and the faid Juftices fhall judge fuch Sufpicion juft and reafonable; then the faid Juftices are hereby impowered and required, to oblige every fuch Person to complained of, as aforefaid, to enter into fuch Recognizance as aforefaid.

AND WHEREAS it is found by Experience, that free Negroes and Mulattoes are idle and flothful, and often prove Burthenfome to the Neighbourhood wherein they live, and are of evil Example to Slaves; Therefore BE IT ENACTED by the Authority aforefaid, *Whoever ma-* That if any Mafter or Miftrefs, fhall, by Will or other-*numits a Slave,* wife, difcharge or fet free any Mulatto or Negro Slave or *&c. fhall give* Slaves, above the Age of *Thirty-five* Years, or decrepid or *Security to in-* infirm, he or fhe, or his or her Executors or Adminiftra-*demnify the* tors, at the next refpective County-Court of Quarter-*County.* Seffions, fhall enter into a Recognizance with fufficient Sureties, to be taken in the Name of the Treafurer of the faid County for the Time being, in the Sum of *Thirty Pounds,* for each Slave fo fet free, to indemnify the County from any Charge they or any of them may be unto the fame, in Cafe of fuch Negro or Mulatto's being fick, or otherwife being rendred uncapable to fupport him or her felf; and that until fuch Recognizance be given, no fuch Mulatto or Negro fhall be deemed free.

AND if any free Negro or Negroes having Children, *The Children of* are not able to maintain or fupport them, it fhall and may *free Negroes to* be lawful to and for the two next Juftices of the Peace, *be bound out to* and they are hereby required, together with the Overfeers *Service.* of the Poor of the Hundred where the faid Negro or Negroes fhall dwell, to bind out to Service fuch Negro Children, the Males until they fhall come to the Age of *Twenty one* Years, the Females until they fhall come to the Age of *Eighteen* Years.

AND BE IT FURTHER ENACTED *Penalty on free* by the Authority aforefaid, That if any free Negro or Mu-*Negroes enter-* latto, fhall harbour or entertain any Servant or Slave, in *taining Servants* his or her Houfe or Habitation, without the Leave and Con-*or Slaves.* fent of fuch Servant or Slave's Mafter or Miftrefs, fuch free Negro or Mulatto fhall forfeit and pay the Sum of *Five Shillings* for the firft Hour, and *Two Shillings* for every Hour

Hour afterwards, during the whole time that such Servant or Slave shall be so harboured or entertained; and if any free Negro or Mulatto shall barter, trade or deal with any Servant, or Negro, or Mulatto Slave, without Licence had as aforesaid, he or she shall make Restitution to the Master or Owner of such Servant or Slave, and also be publickly whipt with any Number of Lashes not exceeding Twentyone.

Free Negroes, &c. dealing with Slaves, shall make Restitution and be whipt.

AND BE IT FURTHER ENACTED by the Authority aforesaid, That if any free Negro or Mulatto shall refuse, or be unable to pay his or her Fine or Forfeiture, or to make Restitution as aforesaid, it shall and may be lawful to and for the Justice, before whom such Matter shall be tried, to order the said free Negro or Mulatto offending, to make Satisfaction to the Party injured, by Servitude.

Or being unable to pay, &c. shall make Satisfaction by Servitude.

AND BE IT FURTHER ENACTED by the Authority aforesaid, That whosoever shall take up any Negro or Mulatto Slave, at above ten Miles Distance from his or her Master or Mistress's Habitation, and not having Leave, in Writing, from his or her Master or Mistress, or not being known by the Taker-up to be about his or her Master or Mistress's Business or Service, and shall convey him or her to the Habitation of his or her said Master or Mistress, if known, such Taker-up shall receive, of the the said Master or Mistress, for his Reward, the Sum of of *Five Shillings*, with reasonable Charges.

Reward for taking up Slaves, above 10 Miles from home.

AND BE IT FURTHER ENACTED by the Authority aforesaid, That no Person shall employ or knowingly harbour, conceal or entertain another's Servant or Slave at his or her House or Plantation without the Master or Owner's Leave and Consent, except in Distress of Weather, or other extraordinary Occasion or Accident, under the Penalty of *Forty Shillings* for every Twenty-four Hours he or she shall entertain any such Servant or Slave as aforesaid, and so in Proportion for any lesser Time.

Penalty on harbouring or concealing Servants or Slaves.

AND BE IT FURTHER ENACTED by the Authority aforesaid, That all the Fines and Forfeitures arising by this Act, together with the respective Costs, shall be recovered by Distress and Sale of the Offender's Goods respectively, by Warrant under the Hands and Seals of the Justice or Justices before whom the Offender

How the Fines, &c. are to be recovered and disposed of.

M m   or

or Offenders fhall be convicted, and fhall be paid, the one Moiety to the Overfeers of the Poor, for the Ufe of the Poor of the Town or Hundred where the Offence or Offences fhall be committed, the other Moiety thereof to the Party or Parties aggrieved.

Signed by Order of the Houfe,

DAVID FRENCH, *Speaker.*

An ACT *impofing a Duty on Perfons convicted of heinous Crimes, and to prevent poor and impotent Perfons being imported into the Government of the Counties of* New-Caftle, Kent *and* Suffex *upon* Delaware.

Preamble.   WHEREAS many Perfons trading into this Government, have, for Lucre and private Gain, imported, fold or difpofed of, and daily do import Paffengers and Servants into this Government, who, by reafon of Age, Impotence or Indigence, have become a heavy Burthen and Charge upon the Inhabitants thereof; and likewife, do frequently import divers Perfons convicted of heinous Crimes, who foon after their Coming into this Government do often commit many Felonies, Robberies, Thefts and Burglaries, to the great Hurt of his Majefty's Subjects trading to and inhabiting the fame.

BE IT THEREFORE ENACTED by the Honourable *GEORGE THOMAS,* Efq; by and with His Majefty's Royal Approbation, Lieutenant Governor and Commander in Chief of the Counties of *New-Caftle, Kent* and *Suffex* upon *Delaware,* and Province of *Pennfylvania,* by and with the Advice and Confent of the Reprefentatives of the Freemen of the faid Counties in General Affembly met, and by the Authority of the fame, That all Mafters of Veffels, Merchants, or others, who

fhall

shall import, land or bring into any Port or Place belong- *Importer of Convicts shall pay 5 l. per Head.*
ing to this Government, at any time after the Publication
of this Act, any Person in the Condition of a Servant, or
otherwise within the Intent and Meaning of this Act, who
hath been convicted of any Murder, Burglary, Rape, Sodomy, Forgery, Perjury, or any other Felony, at any time
before such Importation or Coming into this Government,
shall, before the said Convicts be landed or put on shore,
pay the Sum of *Five Pounds* for every such Convict so imported or otherwise brought in, the one Moiety thereof to
the Governor for the time being, for the Support of Government, and the other Moiety to the Collector appointed
by this Act, or the Informer; and further, shall become *And give Security for their good Behaviour.*
bound with good and sufficient Security, to the Treasurer
of the County, where such Importation shall be made, for
the time being, in the Sum of *Fifty Pounds*, for the good
Behaviour of such convict Person, for the Space of one Year
next after his or her Importation or Coming into this Government.

AND WHEREAS it hath been a Practice for
Masters of Vessels, Merchants, and others, trading into this
Government, with Intent to avoid Complying with the
Payment of the Duties and giving the Security, required by
former Acts of Assembly of this Government, made to prevent the Importation of Convicts and poor and impotent
Persons, to land their Passengers, Servants and Convicts in
some of the adjacent Governments, which Passengers, Servants, impotent People and Convicts have afterwards been
secretly brought into this Government;

THEREFORE to prevent such Practices for the
future, BE IT ENACTED by the Authority *Convicts, &c. found in this Government within twelve Months after their Importation, may be apprehended and examined, &c.*
aforesaid, That if any such Convict as aforesaid, or Servant,
or Passenger, being poor and impotent Persons, shall be imported into the River *Delaware*, after the Publication of
this Act, and shall be found within this Government at any
time within the Space of twelve Months, next after their
being imported as aforesaid, whether such Persons were landed within this Government or elsewhere, it shall and may
be lawful for the Collector of the Duties, appointed by this
Act in each County within this Government, or any Justice
of the Peace within the same, to cause to be apprehended,
taken up, and to examine, upon Oath or Affirmation, all
such Convicts as aforesaid, or Passengers, or Servants, being
poor and impotent Persons, and all other Persons who may
be

be supposed to be able to make any Discovery of the Time and Manner of their being imported or coming into this Government, and from whence they came last, how long they have been come from beyond Seas, of what Country, and in what Vessel, and who was Master or Merchant of such Vessel, and whether such Vessel at the time of such Person or Persons being ship'd or coming on board, was bound to or designed for this Government, and whether such Person or Persons ship'd themselves with Intent to come into this Government: And if, upon Examination, it shall appear to such Collector or Collectors appointed by this Act, in any County within this Government, or any Justice of the Peace as aforesaid, that the said Persons were ship'd or took their Passages for this Government, then the said Collector or Collectors, or Justice of the Peace as aforesaid, before whom such Examination shall be taken, shall demand and compel the Persons, if Convicts, immediately to comply with the Directions of this Act, by paying the Duties hereby imposed on them, and giving the Security directed in the Case of Convicts by this Act; and shall be and are hereby impowered and required to send for the Master or Merchant of such Vessel, or either of them in which such Persons were supposed to be imported, and to examine such Master or Merchant, upon their Oath or Affirmation, concerning the said Passengers, Servants or Convicts, and their Importation or Coming into this Government; and if it shall appear that the said Persons so apprehended, or any other Persons, being Convicts as aforesaid, were shipped and taken on board to be imported into this Government, and put on Shore or permitted to go on Shore by such Master or Merchant in any other Government upon the River *Delaware*, or upon any Island or Place within the said River, without making Report and complying with the Directions of this Act, then and in such Case, the said Master or Merchant shall be obliged forthwith to give Security for his Appearance at the next Court of General Quarter-Sessions of the Peace, to be held for the County where such Examination is taken; and if, upon Presentment or Information he or they shall be legally convicted of such fraudulent Practice, he or they so offending shall forfeit the Sum of *Twenty Pounds* for every Person so by him or them brought in as aforesaid and put or permitted to be put on Shore, and afterwards, at any time within the Space of Twelve-months next after their being landed or put on Shore, shall be found within this Government without making such Entry and paying the Duties, and giving the Security required by this Act,

And shall be compelled immediately to comply with the Directions of this Act.

Penalty on Master or Merchant convicted of acting contrary to this Act.

Act, one half to the Governor for the time being, and the other to the Collector or Informer, and shall further pay the same Duties, and give the same Security for such Convicts as aforesaid, as if such Persons had been imported into this Government, and Report thereof made according to the Direction of this Act.

AND BE IT FURTHER ENACTED by the Authority aforesaid, That upon Information given to any two Justices of the Peace within this Government, that any old Persons, Infants, Maimed, Lunatick, or any vagabond or vagrant Persons are imported, come or brought into this Government, the said Justices to whom such Information shall be given, shall cause such aged Persons, Infants or impotent or vagrant Persons to be brought before them, and if, upon Examination, they shall judge that such Person or Persons are likely to become chargeable to the County where they are found or were imported, it shall and may be lawful for the said Justices as aforesaid, by Warrant or otherwise, to send for the said Master, Merchant, or other Person who imported any such Infant, lunatick, aged, maimed, impotent or vagrant Person or Persons as aforesaid, as are likely to become chargeable as aforesaid, and upon Proof made of their being the Importers or Owners of such Infant, lunatick, aged, maimed, impotent or vagrant Persons, who shall be judged to be likely to become chargeable as aforesaid, the said Justices as aforesaid shall and may compel the said Master, Merchant or Importer of such Infant, lunatick, maimed, aged, impotent or vagrant Person or Persons, to give sufficient Security to carry and transport such Infant, lunatick, maimed, aged, impotent or vagrant Person or Persons to the Place or Places from whence such Person or Persons were imported, or otherwise to indemnify the Inhabitants of this Government from any Charge that may come or be brought upon them by such Infant, lunatick, maimed, aged, impotent or vagrant Person coming into or living within this Government.

Importer of Persons likely to become chargeable, shall give Security to indemnify the Inhabitants.

PROVIDED ALWAYS, That if any Person or Persons shall apprehend him or themselves aggrieved with any such Order or Judgment of the Justices aforesaid who shall make the same, the Person or Persons so aggrieved may appeal to the next Court of General Quarter-Sessions of the Peace to be held for the County where such Order shall be made, whose Judgment then shall be final; but before such Appeal shall be allowed of, the Person or

Persons aggrieved, may appeal to the Court of Quarter-Sessions.

N n

Persons

Perſons appealing ſhall enter into Recognizance with one good Surety, at leaſt, to pay the Coſts and Charges of ſuch Appeal, in caſe the ſaid Order ſhall happen to be confirm'd.

AND for the better Diſcovery of ſuch Convicts, and poor and impotent, or idle, or vagrant Perſons who ſhall hereafter be imported into, and ſhall be likely to become chargable to the Inhabitants of this Government, BE IT FURTHER ENACTED by the Authority *Maſters of Veſ-* aforeſaid, That all Maſters of Veſſels, Merchants and others *ſels, &c to give* who ſhall hereafter bring into any Port or Place belonging to *an Account, on* this Government, by Land or Water, any Men or Women *Oath, of the* Paſſengers or Servants, ſhall, within the Space of Twenty-*Names of all* four Hours after their Arrival into any Port or Place within *Servants, Paſ-* this Government, make Entry, and give or cauſe to be gi-*ſengers, &c.* ven, upon Oath or Affirmation, to the Collector of the ſaid Duties where ſuch Importation is made, a true and juſt Account of all the Names of the Servants and Paſſengers ſo imported or brought in; and the ſaid Collector or Collectors as aforeſaid are hereby impowered and enjoined, immediately, by Warrant, or otherwiſe, to call before them the ſaid Merchant, Maſter, or other Perſon or Perſons importing ſuch Servants or Paſſengers as aforeſaid, and to examine, upon Oath or Affirmation, the ſaid Maſter, Merchant, or other Perſon or Perſons importing ſuch Servant or Servants, or Paſſengers as aforeſaid, and all other Perſon or Perſons who may be ſuppoſed to have any Knowledge of the Character or Circumſtances of ſuch Servants or Paſ-*And ſhall have* ſengers, and thereupon ſhall grant unto the Maſter, Mer-*a Certificate of* chant or Owner, or other Perſon having the Charge or *the Names of* Care of any Servant or Servants, or Paſſengers ſo imported *ſuch as are fit* or brought into this Government, a Certificate, containing *to be landed.* the Names of all the Servants or Paſſengers which ſuch Collector or Collectors ſhall judge fit to be landed or diſpoſed of as Servants, and do not appear to him or them to have been formerly convicted of any of the Crimes mentioned in this Act, or ſuch as do not appear to him or them to be ſuch Infants, lunatick, maimed, aged, impotent or vagrant Perſons as he or they ſhall judge likely to become chargeable to the Inhabitants of this Government; for which Examination, Permit and Certificate, there ſhall be paid to the ſaid Collector where ſuch Importation is made, *Fees to the Col-* the Sum of *Six-Pence,* for every Perſon ſo imported; and *lector.* there ſhall likewiſe be paid to the Collector or Collectors as aforeſaid, for each Bond he ſhall take in Purſuance of any
thing

thing required to be done by Virtue of this Act, the Sum of *Two Shillings and Six-Pence*, and no more.

PROVIDED NEVERTHELESS, AND IT IS HEREBY FURTHER ENACTED by the Authority aforesaid, That if after such Examination taken and Certificate granted, as aforesaid, it shall be made appear, that any of the said Persons so landed or imported are Convicts, the Master, Merchant or other Person who imported such Convict or Convicts, shall be liable to pay the same Duty and give the same Security as if no such Examination had been taken or Certificate granted, any Thing in this Act contained to the contrary notwithstanding.

Duty to be paid, &c. notwithstanding the Certificate granted, if it afterward appears, that any of the Persons imported are Convicts.

AND if any Servant or Servants, or Convict or other Person, shall be imported or brought into and landed in any Port or Place within this Government, without making such Entry, as aforesaid, in the Manner before directed, and paying the Duty and giving the Security required by this Act, and within the Time limited by this Act for that Purpose, and obtaining such Certificate from the Collector or Collectors, as aforesaid, every such Master of a Vessel, Merchant and other Person, so importing, bringing in or landing such Servants or other Persons, shall forfeit and pay, for each Servant or other Person so imported, brought in or landed, contrary to the Directions of this Act, the Sum of *Ten Pounds*, one half, after the Charge of Prosecution deducted, to the Governor, for the Time being, for the Support of Government, and the other half, after such Charges deducted, as aforesaid, to the Collector where such Importation shall be made, or to such Person or Persons as will sue for the same in any Court of Record within this Government, by Bill, Plaint or Information, wherein no Essoin, Protection or Wager of Law shall be allowed.

Penalty on Master, Merchant, &c. not complying with the Directions of this Act.

AND BE IT FURTHER ENACTED by the Authority aforesaid, That all Persons obliged by this Act to make Entry as aforesaid, shall apply to *John Finney*, Esq; for the County of *New-Castle*, *John Holliday*, Esq; for the County of *Kent*, and *Simon Kollock*, Esq; for the County of *Sussex*, who are hereby appointed Collectors of the said Duties hereby imposed, without any Notice or Request made by them.

Persons obliged to make Entry, shall apply to the Collector.

AND

Who are impowered to receive, demand, &c.

AND the said Collectors, and every of them, are hereby impowered to receive, collect, demand and recover, from all Persons importing, landing or bringing in any Servant or Servants, or other Persons, into any Port or Place within this Government, all Forfeitures and Penalties herein before appointed to be set, imposed and levied by Virtue of this Act.

In Case of Death, &c. of any Collector, the Governor may appoint another.

AND BE IT FURTHER ENACTED by the Authority aforesaid, That in Case of the Death or Removal of any of the Collectors or Officers appointed by this Act, it shall and may be lawful for the Governor, for the Time being, to nominate and appoint some fit and proper Person to execute the said Office, in the Room and Stead of the Person so deceased or removed.

Signed by Order of the House,

DAVID FRENCH, *Speaker.*

An ACT about Defalcation.

FOR the avoiding numerous Suits at Law within this Government, BE IT ENACTED by the Honourable *GEORGE THOMAS,* Esq; by and with his Majesty's Royal Approbation, Lieutenant Governor and Commander in Chief of the Counties of *New-Castle, Kent* and *Sussex* upon *Delaware,* and Province of *Pennsylvania,* by and with the Advice and Consent of the Representatives of the Freemen of the said Counties, in General Assembly met, and by the Authority of the same, That if two Men, dealing together, be indebted to each other, upon Bonds, Bills, Bargains and the like, the Defendant may, in his Plea and Answer to the Plaintiff's Declaration, acknowledge the Debt which the Plaintiff demands from him, and defalk what the Plaintiff is indebted to him the said Defendant. PROVIDED ALWAYS, That if the Plaintiff's Demand be a Specialty, the Defendant shall prove the Debt to be defalcated, by the Evidence of one credible Person at the least, or by his or her Book regularly kept, with fair Entries.

Any Person sued on Bond, &c. may defalk what the Plaintiff is indebted to him, &c.

AND

AND BE IT FURTHER ENACTED by the Authority aforesaid, That the Creditor or Plaintiff shall be oblig'd, by Word or Writing, at least Ten Days before Suit brought, to request the Debtor or Defendant, being a Freeholder within this Government, to settle and adjust Accounts; and if the Ballance, upon such Settlement, be made under *Forty Shillings*, the Creditor or Plaintiff may recover the same, by Warrant from a Justice of the Peace, as is directed for the Recovery of Debts under *Forty Shillings*: And if the Debtor or Defendant refuse to come to Account, the Creditor or Plaintiff may sue him for the whole Account, and shall recover his Costs notwithstanding the Ballance due may be found under *Forty Shillings*.

Before Suit brought, the Plaintiff shall request the Debtor to settle.

If the Ballance be under 40 s. it may be recover'd by Warrant.

If the Debtor refuse to settle the Plaintiff may sue for the whole, &c.

BUT if the Defendant doth prove, that before Suit brought, he tendered to the Plaintiff his, the said Defendant's, Account against him, and so much Money as shall, upon Tryal, be found to be due to the Plaintiff, the Plaintiff shall suffer Nonsuit and pay **Costs**.

If the Defendant prove that he tender'd his Account and Ballance, the Plaintiff shall be nonsuit.

AND BE IT FURTHER ENACTED by the Authority aforesaid, That where the Plaintiff and Defendant having Accounts against one another, shall, by themselves or their Attornies or Agents, consent to a Rule of Court for the Referring the Adjustment thereof to indifferent Persons, mutually chosen, or appointed by the Justices in open Court, the Award or Report of such Referrees being made according to the Reference, and approved by the Court, shall be deemed and taken, to be as available in Law as a Verdict of a Jury; and the Party or Parties to whom any Sum of Money shall be awarded or found to be due, shall have Judgment, if he be Plaintiff, and a *Scire facias*, if he be Defendant, and have an Execution for the same, with Costs of that Action, any Law, Custom or Usage to the contrary notwithstanding. **AND** that the former Act of Assembly, entituled, *An Act about Defalcation*, shall be, and is hereby repealed.

If Plaintiff and Defendant consent to a Rule for Referring, the Award shall be binding, &c.

Repeal of the former Act.

Signed by Order of the House,

DAVID FRENCH, *Speaker.*

An ACT *for establishing a Market in the Town of* New-Castle, *for appointing a Clerk of the Market, and directing the Assize of Bread.*

Preamble. WHEREAS the Want of a regular Market in the Town of *New-Castle*, in the County of *New-Castle*, within this Government, hath been attended with great Inconveniencies to the Inhabitants thereof, as well as to such Persons who offer Provisions to Sale in the said Town :   For Remedy whereof;

BE IT ENACTED by the Honourable *GEORGE THOMAS*, Esq; by and with his Majesty's Royal Approbation, Lieutenant Governor and Commander in Chief of the Counties of *New-Castle, Kent* and *Sussex* upon *Delaware*, and Province of *Pennsylvania*, by and with the Advice and Consent of the Representatives of the Freemen of the said Counties, in General Assembly met, and by the *No Provision to be sold on Market Days but at the Market-House, on Pain of Forfeiture.* Authority of the same, That from and after the Publication of this Act, no Person or Persons whatsoever, shall presume either to buy or sell any Kind of Provisions (Fish, Milk and Bread excepted) on Market-Days, within any Part of the Town of *New-Castle* but at the Publick Market-House, under the Penalty of Forfeiting, both by the Buyer and Seller, all such Provisions so sold or bought, or the Value thereof, to be levied, together with Costs, by the Clerk of the Market, for the Use of the Poor of the Town and Hundred of *New-Castle*, by Distress and Sale of the Offender's Goods and Chattels respectively, by Warrant under the Hand and Seal of any one Justice of the Peace of the said Town or County.

AND BE IT FURTHER ENACTED *Poor lean Meat, &c. shall be forfeited, &c.* by the Authority aforesaid, That if any Person or Persons, shall presume to bring to Market and sell, or offer to sale, any Meat or Flesh that shall be poor, lean, or Carrion, or any other Provision, not sound and wholsome, every Person so offending, shall forfeit the same, if sound and wholsome, to the Use of the Prisoners in the common Goal of the said Town or County, if unwholesome or unsound, to be thrown into the River.

AND

AND BE IT FURTHER ENACTED by the Authority aforesaid, That no Person or Persons whatsoever, shall presume to kill or slay any Cattle, Sheep, Calves or Hogs within the said Market House, on Penalty of forfeiting the Sum of *Five Shillings* for every such Offence, to be levied as aforesaid, and applied to the Use of the Poor of the Town and Hundred aforesaid.

Penalty on slaughtering in the Market-House.

AND BE IT FURTHER ENACTED by the Authority aforesaid, That if any Person or Persons whatsoever, shall, by themselves or others, either sell or offer to sale, any Butter, Cheese, Tallow, or any Sort of Provisions, by any false Weights, or for more Weight than the same shall be found to be, by Tryal of the said Clerk of the Market, for the Time being, upon Complaint made, such Person or Persons shall, for every such Offence, forfeit such Butter, Cheese, Tallow or Provision, so sold or offered to sale, as aforesaid, to the Use of the Poor of the Town and Hundred aforesaid; and the Clerk of the Market is hereby empowered to seize the same.

Provisions, &c. sold by false Weights, or wanting weight, shall be forfeited.

AND BE IT FURTHER ENACTED by the Authority aforesaid, That at all Times hereafter, every *Wednesday* and *Saturday* in each Week, and no other Days whatsoever, shall be deemed and taken for the publick and regular Market-Days of the said Town of *New-Castle.*

Wednesday and Saturday shall be the Market-Days.

AND BE IT FURTHER ENACTED by the Authority aforesaid, That no Person or Persons whatsoever, shall presume to hawk or carry about the said Town of *New-Castle*, or expose to sale in the Market-House within the same, any Flesh Meat, on the *Tuesdays* or *Fridays* in each Week, except in the Months of *June, July* and *August*, on Pain of forfeiting such Flesh Meat, or the Value thereof, one half thereof to the Use of the Poor of the Town and Hundred of *New-Castle*, the other half to the Use of the Clerk of the Market, to be recovered in like Manner as other Forfeitures are directed to be recovered by this **Act.**

Flesh Meat expos'd to Sale on Tuesdays or Fridays, shall be forfeited, except, &c.

And for preventing Frauds that may happen to be committed by publick Bakers of Bread, for sale, in the said Town of *New-Castle* · **BE IT ENACTED** by the Authority aforesaid, That from and after the Publication of this Act, every Baker or Bakers of Bread, for sale,

in

Bakers shall mark their Bread, on Penalty of 5s.

in the said Town of *New-Castle*, shall, and are hereby directed and required, to make or impress some Mark, Letter or Name of such Baker, on every such Bread as he or she shall bake for sale, as aforesaid, on Penalty of forfeiting and paying, for every such Neglect, the Sum of *Five Shillings* to the Clerk of the Market, for the Time being.

Justices impowered to appoint the Size and Weight of Bread.

AND BE IT FURTHER ENACTED by the Authority aforesaid, That the Justices of the Court of Quarter-Sessions, shall, and are hereby empowered and required, from time to time, at their Quarterly-Sessions of the Peace for the said County, to settle and appoint the Size and Weight of the several Sorts of Bread, which shall be baked for sale in the said Town of *New-Castle*. AND all Bakers in the said Town, shall conform themselves, and make the Bread, by them baked, for sale, agreeable thereto, on Pain of Forfeiting, for every such Offence, all such Bread, as, upon Tryal of the Clerk of the Market, shall

Penalty on not conforming to such Appointment.

be found to be of lesser Weight; to be, by the said Clerk, seized for the Use of the Poor of the said Town and Hundred, and *Five Shillings* to the said Clerk, to be recovered as aforesaid.

AND that no Baker shall, upon any Pretence whatsoever, make any different or other Sorts of Bread, for sale, but such as shall, by the Justices of the said Court of Quarter-Sessions, be directed and appointed, under the Penalty of Forfeiting the same, as aforesaid, to be applied in Manner aforesaid.

Philip Van Leuvenigh appointed Clerk of the Market.

AND BE IT FURTHER ENACTED by the Authority aforesaid, That *Philip Van Leuvenigh* of the said Town, is hereby appointed and constituted Clerk of the aforesaid Market of the said Town of *New-Castle*, who is hereby strictly charged and commanded, to put this Act, and every Part thereof, in Execution ; and empowered to receive, demand and recover all such Penalties, Fines and Forfeitures, as in this Act are directed to be forfeited and paid, and to enter into all such Places and Houses where he shall suspect any such Bread to be, which is not made agreeable to the Directions of this Act, and to examine the Weights and try the same, for the Purposes in this Act before directed.

Who shall keep fair Accounts.

AND the said Clerk is hereby directed and required to keep a fair and just Account of all Fines, Forfeitures and
Penalties

Penalties that he fhall receive by Virtue of this Act, and *And fettle an-* fettle fuch Account, once in every Year, with the Over- *nually with the* feers of the Poor of the Town and Hundred aforefaid for *Poor, &c.* the time being, and pay to them all fuch Sum and Sums of Money as fhall by him be received for the Ufe of the faid Poor.

AND BE IT FURTHER ENACTED by the Authority aforefaid, That the Clerk of the faid *The faid Clerk* Market, hereby appointed, or that fhall hereafter be ap- *may erect* pointed by Virtue of this Act, is hereby impowered to *Booths and Stalls, and let* make, erect, allot and let out for Hire, Stalls or Booths for *them at the* Accomodating fuch Perfons as fhall attend the Fairs held *Fairs.* within the faid Town of *New-Caftle*, upon the Green, according to the ufual Cuftom and Ufage thereof, and let out the fame on Hire, for fuch Sum and Sums of Money as any three of the Juftices of the faid County fhall appoint and direct: AND for Encouragement and Satisfaction for *His Reward for* his Care in Executing this Act, the faid Clerk fhall receive *putting this Act* and take to his own Ufe the whole Hire of the Stalls erec- *in Execution.* ted on the faid Green, and one Moiety of the Rents of the Stalls in the faid Market-Houfe, and the other Moiety thereof, to be received by the faid Clerk, fhall by him be paid to the Treafurer of the faid County, to remain in his Hands until the fame, by the faid Treafurer, fhall be applied to fuch Ufe and Ufes as the Juftices of the faid Court of Quarter-Seffions fhall from time to time fee fit to order and direct; and that no Perfon or Perfons whatfoever, who are not Inhabitants of the faid County, fhall, without the Approbation of the faid Clerk, make or erect any fuch Stalls or Booths as aforefaid.

AND BE IT FURTHER ENACTED by the Authority aforefaid, That upon the Death, Refufal, *The Clerk dying,* Removal or Inability of the Clerk of the faid Market ap- *&c. the Gover-* pointed by Virtue of this Act, the Governor for the time *nor may appoint* being may, and is hereby impowered, to appoint from time *another.* to time, as often as there fhall be occafion, fome fit and difcreet Perfon to ferve in the Office of Clerk of the faid Market; which faid Clerk of the Market, hereby appointed, or that fhall hereafter be appointed by Virtue of this Act, before he fhall prefume to enter upon his faid Office, or execute the Truft repofed in him, fhall firft take an Oath or *His OATH.* Affirmation before fome Juftice of the Peace of the faid County of *New-Caftle*, that he fhall and will, well and truly demean and behave himfelf in the Office of Clerk of the

P p Market

Market aforesaid, and impartially discharge the Trust reposed in him by Virtue of this Act during his Continuance in that Office.

Repeal of former Acts.

AND BE IT FURTHER ENACTED by the Authority aforesaid, That the several Acts of General Assembly of this Government heretofore made for regulating any Market, the Assize of Bread, or for appointing a Clerk of the Market within the said Town of *New-Castle*, shall be and are hereby repealed, made null and void, any thing in the said Acts contained to the Contrary in anywise notwithstanding.

Signed by Order of the House,

DAVID FRENCH, *Speaker.*

An ACT *providing for the Security and Defence of the Town of* Lewes, *in the County of* Sussex, *within this Government.*

Preamble

WHEREAS the Inhabitants of the Town of *Lewes* having heretofore suffered, and now are in Danger of suffering by the Depredations and Insults of Privateers and Pirates; For Prevention whereof,

BE IT ENACTED by the Honourable *GEORGE THOMAS*, Esq; by and with His Majesty's Royal Approbation, Lieutenant Governor and Commander in Chief of the Counties of *New-Castle, Kent* and *Sussex* upon *Delaware,* and Province of *Pennsylvania,* by and with the Advice and Consent of the Representatives of the Freemen of the said Counties in General Assembly met, and by the Authority of the same, That it shall and may be lawful to and for the Governor,

for

for the Time being, from time to time, and at all Times *The Governor* hereafter, to commission and impower two sufficient and *may appoint* well-qualified Persons or Officers, in the said Town of *Officers, to keep* Lewes, to keep a Military Watch within the said Town, *Lewes, &c.* or in such Place and Places within the Limits herein after particularly described, consisting of such Persons, under such Regulations, and at such Times as to them or either of them shall seem necessary.

AND that all the Inhabitants and Freemen within these Limits, *That is to say,* from the Mouth of *Canary-Run* *Limits.* and *Pagan-Creek* to *Southern's Run* at the King's Road, from thence to the Head of *Pot-hook Creek,* from thence down to *Lewes Creek,* and from thence, down the said *Lewes Creek,* to the Mouth of *Canary-Creek* aforesaid, within the said County of *Sussex,* shall each of them provide and keep, when thereunto required by the said Officer or Officers, these following Arms, *to wit,* a well fixed Firelock or Mus- *Arms to be pro-* ket, one Cartouch-Box with Twelve sufficient Charges of *vided.* Gun-powder and Ball therein, Three good Flints, a Worm and Priming-Wire, to be approved by the said Officer or Officers; and if any Inhabitant or Freeman, as aforesaid, within the Limits aforesaid, shall, for the Space of one Month next after Notice given him by the said Officer or Officers, neglect or refuse to provide the Arms aforesaid, or to produce them to the said Officer or Officers, when thereunto commanded, and be thereof convicted, before any one Justice of the Peace for the said County, every such Person so offending, shall, for the first Offence or Neglect, pay to the said Officer or Officers the Sum of *Ten* *Penalty on Neg-* *Shillings,* and afterwards, for every such Refusal or Neg- *lect, &c. to pro-* lect, monthly, the Sum of *Twenty Shillings,* to be recovered, *vide them.* together with Costs, by Distress and Sale of the Offenders Goods and Chattels, by Warrant under the Hand and Seal of the said Justice; and if no such Goods or Chattels shall be found, the Offender shall be committed to the Goal of the said County, there to remain the Space of Ten Days, for every such Offence.

AND BE IT FURTHER ENACTED by the Authority aforesaid, That all the said Inhabitants *Obedience to the* and Freemen, within the said Town of *Lewes* and Limits *Officers enjoin'd.* aforesaid, shall yield Obedience to the said Officers, and to each of them, in all Things relating to the aforesaid Watch and the Defence of the said Town and Limits aforesaid: And if any Person, being an Inhabitant or Freeman with-

his

Penalty on Non-Attendance or Disobedience. in the said Limits, shall wilfully refuse or neglect to give his Attendance, when commanded by the said Officer or Officers, or disobey them or either of them, in any Matter or Thing relating to the Watch or Defence aforesaid, every such Person so offending, upon Conviction and due Proof thereof made before any one Justice of the Peace for the said County, shall, for every such Offence, forfeit and pay to the said Officer or Officers the Sum of *Five Shillings*, to be recovered, together with Costs, in Manner aforesaid.

AND BE IT FURTHER ENACTED by the Authority aforesaid, That the said Officer and Officers, for the Time being, are hereby empowered and required to call together all and every the Inhabitants and Freemen within the Limits aforesaid, once in every Month, *Days & Times of Exercise.* between the first Day of *April* and the first Day of *October*, and once in every Three Months, between the first Day of *October* and the first Day of *April*, yearly, to exercise or train the said Inhabitants or Freemen, and to view their Arms and Ammunition, that they be in good Order and fit for Service, on all Occasions: And if any Person or Persons, having due Notice, shall neglect or refuse to attend, *Penalty.* or attending, shall wilfully disobey the Commands of such Officer or Officers, or those empowered by them or either of them, every such Person so offending, upon Conviction and due Proof thereof made as aforesaid, shall, for every such Offence, forfeit and pay to the said Officer or Officers the Sum of *Five Shillings*, to be recovered, together with Costs, in Manner aforesaid.

AND BE IT FURTHER ENACTED *What shall be an Alarm.* by the Authority aforesaid, That the Firing three Guns successively or one after another, and the Beating of a Drum, shall be deemed and taken for an Alarm; and that upon every such Alarm given, all the Inhabitants and Freemen within the Limits aforesaid, shall forthwith, either in the Day Time or in the Night, repair, with their Arms and *Place of Rendevous.* Ammunition, to the Market-Street of the said Town of *Lewes*, and from thence whithersoever the Commanding Officer shall direct, and shall obey all and every the Commands of the said Officer and Officers, and those empowered by them for the Defending of the said Town of *Lewes* and Limits, from any Invasion or Descent which shall happen to be made, and shall not depart without the Leave of the said Officer or Officers first had and obtained: And if any Person, being an Inhabitant or Freeman within the
Limits

Limits aforesaid, shall, upon such Alarm given, refuse or neglect to attend, with his Arms and Ammunition, at the said Market-Street, or such other Place or Places whithersoever he shall be commanded by the said Officer or Officers, or those empowered by them or either of them ; or depart without Leave had, as aforesaid, every such Person so offending, upon Conviction and due Proof thereof, made before any Two Justices of the Peace for the said County, shall forfeit and pay to the said Officer or Officers the Sum of *Five Pounds*, to be recovered, together with Costs, by Distress and Sale of the Offenders Goods and Chattels, by Warrant under the Hands and Seals of the said Justices; and if no such Goods or Chattels shall be found, the Offender, for every such Offence, shall be committed to the Goal of the said County, there to remain for the Space of Two Months. AND if any Person or Persons shall, without the Command of the said Officer or Officers, or of such Person or Persons whom they shall empower, presume to make an Alarm within the Limits aforesaid, every such Person so offending, and being thereof legally convicted before any Court of Justice for the said County, shall, for every such Offence, be fined in the Sum of *Five Pounds*, to be paid, the one Moiety thereof to the said Officer or Officers, for the time being, the other Moiety to the Informer.

Penalty on Non-appearance at an Alarm.

Penalty on making an Alarm, without the Command of the Officer, &c.

AND for Prevention of the Danger that may arise by the Piloting into the Bay and River *Delaware* the Ships of Enemies and Pirates, BE IT FURTHER E-NACTED by the Authority aforesaid, That no Person or Persons, who are or shall be Pilots within the Bay and River aforesaid, shall presume to go on Board any inward-bound Vessels, without the Licence of the Governor, for the Time being, first had and obtained, or the Leave or Licence of such Person or Persons as shall or may be appointed by him for that Purpose, upon Pain of Forfeiting the Sum of *Ten Pounds*, the one half thereof to the Use of the Governor, for the Time being, the other half thereof to the Use of such Person or Persons as will sue for the same, to be recovered in any Court of Record within this Government ; and all Pilots within the Bay and River aforesaid are hereby oblig'd to take Notice of the same.

No Pilot shall go on board Vessels, inward bound, without Licence :

Penalty.

AND BE IT FURTHER ENACTED by the Authority aforesaid, That all the Fines and Forfeitures arising by Virtue of this Act, and which the said

Q q

Officer

How the Fines shall be disposed of. Officer or Officers shall receive, shall by him or them be laid out, for the purchasing Arms and Ammunition for the said Town of *Lewes*; and the said Officer and Officers, shall from time to time keep just and fair Accounts thereof, which shall, by him and them, once in every Year, be laid before and approved by the Justices of the said Court of Quarter-Sessions for the said County, at the Time of laying the Levies.

PROVIDED ALWAYS, AND BE IT FURTHER ENACTED by the Authority aforesaid, *Persons, whose Attendance is excused.* That no Person or Persons under the Age of *Fifteen* Years or above *Sixty-three*, and that no Person or Persons, producing to the said Officer or Officers a Certificate from the Meeting he or they frequent, and whose religious Perswasion is against bearing or using Arms, shall, by this Act, be obliged to give his or their Attendance, or be liable to any of the Fines or Forfeitures mentioned in this Act, any Thing therein contained to the contrary notwithstanding.

Signed by Order of the House,

DAVID FRENCH, *Speaker.*

An ACT *for raising the Sum of* One Thousand Pounds, *for defraying the Charges of Victualling and Transporting the Troops raised within this Government for the intended Expedition against some Part of the* Spanish West-Indies.

Preamble. WHEREAS His Majesty has been called upon, by repeated Provocations, to declare War against *Spain,* to vindicate the Honour of His Imperial Crown, to revenge the Injuries done to His Subjects, as well as to assert their undoubted Rights of Commerce and Navigation.

AND

AND WHEREAS His Majesty, by His Instructions under His Royal Sign-Manual, dated at *St. James's* the Second Day of *April*, in the *Thirteenth* Year of His Reign, to the Honourable *GEORGE THOMAS*, Esq; Lieutenant Governor and Commander in Chief of the Counties of *New-Castle*, *Kent* and *Suffex* on *Delaware*, and Province of *Pennsylvania*, hath notified, that His said Majesty hath given Orders for the Equipping and Setting forth of an Expedition against the *Spanish West-Indies*, and hath determined to raise a Body of Troops within His several Governments on the Continent of *America*, to join those to be sent from *Great-Britain* at the Place of General Rendezvous, which will be appointed for that Purpose; and hath directed the said Governor to recommend to the Assembly of this Government, to make Provision for the Victualling and Transporting such Troops as shall be raised within the same to the said Place of Rendezvous, pursuant to His Majesty's said Instructions: And we being willing to exert ourselves, according to our utmost Ability, in so just and necessary an Undertaking, as well as to express our Duty and Loyalty to His Majesty's Person and Government;

BE IT ENACTED by the Honourable *GEORGE THOMAS*, Esq; by and with his Majesty's Royal Approbation, Lieutenant Governor and Commander in Chief of the Counties of *New-Castle*, *Kent* and *Suffex* on *Delaware*, and Province of *Pennsylvania*, by and with the Advice and Consent of the Representatives of the Freemen of the said Counties, in General Assembly met, and by the Authority of the same, That the Sum of *One Thousand Pounds* in Bills of Credit, Part of the Sum of *Six Thousand Pounds*, made current by an Act of General Assembly of this Government, made in the *Thirteenth* Year of His Majesty's Reign, entituled, *An Act for the striking and making current Six Thousand Pounds in new Bills of Credit, to exchange such of the Bills of Credit of this Government, emitted* Anno Domini One Thousand Seven Hundred and Thirty-four, *as are worn and defaced*, shall be put into the Hands of the Honourable *George Thomas*, Esq; Lieutenant Governor, or his Order, for the Use of His said Majesty, to be applied for the Victualling and Transporting the Troops raised within this Government for the Expedition aforesaid; which said Sum of *One Thousand Pounds* shall be paid by the several Trustees of the General Loan-Office within this Government, in Manner following, *That is to say*, The

One Thousand Pounds given for Victualling and Transporting Troops.

Sum

Proportions to be paid by the Trustees of the Loan-Offices of each County.

Sum of *Four Hundred Pounds* by the Trustees of the General Loan-Offices for the County of *New-Castle*: The Sum of *Three Hundred and Thirty-three Pounds Six Shillings and Eight-pence* by the Trustees of the General Loan-Offices for the County of *Kent*: And the Sum of *Two Hundred sixty-six Pounds Thirteen Shillings and Four-pence* by the Trustees of the General Loan-Offices for the County of *Sussex*; for which said Sums, to be paid as aforesaid, the said Trustees shall take Receipts, which said Receipts shall be deemed, taken and allowed to be good and sufficient Discharges to the said Trustees, their Heirs, Executors and Administrators, for the Sums, in Bills of Credit, mentioned and contained therein.

One Fifth Part to be levied annually, and repaid to the Trustees of the Loan-Offices.

AND BE IT FURTHER ENACTED by the Authority aforesaid, That *One Fifth* Part of the said several Sums, amounting in the whole to *One Thousand Pounds*, hereby directed to be paid in Manner aforesaid, shall be annually levied upon the Inhabitants of the respective Counties of *New-Castle*, *Kent* and *Sussex*, in Proportion to the Sums paid by the several Trustees, as aforesaid, at the same Time, and in the same Manner as the County Levies shall be laid and raised; which said Sums, so annually raised, shall be paid by the Collectors of the several Hundreds within the aforesaid Counties, to the several Treasurers within the same, and by them to the several Trustees of the General Loan-Offices aforesaid, in like Bills of Credit as by this Act are directed to be paid to the Lieutenant Governor, or his Order, as aforesaid, for which Sums the Trustees shall give their Receipts to the said Treasurers; which said Receipts shall be allow'd, by the Courts and Grand-Juries, as sufficient Discharges for the Sums of Mo-

And sunk.

ney contained therein. All which Sums annually paid to the Trustees, as aforesaid, shall yearly be sunk and destroyed, in Presence of the several Committees to be appointed by the General Assemblies of this Government, in like Manner as other Bills of Credit of this Government are directed to be sunk by former Acts, until the whole Sum of *One Thousand Pounds* aforesaid, shall be wholly sunk and destroyed.

Signed by Order of the House,

DAVID FRENCH, *Speaker.*

An ACT *for the more eafy and fpeedy Recovery of fmall Debts.*

Preamble.

WHEREAS it is found by Experience, that a great Number of the Law-Suits which are commenc'd in this Government, are brought againſt the poorer Sort of People for ſmall Sums of Money, who are unable to bear the Expences ariſing by the common Method of Proſecution: Therefore for Remedying thereof,

BE IT ENACTED by the Honourable *GEORGE THOMAS*, Eſq; by and with His Majeſty's Royal Approbation, Lieutenant Governor and Commander in Chief of the Counties of *New-Caſtle*, *Kent* and *Suſſex* on *Delaware*, and Province of *Pennſylvania*, by and with the Advice and Conſent of the Repreſentatives of the Freemen of the ſaid Counties, in General Aſſembly met, and by the Authority of the ſame, That all Actions for Debt or other Demand, for the Value of *Forty Shillings* and upwards, and not exceeding *Five Pounds*, except ſuch Actions as are herein after excepted, ſhall, immediately after the Publication of this Act, be and are hereby made cognizable before any Juſtice of the Peace of any of the Counties within this Government, in the County in which the Defendant ſhall be or reſide ; and the ſaid Juſtices are hereby reſpectively impowered and required, upon Complaint to any of them made, for any ſuch Debt or Demand, to iſſue a Warrant in the Nature of a Summons, or Capias, as the Caſe may require, directed to any Conſtable of the County where the Defendant dwells or can be found, commanding him to bring or cauſe ſuch Defendant to appear before him, or ſome other Juſtice of the ſame County, at the Time and in the Manner following, *That is to ſay*, In Caſes where ſuch Proceſs ſhall be in the Nature of a Capias, forthwith, after the Service thereof; but where a Summons ſhall be iſſued, then on ſome certain Day, therein to be expreſſed, not leſs than *Six*, nor exceeding *Ten* Days, from the Date of ſuch Proceſs ; and at the Time appointed for the Hearing of any ſuch Cauſe, the ſaid Juſtice may proceed, with Conſent of Parties, to hear and determine the Matters in

Actions for Debt under 5l. cognizeable before any one Juſtice, &c.

R r Contro-

*Who may de-
termine the
same, or appoint
Referees, &c.*

Controversy ; or, at the Request of the Parties, he is hereby impowered, to nominate and appoint, and by Writing,
under his Hand and Seal, to summons *Three* Freeholders in
the Neighbourhood, Men of good Credit, who are hereby
required to appear before the said Justice, at such Time
and Place as he shall appoint, and proceed, by his Order,
to hear and examine the Proofs and Allegations of the
Plaintiffs and Defendants, and to determine the Matters in Difference in Manner of Arbitrators or Referrees,
and upon Return of such Auditors or Referrees, or any
Two of them, to give his Judgment thereupon, with such
Costs only, as, by the Laws of this Government, are allowed in Debts under *Forty Shillings*, with the additional
Sum of *Two Shillings* for each Referree.

*Process against
a Freeholder to
be by Summons,
&c.*

PROVIDED ALWAYS, That the Process a-
gainst Freeholders, shall be by Summons only, and Service shall be made thereof on the Person, or a Copy thereof left at the House of the Defendant, in the Presence of
one or more of his Family or Neighbours, at least *Four*
Days before the Time appointed for a Hearing; and in
Case the Defendant does not appear at the Time appointed,
then on Oath or Affirmation made by the Constable, that
the said Summons was duly served in Manner aforesaid, the
Justice who granted the said Summons, may either then,
or on such farther Day as he shall deem consistent with
Reason and the Nature of the Case to appoint, and not
otherwise, proceed to hear and determine such Cause or
Causes in the Defendant's Absence, and give Judgment and
award Execution thereupon, as if the Defendant were personally present.

AND BE IT FURTHER ENACTED
by the Authority aforesaid, That after Judgment given in
any of the Cases aforesaid, the Justice who pronounced the
same, or some other Justice of the said County, shall grant
Execution thereupon, directed to any Constable, commanding him to levy the Debt or Damages and Costs, of the
Defendant's Goods and Chattels (who, by Virtue thereof,
after having first publickly advertised the same at least *Six*
Days, shall, within the Space of *Four* Days next following,
expose the same to Sale by Publick Vendue, returning the
Overplus, if any be, to the Defendant) and for Want of
sufficient Effects, to take the Body of such Defendant into
Custody, and him or her to carry or convey to the common Goal of the County; and the Sheriff or Keeper of
such

ſuch Goal, is hereby required to receive the Perſon or Perſons ſo taken in Execution, and him, her or them ſafely
to keep, until the Sum recovered, with Coſts, be fully
paid; and in Default of ſuch ſafe Keeping, to be liable to
anſwer the Damages to the Party aggrieved, in ſuch Manner as by Law is provided in Caſe of Eſcapes. BUT in
Caſe no Effects belonging to the Defendant, ſufficient to
pay the Debt and Coſts, can be found, it ſhall and may be
lawful for the Plaintiff to apply to the Juſtice who pronounced the Judgment, for a Tranſcript thereof, and on
filing the ſame in the Prothonotary's Office of the Court of
Common-Pleas in the County in which the Recovery ſhall
be had, it ſhall and may be lawful for the Plaintiff to levy
the Sum recovered, with Coſts of Suit, on the Lands and
Tenements of the Defendant, either by *Fieri facias, Venditioni exponas,* or Extent, as the Caſe may require, in like
Manner as by Law is provided in other Caſes.

*In Caſe no Ef-
fects can be
found, the Sum
recovered may
be levied on
Lands, &c.*

PROVIDED ALWAYS, That no ſuch Execu-
tion ſhall be iſſued againſt any Freeholder, in leſs than the
Space of *Four* Months next after the Entry of ſuch Judgment, unleſs the Plaintiff, or ſomebody for him or her,
ſhall, on Oath or Affirmation, declare, that he or ſhe hath
good Reaſon to believe, that the Debt will, by ſuch Delay, be loſt, for that at the End of the ſaid Term, or before it, he or ſhe believes, that the Defendant will not have
ſufficient Effects in the County, on which the ſaid Debt
may be levied: And if any Judgment, to be given, as a-
foreſaid, ſhall be againſt a Perſon not a Freeholder, ſuch
Perſon ſhall have the Execution againſt him or her reſpited
for the like Term of *Four* Months, on his or her entering
into a Recognizance to the Plaintiff, with one ſufficient
Security, in the Nature of ſpecial Bail, on Condition to
deliver the Body of the Defendant to the Sheriff of the
County, at the Expiration of the Time ſo to be allowed,
or that the Condemnation Money ſhall then be paid; and
in Default of giving ſuch Security, ſhall be committed to
the common Goal of the County, there to remain until
the Debt and Coſts ſhall be paid, or ſuch Defendant otherwiſe legally diſcharged.

*No Execution
to be iſſued a-
gainſt a Free-
holder, in leſs
than 4 Months,
unleſs, &c.*

PROVIDED ALSO, That where the Plaintiff, in
any Cauſe, ſhall become Non-ſuit, or Judgment ſhall paſs
againſt him, then the Juſtice is hereby required to aſſeſs
the Defendant his reaſonable Coſts, to be levied in Manner
aforeſaid,

PRO-

Insolvent Deb-tors may be re-liev'd, as before. PROVIDED ALSO, That it shall and may be lawful for the Justices in the respective Courts of Common-Pleas, to give such Relief to any insolvent Debtor or Debtors, prosecuted in Pursuance of this Act, as they might have done by the Law now in Force, in Case this Act had not been made.

Persons con-ceiving them-selves aggrieved may appeal, &c. PROVIDED ALSO, That if any Person or Persons shall conceive him, her, or themselves aggrieved by any such Judgment so to be given (Cases determined on the Return of Auditors or Referrees, as aforesaid, only excepted) it shall and may be lawful for such Person or Persons, at any Time within the Space of *Six* Days next following the giving such Judgment, but not after, to appeal therefrom to the next Court of Common-Pleas, to be holden for the County in which such Suit shall be commenced, he, she or they first entering into a Recognizance, with at least one sufficient Security, in double Value of the Debt or Damages sued for, and sufficient to answer all Costs, to prosecute the said Appeal with Effect, and to abide the Order of the said Court, or in Default thereof to be sent, by Mittimus, to the Sheriff of the County, by him to be kept, until he, she, or they shall give such Security, or be otherwise legally discharged.

Justices to make fair En-tries in Books, &c. AND BE IT FURTHER ENACTED by the Authority aforesaid, That the Justices shall cause fair Entries to be made, in Books by them to be provided for that Purpose, of the Names of the Plaintiff and Defendant, in all such Cases as may come before them, with the Debt and Costs adjudged, and the Time when the said Judgment was given; and upon any Appeal made from any such Judgment, the Justice who pronounced the same, shall send a Transcript thereof to the Prothonotary of the Court of Common-Pleas of the County in which such Appeal is made, on or before the first Day of the Term next following any such Appeal; for which Transcript, or any other, obtained by Virtue of this Act, the Justice shall be allowed, in the Costs to be taxed, *Eighteen Pence*, and no more.

Method of Pro-ceeding in Court upon Appeal. AND BE IT FURTHER ENACTED by the Authority aforesaid, That at the Court to which any such Appeal shall be made, the Person so appealing, shall cause an Entry of his Suit to be made by the Prothonotary of such Court, and shall either have his Appearance entered,

entered, or give Bail to the Action, as the Nature of the Case may require, or on Neglect thereof, and Application of the Appellee to the Court for that End, the Appellant's Default shall be recorded, the first Judgment affirmed with reasonable Costs, and Execution shall be issued out of the said Court against the Defendant's Body, Goods or Chattels, as is usual in other Cases; and in Case the Defendant shall appeal, or give Bail, as aforesaid, the Plaintiff or Defendant in the Appeal, as the Case may require, shall file his or her Declaration, and the adverse Party plead to issue in such Time as shall be directed by the Court, so always that the Cause be tried by a Jury of the Country, in the usual Manner, either the Court to which such Appeal is made, or the next Term at farthest, unless the Court, on Cause to them shewn, shall think fit to give the Parties a farther Day; and as the Verdict shall be rendered, in any of the said Causes, the Court shall give Judgment thereupon, as the Nature of the Case may require, with Costs of Suit.

PROVIDED ALWAYS, That if the Parties Appellant and Appellee, shall neglect or refuse to file his or her Declaration, or to plead to Issue in such Time as shall be directed by the Court, a Non-suit or Judgment by Default may be entered for Want thereof, as usual.

PROVIDED ALSO, That the Costs to be taxed in any such Suit, to the several Officers, and others concerned, for the Services by them respectively to be done, shall be the same as the Costs now usually taken in the said Court of Common-Pleas.

Costs taxed in such Suits, to be the same as now usually taken in the Common-Pleas.

PROVIDED ALSO, That none of the Justices, which by Virtue of this Act shall hear and determine any of the Causes aforesaid out of Court, shall afterwards sit on the Hearing and Determining the same Cause, on an Appeal made to any of the Courts of Common-Pleas aforesaid.

Justice who shall determine any Cause out of Court, shall not afterwards, &c.

AND BE IT FURTHER ENACTED by the Authority aforesaid, That if any Person or Persons whosoever, shall commence, sue or prosecute any Suit or Suits, for any Debts or Demands made cognizable, as aforesaid, in other Manner than is directed by this Act, and shall obtain a Verdict or Judgment therein for Debt or Damages, which, without Costs of Suit, shall not amount to

Penalty on commencing Suits made cognizable by this Act, in any other Manner.

S s

more

more than *Five Pounds* (not having caused an Oath or Affirmation to be made, before the Obtaining of the Writ of Summons or Capias, and file the same in the Prothonotary's Office respectively, that he, she or they, so making Oath or Affirmation, did truly believe the Debt due, or Damages sustained, exceeded the Sum of *Five Pounds*) he, she or they so prosecuting, shall not recover any Costs in such Suit, any Law, Usage or Custom to the contrary notwithstanding.

Limitation of this Act.   PROVIDED ALSO, That this Act, nor any thing herein contained, shall be deemed, construed, or understood, to extend to Actions of Debt for Rent, Debt upon Bonds for Performance of Covenants, to Actions of Covenant, to Actions of Replevin, or upon any real Contract; nor to Actions of Trespass on the Case for Trover and Conversion, or Slander; nor to Actions of Trespass for Assault and Battery, or Imprisonment; nor to such Actions where the Titles of Lands shall in any wise come in Question.

How long to be in force.   PROVIDED ALSO, That this Act shall continue in Force for the Space of *Three Years*, and from thence to the End of the next Session of Assembly, and no longer.

Signed by Order of the House,

DAVID FRENCH, *Speaker.*

An ACT *to prevent the Damages which may arise by Firing the Woodlands in the Parts of this Government in this Act mentioned.*

Preamble.   WHEREAS it is found by Experience, that the annual Firing the Woods, as has been customary within this Government, is very prejudicial to Lands, and doth much impoverish the same, as well as destroy many Timber Trees, and prevent the Growth of young Trees and Woods; and also many Fences

ces and Buildings have often been burnt by such Fires:
For Prevention whereof,

BE IT ENACTED by the Honourable
GEORGE THOMAS, Esq; by and with His
Majesty's Royal Approbation, Lieutenant Governor
and Commander in Chief of the Counties of *New-
Castle, Kent* and *Sussex* on *Delaware,* and Province of
Pennsylvania, by and with the Advice and Consent of the
Representatives of the Freemen of the said Counties in
General Assembly met, and by the Authority of the same,
That from and after the Publication of this Act, if any
Person or Persons shall, at any Time or Times whatsoever,
wilfully fire or set on fire, or cause to fire or be set on fire,
any Woodlands, whereby any other Person or Persons
shall suffer Damage, within the Limits herein after expressed, *Limits, within*
That is to say, within the County of *New-Castle,* any Wood- *which Wood-*
lands lying to the Northward of the Publick High-Way, *lands shall not*
called *Nottingham Road,* leading from the Township of *Not-* *be set on fire.*
tingham in *Chester* County to *Christiana-Bridge;* any Woodlands lying to the Eastward of the Road leading from the
aforesaid Bridge to the intersecting of the Road leading
down the said County from the Town of *New-Castle* near
Red-Lion Run; or any of the Woodlands lying to the Eastward of the High-Way, called the Upper-Road, leading
from the said Run down by the Plantation late of *Andrew*
Peterson, Esq; deceased, to *Blackbirds* Bridge, and from the
said Bridge down *Blackbirds Creek* to *Delaware* River: And
within the Count of *Sussex,* any of the Woodlands lying to
the Eastward of the King's High-Way or Road leading
down the said County of *Sussex,* from the Place where the
said Road crosses the *Three Runs* to the *Cool-spring* Branch,
and up the said Branch to the Head thereof, thence, by
the nearest Course, to the Head of *Burdicks* Branch which
issueth into *Rehoboth-Bay,* thence down the said Branch to
the intersecting *Indian-River* Road, thence by the said
Road to a Landing on *Indian-River,* known by the Name
of *Philip Askew's Landing,* and thence down the said River to the Ocean, every such Person or Persons so offending, and being duly convicted thereof, by the Testimony
of one or more credible Witnesses, or Confession of the
Offender or Offenders, before any two Justices of the Peace
of the County where the Offence is or shall be committed,
shall, for every such Offence, forfeit and pay any Sum,
not exceeding *Five Pounds,* current Money of this Govern- *Penalty.*
ment, at the Discretion of the said Justices, to be levied,
together

How to be recovered and disposed of.

together with Cofts, by Warrant under the Hands and Seals of the faid Juftices, before whom the Conviction is had, on the Offender's Goods and Chattels, and paid, within *New-Caftle* County, the one Moiety thereof to the Overfeers of the Poor of the Hundred where the Offence is committed, for the Ufe of the Poor of the faid Hundred; and, within the County of *Suffex*, to the Treafurer of the County, for the Ufe of the Poor of the faid County of *Suffex*; the other Moiety to the Informer: And for Want

For Want of Effects, the Offender shall make Satisfaction by Servitude.

of fuch Goods and Chattels, the Offender or Offenders fhall, by fuch Juftices, be adjudged to make Satisfaction, for the faid Fine and Cofts, by Servitude; and fhall alfo make good all Damages, that, by fuch Firing and Burning, fhall happen to any of the Inhabitants of this Government, to be recovered, together with Cofts, by Bill, Plaint or Information, in any of His Majefty's Courts of Record within this Government. AND if any Negro or Mulatto Slave or Slaves, fhall be duly convicted of fuch Offence, as aforefaid, the faid Juftices fhall, at the Charge or Charges of the Owner or Owners of fuch Slave or Slaves, order and caufe him, her or them to be publickly whipp'd, with any

Punishment of Slaves offending against this act.

Number of Lafhes, not exceeding *Thirty-one*, on his, her, or their bare Back or Backs, well laid on; and if the Owner or Owners of fuch Slave or Slaves, fhall neglect or refufe to pay fuch Charge or Charges, then the faid Juftices fhall commit the faid Slave or Slaves to the common Goal of the County wherein the Offence is committed, there to be kept until the fame, together with the Cofts thereon arifing, be paid and fatisfied.

Signed, by Order of the Houfe, by

THOMAS NOXON, *Speaker.*

An

An ACT *for the more effectual Preventing and Punishing the evil and wicked Practices of Horse-stealing, and other Felonies and Offences committed within this Government.*

WHEREAS the Acts of Assembly of this Government, heretofore made for the Punishment of Horse-Stealing, and other Felonies and Robberies, have been found insufficient to restrain Persons of profligate and dishonest Minds, from committing such Offences; and the Number of such hath, of late Years, greatly increased in this Government, to the great Damage of the Inhabitants thereof: For the more effectual Prevention whereof for the future, and for the more exemplary Punishment of such Offenders,

BE IT ENACTED by the Honourable *GEORGE THOMAS,* Esq; by and with his Majesty's Royal Approbation, Lieutenant Governor and Commander in Chief of the Counties of *New-Castle, Kent* and *Sussex* on *Delaware,* and Province of *Pennsylvania,* by and with the Advice and Consent of the Representatives of the Freemen of the said Counties, in General Assembly met, and by the Authority of the same, That from and after the Publication of this Act, every Person who shall feloniously steal, take or carry away, any Negro or Mulatto Slave, Horse, Gelding, Mare, or Colt, or aid or assist any Person or Persons, in committing any such Offence, and being thereof legally convicted or attainted, by Verdict of a Jury, or Confession of the Party offending; or being indicted thereof, shall stand mute or not directly answer to the Indictment indorsed with the Name or Names of the Prosecutor or Prosecutors, or shall peremptorily challenge above the Number of *Twenty* Persons, legally returned to be of the Jury for the Tryal of such Offenders, shall suffer Death without Benefit of Clergy, in like Manner as such Felons, by the Laws now in Force in that Part of *Great-Britain* called *England,* any Law of this Government to the contrary notwithstanding.

T t   AND

AND BE IT FURTHER ENACTED

by the Authority aforesaid, That every Person who shall feloniously break or enter into any Dwelling-House, Out-House or other House whatsoever, in the Day-time, with an Intent to kill some reasonable Creature, or to commit some other Felony ; or shall aid or assist any Person or Persons in committing any such Offence, and being thereof legally convicted or attainted, by Verdict of a Jury, or Confession of the Party offending, or being indicted thereof shall stand mute, or not directly answer to the Indictment indorsed with the Name or Names of the Prosecutor or Prosecutors, or shall peremptorily challenge above the Number of *Twenty* Persons, legally returned to be of the Jury for the Trial of such Offender, shall suffer Death without Benefit of Clergy, any Law of this Government to the contrary notwithstanding.

AND BE IT ENACTED by the Autho-

rity aforesaid, That if any Person or Persons whatsoever, being in a Dwelling-House, or any other House, whether as a Tenant, Lodger, or otherwise, shall take, steal, or carry away, with an Intent to imbezzle the same, any Money, Furniture, Goods, Wares, or Merchandizes, whether he, she, or they be intrusted with the same, or otherwise, to the Value of *Five Pounds* current Money of this Government, to be valued by any Two Justices of the County where the Offence shall be committed, at the Time of the Complaint made by the Party aggrieved, or the taking such Offender, every such Person so offending, shall be deemed a Felon, and being thereof legally convicted or attainted, by Verdict of a Jury or Confession of the Party offending, or being indicted thereof shall stand mute, or not directly answer to the Indictment indorsed with the Names or Names of the Prosecutor or Prosecutors, or shall peremptorily challenge above the Number of *Twenty* Persons, legally returned to be of the Jury for the Tryal of such Offender, shall suffer Death without Benefit of Clergy, any Law of this Government to the contrary notwithstanding.

AND BE IT ENACTED by the Autho-

rity aforesaid, That every Person who shall enter into any Mansion- or Dwelling-House of another, by Day or by Night, without breaking the same, with an Intent to commit Felony, or being in such House, shall commit any Felony, and shall in the Night-time break the said House to get

get out of the same, shall be taken to be guilty of Burglary, and ousted of the Benefit of Clergy, in the same Manner as if such Person had broken and entered the said House in the Night-time, with an Intent to commit Felony there, any Law of this Government to the contrary notwithstanding.

AND BE IT FURTHER ENACTED by the Authority aforesaid, That every Person who shall receive or buy, of any such Felon or Felons, any Negro or Mulatto Slave, Horse, Gelding, Mare, or Colt, knowing the same to be stolen; or shall knowingly harbour or conceal any Felon or Felons, in this Act before-mentioned, or be assisting to the Escape of such Felon or Felons, knowing him or them to be such, shall be deemed guilty of Felony, and being thereof legally convicted or attainted, by Verdict of a Jury, or Confession of the Party offending; or being indicted thereof shall stand mute, or not directly answer to the Indictment indorsed with the Name or Names of the Prosecutor or Prosecutors, or shall peremptorily challenge above the Number of *Twenty* Persons, legally returned to be of the Jury for the Trial of such Offender, shall suffer Death without Benefit of Clergy, any Law of this Government to the contrary notwithstanding.

Buying or Receiving stolen Horses, Slaves, &c knowingly, Death.

AND BE IT FURTHER ENACTED by the Authority aforesaid, That if any Person or Persons shall take and prosecute any such Felon or Felons to Conviction, within this Government, upon every such Conviction, and procuring a Certificate thereof, under the Hands of the Judges or Justices before whom the Conviction shall be, or either of them, which the said Judges or Justices are hereby directed and required to give, without taking any Fee for the same, such Person or Persons shall receive of the Treasurer of the County where such Conviction shall be had, the Sum of *Five Pounds*, lawful Money of this Government, which the said Treasurer is hereby directed and required to pay out of the Publick Money of the said County in his Hands, which shall be raised upon the Inhabitaints of the said County in like Manner as other County Levies are raised.

Any Person taking and prosecuting such Felons, shall have Five Pounds Reward.

AND BE IT FURTHER ENACTED by the Authority aforesaid, That if any Person shall have committed any such Felony or Felonies, and shall afterwards discover any other Person, who shall have committed such Felony or Felonies, so that he or she be legally convicted

Any Felon discovering & convicting others, shall have Five Pounds, and a Pardon.

convicted thereof, every such Person so discovering, shall receive the like Sum of *Five Pounds*, to be paid and raised as aforesaid, and shall also be entitled to a Pardon of all Felonies by him or her committed within this Government *Exception.* before such Discovery, Treason and Murder excepted.

AND BE IT ENACTED by the Authority *Punishment for* aforesaid, That every Person, who shall receive or buy of *Receiving stolen* any Felon or Felons any Goods, Wares, or Merchandizes, *Goods, Wares,* knowing the same to be stolen, and being thereof legally *&c.* convicted, by Verdict of a Jury or Confession of the Party offending, shall be publickly whipp'd, on his or her bare Back, with *Twenty-one* Lashes, well laid on, and be branded on his or her Forehead with the Capital Letter R; and shall moreover, for all such Goods, Wares or Merchandizes so received or bought, make fourfold Satisfaction to the Party injured, with Costs of Prosecution: And if unable to make such Satisfaction, shall, for the making thereof and Payment of the Costs of Prosecution, as aforesaid, be assigned into Servitude, by the Court where the Conviction is had or made, for any Term of Time not exceeding *Seven Years*, any Law of this Government to the contrary notwithstanding.

Signed by Order of the House,

THOMAS NOXON, *Speaker.*

A Supplementary ACT for

the Amendment of an Act of General-Assembly of this Government, made in the Fourteenth Year of His present Majesty's Reign, entituled, An ACT for the more easy and speedy Recovery of small Debts.

Preamble. WHEREAS the Act of Assembly of this Government, entituled, *An Act for the more easy and speedy Recovery of small Debts,* is found insufficient, as it now stands, to answer all the good Purposes intended thereby; and the same Act is liable to Misconstructions. For the Prevention thereof for the future, and rendering the said Act more effectual,

BE

BE IT ENACTED by the Honourable *GEORGE THOMAS*, Efq; by and with His Majefty's Royal Approbation, Lieutenant Governor and Commander in Chief of the Government of the Counties of *New-Caftle*, *Kent* and *Suffex* on *Delaware*, and Province of *Pennfylvania*, by and with the Advice and Confent of the Reprefentatives of the Freemen of the faid Counties in General Affembly met, and by the Authority of the fame, That the Juftice of the Peace before whom the Parties fhall appear, upon the Return of either of the Procefs directed by the faid Act, is hereby impowered and directed to hear and determine the Matter in Controverfy, unlefs either Plaintiff or Defendant objects againft being tried by fuch Juftice; then and in fuch Cafe, the faid Juftice is hereby directed to appoint, by a Summons in Writing, under His Hand and Seal, *Three* Freeholders to appear before him, to hear and determine the Matters in Difference between the faid Parties, according to the Direction of the faid Act; for which Summons the faid Juftice is hereby empowered to take *Eighteen-Pence*, and no more.

Plaintiff or Defendant objecting againft being determined by the Juftice, 3 Freeholders fhall be fummoned, &c.

AND BE IT FURTHER ENACTED by the Authority aforefaid, That if any Arbitrator or Referree, being legally fummoned, fhall neglect or refufe to appear and proceed to hear and determine, according to the Directions of the aforefaid Act, every fuch Perfon, fo neglecting or refufing, fhall forfeit and pay the Sum of *Twenty Shillings*, current Money of this Government (unlefs he fhew fufficient Caufe for fuch Neglect or Refufal, to be allowed of by fuch Juftice as aforefaid) to be levied, by Warrant under the Hand and Seal of fuch Juftice, by Diftrefs and Sale of the Offender's Goods and Chattels, and applied to the Ufe of the Poor of the County or Hundred where the Offence arifes; and the faid Juftice is hereby empowered and required, by Summons, to appoint another Referree or Arbitrator, to ferve for the Purpofes aforefaid.

Referree fummoned, not appearing, fhall be fined 20f to the Ufe of the Poor;

And others appointed.

AND BE IT FURTHER ENACTED by the Authority aforefaid, That if the Debtor, againft whom any Judgment fhall have paffed, and who fhall have given Security, according to the Directions of the beforementioned Act, fhall neglect to fatisfy fuch Judgment, or to furrender his Body according to the Tenour of his Recognizance, it fhall and may be lawful for the Juftice who gave fuch Judgment, or any other Juftice of the fame County, who is hereby required, on Application made by

Debtor neglecting to fatisfy the Judgment, the Security fhall be fummoned;

V v   the

the Plaintiff in the Suit, his Executors or Administrators, to issue out a Precept, in the Nature of a Summons, commanding such Security to appear before him, within *Ten* Days, and not less than *Five* Days, to shew Cause, why Execution should not issue against such Security's Body or Effects, for satisfying the Judgment aforesaid, and the accruing Costs, as ought or might have issued out against the original Debtor: A N D in Case such Security, as aforesaid, shall fail to shew sufficient Cause to the said Justice, why such Execution should not issue, it shall then be lawful for such Justice, and he is hereby required, at the Prayer of the aforesaid Plaintiff, his Executors or Administrators, to issue out Execution against such Security, for such Judgment and the Costs as aforesaid, in like Manner as might or ought to have been granted against the Original Debtor, for Satisfaction to the Creditor, as aforesaid.

To appear within 10 Days;

And not shewing sufficient Cause to the contrary, Execution may issue against him.

A N D B E I T F U R T H E R E N A C T E D by the Authority aforesaid, That all Specialties, where the real Debt and Interest thereon arising, which are demanded by the Plaintiff or Obligee, shall not exceed the Sum of *Five Pounds* in the whole, shall be recovered in like Manner as other Debts and Demands are recoverable by Virtue and according to the Directions of the aforesaid Act.

Specialties under 5 l. may be recovered as other Debts, by the said Act.

A N D B E I T F U R T H E R E N A C T E D by the Authority aforesaid, That all Writs of Attachment, for any Debt or Demand exceeding *Forty Shillings*, shall be issued out of the Prothonotary's Office, and prosecuted in the Courts of Common-Pleas, in the respective Counties within this Government, in like Manner as the same hath been done before the aforesaid Act was made.

Attachments for any Demand exceeding 40 s. shall be prosecuted in the Courts of Common-Pleas.

A N D B E I T F U R T H E R E N A C T E D by the Authority aforesaid, That this Act shall continue and be in full Force for and during the Continuance of the first before-mentioned Act, and no longer, any thing therein contained to the contrary in any wise notwithstanding.

Continuance of this Act.

Signed, by Order of the House, by

T H O M A S N O X O N, *Speaker.*

An

An ACT *for establishing a Militia within this Government.*

WHEREAS His Majesty, for vindicating the *Preamble.* Honour of His Crown and maintaining the Rights of His Subjects, is at this Time engaged in a War with *Spain*; and there is just Reason to apprehend that a Rupture with *France* is unavoidable. AND WHEREAS, from the Defenceless State of this Government, it is exposed not only to the Invasions of a foreign Enemy, but to the Insults also or Insurrections of our own Slaves.

FOR the better Security of the Lives, Liberties and Properties of His Majesty's Subjects, Inhabitants thereof, BE IT ENACTED by the Honourable *GEORGE THOMAS,* Esq; by and with His Majesty's Royal Approbation, Lieutenant Governor and Commander in Chief of the Counties of *New-Castle, Kent* and *Sussex* on *Delaware,* and Province of *Pennsylvania,* by and with the Advice and Consent of the Representatives of the Freemen of the said Counties, in General Assembly met, and by the Authority of the same, That every Freeholder and taxable *Every Taxable* Person residing in this Government (except such as are *shall be provided* hereafter excepted) shall, on or before the *First* Day of *with Arms & Ammunition;* *March* next, provide himself with the following Arms and Ammunition, *viz.* One well fixed Musket or Firelock, one Cartouch-Box, with *Twelve* Charges of Gun-Powder and Ball therein, and *Three* good Flints, to be approved of by the Commanding Officer of the respective Company to which he belongs, and shall be obliged to keep such Arms and Ammunition by him, during the Continuance of this Act; and on each Default thereof, such Person or Persons so offending, shall forfeit and pay the Sum of *Forty Shil- On Penalty of lings,* current Money of this Government aforesaid. *40s.*

AND BE IT FURTHER ENACTED by the Authority aforesaid, That all Male Persons, above *All Males, be- Seventeen* and under *Fifty Years* of Age (except such as are *tween 17 and* hereafter excepted) shall be inlisted, by themselves, their *50 Years of* Parents or Masters, on or before the *First* Day of *March Age, shall be* inlisted,

next,

next, as aforesaid, under the respective Officer or Officers that shall be appointed for that Purpose, by the Governor for the Time being, in every Hundred in each of the Counties within this Government: And, being so inlisted, shall appear and attend in their own proper Persons, with their Muskets or Firelocks, Cartouch-Boxes and *Six* Charges of Powder and Ball, each, together with *Three* Flints, all in good Order and fit for Service, at the respective Places of Meeting that shall be appointed by the commanding Officer under whom they are inlisted, *Four* Times in every Year, *viz.* On the last *Saturday* in *March*, on the last *Saturday* in *May*, on the last *Saturday* in *July*, and on the last *Saturday* in *September*, each Day, at the Hour of *Twelve*; and shall continue under Arms, any Time not exceeding *Four* Hours, in order to be taught and improved in military Exercise; who are hereby strictly required and obliged, to render due Obedience unto the Commands of their respective Officers (according to the Rules of military Discipline) for that Purpose: And every Person that refuses to inlist, as aforesaid, or being inlisted, as aforesaid, neglects or refuses to appear in the Manner aforesaid (unless he shew to the commanding Officer sufficient Reason for such Neglect or Refusal) or appearing in the Manner aforesaid, shall wilfully disobey the Officers aforesaid, upon every such Default, being duly convicted thereof, before one Justice of the Peace, shall forfeit and pay the Sum of *Five Shillings*, current Money aforesaid.

And shall appear with their Arms, &c. 4 times a Year, in order to be instructed in military Exercise.

Penalty on refusing to inlist, or not appearing when inlisted.

AND BE IT FURTHER ENACTED by the Authority aforesaid, That the whole Militia of each respective County within this Government, shall be obliged to appear and attend, as often, and at such Place as the Governor, for the time being, shall see meet to appoint or direct a General Review, he being present. And every Person, inlisted as aforesaid, having due Notice thereof, that shall neglect or refuse to appear at and attend the said General Review (unless he shew unto the commanding Officer of the Company to which he belongs sufficient Reason for such Neglect or Refusal) or attending, shall wilfully disobey the Commands of the said Officer or Officers (or those impowered by him or them) upon due Conviction thereof, as aforesaid, shall forfeit and pay the Sum of *Five Shillings*, current Money aforesaid.

The whole Militia of each County shall appear at General Reviews.

Penalty on Neglect, or Disobedience.

AND BE IT FURTHER ENACTED by the Authority aforesaid, That the Firing *Four* Muskets

or

or Firelocks fucceffively, and diftinct one after another, and the Beating of a Drum; or the Firing two great Guns at *Four* Minutes diftance of Time, and beating the Drum, fhall be deemed and taken for an Alarm. And that the commanding Officer of each Company, who fhall firft receive an Account of fuch Alarm, fhall forthwith caufe Notice thereof to be given to the commanding Officer of the Company that fhall be in the adjoining Diftrict, which faid commanding Officer, fo receiving Notice, fhall, in like Manner, caufe Notice thereof to be given to the commanding Officer of the next adjoining Company to him, and fo on, in the like Manner, till Notice thereof be given, generally, through the whole County; which faid commanding Officer, and every of them, fhall alfo forthwith caufe an Alarm to be made, for the Raifing the feveral Companies; and when raifed, whether the fame be in the Day-time or in the Night, fhall forthwith march the fame to the Place where the Alarm firft arofe, in order to defend the Town or Place where any Invafion, Defcent or Infurrection fhall or may happen to be made, under the Penalty of *Five Pounds*, for each and every fuch Neglect or Default.

What fhall be deemed an Alarm, and how the fame fhall be communicated.

Duty of the Companies, when raifed.

Penalty on Neglect.

AND BE IT FURTHER ENACTED by the Authority aforefaid, That every Perfon (except fuch as fhall be hereafter excepted) receiving an Account of fuch Alarm, fhall obey all and every the Commands of the faid Officer and Officers, and thofe impowered by them for the Defending of the Town or Place, within the faid County, from any Invafion, Defcent or Infurrection, which fhall or may happen to be made, and fhall not depart, without Leave of the faid Officer or Officers firft had and obtained. AND if any Perfon, being an Inhabitant within the Limits aforefaid, who is obliged, by the Directions of this Act, to attend the common Mufter or Exercife, or to provide and keep by him Arms and Ammunition, *&c.* fhall, upon fuch Alarm given, neglect or refufe to attend (unlefs he fhew to the commanding Officer fufficient Reafon for fuch Neglect or Refufal) with his Arms and Ammunition, at the Place or Places whitherfoever he fhall be commanded by the faid Officer or Officers, or thofe impowered by them or either of them, as aforefaid; or attending, fhall wilfully difobey their or either of their Commands relating to the Defence aforefaid; or depart from the faid Town or Place, without having Leave as aforefaid, every fuch Perfon fo offending, upon due Conviction

Obedience enjoined.

Penalty on Non-appearance, or Difobedience.

X x   tion

tion made before any Two Juſtices of the Peace for the ſaid County wherein ſuch Offence is committed, ſhall forſeit and pay the Sum of *Forty Shillings*, current Money aforeſaid.

A N D if any Perſon or Perſons ſhall, without the Command of the ſaid Officer or Officers, or of ſuch Perſon or Perſons whom they or either of them ſhall impower, preſume to make an Alarm within the Limits aforeſaid, every ſuch Perſon ſo offending, and being thereof legally convicted before any Court of Juſtice for the ſaid County, ſhall, for every ſuch Offence, be fined in the Sum of *Five Pounds*, current Money aforeſaid; the one Moiety whereof ſhall be paid to the Informer, and the other Moiety as ſhall be hereafter directed.

A N D   B E   I T   E N A C T E D   by the Authority aforeſaid, That the ſeveral Treaſurers of the reſpective Counties within this Government, ſhall, at the publick Expence, provide for each Company in the ſeveral Counties, *One* good Drum, a Pair of Colours, and *Two* Halberts; which Expence, and Coſts, is hereby ordered to be raiſed and levied by the Court and Grand-Jury, at the Time for laying the Levies for the ſeveral Counties aforeſaid.

A N D   B E   I T   E N A C T E D   by the Authority aforeſaid, That during the Time the Officers and their Companies ſhall be under Arms, they ſhall be obedient to their ſuperiour Officers, and ſhall obſerve and keep all and every the Rules and Orders that the Governor, for the time being, ſhall think proper to make and direct; provided the ſame do not exceed, in Severity, the Rules and Orders eſtabliſhed for the regulating the Militia in that Part of *Great-Britain* called *England*. And in Order that the ſeveral Companies may the better learn and know their Duty, the ſeveral Captains thereof are hereby directed, to cauſe ſuch Rules and Orders, as aforeſaid, to be publickly read at the Head of each of their Companies, on each of the Days they ſhall muſter, during the Time they are under Arms, on Pain of forfeiting the Sum of *Forty Shillings*, current Money, for each Neglect.

A N D   B E   I T   E N A C T E D   by the Authority aforeſaid, That the ſeveral Captains within this Government, ſhall appoint their ſeveral Companies to meet and muſter, on the Days and Times herein before directed, at the

the moft convenient Place or Places in the feveral Hundreds to which their Companies belong ; provided the *The fame not*
fame be not within the Diftance of *One* Mile of any Ta- *being within one*
vern or Inn (the Town Companies within this Govern- *vern, &c.*
ment only excepted) under the Penalty or Forfeiture of
Forty Shillings, current Money aforefaid, for each Neglect
or Offence.

AND BE IT FURTHER ENACTED
by the Authority aforefaid, That if any Perfon or Perfons *Penalty on fel-*
whatfoever, fhall fell, or expofe to Sale, at fuch Places of *ling Drink at*
Mufter as aforefaid, any Sort of ftrong Drink whatever, *the Places of*
fuch Perfon fo offending, fhall forfeit and pay the Sum of *Muftering.*
Forty Shillings, current Money aforefaid.

AND BE IT FURTHER ENACTED
by the Authority aforefaid, That (in order to prevent any *Penalty on fi-*
falfe Alarms being made by Firing Guns in the Night- *ring Guns in*
time after the *Firft* Day of *March* next as aforefaid) if any *the Night, &c.*
Perfon whatfoever, fhall prefume to fire any fmall Arms
or Guns from *Two* Hours after Sun-fet until *One* Hour before Sun-rife, unlefs in Cafe of Invafion, Defcent or Infurrection, or other lawful Occafion, every Perfon fo offending, fhall forfeit and pay the Sum of *Forty Shillings,* current Money, for every fuch Offence. AND, that no
Captain, Mafter, or Commander of any Ship, or Veffel,
within any Harbour belonging to this Government, or in
the River *Delaware,* fhall fire or fuffer to be fired any great
Guns or fmall Arms, from *Two* Hours after Sun-fet until
One Hour before Sun-rife, as aforefaid (the Commanders of
His Majefty's Ships of War only excepted) under the Penalty and Forfeiture of the Sum of *Twenty Shillings,* current Money as aforefaid, for every Gun fo fired.

AND BE IT ENACTED by the Authority
aforefaid, That the Drummers belonging to the feveral *Drummers,*
Companies within this Government, fhall each of them be *their Pay.*
paid the Sum of *Twenty Shillings per Annum,* for their Service in the Militia, by the Treafurer of the refpective
Counties to which they belong ; which faid Sums fhall be
levied and raifed as other County Levies are, as aforefaid.

AND BE IT ENACTED by the Authority
aforefaid, That any one Juftice of the Peace, in or neareft
to the Town of *New-Caftle* (who is not of the People called *Quakers)* together with the commanding Officer of the
Company

Watch to be kept in the Town of New-Castle. Company to which the Inhabitants of the said Town belongs, shall, and are hereby impowered, to give the necessary Directions and Orders (as they shall think fit) for the keeping a Night-Watch in the Town aforesaid, for the Security of the same: And after such Directions and Orders given, every Person (except such as are hereafter excepted) having due Notice thereof, neglecting or refusing to attend on the said Watch (unless he shew unto the said Justice or Officer sufficient Reason for such Neglect or Refusal) shall forfeit and pay the Sum of *Five Shillings*, current Money aforesaid.

Quakers exempted from bearing Arms, &c. AND BE IT ENACTED by the Authority aforesaid, That every Person who is of the religious Society of the People called *Quakers*, is entirely exempted and excused from providing and bearing Arms, as aforesaid, in the Militia, attending the Exercise, and keeping the Watch, and from every Part thereof; he paying, for every Day that others are obliged to attend the said Muster, Exercise, or Watch (in Consideration of the said People, called *Quakers*, maintaining their own Poor, and contributing towards the Support of the Poor of other Societies also) but the Sum of *Two Shillings and Six-pence*, current Money aforesaid.

Producing a Certificate from the Meeting they belong to, if required. PROVIDED that such Person produces unto the commanding Officer, in the District where such Person dwells, within *Two* Months after he shall be by the said Officer thereunto required, a Certificate from the Meeting to which he says he belongs, testifying that he is actually deemed to be a Member of the said Society; which said Fine of *Two Shillings and Six-pence*, for every such Person, shall be paid unto the Collector of the Hundred wherein such Person dwells, for the Use of the Poor, within *Ten* Days after suchDays of Mustering as aforesaid; and upon Default thereof, the said Fine shall be recovered by Warrant under the Hand and Seal of any one Justice of the Peace (who is not a *Quaker*) within the County where the Person dwells, by Distress and Sale of the Offender's Goods and Chattels.

Justices and others exempted; AND also, that all Justices of the Peace, Physicians, Lawyers, and Millers, and Persons incapable through Infirmities of Sickness or Lameness, shall be exempted and excused from appearing to muster, except in Case of an *But shall nevertheless provide Arms, &c.* Alarm: They being nevertheless obliged, by this Act, to provide and keep by them Arms and Ammunition as aforesaid, as well as others. And if an Alarm happen, then all those, who by this Act are obliged to keep Arms as aforesaid,

aforesaid, as well as those who are obliged to attend the General Muster or Exercise, shall join the General Militia, and yield Obedience as aforesaid, under the Penalty and Forfeiture of the Sum of *Forty Shillings*, as aforesaid. All Ministers being intirely exempt from any Duties or Fines whatsoever required of others (*viz.* of those that are not Ministers) by Virtue of this Act.

And join the General Militia on an Alarm, under Penalty of 40s.

AND BE IT ENACTED by the Authority aforesaid, That all the Fines, amounting to and not exceeding the Sum of *Five Shillings*, mentioned in this Act, shall be paid to the Captain of the Company where such Fines and Forfeitures arise, within *Ten* Days after the Offence or Offences are committed (which occasions the said Fines) by the Person or Persons offending as aforesaid : And upon Non-payment thereof, the same shall be recovered by Warrant under the Hand and Seal of any Justice of the Peace of the County where such Fines and Forfeitures arise, in like Manner as Debts under *Forty Shillings* are recovered, and paid to the said Captain as aforesaid, to be applied to the purchasing of Arms and Ammunition for those who are not Taxables, and who are nevertheless obliged to appear, as by this Act is directed; which said Captain is hereby ordered and directed, to account once in each Year with the Treasurer of the County where such Captain dwells.

Fines of 5s. & under, to be paid to the Captain, within Ten Days, or recovered by Warrant, &c.

The Captain to account yearly.

AND all Fines and Forfeitures, exceeding the Sum of *Five Shillings*, already mentioned in this Act, shall, upon the Offender's refusing to pay the same, be recovered by Warrant under the Hands and Seals of any two Justices of the Peace of the County where such Fines and Forfeitures arise, by the Distress and Sale of the Offender's Goods and Chattels, and paid to the Treasurer of the said County, to be applied as aforesaid (except such Part as by Virtue of this Act shall belong to any Informer or Informers) and for Want of such Goods and Chattels, such Offender or Offenders as aforesaid, shall be committed to the Goal of the County aforesaid, and there remain until the Fine or Fines and Costs be fully paid and satisfied.

Fines exceeding 5s how to be recovered.

AND BE IT ENACTED by the Authority aforesaid, That all Magistrates and Officers, that shall be appointed by the Governor for the Time being, (and being qualified as such) for the putting this Act in Execution, who shall neglect or refuse to do their Duty, and shall be duly convicted thereof, by the Testimony of two sufficient

Magistrates & Officers refusing to put this Act in Execution, forfeit 5l.

Y y

Witnesses,

Witnesses, or the Confession of the Party offending, before the Justices of the Court of *Quarter-Sessions* for the County wherein the Offence is committed, shall, for every such Default, forfeit and pay the Sum of *Five Pounds,* current Money aforesaid, to be levied, with Costs, by Distress and Sale of the Offender's Goods and Chattels, and to be applied as aforesaid.

Penalty on Officers taking more Goods than treble Value in Execution.

AND BE IT ENACTED by the Authority aforesaid, That no Officer shall presume to take more Goods or Chattels in Execution, by Virtue of this Act, than Treble the Value of the Sum mentioned in the Precept by Virtue of which he executes the same, under the Penalty of *Forty Shillings,* to be recovered and applied as aforesaid, the Overplus (if any there be) to be returned to the Owner. AND also that no Person or Persons whatsoever, that by this Act is directed to appear and muster as aforesaid, shall be liable to be taken by any Officer, in any Civil Action whatsoever, on the Day whereon such Person is directed to appear, nor in the Night following after such Day of Appearance.

Persons hereby directed to appear &c. exempted from Arrests on Mustering Days, &c.

No Servant or Slave shall be allowed to bear Arms, &c.

AND BE IT FURTHER ENACTED by the Authority aforesaid, That no bought Servant, or Negro or Mulatto Slave, shall, upon any Pretence whatsoever, be allowed to bear Arms, or to be mustered in any of the Companies of the Militia within this Government.

The Act for securing Lewes shall remain in force.

AND BE IT FURTHER ENACTED by the Authority aforesaid, That an Act of General Assembly of this Government, made in the *Thirteenth* Year of His present Majesty's Reign, entituled, *An Act providing for the better Security and Defence of the Town of* Lewes *in the County of* Sussex, *within this Government,* and every Part thereof, shall be and remain in full Force, any thing in this Act contained to the contrary notwithstanding.

Limitation of this Act.

AND BE IT ENACTED by the Authority aforesaid, That this Act shall continue and be in full Force for and during the Space and Term of *Three Years* from and after the Publication of the same; or so long as any War shall subsist with *Great-Britain,* which ever shall first happen to expire.

Signed by Order of the House,

THOMAS NOXON, *Speaker.*

An ACT appointing Persons to lay out Two Hundred Acres of Land in Lots adjoining to the Court-House of the County of Kent, and to dispose of the same to the Use of the Publick.

Vide supra pag. 130.

NOTHING being of more Consequence to a Country than the Improvement thereof by the Addition of Tradesmen, and others in such measure as may not be of great Expence to the New-Settlers; BE IT THEREFORE ENACTED by the Honourable *WILLIAM KEITH*, Esq; by His Majesty's Royal Approbation Lieutenant - Governor of the Counties of *New-Castle, Kent* and *Suffex* on *Delaware*, and Province of *Pennsylvania*, by and with the Advice and Consent of the Freemen of the said Counties in General Assembly met, and by the Authority of the same; That it shall and may be lawful, and it is hereby made lawful for *Benjamin Shurmer, William Brinkloe* and *Richard Richardson*, or any two of them, to survey and lay out into Lots a certain Tract of Land in the County of *Kent*, adjoining to the Court-House of said County, and purchased by the People thereof, and commonly called the Town of *Dover*, in such Measures and Proportions as to them shall seem meet and convenient, and the said Lots so surveyed and laid out, as aforesaid, to dispose of and sell to such Persons as are willing to purchase and buy; And further, that it shall and may be lawful, and is hereby made lawful for the Persons above-mentioned, to grant, execute and perform Deed or Deeds, Conveyance or Conveyances, Bargains or Sales, for the said Lot or Lots, to any such Person or Persons as shall purchase the same; which said Deeds, Conveyances, Bargains or Sales shall be good and valid in Law to the Parties purchasing to them, their Heirs and Assigns for ever.

Preamble.

Benjam. Shurmer, &c. impowered to lay out into Lots a Tract of Land in the Town of Dover,

AND BE IT FURTHER ENACTED by the Authority aforesaid, That the above-mentioned *Benjamin Shurmer, William Brinkloe* and *Richard Richardson*, or any two of them, may and are hereby impowered to sue for, ask, levy and recover every such Sum or Sums of Money, as shall arise due from the Sale of the said Lot or Lots.

And to recover the Money for said Lots,

Z z

AND

AND BE IT FURTHER ENACTED,

And render an Account of the Money receiv'd, &c. That the said *Benjamin Shurmer, William Brinkloe* and *Richard Richardson,* shall, and are hereby made liable, upon all Demands hereafter, to render an Account of Money or Monies received on Account of the abovesaid Lots, to any Person or Persons whom the Justices of the Peace for the time being and Grand-Jury of said County shall appoint; whose Receipt shall discharge the said above-mentioned Persons from any farther Demand: And the said *Benjamin Shurmer, William Brinkloe* and *Richard Richardson* are hereby allowed, and it may be lawful for them to reserve for themselves out of the Monies so as aforesaid to be received, every such Part or Proportion of the same as by them and any other three Persons whom the Court and Grand-Jury shall nominate for the said Purpose, shall agree upon and think fit.

PROVIDED ALWAYS, and it is hereby meant and intended, That the said Survey and Allotment and laying-out shall be finished and compleated at or before the *Tenth* Day of *March* next.

Signed by Order of the House,

JOHN FRENCH, *Speaker.*

An ACT *for the better Confirmation of the Owners of Lands and Inhabitants of this Government in their just Rights and Possessions.*

Preamble: WHEREAS divers Laws have been enacted in this Government, that made all Lands and Tenements (without any Regard to the Fee-simple or other Tenures by which they are held) as liable to pay Debts as Chattels, and be taken and sold upon Executions, or by Decrees in Courts of Equity, or to be sold by such Executors as had no Power by their Testators Wills for so doing, and in certain Cases to be sold by Administrators, as also to be divided, allotted and distributed amongst the Children of Intestates; in Pursuance of which Laws, divers Lands, Tenements and Hereditaments in this Government **have**

have been sold, delivered, affessed, allotted or diftributed accordingly : Now to the end that thefe Sales, Deliveries, Affignments and Allotments or Diftributions may have Effect according to the Tenor and true Meaning of the faid Laws, and that the Poffeffors and Owners of the faid Lands and Hereditaments fo fold, delivered, affigned and diftributed, and their Heirs and Succeffors, may quietly have, hold and enjoy the fame ;

BE IT ENACTED, &c. That all and fingular the Bargains and Sales, being made *bona fide* and for valuable Confideration, as alfo all Affignments, Grants and Allotments or Diftributions made to any Perfon or Perfons whatfoever, of any Lands, Tenements or Hereditaments made in this Government according to the Tenor and Direction or the true Intent and Meaning of the faid Laws in thofe Cafes made and provided, before the *firft* Day of *December*, in the Year 1721 ; are hereby declared to be good and effectual, and fhall ftand, and be taken, deemed and adjudged good, fure and available in Law, againft all Perfons whatfoever, according to the Tenor and Effect of the fame Bargains, Sales, Affignments, Grants, Allotments or Diftributions ; and that every Perfon or Perfons, Bodies politick and corporate, their Heirs and Succeffors, and all claiming by, from or under them or any of them, for and according to their and every of their feveral Eftates and Interefts, of, in and to the faid Lands, Tenements and Hereditaments, with their Appurtunances fo as aforefaid fold, delivered, affigned or allotted, fhall and may quietly or peaceably have, hold and enjoy the fame Lands, Tenements, Hereditaments and Premiffes, and every part thereof, againft all and every Perfon and Perfons, their Heirs and Affigns, having, claiming or pretending to have any Eftate, Right, Title, Intereft, Claim or Demand whatfoever, of, in or to the fame : SAVING NEVERTHELESS to all and every Perfon and Perfons, Bodies politick and corporate (others than to the Perfon or Perfons for Payment of whofe Debts and Maintenance of whofe Widows and Children any of the faid Lands, Tenements, Hereditaments have been fold, delivered or conveyed as aforefaid, and his and their Heirs, and others than to the Heirs at Law of the faid Inteftates, or any claiming under them who attempt to avoid or annul the faid Divifions, Allotments or Diftributions which have been made of the faid Inteftates Lands and Hereditaments amongft their Children by Virtue or in Purfuance of the faid Laws) all fuch Actions, Eftates, Poffeffions,

Rights,

Rights, Titles, Interests, Rents, Profits and Demands as they or any of them have, shall, may or ought to have of, in or to all or any of the said Lands, Tenements and Hereditaments, or any part thereof, in such Manner and Form as if this Act had never been made; so that they do pursue their said Rights, Titles, Claims and Interest, by way of Action or lawful Entry before the first Day of *October*, which will be in the Year of Lord *One Thousand Seven Hundred and Twenty-two*. PROVIDED ALWAYS, That all and every the Children of Intestates, to or amongst whom any Lands, Tenements and Hereditaments have been allotted or distributed by virtue of the said Laws, and all and every Person and Persons to whom any Parts or Purports of Lands, Tenements or Hereditaments have as aforesaid been or hereafter shall be sold or delivered upon Executions, shall hold and enjoy their said respective Parts, Purports or Allotments in Severality, or as Tenants in Common, and not as Joint-Tenants.

Lands divided amongst Children of Intestates, and those sold upon Executions, to be held in Common Tenancy.

WHEREAS divers Persons living out of this Government, are and have been Owners of Lands within the same, such Persons have usually appointed Attornies to sell and dispose thereof: To the end therefore that those who have so purchased, and their Heirs or Assigns forever hereafter to be secured in their Titles and Estates, BE IT EN- ACTED, *&c.* That all Sales of Lands, Tenements and Hereditaments formerly made by any Attornies or Agents who have been appointed by any Person or Persons who had Right so to do, and especially giving them Power or Directions therein to sell or convey Land, are and shall be deemed and adjudged good and effectual in Law, to all Intents, Constructions and Purposes whatsoever, as fully as if the said Owners of such Lands had by their own Deeds, Bargains and Sales, actually and really sold and conveyed the same; and all and singular the Lands, Tenements and Hereditaments sold and conveyed as aforesaid, shall be and remain to such Purchasers respectively, their Heirs and Assigns, forever, as they were or ought to have been to the Owner or Owners of such Lands or Premisses so imploying his or their Attornies and Agents as aforesaid.

Sales, &c. which have been made by Attornies, are adjudged good.

AND BE IT FURTHER ENACTED, *&c.* That all and every Bonds, Specialties, Letters of Attorney, and other Powers in Writing, which shall be produced in any Court, or before any Magistrate in this Government, the Execution whereof being proved by two or more of the Wit-

Bonds, &c. proved before any Magistrate, are good in Law.

Witnesses thereunto before any Mayor or chief Magistrate or Officer of the Towns or Places where such Bonds, Letters of Attorney or other Writings are or shall be made or executed, and accordingly certified under the Common or Publick Seal of the Towns or Places where the said Bonds, Letters of Attorney or other Writings are so proved respectively; shall be taken and adjudged as sufficient in Law, as if the Witnesses therein named had been present, and such Certification shall be sufficient Evidence to the Court and Jury for the Proof thereof.

AND BE IT FURTHER ENACTED, &c. That all Sales or Conveyances of Lands, Tenements or Hereditaments which shall hereafter be made by Virtue of any Letters or Powers of Attorney, or Agency duly executed, which do or shall expresly give Power to sell Lands or other Estates, and be certified to have been proved as aforesaid, or shall be proved in this Government before any Court of Common Pleas within this Government by one or more of the Witnesses thereto; shall be good and effectual in Law, to all Intents, Constructions and Purposes whatsoever, as if the said Constituent or Constituents had by their own Deeds, Bargains and Sales, actually and really sold and conveyed the same.

Sales of Lands, &c. made by Letters of Attorney expresly giving Power, &c. shall be good, &c.

PROVIDED ALWAYS, That no Sale of Lands, Tenements and Hereditaments made by Virtue of such Power or Powers of Attorney or Agency as aforesaid, shall be good and effectual unless such Sale be made and executed while such Power is in Force; and all such Powers shall be accounted, deemed and taken to be in Force, until the Attorney or Agent shall have due Notice of a Countermand, Revocation, or Death of the Constituent.

Signed by Order of the House, by

JOHN FRENCH, *Speaker.*

See the Supplement to this Act, pag. 70.

A a a

191

An

An ACT for regulating Attachments within this Government.

Preamble. WHEREAS the Laws of this Government have hitherto been very deficient in refpect to Attachments, fo that the Effects of Perfons abfenting themfelves have not been by the faid Laws effectually fecured to make Satisfaction for the Debts contracted or owing within this Government, and the prefent Method of Proceeding in the Courts of Judicature againft the Effects of abfent Perfons is attended with fo great an Expence, that oftentimes the greateft part of the Goods attached are fwallowed up in Cofts and Charges : To the end therefore that the Goods of abfent Perfons may be effectually fecured for the Benefit of their Creditors within this Government, and at a moderate Expence, and yet that no Perfon may be hurt or wronged in his Intereft whofe Effects are not by the Laws of this Government liable to be attached ;

BE IT ENACTED by the Honourable *PATRICK GORDON*, Efq; Lieutenant-Governor of the Counties of *New-Caftle*, *Kent* and *Suffex* on *Delaware*, and Province of *Pennfylvania*, by and with the Advice and Confent of the Reprefentatives of the Freemen of the faid Counties in General Affembly met, and by the Authority of the fame ; *Oath or Affirmation to be taken before Attachments are granted.* That no Writ of Attachment fhall iffue out of any Court within this Government, before the Perfon or Perfons requefting the fame, or fome other credible Perfon for him, her or them, fhall upon Oath or Affirmation declare that the Defendant is indebted to the Plaintiff in the Sum of *Forty Shillings* or more, and that the Defendant is abfconded from the Place of his ufual Abode, or is gone out of the Government with an Intent to deceive his or her Creditors as it is believed ; which Oath or Affirmation fhall or may be adminiftred by the Officer who grants the Writ of Attachment, and fhall be filed in the Court to which fuch *Tenor of the Writ of Attachment.* Attachment is returnable : Which Oath or Affirmation being made, an Attachment fhall be granted, by which the Sheriff fhall be commanded to attach the Defendant by all his Goods and Chattels, Lands and Tenements, in whofe Hands or Poffeffion foever the fame may be found in his County or Bailiwick, fo that the Defendant appear at the next Court of Common Pleas to be held, &c. to anfwer, &c. and that he fummon the Garnifhees to appear at the Court

at

at the Return of the said Writ, to declare what Goods or Effects of the Defendant's such Garnishee hath in his or her Hands.

AND to prevent the unreasonable Charges with which the usual Method of prosecuting Writs of Attachment is attended, BE IT FURTHER ENACTED by the Authority aforesaid, That no Writ of Attachment shall issue out of any Prothonotary's Office, or from any Magistrate, but one only against one Person's Estate in one County, before the Return of the said Writ, which is to be executed in the Manner following, *That is to say*, Where the Officer cannot come at the actual Possession of the Goods, Chattels or Effects of the Defendant, he shall go to the Person in whose Hands or Possession the Defendant's Goods or Effects are supposed to be, and there declare in the Presence of one or more credible Persons, that he attacheth all the Goods or Effects of the Defendant in the Hands or Possession of the said Garnishee, at the Suit of the Plaintiff for the Use of the Creditors of the Defendant, and that he doth summon the Garnishee to appear at the next Court, &c. to declare upon Oath or Affirmation what Goods or Effects such Garnishee hath in his or her Hands or Possession belonging to the Defendant; from and after which Declaration the Goods, Money or Effects so attached, shall be delivered to the Sheriff, and be by him secured in order to abide the Judgment of the Court, unless the Garnishee will give Security for the same; but if such Goods and Effects be not actually delivered to the Officer, yet the same shall be deemed to be in his Possession to answer the Judgment of the Court in that Case. But if the Defendant in the Attachment, or some sufficient Person or Persons for him or her, will at any time before Judgment be entered against him or her, put in Special Bail to the Plaintiff's Action, and to the several Demands made against him or her as they appear to be entered in the Prothonotary or Clerk's Office, out of which such Attachments issued according to the Directions of this Act, then the Goods and Garnishee shall thereupon be immediately discharged.

But one Attachment to issue against one Person's Estate.

Manner of Executing it.

AND BE IT FURTHER ENACTED by the Authority aforesaid, That instead of other Creditors taking out new Writs of Attachment, they shall only be obliged to cause their Names and Demands to be entered in the Prothonotary's Office out of which the Attachments issued,

Other Creditors to enter their Names & Demands with the Prothonot:

issued, which the Prothonotary or his Deputy is hereby required to enter, in Order, as the Creditors of the Defendant or any Person for them shall apply, and shall set down the Time of their respective Applications; which Entry in the Prothonotary's Office shall be as sufficient to entitle such Claimant or Creditor to recover his, her or their Debts out of the Effects that shall remain after the prior Attachments or Demands, and Costs of Suit are satisfied, as if each Creditor had taken out a separate Attachment for their respective Debts. PROVIDED ALWAYS, That every Creditor who makes such Entry, shall likewise make due Proof of his Debt or Demand in the usual Way, as the Court shall direct, and thereupon shall obtain Judgment the third Court after the Issuing of the said Attachment.

And make due Proof, &c.

AND forasmuch as it is reasonable, that every Creditor, who is to bear the Charges of his own Suit, should have the Benefit of his own Discovery of the Defendant's Effects, BE IT FURTHER ENACTED by the Authority aforesaid, That any Creditor, after the Writ of Attachment has issued against any Person's Effects, may cause his or her Claim or Demand to be entered with the Prothonotary, and at the same time enter the Names of such Persons as he or she believes are indebted to the Defendant, or in whose Hands or Possession he or she knows or believes there are any Effects of the Defendant, and shall take a Memorandum of such Debtors Names, and deliver the same to the Sheriff or Officer who hath the Execution of the said Writ of Attachment; which Officer is hereby obliged to serve the Attachment in the Manner by this Act directed, upon the Effects of the Defendant, in the Hands of every such Debtor where the Attachment has not been already served in the Name of the first Person or the Plaintiff named in the Writ of Attachment, and shall make Return thereof as before is directed.

Creditors to have the Benefit of their own Discovery of the Defendant's Effects.

PROVIDED NEVERTHELESS, and it is hereby enacted, That the Effects attached in the Hands of such Debtor, tho' the same be done in the Name of the first Plaintiff or Claimant, shall be liable to answer the Debt and Costs of that Creditor who made the Discovery, or at whose Instance the same were attached, and the Residue of such Effects, if any remain, shall go towards the Satisfaction of the next Claimant or Creditor.

PRO-

PROVIDED ALSO, That where an Attachment is laid in the Hands of any Person or Persons supposed to have in his or her Hands or Possession any Goods or Effects of a Defendant in any Attachment, and such Person or Persons will go before a Magistrate of the County where the Effects were attached, and upon his or her Oath or Affirmation, in the Presence of the Party at whose Instance the Attachment is made, declare whether he hath any Effects, and (if any) what Effects he or she hath in his or her Hands or Possession, or in the Hands or Possession of any other Person, for the Use of such Deponent belonging to the Defendant in the Attachment named, and shall deliver the said Effects (if any) to the Sheriff or Officer as aforesaid; that then the said Debtor or Garnishee shall not be obliged to give any farther Attendance in Court at the Return of the Writ of Attachment, or at any time after, unless the Creditor shall be dissatisfied with, or refuse to accept of such Oath or Affirmation; and in such Case the Garnishee shall appear at Court according to the Directions of this Act: And if there prove to be no Effects of the Defendant's, or no more Effects in the Hands of such Garnishee than was before by him or her discovered, then the said Garnishee shall have the Charges of his, her or their Attendance defrayed by the Creditor requiring his, her or their Appearance as aforesaid, and not otherwise.

Garnishee delivering up Defendant's Effects, shall not be obliged to attend, &c.

AND to the end that it may be known, as well what Lands or Effects of the Defendant's are come to the Sheriff's Hands, as in whose Hands such Effects are attached, BE IT FURTHER ENACTED by the Authority aforesaid, That the Sheriff shall return into the Court a particular Account, as well of all the Lands and Tenements, as of the Goods, Chattels and Effects of the Defendant by him attached, and at whose Suit or Application, or on whose Discovery, and the Names of the Persons in whose Hands the same were attached; whereupon the Court shall, if they see Occasion, order such of the said Goods or Effects as are come to the Sheriff's Hands, to be appraised; and if they be perishable, or such as will create an Expence in the keeping of them, the Court, or in the Vacation three Magistrates of the County, may order the Sheriff in such Cases to sell such perishable Goods, and retain the Money in his Hands, or deliver the same into the Court until Judgment be obtained against the Defendant in the Attachment; and after Judgment all the Goods in the Sheriff's Hands shall be sold, and the Sheriff shall without any

Sheriff shall return an Account of Goods, &c. attached.

How to be disposed of.

Writ of Execution (unless it be when the Defendant's Lands
or Tenements are attached, in which Case one Execution
only shall issue against the said Lands or Tenements) proceed to take the same in Execution, and sell the same, as
by an Act of Assembly of this Government for taking
Lands in Execution, is directed, and shall pay to the respective Creditors their Debts and Costs of Suit out of the
Defendant's Effects, in order as they laid their Attachments
or entered their Claims with the Prothonotary, as in this
Act is directed.

PROVIDED ALWAYS, That there shall no more
of the Defendant's Effects be applied to the Payment of any
one Creditor, than happened to be in the Hands of the
Garnishee or Garnishees whose Names were entered by such
Creditor with the Prothonotary, unless there be no subsequent or other Creditor to claim the same.

AND BE IT FURTHER ENACTED
by the Authority aforesaid, That if the said Garnishee or
Garnishees shall fail to appear and declare upon Oath or
Affirmation what Goods or Effects of the Defendant's he or
she had in his or her Hands or Possession at the Time of
the Attachment laid, or at any Time after, it shall in such
Case be presumed that such Garnishee (not having before
made Oath or Affirmation before any Magistrate as in this
Act is directed) hath sufficient Effects of the Defendant's
in his Hands to satisfy the Demands of the Plaintiff, and
Judgment shall be entered, and Execution issue against the
said Garnishee, his Body or Estate, for the Sum recovered
by the Plaintiff at whose Instance the Attachment was laid
against the Defendant, as if a Verdict had passed against
such Garnishee : But if the Garnishee do appear, and the
Plaintiff or Claimant shall require that the Garnishee or
Garnishees shall upon Oath or Affirmation declare that he
had no Effects of the Defendant in his Hands or Possession
at the Time of the Attachment laid, or at any Time after,
then such Garnishee shall be discharged ; but if the Plaintiff
shall require the Garnishee to plead that he had no Effects
of the Defendant in his Hands or Possession at the Time of
the Attachment laid, or at any Time after, then the Plaintiff may take Issue upon such Plea ; and if upon Trial it
appear to the Jury that the Garnishee had any Goods or
Effects of the Defendant's as the Plaintiff shall alledge, in
such Case the Jury shall find for the Plaintiff, and say what
Goods and Effects are or were in the Garnishee's Hands at

Garnishees fail-
ing to appear,
&c. Judgment
may be entered
against them,
&c.

the

the Time of the Attachment laid, or at any Time after, and Judgment shall be entered that the Plaintiff recover the Goods, or the Value thereof; whereupon the Court may appoint indifferent Persons to appraise such Goods and Effects: And if the Garnishee will not deliver the Goods to the Sheriff, the Plaintiff shall at his Election have Execution against such Garnishee, his Body or Goods, for the appraised Value of the Goods or Effects found to be in his, her or their Hands, together with the Costs of Suit. And *Sheriff's Fees.* that the Sheriff's Fees for serving an Attachment, shall be as follows, *To wit*, For serving the Writ of Attachment in the Hands of the two first Garnishees, and Summons, the Sum of *Six Shillings* each, and for serving the same in the Hands of every other Garnishee, the Sum of *One Shilling and Six Pence*, and no more, and for his Trouble in securing the Effects of the Defendant, to be paid such reasonable Charges as the Court shall think fit to allow.

PROVIDED ALWAYS, That the Overplus of *Overplus to be* the said Debtor's Estate (if any) after all Debts and lawful *returned.* Charges are deducted, shall be returned to such Defendant, his Executors or Administrators, any thing herein contained to the contrary notwithstanding.

AND BE IT FURTHER ENACTED by the Authority aforesaid, That one Act of Assembly of *Repeal of a* this Government, entituled, *An Act about Attachments*, be *former Act.* and is hereby repealed.

PROVIDED ALWAYS, AND BE IT ENACTED by the Authority aforesaid, That it shall and may be lawful for any Person or Persons who have prosecuted any Writ or Writs of Attachment in any Court of Record within this Government, and which are now depending, to proceed thereupon in the usual Manner, and to obtain Judgment and Execution for his, her or their Debt or Damages, any thing herein contained to the contrary notwithstanding.

AND WHEREAS it oftentimes happens that the *In Cases where* Persons or Garnishees in whose Hands the Defendant's Goods *Garnishees re-* or Effects are attached, are Persons residing in another *side in another* County or Government, and at other times it happens that *Government,* Garnishees are likely to depart the Government, or remove *&c.* out of the County where the Attachment is served, and so the Plaintiff loses the Benefit of his Writ; and whereas it also

also often falls out that Persons who are indebted in confiderable Sums of Money to the Inhabitants of this Government, remove themfelves and Effects out of the fame before the Days of Payment of their faid Debts, and the Creditor is without all Relief, except in a Courfe of Equity, which is both very troublefome and expenfive, efpecially where the Debts are fmall: For remedying which Inconveniency, and the better to fecure the Inhabitants of this Government againft fuch difhoneft Practices, B E I T FURTHER ENACTED by the Authority aforefaid, *The Plaintiff fhall declare, &c.* That if any Plaintiff in any Writ of Attachment profecuted within this Government, or any Creditor claiming any Benefit by or under fuch Writ of Attachment, fhall upon Oath or Affirmation declare, that he verily believes the Garnifhee or Garnifhees is or are not Inhabitants of this Government, or the County where the Attachment is depending, or that fuch Garnifhee is about to depart this Government, or the County where the Attachment is laid or to be laid, and that fuch Deponent does alfo believe that fuch Garnifhee hath fome Goods or Effects of the Defendant's in his or her Hands or Poffeffion, or oweth Money to the Defendant, altho' the fame fhall happen at that Time *And may take a Writ againft fuch Garnifhee, &c.* not to be due ; that then and in fuch Cafe it fhall and may be lawful for fuch Plaintiff or Creditor to take a Writ againft the faid Garnifhee or Garnifhees, as the Cafe may require, and oblige the Garnifhee to find Sureties to appear at Court, and make fuch Anfwer as in this Act is required, and further to abide the Judgment of the Court.

AND BE IT FURTHER ENACTED by the Authority aforefaid, That if any Perfon be indebted to any Inhabitant of this Government, in any Sum of Money exceeding *Forty Shillings*, and the Day of Payment be not then come, and if the Creditor or fome credible Perfon for him or her, will on Oath or Affirmation declare, that the Defendant or Debtor is indebted to him or her in a Sum of Money exceeding *Forty Shillings*, and that the Day *Debtors about to depart, may be obliged to give better Security.* of Payment is not then come, and that fuch Deponent does verily believe upon good Grounds, that the Debtor is about to depart this Government, and to remove his Effects, and that fuch Debtor hath refufed to give better Security for Payment of the Money when the fame fhall become due ; it fhall then be lawful for fuch Creditor or Creditors to arreft or caufe to be arrefted the faid Debtor or Debtors, who upon his Appearance in Court, at the Return of the Writ, fhall be obliged to give better Security for the Debt due to the

the Plaintiff, if the Court shall see Cause, on the hearing the Allegations of Plaintiff and Defendant, so to order it; in which Case the Defendant shall pay the Costs of such Prosecution: But if the Court shall be of Opinion that there was not a sufficient Cause for demanding better Security of the Defendant, and for causing him to be arrested, the Plaintiff shall pay to the Defendant such Costs for his Trouble, and Charges as the Court shall think fit to direct, and the Suit shall be discontinued.

PROVIDED ALWAYS, That before any Execution issue upon any Attachment, and before the Effects of the Defendant, or the Money for which they shall be sold, be delivered to the Plaintiff or Claimant in the Attachment, every such Plaintiff or Claimant shall be obliged to find Sureties, who shall undertake to the Defendant in the Attachment, that if such Defendant shall within a Year and a Day next following, by him or her self, or by his or her Attorney come into Court, and disprove or avoid the Debt recovered by the Plaintiff or Claimant, or any Part of it, that then the Plaintiff or Claimant shall restore to the Defendant the Goods or Effects so attached, if the same be not sold; but if the Effects be sold, then to restore the Value thereof, with Costs of Suit, or so much thereof as shall be disproved.

Before the Effects of Defendants are delivered to the Plaintiffs, Security shall be given, &c.

Signed by Order of the House,

A. HAMILTON, *Speaker.*

An ACT *for erecting a Pound in the Town of* New-Castle.

WHEREAS many of the Inhabitants of the Hundred of *New-Castle* have received great Injury and Damage by unruly Horses and Cattle breaking into their Fields and Inclosures; For Remedy whereof, BE IT ENACTED by the Honourable *GEORGE THOMAS*, Esq; Lieutenant-Governor of and in the Counties of *New-Castle, Kent* and *Suffex* on *Delaware*, and Province of *Pennsylvania*, by and with the Advice and Consent of the Representatives of the Freemen of the said Counties in General Assembly met, and

Preamble.

C c c

by

A Pound to be erected in N. Castle.

by the Authority of the same; That a Pound shall be erected in the Town of *New-Castle* in the County of *New-Castle* on *Delaware*, at the proper Cost and Charge of the Inhabitants of the said Hundred: And if any

Cattle, &c. breaking into Inclosures, shall be impounded,

Horses or Cattle shall at any time hereafter break into any Field or Inclosure of any of the Inhabitants of the aforesaid Hundred, being fenced as the Law of this Government directs, then and in that Case it shall and may be lawful for the Owner or Possessor of such Field or Inclosure, to put such Horses or Cattle in the Pound aforesaid, there to remain until the Damages which shall be adjudged by the Viewers of the Fences within the said Hundred to have been sustained, are paid by the Owner or

Pound-Keeper shall give public Notice, &c.

Owners of such Horses or Cattle so impounded: But in case the Owner or Owners of such Horses or Cattle are not known, or do not appear, the Keeper of the Pound shall, and is hereby ordered immediately to cause Notes to be affixed at the most publick Places in the said Hundred, describing the Marks and Colour of such Horses or Cattle in his Possession, and shall in the mean Time provide the said Horses or Cattle with sufficient Food and Water. And

Owner not appearing within 10 Days, Appraisment and Sale shall be made, &c.

if the Owner or Owners of such Horses or Cattle do not appear within the space of Ten Days after such Impounding, it shall and may be lawful for the said Keeper of the said Pound, to cause the said Horses or Cattle to be appraised by Two creditable Men, Inhabitants of the said Hundred (they being first lawfully qualified) and to cause them to be sold at publick Vendue, at the Market-place within the Town of *New-Castle* aforesaid; and out of the Money arising by the Sale aforesaid, to pay all Charges of keeping such Horses or Cattle in the Pound, and other Costs, together with such Damages as the Owners of such Field or Inclosure shall have sustained; and the Overplus (if any be) to be lodged in the Hands of the County-Treasurer for the Time being, there to remain for the full space of One Year; and if the Owner or Owners of such Horses or Cattle during that Time do not appear, then the Money so lodged in the Treasurer's Custody, to be applied for the Use and Benefit of the Poor of the Hundred aforesaid But if it shall be found upon View by the Overseers of the Fences within the Hundred aforesaid, that the Fences of such Fields or Inclosures, wherein such Horses or Cattle have been taken trespassing, are not sufficient or lawful Fences, then and in such Case the Owner or Owners of such Field or Inclosure shall pay all Costs and Damages which have accrued or shall accrue thereon.

AND

AND in order that the Defign of erecting the Pound aforefaid may not be defeated, BE IT ENACTED by the Authority aforefaid, That the Juftices of *New-Caftle* County, in their next Court of Quarter-Seffions, together with the Affeffor of the faid Hundred, fhall, and are hereby impowered to affefs every Freeholder and Inhabitant of the Hundred aforefaid, in all fuch Sum and Sums of Money, as may be neceffary to erect the fame.

Juftices, &c. impowered to affefs for erecting the Pound.

AND BE IT FURTHER ENACTED by the Authority aforefaid, That the faid Juftices, at their Seffions aforefaid, or any fucceeding Seffions, fhall, and are hereby impowered to appoint a proper Officer for keeping of the faid Pound, and to eftablifh fuch Fees to be paid to the faid Officer for his Services, and for keeping the faid Pound in Repair, as they from time to time fhall think proper.

Juftices to appoint Pound-Keeper, eftablifh Fees, &c.

Signed by Order of the Houfe,

DAVID FRENCH, *Speaker.*

An ACT *for laying out Roads, and for erecting, repairing and maintaining Bridges, Caufeways and Highways within this Government.*

WHEREAS the prefent Manner and Method of repairing and amending the publick Highways, Caufeways and Bridges in the feveral Hundreds of the refpective Counties of this Government, is by Experience found to be very burthenfome and expenfive to the Inhabitants, and the fame are not kept in fuitable Repair and Order;

Preamble.

BE IT THEREFORE ENACTED by the Honourable GEORGE THOMAS, Efq; by and with His Majefty's Royal Approbation, Lieutenant-Governor and Commander in Chief of the Counties of *New-Caftle,* *Kent* and *Suffex* on *Delaware,* and Province of *Pennfylvania,* by and with the Advice and Confent of the Reprefentatives of the Freemen of the faid Counties in General Affembly met,

Justices im-
powered to ap-
point Overseers
of Highways,
&c.

met, and by the Authority of the same; That the Justices of the respective Courts of Quarter-Sessions for the several Counties of this Government, are hereby impowered and required, in *May*-Sessions yearly and every Year to nominate and appoint in each of the Hundreds of their respective Counties, one or more discreet and substantial Inhabitant or Inhabitants, to be Overseer or Overseers of the Highways, Causeways and Bridges of the several Parts of their respective Hundreds for the ensuing Year, as to the said Courts respectively shall seem necessary and most convenient: And that the said Court of Quarter-Sessions in the several Counties of this Government, or any three or more of the Justices of the said Court, within three Days next after the Ending of their respective Sessions, with the Approbation of the Overseer or Overseers of the Highways of any Hundred or Hundreds in their respective County, or

And with the
Overseers to
employ Persons
to keep High-
ways, &c. in
Repair.

the Majority of them; are hereby impowered to agree with and employ some proper Person or Persons (if any such can be had) to keep in Repair and amend, during the Term of One Year then next ensuing, all the publick Highways, Causeways and Bridges of the Hundred or Hundreds to which such Overseer or Overseers respectively belong (except such Roads, Causeways and Bridges, as by virtue of any Act of General Assembly of this Government, or otherwise, have been or shall be laid out, made or erected for the private Interest of any Person or Persons, or for passing over which, Travellers and other Passengers do or shall be obliged to pay any Sum or Sums of Money to any Person

And to make
new Roads, &c:

or Persons whatsoever) and also to make new Roads, Causeways and Bridges in such Part or Parts of the said Hundred or Hundreds, as shall by the said Court be judged necessary and laid out by virtue of this Act: Which Agreement, if any such shall be, shall by the Clerk of the said Court be entered on the Records of the said Court, thence after to be made Use of as Occasion may require:

And shall draw
Orders on the
Treasurer for
Payment, &c.

And the said Court shall draw an Order or Orders on the Treasurer of the respective County from time to time, for the Sum or Sums of Money in such Agreement or Agreements mentioned payable to such Person or Persons so undertaking the Repairing, Making or Erecting of any such Highways, Causeways, Roads or Bridges aforesaid, or to his or their Order; which said Sum and Sums of Money the said Treasurer is hereby required to pay out of the publick Money of the said County in his Hands.

BUT

BUT in cafe no fuch Agreement, during the faid Seffions, or the fpace of Three Days next following, fhall be made, then the Overfeer of the Highways of the Hundred for which fuch Agreement fhall not be made, as aforefaid, or each Overfeer of fuch Parts of the Highways of the faid Hundred, as by the faid Court fhall be allotted to him, together with the nigheft Juftice of the Peace of the fame County, are hereby impowered and required, to employ Labourers and Workmen to repair or amend, make or erect fuch Highways, Roads, Caufeways and Bridges, as aforefaid; which faid Labourers and Workmen fhall be paid, and receive their Wages by Orders drawn by the faid Juftice and Overfeer or Overfeers on the faid Treafurer, who is hereby required to pay the fame as aforefaid.

No Agreement being made; the Overfeer with a Juftice fhall employ Labourers, &c.

To be paid by the Treafurer.

AND that the Inhabitants of each Hundred fhall pay for the repairing and maintaining that Part of the King's-Roads or Highways which lies in their refpective Hundred, and that the fame be well performed by fome Undertaker by Agreement to be made, or by the Overfeer, as by this Act is before directed. And that the Account of the Charges thereof be brought into the Court of Appeal next following, in order that the fame may be levied on the faid Inhabitants. And that all Bridges over Creeks and deep Waters, lying on the King's Highways, together with the Caufeways thereunto belonging, leading through any of the Counties aforefaid, fhall be erected, repaired and maintained at the Common Expence of the refpective County wherein fuch Bridges and Caufeways fhall be.

Account to be brought to the next Court of Appeal.

Bridges to be erected by the refpective Counties.

AND BE IT FURTHER ENACTED by the Authority aforefaid, That all and every the Sum and Sums of Money which fhall hereafter be paid by the Treafurer or Treafurers of the refpective Counties of this Government, for repairing, making or erecting any Roads, Caufeways or Bridges within any of the faid Counties by virtue of this Act, fhall be affeffed and raifed upon the Inhabitants of the fame County or Hundred refpectively, in the Manner as other County-Levies are raifed.

Money paid by the Treafurer, to be affeffed & levied on the Inhabitants, &c.

AND BE IT FURTHER ENACTED by the Authority aforefaid, That where any Bridge or Bridges already erected or hereafter to be erected within this Government by virtue of this Act, is, are or fhall be the Boundary or Boundaries between any Two of the Counties of this Government, the faid Bridge or Bridges

Boundary Bridges to be erected and maintained at the Joint-Expence of the Counties or Hundreds.

Ddd

fhall

shall be erected, and from time to time supported and maintained at the Joint-Expence and Charges of the Two Counties between which the said Bridge or Bridges do or shall stand or be erected, or at the Joint-Expence of the Two Hundreds between which the same Bridge or Bridges do or shall stand.

AND BE IT FURTHER ENACTED by the Authority aforesaid, That all King's-Roads or Highways within this Government, shall be of the Breadth of Forty Feet, whereof Twenty Feet shall be grubbed, and the Branches and Limbs of Trees adjoining to the said Roads or Highways shall be cut down, at least Ten Feet from the Ground, and all dead Trees standing near the said Roads or Highways, and which, if falling, might reach the same, shall be cut down. And that all Causeways and Bridges shall be of the Breadth of Twelve Feet at least, and Bridges standing over deep Waters shall be railed in, at the Distance of Ten Feet from Rail to Rail, and of the Height of Three Feet from the Plank or Floor of the Bridge.

King's High-
ways to be 40
Feet broad.

Breadth of
Causeways and
Bridges.

AND BE IT FURTHER ENACTED by the Authority aforesaid, That the said Overseers and Persons to be employed as herein before is directed, shall have Power to cut down, fall and carry away any Timber or Trees, and dig Earth or Gravel, for the supporting or maintaining, making and erecting of the said Roads, Causeways and Bridges, in any Place lying within Ten Feet of each Side of the Roads, or any of them : And if no suitable Timber or Trees shall be found within the Distance of One Mile (within Ten Feet on each Side of any such Road as aforesaid) from the Place where any Bridge, Causeway or Road is to be erected, made or amended; then the Overseer or Overseers, or Person or Persons to be employed as aforesaid, shall and is or are hereby directed, to make Application to One of the nearest Justices of the Peace of the County where such Timber or Trees are wanting, which said Justice is hereby impowered and required to issue out his Warrant or Precept, in the Nature of a Summons, requiring Two good and substantial Freeholders of the Hundred where such Timber is wanting, to appear before him at a certain Day and Place ; and the said Freeholders upon their Appearance shall upon Oath or Affirmation, by the said Justice or some other Justice to be administred, value all such Timber and Trees as shall be needful, and stand most

Overseers, &c.
impowered to
fell Trees, dig
Gravel, &c.

Method of Valu-
ing Timber
necessary for
Bridges, &c.

moft convenient to the Place where the fame fhall be wanting, in the Prefence of the Owner or Poffeffor of the Land
whereon fuch Timber or Trees grow, if fuch Owner or
Poffeffor will appear, after One Day's Notice to him or her
given, or at his or her Dwelling-Houfe left by fuch Overfeer or Overfeers or Perfon or Perfons employed as aforefaid: And after fuch Valuation it fhall and may be lawful
to and for fuch Overfeer or Overfeers, or Perfon or Perfons
employed as aforefaid, or others by their or any of their
Order, to fall or cut down and carry away all fuch Timber
and Trees fo valued, and neceffary for any of the Purpofes
aforefaid. And the faid Juftice and Overfeer or Overfeers
fhall draw on the Treafurer of the County, for the Value
of the faid Timber and Trees, payable to the faid Owner
or Poffeffor; which Value the faid Treafurer is hereby directed and required to pay; and the fame fhall be affeffed
and raifed as aforefaid. And if any Owner or Poffeffor of
Land fhall bring any Action or Suit againft any Perfon for
proceeding as in and by this Act is directed, the Defendant
may plead the General Iffue, and give this Act in Evidence,
and the Plaintiff fhall become non-fuited, and pay unto the
Defendant his treble Cofts.

AND if any Freeholder being fummoned to value any
Timber or Trees as aforefaid, fhall neglect or refufe to appear, be qualified, or value the fame as aforefaid, every
fuch Perfon fo neglecting or refufing, fhall for fuch Neglect
or Refufal forfeit the Sum of *Twenty Shillings*, to be levied
together with Cofts, by Diftrefs and Sale of the Offender's
Goods and Chattels, by Warrant under the Hand and Seal
of the fame or any other Juftice, and paid to the Overfeer
or Overfeers of the Highways of the Hundred wherein the
Offence is committed, by him or them to be applied towards the defraying the Charge of the Road, Caufeway or
Bridge, for which fuch Timber or Trees fhall be fo wanting
as aforefaid: And the faid Juftice fhall and is hereby impowered and required to fend out another Precept, requiring
another Freeholder to appear and ferve in the room and
ftead of fuch Perfon fo refufing or neglecting as aforefaid,
and appoint another Time of Appearance, and fo *toties
quoties*, until fome fufficient Perfons fhall be got to do what
is required of them by virtue of this Act.

Penalty on Freeholders refufing to appear, &c.

PROVIDED ALWAYS, That no more Timber or
Trees fhall be valued, than what are really neceffary for the
Work for which they fhall be fo wanting as aforefaid.

AND

AND BE IT FURTHER ENACTED

Breadth of Publick Roads, &c. by the Authority aforesaid, That all publick Roads, which are not properly King's-Roads or Highways, shall be of the Breadth of Thirty Feet, Twenty Feet of which shall be grubbed and cleared, in like Manner as King's-Roads; and if no Timber or Trees shall be found within the Breadth allowed for the said Roads for the space of One Mile from the Place where any Bridge, Causeway or Road is to be erected, repaired or amended, suitable for that Purpose, then the Overseer or Overseers, or Person or Persons to be employed as aforesaid, shall and is or are hereby required, to make Application for, and to get Timber and Trees for the Uses aforesaid, in like Manner as is herein before directed for repairing of the King's-Highways.

AND BE IT FURTHER ENACTED

Penalty on Overseers, &c. neglecting or refusing to do their Duty. by the Authority aforesaid, That if any Overseer or Overseers hereafter appointed by the Direction of this Act, or any other Person or Persons employed or undertaking as aforesaid, shall neglect or refuse to do his or their Duty by this Act required, or after Notice to him or them given by some Justice of the Peace of the same County, shall for the space of Ten Days suffer any of the said Roads, Causeways or Bridges within his or their District or Charge, or by him or them undertaken as aforesaid, to remain incumbred, unpassable or unrepaired, upon the View of any one Justice of the Peace of the respective County, or Complaint and due Proof thereof made before any such Justice; every such Overseer, or Person employed or undertaking as aforesaid, shall for every such Offence or Neglect, forfeit the Sum of *Five Pounds*, to be levied together with the Costs by Distress and Sale of the Offender's Goods and Chattels, by Warrant under the Hand and Seal of such Justice, and paid to the Treasurer of the County towards defraying the Charge of repairing the Roads of the Hundred wherein such Fine shall arise.

AND BE IT FURTHER ENACTED

Justices impowered to appoint Freeholders to view Places where Roads, &c. are petitioned for. by the Authority aforesaid, That the Justices of each Court of Quarter-Sessions within this Government, shall by virtue of this Act have Power, as often as they shall find Occasion, in open Court to order and appoint Five sufficient Freeholders of the Neighbourhood, inhabiting near the Place where a Road or Cart-way, Causeway or Bridge, leading unto the Publick Road, shall be petitioned for by any Person or Persons, who shall view the said Place:

          And

And if such Freeholders, or any Three of them, shall be satisfied that there is Occasion for a Bridge, Causeway, Road or Cartway to be laid out according to such Petition or Petitions, then they shall and may lay out the same, in and through such convenient Places as they shall think may be *Who may lay out the same.* least to the Damage, Injury or Inconvenience of the Neighbours or Parties concerned, and to the Settlements thereabouts, and of such Breadth as the Justices shall order and appoint, so that any such Road or Cartway shall not exceed Thirty Feet in Breadth; and shall make Return thereof under their Hands, to the next County-Court after it is laid out: And if then and there the Justices shall approve *And the Justices approving thereof, it shall be recorded.* the same, and the Requisites hereafter mentioned shall be complied with and performed, it shall at the same Court be entered upon Record, and from thenceforth shall be deemed, taken and allowed to be a lawful Common Bridge, Causeway, Road or Cartway. And whenever it shall be found necessary and convenient by such Five Freeholders or any Three of them, that such Road or Roads should run or go through the improved Land of any Person or Persons, then and in such Case such Five Freeholders, or any Three of them, shall, together with the Return of the View of such Road or Roads, make Return to the respective County-Court aforesaid, upon Oath or solemn Affirmation to be taken before any Justice of the Peace of the County where such Lands lie, of the Damages that may be sustained by such Person or Persons as shall be Owners of such improved Lands, by Reason or Means of laying out such Road or Roads through the same; and the Road or Roads so re- *Damages sustained by means of laying out Roads, to be made good.* turned, shall not be confirmed until the Person or Persons petitioning for the same shall pay to the Owner or Owners of such improved Lands all such Damages as shall be so returned by such Five Viewers, or any Three of them, as aforesaid. And the Petitioner or Petitioners for such Road *Petitioners for Roads to pay the Charges.* and Roads shall pay and satisfy all Costs and Charges whatsoever, that shall or may happen to accrue for or on Account of laying out such Road or Roads.

AND to prevent any Difference that may arise among Neighbours about Roads or Cartways already laid out by Order of the Governor and Council, or any of the County-Courts of this Government, and which are or shall be entered upon Record, either before or after the making and publishing of this Act; BE IT ENACTED by the Authority aforesaid, That all such Roads and Cartways, as *Roads so laid out, shall be deemed free, &c.* aforesaid, shall be taken, deemed and allowed to be free,

open

open and lawful Common Roads and Cartways, from the Time of their being so laid out and recorded as aforesaid.

AND BE IT FURTHER ENACTED by the Authority aforesaid, That if any Person or Persons who shall be appointed by the respective County-Courts aforesaid to view and make Return of such Road or Roads as shall be proper and convenient as aforesaid, shall neglect or refuse to perform and execute such Charge and Duty, (unless prevented and hindered by unavoidable Accidents) such Person or Persons so neglecting or refusing, being thereof convicted by his or their own Confession, or by the Oath or Affirmation of One Witness before any Magistrate of the respective County where such Order for viewing any Road or Roads shall be made as aforesaid, shall forfeit and pay to the Overseer or Overseers of the Hundred wherein such Road shall be petitioned for, the Sum of *Ten Shillings* for every such Default; and in case of Non-Payment thereof, the same shall be levied of the Goods and Chattels of such Defaulter or Defaulters, by Distress and Sale thereof, by virtue of a Warrant from any Justice of the Peace of the respective County as aforesaid; and such Fine or Fines shall be applied towards defraying and paying the Charge of the laying out such Road or Roads as aforesaid.

AND BE IT FURTHER ENACTED by the Authority aforesaid, That an Act of General Assembly of this Government, entituled, *An* ACT *for erecting Publick Bridges, and maintaining Highways, and also a Pound and Gates for the Town of* Lewes; shall be and is hereby repealed.

Signed by Order of the House,

JEHU CURTIS, *Speaker.*

Vid. supra pag. 8.

A Supplementary Act to an Act of General Assembly of this Government, entituled, An Act for the Advancement of Justice, *and more certain Administration thereof.*

WHEREAS the Act of General Assembly of this Government, made in the Sixth Year of the Reign of His late Majesty King GEORGE the First, entituled, *An* ACT *for the Advancement of Justice,*

and

and more certain Adminiſtration thereof; doth not clearly appear to have ſufficiently provided for the Manner of Trial and Puniſhment of Petty-Treaſon, Miſpriſion of Treaſon, Murder, Manſlaughter, Homicide, Beſtiality, Inceſt and Bigamy;

BE IT THEREFORE ENACTED by the Honourable *GEORGE THOMAS*, Eſq; by and with His Majeſty's Royal Approbation, Lieutenant-Governor and Commander in Chief of the Counties of *New-Caſtle*, *Kent* and *Suſſex* on *Delaware*, and Province of *Pennſylvania*, by and with the Advice and Conſent of the Repreſentatives of the Freemen of the ſaid Counties in General Aſſembly met, and by the Authority of the ſame, That every Perſon or Perſons who ſhall be guilty of any Petty-Treaſon, Miſpriſion of Treaſon, Murder, Manſlaughter, Homicide, Beſtiality, Inceſt or Bigamy, ſhall be tried in like Manner as other Felons by the ſaid Act are directed to be tried, and puniſhed in the like Manner as Perſons guilty of the like Crimes and Offences are puniſhable by the Laws and Statutes of that Part of *Great-Britain* called *England.*

Signed by Order of the Houſe,

JEHU CURTIS, *Speaker.*

An ACT *againſt forceable Entry, Bar-ratry, Maintenance, Champerty and Embracery.*

BE IT ENACTED by the Honourable *GEORGE THOMAS*, Eſq; by and with His Majeſty's Royal Approbation, Lieutenant-Governor and Commander in Chief of the Counties of *New-Caſtle*, *Kent* and *Suſſex* on *Delaware*, and Province of *Pennſylvania*, by and with the Advice and Conſent of the Repreſentatives of the Freemen of the ſaid Counties in General Aſſembly met, and by the Authority of the ſame; That whoſoever ſhall forceably enter into the Houſe, Lands or Poſſeſſions of any other Perſon, or being entered peaceably, ſhall forceably hold the Houſe, Lands or Poſſeſſions of any other Perſon within this Government, ſhall be proceeded againſt
and

and puniſhed as by the ſeveral Statutes made againſt forceable Entries and Detainures in that Part of *Great-Britain* called *England*, is provided and directed.

AND BE IT FURTHER ENACTED by the Authority aforeſaid, That if any Perſon within this Government be a common Barrator, vexing others with unjuſt and vexatious Suits, or ſhall promote or encourage others ſo to do, or ſhall be guilty of Maintenance, Champerty or Embracery ; every ſuch Perſon ſo offending ſhall be proceeded againſt, and puniſhed for his Offence, as by the Common Law and the ſeveral Statutes made againſt ſuch Offences in that Part of *Great-Britain* called *England*, is provided and directed.

Signed by Order of the House,

JEHU CURTIS, *Speaker.*

An ACT directing the Puniſhment of Petty-Larceny.

BE IT ENACTED by the Honourable *GEORGE THOMAS*, Eſq; by His Majeſty's Royal Approbation, Lieutenant-Governor and Commander in Chief of the Counties of *New-Caſtle*, *Kent* and *Suſſex* on *Delaware*, and Province of *Pennſylvania*, by and with the Advice and Conſent of the Repreſentatives of the Freemen of the ſaid Counties in General Aſſembly met, and by the Authority of the ſame ; That if any Perſon within this Government ſhall at any Time hereafter be duly convicted by the Teſtimony of one or more credible Witneſſes, or Confeſſion of the Party offending, before any Two Juſtices of the Peace in any of the Counties of this Government, of having ſtolen from any Perſon or Perſons within the ſame, any Money or Goods under the Value of *Five Shillings*; every ſuch Perſon ſo offending ſhall by the ſaid Juſtices be ordered to be publickly whipt on his or her bare Back, with any Number of Laſhes not exceeding Fifteen; and alſo ſhall by the ſaid Juſtices be adjudged to return to the Party or Parties aggrieved, the Money or Goods ſo ſtolen, if the ſame can be found, and alſo the Value thereof, according to the Valuation of the ſaid Juſtices, who are hereby directed and required to value the ſame, together

Puniſhment of Petty-Larceny.

with

with the Cofts of Profecution and Whipping ; and in cafe the faid Goods be not found, double the Value of the faid Money or Goods ; and fhall alfo be adjudged to pay all the Charges of fuch Profecution and Whipping, to be levied and raifed by Diftrefs and Sale of the Offender's Goods and Chattels, by Warrant under the Hands and Seals of the faid Juftices, or either of them : And for want of fuch Goods or Chattels, the faid Offender fhall be adjudged by the faid Juftices to make Satisfaction for the adjudged Values and Charges by Servitude for any Term of Time at the Difcretion of the faid Juftices ; provided the fame do not exceed One Year.

Signed by Order of the Houfe,

JEHU CURTIS, *Speaker.*

An ACT *for acknowledging and recording Deeds.*

BE IT ENACTED by the Honourable *GEORGE THOMAS*, Efq; by and with His Majefty's Royal Approbation, Lieutenant-Governor and Commander in Chief of the Counties of *New-Caftle*, *Kent* and *Suffex* on *Delaware*, and Province of *Pennfylvania*, by and with the Advice and Confent of the Reprefentatives of the Freemen of the faid Counties in General Affembly met, and by the Authority of the fame ; That there fhall be an Office of Record in each County of this Government, which fhall be called and ftiled, *The Office for recording of Deeds*; and fhall be kept in fome convenient Place in the faid refpective Counties ; and the Recorder fhall duly attend the Service of the fame, and at his own proper Cofts and Charges fhall provide good large Books of Royal or other large Paper, well bound and covered, wherein he fhall record, in a fair and legible Hand, all Deeds and Conveyances which fhall be brought to him for that Purpofe, according to the true Intent and Meaning of this Act.

An Office of Record to be kept in each County.

AND BE IT FURTHER ENACTED by the Authority aforefaid, That all Bargains and Sales, Deeds and Conveyances of Lands, Tenements and Hereditaments within this Government, fhall be recorded in the faid Office within One Year after the Execution thereof:

All Deeds, &c. fhall be recorded.

But

But first to be acknowledged, &c. But before the same shall be so recorded, the Grantee or Grantees, or some other proper Person for such Grantee or Grantees, shall procure the Grantor or Bargainor named in every such Deed, or his, her or their Attorney or Attornies for that Purpose appointed, to acknowledge that such Deed or Deeds, Conveyance or Conveyances, is or are the Act or Acts, Deed or Deeds of such Grantor or Grantors, to appear before the Court of Common Pleas of the proper County where the Lands lie; which said Court is hereby impowered to take an Acknowledgment of the Grantor, if one, or one of the Grantors, if more, or his, her or their Attorney or Attornies, that the same is his, her or their Act and Deed. But in case the Grantor be dead, or cannot appear, and no Attorney be appointed as aforesaid, the Grantee or Grantees, or some proper Person for such Grantee or Grantees, shall and may procure one or more of the Witnesses that were present at the Execution thereof, to be brought before such Court, who shall be examined upon *Or proved.* Oath or Affirmation to prove the Execution of the Deed or Conveyance then produced; whereupon the Clerk of the said Court, under his Hand and Seal of the County, shall certify such Acknowledgment or Proof upon the Back or at the Foot of the Deed or Conveyance as aforesaid, with the Day and Year when the same was made, and by *Recording to be certified.* whom: And after the same shall be recorded, the Recorder shall certify on the Back or at the Foot thereof, under his Hand and Seal of his Office, the Day he recorded the same, and the Name or Number of the Book and Page wherein it is recorded.

AND BE IT FURTHER ENACTED *Deeds, &c. made out of the Government, shall be proved, &c.* by the Authority aforesaid, That where any Deed or Deeds, Conveyance or Conveyances, or Power of Attorney for granting or conveying of any Lands or Tenements within this Government, or Power of Attorney to acknowledge such Deed or Deeds, Conveyance or Conveyances, shall hereafter be made or executed by any Person or Persons out of this Government, such Deed or Deeds, Conveyance or Conveyances, or Power of Attorney, shall be proved by one or more of the Witnesses to such Deed or Deeds, Conveyance or Conveyances, or Power of Attorney, in open Court, in the County where the Lands or Tenements lie; and such Witness or Witnesses shall upon a legal Qualification declare, that he, she or they was or were present and saw such Deed or Deeds, Conveyance or Conveyances, or Power of Attorney, duly signed, sealed **and**

and delivered by the Party or Parties making such Deed or Conveyance or Power of Attorney.

AND BE IT FURTHER ENACTED by the Authority aforesaid, That all Deeds and Conveyances made and to be made, and proved or acknowledged and recorded as aforesaid, which shall appear so to be by Certificate made thereon, according to the true Intent and Meaning of this Act, shall be of the same Force and Effect here for the giving Possession and Seizin, and make good the Title and Assurance of the Lands, Tenements and Hereditaments, as Deeds of Feoffment with Livery and Seizin, or Deeds enrolled in any of the King's Courts of Record at *Westminster*, are or shall be in that Part of *Great-Britain* called *England*; and the Copies or Exemplifications of all Deeds so enrolled, being examined by the Recorder and certified under his Hand and Seal (which the Recorder or Keeper of the Records is hereby required to affix thereto) shall be allowed in all Courts of Law where produced, and are hereby declared and enacted to be as good Evidence, and as valid and effectual in Law, as the Original Deeds or Conveyances, or as Bargains and Sales enrolled at the said Courts at *Westminster* and Copies thereof can or may be, and the same may be sued, pleaded and made use of accordingly.

Deeds. &c. so proved, or acknowledged and recorded, shall be good, &c.

AND BE IT FURTHER ENACTED by the Authority aforesaid, That in all Deeds to be recorded in pursuance of this Act, whereby any Estate of Inheritance in Fee-simple shall hereafter be conveyed to the Grantee and his Heirs or Assigns, the Words [Grant, Bargain, and Sell] shall be judged an express Covenant to the Grantee, his Heirs and Assigns, *To wit*, That the Grantor was seized of an indefeazable Estate in Fee-simple, freed from all Incumbrances done or suffered by the Grantor (excepting the Rents and Services due to the Lord of the Fee) as also for quiet Enjoyment against the Grantor, his Heirs and Assigns, unless limited by express Words contained in such Deeds; and that the Grantee, his Heirs, Executors, Administrators and Assigns, may in any Action assign Breaches as if such Covenants were expressly inserted.

Force of the Words Grant, Bargain & Sell, &c.

PROVIDED ALWAYS, That this Act shall not extend to Leases on Rent, or to Leases not exceeding Twenty-one Years, where the actual Possession goes with the Lease.

AND BE IT FURTHER ENACTED,

No Mortgage shall be good, unless recorded.

That no Mortgage-Deed or Defeazable Deed in the Nature of Mortgages hereafter to be made, shall be good or sufficient to pass any Freehold or Inheritance, or to grant any Estate therein for Life or Years, unless such Deed be acknowledged or proved and recorded in the County where the Lands or Tenements lie, within Twelve Months after the Date thereof, as herein is before directed for other Deeds.

AND BE IT FURTHER ENACTED,

Mortgagee having received Payment, shall enter Satisfaction on the Margin of the Record.

That every Mortgagee within this Government, his or her Heirs, Executors, Administrators or Assigns, having received full Satisfaction and Payment of all such Sum and Sums of Money as are really due to him or them by such Mortgage, shall at the Request of the Mortgagor, his Heirs or Assigns, enter Satisfaction upon the Margin of the Record of such Mortgage recorded in the said Office, which shall for ever thereafter discharge and release the same, and shall likewise bar all Actions brought or to be brought thereon. And if any such Mortgagee, his Heirs, Executors, Administrators or Assigns, by him or themselves, or his or their Attorney, shall not within Three Months next after Request and Tender made for his or their reasonable Charges, repair to the said Office, and there cause such

Forfeit on Neglect or Refusal.

Satisfaction to be entered as aforesaid; he or they neglecting or refusing so to do, shall for such Neglect or Refusal forfeit and pay unto the Party or Parties aggrieved, any Sum or Sums of Money not exceeding the Consideration mentioned in the Mortgage-Deed, to be recovered, together with Costs, in any Court of Record within this Government by Bill, Plaint or Information.

AND WHEREAS it hath been customary for some Persons to let out Money at Interest upon Mortgage of Lands, Tenements and Hereditaments within this Government, and to take of the Mortgagors absolute Deeds of Bargain and Sale, or Deeds of Lease and Release which have been acknowledged and recorded, and to give them separate Defeazances which have not been recorded, and upon Discharge or Payment of the Mortgage-Money and Interest to return to the Mortgagor, his Heirs or Assigns, the said Deeds with short Releases thereon indorsed, which have not been acknowledged or recorded; whereby great Difficulties will hereafter arise to the true and rightful Owners of the said Lands, Tenements or Hereditaments, and Suits for the same may be brought against them by the Heirs of such Mortgagees;   B E

BE IT THEREFORE ENACTED by
the Authority aforesaid, That where any Person shall
after the Publication of this Act, take or receive any absolute Deed of Conveyance, or Deed of Lease and Release
from the Mortgagor of any real or personal Estate as aforesaid, and shall give or make any Defeazance or other Contract in Writing in the nature of a Defeazance, for Redemption and Discharge of such Estate mortgaged ; every such
Mortgagor shall, and is hereby required to cause such Defeazance, or other Contract in Writing, as aforesaid, to be
acknowledged or proved and recorded, within the space of
Twelve Months next after the Execution thereof: And if
such Mortgagor shall neglect so to do, he or she shall lose
all Benefit whatsoever of the said Defeazance, and the same
shall be utterly null and void.

Mortgages to be acknowledged, &c. within 12 Months.

AND BE IT FURTHER ENACTED
by the Authority aforesaid, That whenever any Deed or
Conveyance, which shall be defeazanced as aforesaid in the
nature of a Mortgage or Mortgages, shall be paid off, and
satisfied to the Mortgagee or Mortgagees, his or their Heirs,
Executors, Administrators or Assigns, they and every of
them shall at the reasonable Request, and at the proper Cost
and Charges of the Mortgagor, his Heirs, Executors, Administrators or Assigns, by good and sufficient Deeds and
Conveyances in the Law, reconvey unto such Mortgagor
or Mortgagors, his or their Heirs, Executors, Administrators or Assigns, for the Use of the said Mortgagor or Mortgagors, his or their Heirs and Assigns, all and every the
Lands, Tenements and Hereditaments so conveyed as aforesaid, with the Appurtenances, under the Penalty of the
Value of the Lands and Tenements so mortgaged, to be
recovered in Manner aforesaid for the Use of the Mortgagor, his Heirs or Assigns.

Mortgages being paid off, Reconveyances to be made.

AND BE IT FURTHER ENACTED
by the Authority aforesaid, That before any of the said
Recorders shall enter upon their respective Offices, they
shall find Sureties, as follows, *viz.* The said Recorder of
Deeds shall give Bond to the County-Court or to the
County-Treasurer within the County where such Recorder
shall be appointed for the Time being, with one or more
sufficient Sureties in a Bond of *Five Hundred Pounds* conditioned for the true and faithful Execution of his Office, and
for delivering up the Records and other Writings belonging
to the said Office, whole, safe and undefaced to his Successor

Recorders to find Sureties, &c.

in the said Office ; and shall take a Receipt for the same, which shall contain a List thereof ; which said Bond and Receipt shall be preserved and kept safely by the Justices of the said Court or County-Treasurer, in order to be sued and prosecuted, for making Satisfaction to the Parties that shall be damnified or aggrieved, or for not delivering the same in Manner aforesaid, as is or shall be in such Cases *Penalty on offi-* directed by the Laws of this Government. And that no *ciating before* Recorder of Deeds whatsoever hereafter appointed as afore-
Security given. said, shall enter upon, or officiate in the said Office, before he hath given such Surety as aforesaid, upon Pain of for-feiting the Sum of *One Hundred Pounds,* the one Half to the Governor for Support of Government, and the other Half to him or them that will sue for the same, to be recovered as aforesaid.

AND BE IT ENACTED by the Authority *Former Acts* aforesaid, That all Acts of Assembly, and Laws of this *repealed.* Government heretofore made or enacted, any Way relating to, or concerning the Recording of any Deeds or Convey-ances, or Mortgages, or the proving or acknowledging them or any of them, or of any Letters or Powers of At-torney for the conveying of Lands or Tenements, or ac-knowledging of any such Deeds or Conveyances as afore-said, contrary to this Act ; be, and the same are hereby repealed, and declared to be null and void to all Intents and Purposes whatsoever.

Signed by Order of the House,

JEHU CURTIS, *Speaker.*

An ACT *for Relief of the Poor.*

FOR the Prevention of straggling and indigent Per-sons from coming into and being chargeable to the Inhabitants, and for the better Relief of the Poor of this Government ; BE IT ENACTED by the Honourable *GEORGE THOMAS,* Esq; by and with His Majesty's Royal Approbation, Lieutenant-Governor and Commander in Chief of the Counties of *New-Castle, Kent* and *Sussex* on *Delaware,* and Province of *Pennsylvania,* by and with the Advice and Consent of the Representatives of the Freemen of the said Counties in General Assembly met,

met, and by the Authority of the same; That the Justices of the Peace of the several Counties of this Government, or any three or more of them, at the Time and Place of laying the County-Levies, shall nominate and appoint one or more substantial Inhabitant or Inhabitants of each of the Hundreds within their respective Counties, to be Overseer or Overseers of the Poor of the said respective Hundreds, who shall then and there, by the said Justices or some of them, be qualified upon Oath or Affirmation, for the due Execution of his or their Office, as herein after directed, for the ensuing Year.

Justices to nominate Overseers of the Poor;

Who shall be qualified.

AND if any Person hereafter appointed to the Office of Overseer of the Poor as aforesaid, shall refuse or neglect to be qualified as aforesaid, the said Justices shall in the room and stead of such Person so refusing or neglecting, appoint some other fit Person, and so *toties quoties*, until some proper Person or Persons shall be appointed and qualified as aforesaid. And every such Person so refusing or neglecting, shall for such Contempt forfeit the Sum of *Five Pounds*, to be levied, together with Costs, by Distress and Sale of the Goods and Chattels of such Person so refusing or neglecting, by Warrant under the Hands and Seals of any two of the said Justices, and paid to the Treasurer of the same County for the Use of the Poor of the said County.

Penalty on refusing to serve.

AND BE IT FURTHER ENACTED by the Authority aforesaid, That the Constables and Overseers of the Poor in each Hundred within the several Counties of this Government, shall and are hereby required to make diligent Inspection and Enquiry in their respective Districts after all vagrant, poor and impotent Persons coming into the same in order to settle or otherwise; and if any such shall be found as aforesaid, such Overseer or Constable shall and is hereby required to make Report thereof to the next Justice of the Peace of the said County; and the said Justice shall and is hereby required, by Warrant under his Hand and Seal, to cause such vagrant, poor or impotent Person to be apprehended, and brought before him or some other Justice of the Peace of the same County; and if it appear to the Justice before whom such Person is or shall be brought, that such Person is likely to become chargeable as aforesaid, such Justice shall and is hereby required to order such vagrant, poor or impotent Person, if able to travel, immediately to depart the County, or to give sufficient Security to indemnify the County, as herein after mentioned;

Constables and Overseers to enquire after Vagrants, Poor, &c.

Vagrants, &c. to be apprehended, &c.

mentioned; and upon Refufal or Negle&t of fuch vagrant, poor or impotent Perfon to depart or give Security as aforefaid, it fhall and may be lawful to and for any Two Juftices of the Peace of the fame County, to caufe every fuch Perfon fo refufing or negle&ting, to be publickly whipp'd at the common Whipping-Poft, with any Number of Lafhes not exceeding Fifteen, and the fame Punifhment to be repeated every Day, or fo often as he or fhe fhall be found in the faid County, until he or fhe fhall depart the fame as aforefaid.

Poor not having a legal Settlement, to be fent to the Place of their laft Abode.

AND BE IT FURTHER ENACTED by the Authority aforefaid, That if any poor or impotent Perfon fhall be found in any of the Counties of this Go- vernment, who is not an Inhabitant of the fame County, fuch Perfon, before he or fhe fhall have gained a legal Settle- ment as by this A&t is dire&ted, fhall by Warrant under the Hands and Seals of any Two Juftices of the Peace of the fame County, be fent from Conftable to Conftable through the feveral Hundreds within this Government, as the Cafe may require, the nigheft Way towards the Place of his or her laft Abode; and the Conftables of the refpe&tive Hundreds within this Government, fhall and are hereby required to receive fuch Perfon, and him or her to convey or forward to the next Conftable, and fo from Conftable to Conftable, until he or fhe fhall be delivered to the nigheft Juftice of the Peace of the County wherein fuch Perfon did laft refide or dwell, or of the next County lying in the Way to the Place of fuch Perfon's laft Settlement or Abode.

AND BE IT FURTHER ENACTED by the Authority aforefaid, That if any poor or impotent Perfon, being a Refident of any one of the Counties of this Government, fhall tranfport him or her felf, or go into an- other of the faid Counties, in order fettle or refide in fuch County, or otherwife, and fhall be likely to become charge- able to the County into which he or fhe hath laft gone; it fhall and may be lawful for any two Juftices of the Peace of the faid County, and they are hereby required, before fuch Perfon fhall have gained a legal Settlement therein, by Warrant under their Hands and Seals, to caufe the faid Perfon to be fent from Hundred to Hundred, and from Conftable to Conftable, the nigheft Way to the County wherein fuch Perfon did laft refide, and to be delivered to the nigheft Juftice of the Peace of the faid County, or to the nigheft Juftice of the Peace of the next County lying **in** in the Way to the Place of such Person's last Settlement; which said Justice is hereby required to receive such Person if he or she be a Resident of the said County, or otherwise to cause such Person to be sent forward, from Constable to Constable, towards the County wherein he or she had his or her last Settlement or Abode as aforesaid.

AND BE IT FURTHER ENACTED by the Authority aforesaid, That if any Person or Persons inhabiting within any of the Counties of this Government, shall for above the space of Three Days, harbour or entertain any such vagrant, poor or impotent Person or Persons coming into the same County, without making Report or giving Notice thereof to the Overseer or Overseers of the Poor of the Hundred, or to the nigheft Justice of the Peace of such County; every such Person so harbouring or entertaining any such vagrant, poor or impotent Person, for every Twenty-four Hours he or she shall harbour or entertain such vagrant, poor or impotent Person, upon due Proof thereof made before any Justice of the Peace, shall forfeit the Sum of *Five Shillings*, to be levied, together with Costs, by Distress and Sale of the Offender's Goods and Chattels, by Warrant under the Hand and Seal of the said Justice, and paid to the Treasurer of the County for the Time being for the Use of the Poor of the said County; and shall lose all such Debt or Account which shall be owing to him or her from such vagrant, poor or impotent Person, so that he or she may not for the same be detained within such County; and shall also, by Order of the said Justice, at his or her Expence cause such vagrant, poor or impotent Person to be removed out of the said County within the space of Three Days; and if any Person so harbouring or entertaining any such vagrant, poor or impotent Person without giving such Notice as aforesaid, shall neglect or refuse at his or her Expence to cause such vagrant, poor or impotent Person to be removed out of the said County within the Time above limited, every such Person shall for such Neglect or refusal forfeit the Sum of *Five Pounds*, to be levied, together with Costs, by Distress and Sale of the Offender's Goods and Chattels, by Warrant under the Hands and Seals of any Two Justices of the same County, and paid to the Treasurer of the County for the Use of the Poor of the said County; and the said vagrant, poor or impotent Person shall by Warrant of the said Justices be removed out of the County, in Manner herein before directed.

Penalty on entertaining Vagrants, &c.

AND for the better afcertaining what Continuance fhall render any Perfon an Inhabitant of any of the Counties of this Government, BE IT ENACTED by the Authority aforefaid, That where any unmarried Perfon, not

What fhall render any Perfon an Inhabitant, &c.

having Child or Children, is or fhall be lawfully hired as a Servant in any Town, Village or Hundred within this Government, and did or fhall continue or abide in the fame Service during the fpace of One whole Year, without being warned to depart or give Security as aforefaid, fuch Service fhall be adjudged and deemed a good and legal Settlement. And where any unmarried Perfon, not having Child or Children, fhall by Indenture be bound Apprentice or Servant, and inhabit in any County of this Government until the Time of his or her Apprenticefhip or Servitude be expired; fuch Binding and Inhabiting fhall be adjudged and deemed a good and legal Settlement; provided that the Term of fuch Apprenticefhip or Servitude be not lefs than Two Years. And if any Perfon who fhall hereafter come to inhabit in any of the Counties of this Government, fhall for himfelf and of his own Account execute any publick or annual Office or Charge within the faid County, during One whole Year, or fhall be charged with, and pay his Share towards the County-Taxes or Levies; fuch Perfon fhall be adjudged and deemed to have a good and legal Settlement in the fame. And that no other Perfon or Perfons, who fhall be imported or come into any of the Counties of this Government, fhall be adjudged or deemed to have procured a legal Settlement in fuch County, unlefs he, fhe or they fhall really. and *bona fide*, take a Leafe of fome Tenement or Plantation within the fame County, of the yearly Value of *Fifty Shillings*, and continue thereon One whole Year without being warned to depart; or unlefs he, fhe or they give fufficient Security to the Treafurer of the County for the Time being, to indemnify the faid County from any Charge that may accrue by reafon of fuch Perfon's coming into fuch County, to be allowed by any Two Juftices of the Peace or Magiftrates of the faid County.

AND BE IT FURTHER ENACTED

What Relations are to maintain their Poor, &c.

by the Authority aforefaid, That the Father and Grandfather, Mother and Grand-mother, being of fufficient Ability, fhall at their own Charges relieve and maintain their poor, blind, lame and impotent Children and Grand-children, as the Juftices of the Peace at their General Court of Quarter-Seffions fhall order and direct; and the Children and Grand-children, being of Ability, fhall, by fuch Order of of the Juſtices as aforeſaid, at their own Charges relieve and maintain their Fathers and Mothers, Grand-fathers and Grand-mothers, not having any Eſtate, nor being of Ability to work ; upon Pain of forfeiting *Forty Shillings* for every Month they or any of them ſhall fail therein, to be levied monthly, together with Coſts, by Diſtreſs and Sale of the Goods and Chattels of ſuch Father, Mother, Grand-father, Grand-mother, Child or Children reſpectively, by Warrant under the Hands and Seals of any Two Juſtices of the Peace of the ſame County, and paid to the Treaſurer for the Uſe of the Poor of the ſame County.

Penalty on Neglect, &c.

AND BE IT FURTHER ENACTED by the Authority aforeſaid, That any Two Juſtices of the Peace of the County, with the Conſent and Approbation of the Overſeer or Overſeers of the Poor of the reſpective Hundred, are hereby impowered and required to bind out Apprentices to Trades or otherwiſe, the Children of all ſuch who ſhall not by the ſaid Juſtices and Overſeer or Overſeers be thought of Ability to maintain and educate them, for ſuch Term and Terms as the ſaid Juſtices and Overſeer or Overſeers in their Diſcretion ſhall ſee meet, ſo as that any ſuch Male-Child be not be not bound longer than until he ſhall arrive at the Age of Twenty-one Years, and a Female until ſhe ſhall arrive at Sixteen Years.

Juſtices impowered to bind out poor Children, &c.

AND BE IT ENACTED by the Authority aforeſaid, That the Juſtices of the Peace, together with the Aſſeſſors, and Eight of the Grand-Jury, or ſo many of them as ſhall be preſent at the laying the Levies for the reſpective Counties of this Government, ſhall from time to time be, and are hereby declared to be Judges of all ſuch Poor within their County, who ſhall receive Relief out of the publick Stock of the ſaid County, and of the weekly, monthly, quarterly or yearly Sums of Money, to be paid them, or to any other Perſon or Perſons, for their Uſe, by the Treaſurer of the ſaid County ; which Sums of Money the ſaid Treaſurer is hereby impowered and required to pay, in ſuch Manner as the Court of Levies ſhall direct, out of the publick Money of the ſaid County in his Hands, or to come to his Hands ; and the ſaid Sums of Money by proper Receipts appearing to be paid, ſhall be allowed to the ſaid Treaſurer in the making up his Accounts at the next Court for the laying the Levies for the ſaid County.

Juſtices, Aſſeſſors, and 8 of the Grand Jury to judge what Poor ſhall receive Relief, &c.

AND

Persons falling into Poverty between two Courts, how to proceed.

AND if any Person or Persons having a legal Settlement within any of the Counties of this Government, shall fall into Decay or Poverty, between any Two Courts for laying the Levies for the same County, upon Complaint or Application by him, her or them made to the Overseer or Overseers of the Poor of the Hundred to which such poor Person or Persons doth or do belong, and any Two Justices of the Peace of the same County, if the said Justices and Overseer or Overseers shall judge such Person or Persons entituled to Relief out of the publick Stock of the County, then the said Justices and Overseer or Overseers shall under their Hands certify the same to the Treasurer of the County, which Certificate shall contain an Order on the Treasurer for such Sum or Sums of Money that shall from time to time be paid to such poor Person or Persons, and the Time or Times when the same shall be paid, whether weekly, monthly or quarterly, until the next Court for laying the Levies; which Sum or Sums of Money the said Treasurer shall and is hereby impowered and required to pay to such Person or Persons, or to some other proper Person for him, her or them; and the said Certificate or Certificates, with proper Receipts for the Sum or Sums of Money by virtue thereof paid, being produced by the Treasurer at the next Court for laying the Levies, shall be allowed to, and discharge the said Treasurer, for so much Money by him paid to any such poor Person or Persons as aforesaid.

Poor Persons to wear a Badge, &c.

AND BE IT FURTHER ENACTED by the Authority aforesaid, That every poor Person, whose Name shall stand on the List of any of the Counties of this Government as one of the Poor of the said County, shall on the Right Sleeve, or on the Back of his or her upper Garment, in an open and visible Manner, wear such Badge or Mark as herein after is mentioned and expressed, *That is to say*, A large Roman or Capital P, together with the first Letter of the Name of the County whereof such poor Person is an Inhabitant, cut either in Red or Blue Cloath, as by the Overseers of the Poor of the Hundred wherein such poor Person doth reside, shall be directed and appointed: And if any such poor Person within any County within this Government, shall at any time neglect or refuse to wear such Badge or Mark as aforesaid, upon Complaint and due Proof thereof made before any One Justice of the Peace of the said County, or upon the View of such Justice, the said Justice shall, and is hereby required

by

by Writing under his Hand to the Treasurer directed, stop Payment of such poor Person's Relief or usual Allowance, until the next Time of the laying the Levies for the said County: And if any Treasurer of any of the Counties of this Government, shall, after such Writing as aforesaid to him shewn, pay to such poor Person any Sum or Sums of Money; the same shall be at his own Risque, and shall not be allowed him in the making up his Accounts of the publick Money by him received.

AND BE IT FURTHER ENACTED by the Authority aforesaid, That all and every Act and Acts of Assembly of this Government heretofore made for the Relief of the Poor, and every Article, Clause and Thing in all and every such Act and Acts contained, be, and the same are hereby, repealed, annulled and made void, to all Intents and Purposes whatsoever.

Former Acts repealed.

Signed by Order of the House,

JEHU CURTIS, *Speaker.*

An ACT *against spreading false News and Defamation.*

FOR the restraining of evil-minded Persons who by seditious Words or Libels may endeavour to disturb the publick Peace and Quiet of this Government, or defame any of the Inhabitants thereof;

BE IT ENACTED by the Honourable GEORGE THOMAS, Esq; by and with His Majesty's Royal Approbation, Lieutenant-Governor and Commander in Chief of the Counties of New-Castle, Kent and Sussex on Delaware, and Province of Pennsylvania, by and with the Advice and Consent of the Representatives of the Freemen of the said Counties in General Assembly met, and by the Authority of the same; That if any Person shall speak or write any Thing tending to the Disturbance of the Peace of this Government, or shall maliciously report and spread abroad false News tending thereto, such Person, being thereof legally convicted in any Court of Quarter-Sessions in this Government, upon Presentment or Indictment, shall

Iii   be be fined by the said Court in any Sum not less than *Five Pounds*, nor exceeding *Twenty Pounds*, or suffer Three Months Imprisonment at hard Labour in the House of Correction. And that all the Fines and Forfeitures arising by this Act, shall be paid to the Governor for the Time being, for the Support of Government.

AND BE IT FURTHER ENACTED by the Authority aforesaid, That whosoever shall slander or defame any Person whatsoever within this Government, the Person or Persons so slandered or defamed may bring his or their Action at Law against such Slanderer or Slanderers; and if the Plaintiff in such Action shall obtain a Verdict, although the Damages given may be under *Forty Shillings*, the Plaintiff in such Action or Actions shall recover his or her Costs, in such Manner as he or she should have done in case the Jury had found Damages to the Value of above the Sum of *Forty Shillings*. And all former Acts of Assembly of this Government concerning Defamation and Slander, are hereby repealed.

Signed by Order of the House,

JEHU CURTIS, *Speaker.*

An ACT *about Contracts and Assumptions.*

BE IT ENACTED by the Honourable *GEORGE THOMAS*, Esq; by and with His Majesty's Royal Approbation, Lieutenant-Governor and Commander in Chief of the Counties of *New-Castle, Kent* and *Sussex* on *Delaware*, and Province of *Pennsylvania*, by and with the Advice and Consent of the Representatives of the Freemen of the said Counties in General Assembly met, and by the Authority of the same; That from and after the Publication of this Act, all Promises and Assumptions for any Matter under the Value of *Forty Shillings*, whereby any Person shall undertake to answer or pay for the Default, Miscarriage or Debt of another, being proved by the Oath or Affirmation of the Person or Persons to whom any such Promise or Assumption is or shall be made, are hereby declared to be good and valid to charge the Party or Parties making such Promise or Assumption.

AND

AND BE IT FURTHER ENACTED by the Authority aforesaid, That no Contract or Agreement whatsoever for any Matter of the Value of *Forty Shillings* or upwards, and not exceeding *Ten Pounds,* shall be good or effectual to charge any of the Parties thereto, unless the same be proved by the Oath or Affirmation of One legal Witness, or shall be reduced into Writing signed or subscribed by the Party or Parties to be charged thereby, except for Goods sold and delivered, in which Case the Oath or Affirmation of the Plaintiff, joined to a Book regularly, and fairly kept, shall be good and sufficient Evidence.

AND BE IT FURTHER ENACTED by the Authority aforesaid, That an Act of General Assembly of this Government, entituled, *An Act about verbal Contracts,* shall be, and the same is hereby repealed.

Signed by Order of the House,

JEHU CURTIS, *Speaker.*

An ACT *to encourage the Killing of Wolves within this Government.*

BE IT ENACTED by the Honourable *GEORGE THOMAS,* Esq; by and with His Majesty's Royal Approbation, Lieutenant-Governor and Commander in Chief of the Counties of *New-Castle, Kent* and *Sussex* on *Delaware,* and Province of *Pennsylvania,* by and with the Advice and Consent of the Representatives of the Freemen of the said Counties in General Assembly met, and by the Authority of the same; That if any Person shall kill any Wolf, and shall bring the Head thereof to any Justice of the Peace of any of the Counties of this Government, and upon Oath or Affirmation declare that such Wolf was kill'd within the County to which such Justice doth or shall belong; every such Person shall receive for killing a grown Wolf, the Sum of *Fifteen Shillings,* and for killing a Whelp or Puppy, the Sum of *Ten Shillings,* to be paid by the Treasurer of the County out of the publick Money of the said County, raised or to be raised as County-Levies

Levies are; and the said Justice shall cause the Ears of every such Wolf or Puppy to be cut off, and shall give unto such Person a Receipt and Certificate to the said Treasurer, who is hereby directed and required to pay the said Money to the Person who killed such Wolf, or his Order.

Signed by Order of the House,

JEHU CURTIS, *Speaker.*

An ACT to prevent Abuses committed by destroying Timber and other Trees within this Government.

Penalty on falling Timber on the Land of others.

BE IT ENACTED by the Honourable GEORGE THOMAS, Esq; by and with His Majesty's Royal Approbation, Lieutenant-Governor and Commander in Chief of the Counties of *New-Castle,* *Kent* and *Sussex* upon *Delaware,* and Province of *Pennsylvania,* by and with the Advice and Consent of the Representatives of the Freemen of the said Counties in General Assembly met, and by the Authority of the same; That if any Person or Persons shall fall or cut down any Timber, Tree or Trees upon the Land of any other Person or Persons within this Government, without Leave first had of the Owner or Oweners thereof, every such Person so offending shall for every such Tree so fallen or cut down, forfeit the Sum of *Fifty Shillings,* to be recovered with Costs of Suit, by Action of Trespass to be brought upon this Act by the Party injured; and in case such Trespasser or Trespassers shall not be able to pay such Damages and Costs as aforesaid, he or or they shall be adjudged by the Justices of the Court, wherein a Verdict shall be obtained against such Offender or Offender or Offenders, to make Satisfaction for the said Damages and Costs, by Servitude for any Term of Time not exceeding Four Years.

What shall be deemed a Timber Tree.

AND that every Tree which at the Distance of Two Feet from the Ground shall be found or deemed to measure One Foot over, or more, shall be adjudged a Timber Tree.

AND

AND BE IT FURTHER ENACTED by the Authority aforesaid, That if any Person or Persons shall fall or cut down any Fire- or Under-Wood on the Land of another Person or Persons within this Government, without Leave first had as aforesaid, every such Person so offending shall forfeit treble the Value of all such Fire- or Under-Wood so fallen or cut down, with Costs of Suit, to be recovered in Manner above-mentioned; and for want of Goods and Chattels to satisfy such Damages and Costs, the Offender shall be adjudged by the Justices of the Court wherein a Verdict shall be given against such Offender or Offenders, to make Satisfaction for the said Damages and Costs by Servitude as aforesaid.

AND BE IT FURTHER ENACTED by the Authority aforesaid, That an Act of Assembly of this Government, entituled, *An Act about cutting Timber Trees*, shall be and is hereby repealed.

A former Act repealed.

Signed by Order of the House,

JEHU CURTIS, *Speaker.*

An ACT *against trusting Mariners.*

TO the end that no Ship or Vessel may be detained from proceeding in the intended Voyage by the Arrest of any Sailor or Mariner shipped or belonging to any such Ship or Vessel in any Port or Harbour within this Government; BE IT ENACTED by the Honourable *GEORGE THOMAS*, Esq; by and with His Majesty's Royal Approbation, Lieutenant-Governor and Commander in Chief of the Counties of *New-Castle, Kent* and *Sussex* on *Delaware,* and Province of *Pennsylvania,* by and with the Advice and Consent of the Representatives of the Freemen of the said Counties in General Assembly met, and by the Authority of the same; That no Tavernkeeper or Innholder or other Person within this Government, shall trust any Sailor or Mariner shipped or belonging to any Ship or Vessel in any Port or Harbour within this Government, above the Sum of *Ten Shillings,* unless the Master, Commander or Owner of such Ship or Vessel, to which such Sailor or Mariner belongs, give his

K k k

or

or their Orders or Confent for the trufting fuch Sailor or Mariner. And that no Perfon trufting any Sailor or Mariner belonging to, or fhipp'd as aforefaid, for any Value above the Sum of *Ten Shillings*, without fuch Order or Confent as aforefaid, after Tender to him or her made of the faid Sum of *Ten Shillings*, and Cofts, if any fhall have arifen, fhall ftop or hinder fuch Sailor or Mariner from proceeding the intended Voyage for which he fhall then be fhipp'd, any Law, Cuftom or Ufage to the contrary notwithftanding.

Signed by Order of the Houfe,

JEHU CURTIS, *Speaker.*

An ACT to prevent Duelling and fighting of Duels within this Government.

FOR preventing of Duelling and fighting of Duels within this Government; BE IT ENACTED by the Honourable *GEORGE THOMAS*, Efq; by and with His Majefty's Royal Approbation, Lieutenant-Governor and Commander in Chief of the Counties of *New-Cafle*, *Kent* and *Suffex* on *Delaware*, and Province of *Pennfylvania*, by and with the Advice and Confent of the Reprefentatives of the Freemen of the faid Counties in General Affembly met, and by the Authority of the fame; That if any Perfon within this Government fhall challenge any other Perfon to fight with Sword, Piftol, Rapier, or any other dangerous and deftructive Weapon, every fuch Perfon fo challenging, being legally convicted thereof, by Bill, Plaint or Information, in any Court of Quarter-Seffions within this Government, fhall forfeit and pay the Sum of *Twenty Pounds*, or fuffer Three Months Imprifonment in the common Goal of the faid County.

AND if any Perfon fhall carry or deliver to another Perfon any fuch Challenge, knowing it to be fuch, every fuch Perfon carrying or delivering fuch Challenge, being legally convicted as aforefaid, fhall forfeit and pay the like Sum of *Twenty Pounds*, or fuffer Three Months Imprifonment as aforefaid.

AND

AND if any Person shall accept any such Challenge, and meet the Person challenging in order to fight as aforesaid, every such Person so offending, and being thereof legally convicted as aforesaid, shall forfeit and pay the Sum of *Ten Pounds*, or suffer Six Weeks Imprisonment as aforesaid.

Signed by Order of the House,

JEHU CURTIS, *Speaker.*

An ACT *to prevent Ston'd Horses under Size from running at large within this Government.*

FORASMUCH as the Generation and Breed of good and strong Horses within this Government, is of great Benefit and Profit to the Inhabitants thereof; Therefore, for the Increase of such,

BE IT ENACTED by the Honourable *GEORGE THOMAS*, Esq; by and with His Majesty's Royal Approbation, Lieutenant-Governor and Commander in Chief of the Counties of *New-Castle*, *Kent* and *Sussex* on *Delaware*, and Province of *Pennsylvania*, by and with the Advice and Consent of the Representatives of the Freemen of the said Counties in General Assembly met, and by the Authority of the same ; That from and after the *First* Day of *June*, in the Year of our Lord *One Thousand Seven Hundred and Forty-two*, between the *First* Day of *March* and the *First* Day of *November* yearly and every Year, no Ston'd Horse or Horses above the Age of Two Years, and not being of the Height of Thirteen Hands and an Half, to be measured from the lowest Part of the Hoof of the Fore-Foot to the highest Part of the Wither, and each Hand to contain Four Inches, shall by the Owner or Owners thereof be permitted to range or run at large in any of the Wood-lands or Marshes within this Government. And if any such Horse, above the Age of Two Years, and under the Height of Thirteen Hands and an Half as aforesaid, shall within the Time above-limited be found at large as aforesaid, it shall and may be lawful to and for any Freeholder within this Government, finding such Horse,

No Ston'd Horse under Thirteen Hands and a half, shall be permitted to go at large.

to

to take up the same, and him to bring to the next Juſtice of the Peace of the County wherein the ſaid Horſe ſhall be taken up; which ſaid Juſtice ſhall cauſe ſuch Horſe's Age and Height to be enquired into, or examined and meaſured, and upon finding him to be above the Age of Two Years, and under the Height by this Act required, the ſaid Juſtice ſhall, and is hereby impowered and required to adminiſter an Oath or Affirmation to the Perſon or Perſons taking up ſuch Horſe, that he or they did find the ſaid Ston'd Horſe at large within the ſaid County, and that neither he or they or any other Perſon or Perſons for him or them, or by his or their Means, Privity or Procurement, or to his or their Knowledge, did drive or turn the ſaid Horſe out of the Incloſure of any Perſon or Perſons whatſoever, or did pull or lay down the Fence or Fences or any Part thereof, or open any Gate or Door of any Perſon or Perſons, with Intent that the ſaid Horſe might go out of ſuch Incloſure: Whereupon the ſaid Juſtice ſhall cauſe Notice to be given to the Owner of ſuch Horſe, if known, requiring him immediately to appear before him; and upon Appearance of ſuch Owner or ſome other proper Perſon for him, the ſaid Juſtice ſhall order the ſaid Owner to pay unto the Perſon or Perſons taking up the ſaid Horſe, the Sum of

Penalty. *Twenty Shillings*, to be recovered, together with Coſts, in like Manner as Debts under *Forty Shillings*. And the ſaid Juſtice ſhall cauſe the ſaid Horſe to be delivered to ſuch Owner or other proper Perſon for him, and order him to have the ſaid Horſe cut or gelded within the ſpace of Three Days then next following. And if the Owner of ſuch Horſe ſhall neglect or refuſe to cauſe the ſaid Horſe to be gelded as aforeſaid, and the ſame Horſe ſhall afterwards be found at large, and not gelded, upon Complaint and due Proof thereof made before any Two Juſtices of the Peace of the ſaid County, the Owner of the ſaid Horſe ſhall forfeit

Farther Penalty the ſaid Horſe, or pay the Sum of *Five Pounds*, to be recovered by Diſtreſs and Sale of ſuch Owner's Goods and Chattels, by Warrant under the Hands and Seals of the ſaid Juſtices, and paid, the one Moiety thereof to the Treaſurer of the County for the Uſe of the Poor of the ſaid County, the other Moiety to the Informer; or the Horſe forfeited ſhall be gelded and ſold as in this Act after directed; and after Payment of all neceſſary Charges, the Money ariſing by the Sale, ſhall be applied and paid as aforeſaid.

AND

AND if upon Notice given to the Owner of any Ston'd Horse taken up, and found under Size as aforesaid, the Owner shall refuse or neglect to appear before the said Justice, or to send some proper Person in his Behalf or Stead, or if the Owner of any such Horse shall not be known, then the said Justice shall order the Taker-up of any such Horse to lead or take him to some proper and skilful Person, by the said Justice to be named, and the same Horse to cause to be cut or gelded at the Risque of the Owner thereof, and the Taker-up shall take into his Care and Keeping the said Horse, until cured ; for which Cutting, Keeping and Service there shall be paid to the said Taker-up by the Owner of such Horse, or out of the Money arising by the Sale thereof, the Sum of *Ten Shillings* over and above the aforesaid Sum of *Twenty Shillings :* And the said Taker-up shall put up in Three of the most publick Places of the Hundred wherein the said Horse was taken up, Advertisements describing the Size, Colour, Age and Marks of the said Horse, and setting forth, that if the Owner thereof shall not before the End of Fifteen Days then next following, come in, and prove his Property, and pay the Charges, the said Horse will be sold at publick Vendue. And in case no Owner shall within the said Fifteen Days claim the said Horse and pay Charges as aforesaid, then the said Horse, being duly advertised as aforesaid, shall by Order of the said Justice be sold at publick Vendue, by some Constable of the same Hundred, and the Money arising by the Sale shall be delivered to the said Justice, who out of the same shall pay to the Taker-up his Charges for taking up, cutting and keeping the said Horse, and his own and the Constable's Fees ; and the Overplus, if any be, shall remain in the Hands of the said Justice, for the Use of the Owner of such Horse, if within Six Months after such Sale, he shall come in, and to the Satisfaction of such Justice prove his or her Property therein. And in case no Owner shall, within the space of Six Months aforesaid, prove his or her Property aforesaid, the said Overplus Money shall by the said Justice be paid to the Treasurer of the County, for the Use of the Poor of the said County ; and the said Owner shall for ever after be foreclosed and debarred from any Title or Claim thereto.

The Owner not appearing, or not being known, the Justice shall order such Horse to be cut, &c:

Advertisements to be put up.

No Claim being made in 15 days the Horse shall be sold, &c:

AND BE IT ENACTED, That no Person other than a Freeholder within this Government, shall be entituled to any Reward for taking up any such Ston'd Horse under Size as aforesaid.

None but Freeholders may claim the Reward, &c.

AND BE IT FURTHER ENACTED

Sales of Horses by virtue of this Act, shall be good. by the Authority aforesaid, That all and every Sale and Sales of any Horse and Horses hereafter to be made by virtue of this Act, shall be good and available in Law, to all Intents and Purposes whatsoever; and that the Buyer and Buyers of every such Horse and Horses, shall, or lawfully may hold and retain the same Horse and Horses and every of them, to his and their own proper Use, as his and their own proper Goods and Chattels, without any Let, Interruption, Vexation, Suit or Trouble of the former Owner or Owners of them or any of them, or any other Person or Persons whatsoever.

AND BE IT FURTHER ENACTED

Repeal of a former Law. by the Authority aforesaid, That an Act of General Assembly of this Government, entituled, *A Law preventing Stoned Horses under the Height of Thirteen Hands and an Half, from running at large,* shall be, and the same is hereby repealed.

Signed by Order of the House,

JEHU CURTIS, *Speaker.*

An ACT concerning Rangers and Strays.

WHEREAS many and great Abuses have been and daily are committed within this Government by Persons taking up, working, riding and abusing stray Creatures, and marking or branding such unmarked Creatures as do not belong to them; For Prevention whereof,

BE IT ENACTED by the Honourable *GEORGE THOMAS*, Esq; by and with His Majesty's Royal Approbation, Lieutenant-Governor and Commander in Chief of the Counties of *New-Castle*, *Kent* and *Sussex* on *Delaware*, and Province of *Pennsylvania*, by and with the Advice and Consent of the Representatives of the Freemen of the said Counties in General Assembly met, and by the *No Horse, &c. to be deemed stray, if under 18 Months old, unless &c.* Authority of the same; That no Horse, Mare, Colt or horned Cattle shall be taken or deemed to be stray, unless the same be of the Age of Eighteen Months at the least, except such as follow their Dams being Strays; and that no Person

son or Persons whatsoever, at any Time after the Publication of this Act, shall take up as a Stray any unmark'd Horse, Gelding, Mare, Colt, or any other Cattle, that shall be under the Age of Eighteen Months, except such as are before excepted, under the Penalty of *Five Pounds,* to be recovered in Manner as herein after directed. But if any such Beasts or Cattle, as aforesaid, of the Age of Eighteen Months or upwards, be found at large, it shall and may be lawful to take up and carry the same to the Ranger of the respective County wherein such Beasts or Cattle shall be so taken up, to be secured and disposed of according to Law. And every Person who shall mark or brand any Horse, Gelding, Mare, Colt, or Horned Cattle, not belonging to him or her, shall be deemed, and is hereby declared guilty of Felony, and shall be prosecuted and punished accordingly.

Penalty on taking up such young Creatures

Marking the Horses, &c. of others, is Felony

AND BE IT FURTHER ENACTED by the Authority aforesaid, That no Person or Persons whatsoever shall presume to take up any mark'd Horse, Gelding, Mare, Colt, or other Cattle, before the same shall have been astray from the Owner for the space of Two Months next before, unless such Horse, Gelding, Mare, Colt, or other Cattle shall trespass upon, or prejudice such Person or Persons; and then and in such case the Person taking up any such Creature or Creatures, and not knowing the Owner or Owners thereof, shall take or lead the same to the next Justice of the Peace of the County wherein the said Trespass shall be committed, and shall upon Oath or Affirmation declare, that he doth not know who is the Owner or Owners thereof, and that the said Stray or Strays hath or have really trespassed upon him or her, without his or their Default; which Oath or Affirmation such Justice is hereby impowered and required to administer, and shall award to such Person or Persons for his or their Trouble of taking up, leading or driving to the Ranger such trespassing Creature or Creatures, such Satisfaction, as to the said Justice shall seem reasonable: For doing whereof, administring the said Oath or Affirmation and certifying the same under his Hand and Seal, the said Justice shall receive the Sum of *Eighteen Pence,* and no more; And the Sum awarded by such Justice, together with the said Sum of *Eighteen Pence,* shall by the Ranger of the County be paid to the said Person or Persons so trespassed upon, when the said trespassing Creature or Creatures shall by the Ranger be delivered to the Owner or Owners thereof, or after Sale thereof made by the Ranger, and Deduction of his Fees and Charges of

No Horse, &c. to be taken up, until it has been astray 2 Months, unless trespassing, &c,

The Method of proceeding with Trespassing Creatures.

keeping

keeping the same. And the said Person or Persons so trespassed upon as aforesaid, then and not before shall and lawfully may take, and deliver to the Ranger, together with the said Certificate, such Horse, Gelding, Mare, Colt, or other Cattle, in order to be entered in his Book.

How to proceed with Estrays not trespassing.

AND that no Person or Persons shall take up any mark'd Creature or Creatures not committing Trespass, unless the same shall have been stray'd or absent from the Owner at least for the space of Two Months; after which Time it shall and may be lawful to take up, and take and lead the same before a Justice as aforesaid, who shall administer such Oath or Affirmation as before directed, and make such reasonable Allowance as before mentioned, to be paid together with the like Fee to the Justice by the Ranger as aforesaid, and the Stray or Strays shall be delivered to the Ranger, in the Manner before appointed.

AND BE IT FURTHER ENACTED by the Authority aforesaid, That any Person or Persons who shall ride, work, use or abuse any Stray or Waif, upon Complaint and due Proof thereof made to any Two Justices of the Peace of the County wherein the Offence shall be committed, shall for the first Offence, forfeit by the Judgment of such Justices, the Value of such Stray or Waif, to be recovered together with Costs, by Distress and Sale of the Offender's Goods and Chattels, by Warrant under the Hands and Seals of the said Justices, and paid, the one Moiety thereof to the Informer, and the other Moiety to the Owner or Owners of such Stray or Strays, if known, and if not known, to one of the said Justices, for the Use of such Owner or Owners: But if within Six Months next after such Conviction, the said Owner or Owners shall not to the Satisfaction of such Justice, prove his or their Right to the Moiety of the said Fine, then the same shall by the said Justice be paid to the Treasurer of the County wherein the Offence is or shall be committed, for the Use of the Poor of the said County; and for every other Offence as aforesaid, such Offender or Offenders shall forfeit and pay double the Value of such Waif or Waifs, Stray or Strays, to be valued, recovered and disposed of, in Manner aforesaid. And if such Offender or Offenders shall not be able to pay such Forfeiture or Forfeitures as aforesaid, he or they shall and may be bound by such Two Justices of the respective County where such Offence shall be committed as aforesaid, to any Person or Persons, as such Two Justices shall think

Penalty on riding, working, &c. of Estrays.

proper,

proper, for any Term not exceeding Two Years, to make Satisfaction for the Forfeitures aforesaid.

PROVIDED NEVERTHELESS, That it shall and may be lawful to and for any Ranger within this Government, reasonably and moderately to work, ride and make use of, or to suffer or permit any other Person, reasonably and moderately to work, ride or make use of any such Stray as aforesaid, in order to defray the Charge of pasturing or keeping the same, so as such Stray so worked or used, shall have on and wear, at the Time of being so used or worked, a Wyth about the Neck of the same, and not otherwise. And if any Person or Persons shall work, ride or use any such Stray without a Wyth as aforesaid, every such Person shall for every such Neglect, forfeit the Sum of *Ten Shillings*, to be recovered and applied as aforesaid.

Ranger's may moderately work Estrays, &c.

AND BE IT FURTHER ENACTED by the Authority aforesaid, That every Ranger within this Government, shall and is hereby required to receive into his Custody every Horse, Gelding, Mare, Colt, and other Cattle brought to him with such Certificate, and shall enter the same in his Book; and the said Ranger shall and is hereby required to keep a fair Book, in which he shall enter in a fair and legible Hand-Writing, the Colours, Flesh-Marks and Brands of all Stray and Strays which any such Ranger shall take up, or which shall be brought to him, with the Date or Time when he shall take up the same, or they shall be brought to him; and shall within one Week after the Receipt of any such Stray or Strays, fix up at Three publick Places at least of the County to which such Ranger doth belong, Advertisements describing the Colour, Marks and Brands of such Stray or Strays; and if within One Month next after the bringing to the Ranger any such Stray, the Owner thereof shall come to the Ranger and prove his Property in the same as before directed, and shall pay to him for his Trouble the Sum of *Five Shillings*, and his reasonable Charges of keeping the same, and also the Sum awarded to the Taker-up, and Justice's Fee as aforesaid, then the Ranger shall deliver to such Owner the said Stray: And in case after the Expiration of the said Month, and before the Sale of any such Stray, the Owner thereof shall come in, and prove his Property in the same as aforesaid, if the Owner and Ranger do not agree as to the Value of the Stray, the same shall be valued by Two substantial,

Ranger to receive Estrays, and enter them in a Book, &c.

And put up Advertisements, &c.

M m m

honest

honeſt and judicious Freeholders of the reſpective County, to be qualified for that Purpoſe upon their Oath or Affirmation by ſome Juſtice of the Peace of the ſame County, and the Stray ſhall be delivered to the Owner, upon his paying to the Ranger for his Trouble at the Rate of *Three Shillings* in the *Pound* according to ſuch Valuation, and his reaſonable Charges of keeping, and the Charge for taking up, appraiſing, and Juſtice's Fees ariſen thereon.   But in caſe the Owner ſhall refuſe to pay the aforeſaid Charges, or ſhall not appear within the Times herein after limited for the Sale of Strays, then the Ranger ſhall cauſe ſuch Stray to be ſold at publick Vendue to the higheſt Bidder, and out of the Money ariſing by the Sale, ſhall reſerve to himſelf for his Trouble, at the Rate of *Three Shillings* in the *Pound* according to ſuch Sale, and his reaſonable Charges of keeping the Stray, whereof any Juſtice of the Peace of the ſame County ſhall and is hereby declared to be a proper Judge, and out of the Reſidue of the Money, if any be, ſhall pay to the Juſtice and Taker-up their reſpective Dues as aforeſaid.   And after Payment of all neceſſary Charges, the Reſidue of the Money ariſing by the ſaid Sale, if any be, ſhall remain in the Ranger's Hands, by him to be paid to the Owner of ſuch Stray, if within the ſpace of Six Months next after ſuch Sale he appear, and prove his Right to the ſame, to the Satisfaction of any One Juſtice of the Peace of the County to which ſuch Ranger belongs.   And if within the ſaid Six Months no ſuch Owner appear and prove his Right thereto as aforeſaid, then the Ranger ſhall account with the Proprietor for the ſame, as has been uſual heretoſore.

Owner refuſing to pay the Charges, &c. Eſtrays to be ſold, &c.

AND BE IT FURTHER ENACTED

by the Authority aforeſaid, That the Times of ſelling any Strays brought to the Ranger and entered on his Book, ſhall be as follows, *That is to ſay*, A treſpaſſing Stray ſhall and may be ſold at the End of Six Months, and other Strays at the End of Four Months next after the Entry thereof on the Ranger's Book, and not before: And the Ranger ſhall, and is hereby required, at every Court of Quarter-Seſſions, to be held for the County to which he belongs, to fix up at the Court-Houſe-Door, Advertiſements of all Strays on his Book, deſcribing the Age, Colour, Marks and Brands of ſuch Strays, and the Times when the ſame came to his Hands.

Times of ſelling Eſtrays.

AND

AND BE IT FURTHER ENACTED by the Authority aforesaid, That all Sale and Sales of any Stray and Strays, to be made by virtue of this Act, shall be good and available in Law, to all Intents and Purposes whatsoever; and that the Buyer and Buyers of any such Stray and Strays shall and lawfully may hold and retain the same, and every of them, to his and their own proper Use, as his and their proper Goods and Chattels, without any Let, Interruption, Vexation, Suit or Trouble of the former Owner or Owners of them or any of them, or any other Person or Persons whatsoever.

Sales made by virtue of this Act, shall be good.

AND BE IT FURTHER ENACTED by the Authority aforesaid, That if any Person shall without Leave take any Stray entered upon the Book of any Ranger within this Government, or Waif out of the Inclosure of such Ranger, or of any other Person to whom the same shall by the said Ranger be delivered to be kept; every such Offender shall be deemed a Horse-stealer, and being legally convicted thereof, shall be punished as such.

Taking Estrays out of the Ranger's Enclosure without leave, shall be deemed Horse stealing.

AND BE IT FURTHER ENACTED by the Authority aforesaid, That nothing in this Act contained, shall be construed, deemed or taken to repeal an Act of General Assembly of this Government, made in the Twelfth Year of His Majesty's Reign, entituled, *An Act for erecting a Pound in the Town of* New-Castle; or any Part thereof: And that an Act of Assembly of this Government, entituled, *An Act preventing Abuses committed by Rangers, and other Inhabitants of this Government*, shall be, and the same is hereby repealed.

A former Act repealed.

PROVIDED, That this Act shall continue in Force for Three Years, from the *Twentieth* Day of *October* next, and no longer.

Limitation.

Signed by Order of the House,

JEHU CURTIS, *Speaker.*

An

An ACT *directing and impowering the several Sheriffs within this Government, to summon a sufficient Number of Freeholders to serve as Jurors in the several Counties thereof.*

Sheriffs shall summon 24 G. and 48 Petit Jurors, ten Days before the Court.

BE IT ENACTED by the Honourable GEORGE THOMAS, Esq; by and with His Majesty's Royal Approbation, Lieutenant-Governor and Commander in Chief of the Counties of *New-Castle, Kent* and *Sussex* on *Delaware*, and Province of *Pennsylvania*, by and with the Advice and Content of the Representatives of the Freemen of the said Counties in General Assembly met, and by the Authority of the same; That the Sheriffs of the respective Counties within this Government, shall upon receiving a Writ of *Venire facias*, to be to them respectively directed for summoning a Jury to attend a Court of Oyer and Terminer within any of the said Counties, forthwith proceed to summon Twenty-four of the most able, sufficient and substantial Freeholders within their respective Bailywick to serve as Grand-Jurors, and Forty-eight of the most discreet and judicious Freeholders to serve as Peti-Jurors, at the Court aforesaid; which said Grand-Jurors and Petit-Jurors shall be summoned at least Ten Days before the Day appointed for holding the said Courts within the said Counties. And if any of the said Jurors

Penalty on their not attending.

so summoned as aforesaid, shall refuse or neglect to attend at the said Courts, they and every of them shall be fined by the said Court, according to the Directions of an Act of General Assembly of this Government, entituled, *An Act against Jurors absenting themselves, being lawfully summoned to attend the several Courts of Judicature within this Government.*

Penalty on Sheriffs returning Jurors not so summoned.

AND BE IT FURTHER ENACTED by the Authority aforesaid, That if any Sheriff or Sheriffs from and after the End of this present Sessions of Assembly, shall or do return any Person or Persons to serve as aforesaid, when in Truth such Person or Persons shall not have been summoned according to the Directions aforesaid, such Sheriff or Sheriffs shall for every such Offence, be fined by the said Court, in any Sum not exceeding *Ten Pounds*, and shall be committed till such Fine shall be paid. And if any Sheriff or Sheriffs shall refuse or neglect to summon **and**

and return Persons to serve on the Juries as before directed, whereby Justice may be delayed, if not altogether eluded; such Sheriff or Sheriffs shall for every such Refusal or Neglect, be fined by the said Court in any Sum not exceeding *One Hundred Pounds*, and shall be committed until such Fine be paid, and be disabled from holding or exercising the said Office, during the Term of Three Years then next ensuing.

AND BE IT FURTHER ENACTED by the Authority aforesaid, That the respective Sheriffs of the several and respective Counties within this Government, shall, at least Ten Days before *May*-Sessions yearly and every Year, without any Writ of *Venire facias*, proceed to summon and return Twenty-four substantial and judicious Freeholders, lawful Men, and Inhabitants of his Bailywick, to serve as Grand-Jurymen at the next *May*-Sessions aforesaid; which said Persons, or a sufficient Number of them, so summoned and returned, shall be and remain the standing Grand-Jury for that Year: But the Justices of the respective Courts of Quarter-Sessions are hereby required to administer or cause to be administred to the said Jurors every Sessions the Qualifications usual for the faithful Discharge of their Duty and Trust. And the Sheriffs of the said respective Counties are hereby required to summon Twenty-four able, discreet and judicious Freeholders, legal Men, and Inhabitants in the Bailywick to such Sheriffs respectively belonging, at least Ten Days before each and every Court of Quarter-Sessions, to serve as Petit-Jurymen for the Court or Sessions to which they are summoned, and make Return of the Persons so summoned, at the respective Sessions; which Persons so summoned and returned by the Sheriffs as aforesaid to serve as Grand- and Petit-Jurors, are hereby required to attend the respective Courts, upon Pain of being fined by the Courts for such their Default, according to the Directions of the Act of Assembly aforesaid. Provided always, That no Person shall be obliged to serve as a Grand-Juryman for Two Years successively in any of the said Counties.

A standing Grand Jury to be summoned for the Year.

But to be qualified every Sessions.

Petit-Jurors to be summoned, &c.

AND BE IT FURTHER ENACTED by the Authority aforesaid, That the Sheriffs of the respective Counties of this Government, shall, and are hereby required and authorized, from time to time and at all Times hereafter, when and as often as Occasion may require, to summon all and every other Inquests, or Jurors which

Sheriffs to summon all other Inquests, &c.

Sheriffs

Sheriffs ought to summon, or Evidences requisite and necessary for the executing Justice within their respective Counties, who are hereby required to give due Attendance accordingly; and the Neglects or Defaults of the Sheriffs aforesaid, or any of them, shall be punished by Fine as aforesaid.

Duty of Coroners in particular Cases.

AND BE IT FURTHER ENACTED by the Authority aforesaid, That the Coroners of the respective Counties aforesaid, shall and are hereby required to conduct, regulate and behave themselves in summoning Juries, or other Matters where the Sheriff cannot legally do it by reason of his Affinity to any Suitors, or otherwise, in the same Manner and Form as the Sheriffs are by this Act directed and impowered, under the like Penalties to be inflicted and laid upon Sheriffs for Neglects and Defaults contrary to this Act. And all Persons are hereby required, in such Cases, to pay the same Obedience and Attendance to the Precepts and Summons of such Coroner or Coroners as before directed, to the Precepts and Summons of the Sheriffs aforesaid, under the like Penalties as above-mentioned; and generally to do and execute all other Matters and Things, which to their Offices by the Laws of that Part of *Great-Britain* called *England*, appertain, under the Penalties inflicted by the Laws of *England*, for such their Neglect or Default, so far as the same have received no Alteration by this Act.

Fines how to be disposed of.

AND BE IT FURTHER ENACTED by the Authority aforesaid, That all the Fines and Forfeitures arising or becoming due by virtue of this Act, shall be and remain the one Moiety thereof to the Governor for the Time being, towards the Support of Government, the other Moiety to be paid to the Treasurer of the County, for the Use of the Poor of the County where the Offence is or shall be committed.

Repeal of a former Act.

AND BE IT FURTHER ENACTED by the Authority aforesaid, That an Act of Assembly of this Government, entituled, *An Act for summoning of Juries and about Tryals by Twelve Men*, shall be and the same is hereby repealed.

Signed by Order of the House,
JEHU CURTIS, *Speaker.*

An

An ACT *for Limitation of Actions, and proving Accounts against the Estates of Persons dying within this Government.*

BE IT ENACTED by the Honourable *GEORGE THOMAS*, Eſq; by and with His Majeſty's Royal Approbation, Lieutenant-Governor and Commander in Chief of the Counties of *New-Caſtle*, *Kent* and *Suſſex* on *Delaware*, and Province of *Pennſylvania*, by and with the Advice and Conſent of the Repreſentatives of the Freemen of the ſaid Counties in General Aſſembly met, and by the Authority of the ſame ; That no Perſon or Perſons that now hath or have any Right or Title of Entry into any Lands, Tenements or Hereditaments, now held from him or them, ſhall thereinto enter, but within Twenty Years next after the End of this preſent Seſſion of General Aſſembly, or within Twenty Years next after any other Title of Entry accrued ; and that no Perſon or Perſons ſhall at any Time hereafter, make any Entry into any Lands, Tenements or Hereditaments, but within Twenty Years next after his or their Right or Title, which ſhall hereafter firſt deſcend or accrue to the ſame : And in Default thereof, ſuch Perſon or Perſons ſo not entering and bringing his or their Action or Actions, and their Heirs, ſhall be utterly excluded and diſabled from ſuch Entry or Action to be made or brought, any former Law, Statute or Act of Aſſembly to the contrary notwithſtanding.

Perſons having Right of Entry into Lands, &c. ſhall not enter after 20 Years, &c.

AND BE IT FURTHER ENACTED by the Authority aforeſaid, That all Actions of Treſpaſs, Treſpaſs *vi et armis*, *Quare clauſum fregit*, all Actions of Detinue, Trover and Replevin for taking away Goods or Cattle, all Actions upon Account and upon the Caſe, (other than ſuch Accounts as concern the Trade of Merchandize between Merchant and Merchant, their Factors and Servants) all Actions of Debt grounded upon any Lending or Contract without Specialty, all Actions of Debt for Arrearages of Rent (the Proprietor's Quit-rent excepted) all Actions of Treſpaſs, Aſſault, Menace, Battery, Wounding and Impriſonment, or any of them, which ſhall be ſued or brought at any Time after the Publication of this Act, ſhall be commenced and ſued within the Time and Limit hereafter expreſſed, and not after, *That is to ſay,* The ſaid Actions upon the Caſe (other than for Slander) **and**

Actions of Treſpaſs, &c. within what Time to be commenced.

and the said Actions of Account, and said Actions of Debt, Detinue and Replevin for Goods or Cattle, within Three Years after the Cause of such Actions or Suits, and not after. And the said Actions of Trespass, other than for Assault, Battery, Menace, Wounding or Imprisonment, and the said Actions of Trespass *quare clausum fregit*, within Three Years after the Cause of such Actions or Suits, and not after. And the said Actions of Trespass for Assault, Menace, Battery, Wounding, Imprisonment, or any of them, within One Year next after the Cause of such Actions or Suits, and not after. And the said Actions upon the Case for Words, within One Year next after the Words spoken, and not after.

AND NEVERTHELESS BE IT EN-ACTED, That if in any of the said Actions or Suits, Judgment be given for the Plaintiff or Plaintiffs, and the same be reversed by Error, or a Verdict pass for the Plaintiff or Plaintiffs, and upon Matter alledged in Arrest of Judgment, the Judgment be arrested and stayed, and Judgment therefore be given that the Plaintiff or Plaintiffs take nothing by his or their Plaint, Writ or Bill, That in all such Cases the Plaintiff or Plaintiffs, and his or their Heirs, Executors or Administrators, as the Case may require, where the Action shall not by Law die with the Person, may commence a new Action or Suit from time to time within a Year after such Judgment reversed, stayed or given against the Plaintiff or Plaintiffs as aforesaid, and not after.

In what Cases a new Action may be commenced.

AND BE IT FURTHER ENACTED, That in all Actions of Trespass *quare clausum fregit*, hereafter to be brought, wherein the Defendant or Defendants shall in his or their Plea disclaim any Title or Claim to the Land in which the Trespass shall be in the Declaration supposed to be done, and the Trespass be by Negligence or involuntary, the Defendant or Defendants shall be admitted to plead a Disclaimer, and that the Trespass was by Negligence or involuntary, and a Tender or Offer of sufficient Amends for such Trespass before the Action brought; whereupon, or upon some of them, the Plaintiff or Plaintiffs shall be enforced to join Issue; and if the said Issue be found for the Defendant or Defendants, or the Plaintiff or Plaintiffs shall be non-suited, the Plaintiff or Plaintiffs shall be clearly barred from the said Action or Actions, and all other Suit concerning the same.

Defendant in Actions of Trespass, &c. may plead a Disclaimer, &c.

PRO-

PROVIDED ALWAYS NEVERTHE-
LESS, That if any Person or Persons, who is or shall
be entitled to any such Action of Trespass, Detinue, Trover, Replevin, Actions of Account or Debt, Actions of
Trespass for Assault, Menace, Battery, Wounding or Imprisonment, Actions upon the Case for Words, are or at
the Time of any Cause of such Action given, or accrued,
fallen or come, shall be within the Age of Twenty-one
Years, Feme Covert, *non compos mentis*, imprisoned, or beyond Sea, or out of this Government ; That then and in
such Case, such Person or Persons shall be at Liberty to
bring the same Actions, so as the same be brought within
such Times as are hereby before limited, after their coming
to or being of full Age, Discoverture, of sound Memory,
at large, or returning into this Government.

Persons within Age, non compos, &c. being entituled to Actions, may afterwards bring the same, so as, &c.

AND if any Person or Persons, against whom any of
the Causes of Action beforementioned do arise, shall at the
Time of the Cause of Suit or Action arising, or afterwards
before the Time of bringing such Action be expired, be
beyond Seas, or go out of his Government; then the Person
entituled to such Suit, may bring an Action after the Return of such Person, so as he bring the same within such
Time after the Return, as is before limited by this Act.

AND forasmuch as many Evils may arise, and great
Frauds be committed, by suffering Persons to prove Accounts of long standing against the Estates of Persons dying
within this Government ; for Prevention whereof, BE IT
ENACTED by the Authority aforesaid, That no Person or Persons whatsoever, from and after the Publication
of this Act, who doth not or shall not keep a Day-Book
or other regular Book of Account, shall be admitted to
prove or require Payment of any Account or Demand against
the Estate of any Person or Persons dying within this Government, if such Account or Demand shall appear to be
older or of any longer standing than One Year next before
the Death of the deceased Person, unless such Person or
Persons so pretending to be a Creditor or Creditors of the
Deceased, shall be able clearly to make appear by one good
and sufficient Evidence at least, that his Debt or Demand
is just and true : And that no Person or Persons whatsoever
who do or shall keep regular Books of Account, shall be
admitted to prove or require Payment of any Account or
Demand against the Estates of Persons so dying as aforesaid,
if such Account or Demand shall appear to be older or of

Accounts a-gainst the E-states of Persons deceased, may not be proved, unless, &c.

any

any longer ftanding than Three Years next before the Death
of fuch Perfon or Perfons fo dying or deceafed as aforefaid.

AND BE IT FURTHER ENACTED
Repeal of a by the Authority aforefaid, That the Act of Affembly
former Act. of this Government, entituled, *An Act for the Limitation
of Actions*, be and is hereby repealed.

Signed by Order of the Houfe,

JEHU CURTIS, *Speaker.*

An ACT *to prevent Frauds by clandeftine Bills of Sale.*

WHEREAS many Frauds have been and daily
are committed, by making clandeftine Bills of
Sale for Goods and Chattels within this Government, to the Prejudice of Creditors, who by that Means
are defrauded of their juft Debts; For Prevention whereof,

BE IT ENACTED by the Honourable
GEORGE THOMAS, Efq; by and with His Majefty's
Royal Approbation, Lieutenant-Governor and Commander
in Chief of the Counties of *New-Caftle*, *Kent* and *Suffex* on
Delaware, and Province of *Pennfylvania*, by and with the
Advice and Confent of the Reprefentatives of the Freemen
of the faid Counties in General Affembly met, and by the
Bill's of Sale Authority of the fame; That no Sale or Bill or Bills of
not good with- Sale which fhall hereafter be made of any Goods or Chat-
out valuable tels within any of the Counties of this Government, fhall
Confideration, be good or available in Law, or fhall change or alter the
&c. Property of fuch Goods or Chattels, unlefs a valuable Confideration fhall be paid, or really and *bona fide* fecured to be
paid for fuch Sale or Bill or Bills of Sale, and unlefs the
Goods and Chattels fold or contained in fuch Bill or Bills
of Sale, fhall be actually delivered into the Poffeffion of
the Vendee or Vendees, as foon as conveniently may be,
after the making of fuch Sale or Bill or Bills of Sale.

AND if fuch Goods and Chattels fold or contained or
mentioned in fuch Bill or Bills of Sale, fhall afterwards return or come into, and continue in the Poffeffion of fuch

Vendor

Vendor or Vendors, the fame fhall be chargeable and liable to the Demands of all Creditors of fuch Vendor or Vendors as aforefaid.

PROVIDED ALWAYS, AND BE IT FURTHER ENACTED by the Authority aforefaid, That all Bills of Sale made of Goods or Chattels within any of the Counties of this Government, by any Perfon or Perfons within the fame to any other Perfon or Perfons, fhall be good and effectual againft the Vendor or Vendors of fuch Goods and Chattels, any Thing herein contained to the contrary notwithftanding.

Signed by Order of the Houfe,

JEHU CURTIS, *Speaker.*

An ACT *for afcertaining the Proportion of the Government-Charges hereafter to be paid by the feveral Counties of* New-Caftle, Kent *and* Suffex *on* Delaware.

WHEREAS the Quotas or Sums of Money from time to time heretofore paid by the Inhabitants of the feveral Counties of this Government, towards the Support of the Governor, Travelling-Charges and Wages of Affemblymen, and other Charges of Seffions of Affembly, have not been duly proportioned according to the Abilities of the Inhabitants of the faid Counties refpectively;

BE IT THEREFORE ENACTED by the Honourable GEORGE THOMAS, Efq; by and with His Majefty's Royal Approbation, Lieutenant-Governor and Commander in Chief of the Counties of New-Caftle, Kent and Suffex on Delaware, and Province of Pennfylvania, by and with the Advice and Confent of the Reprefentatives of the Freemen of the faid Counties in General Affembly met, and by the Authority of the fame; That all and every Sum and Sums of Money at any time or times hereafter to be raifed upon the Inhabitants of this Government for all or any of the Purpofes aforefaid, fhall be raifed and paid in Manner following, *That is to fay,*

Five

Five Tenth Parts, or One Half thereof, ſhall be raiſed upon and paid by the Inhabitants of the County of *New-Caſtle*, Three Tenth Parts thereof by the Inhabitants of the County of *Kent*, and Two Tenth Parts thereof by the Inhabitants of the County of *Suſſex*; any Law, Cuſtom or Act of Aſſembly of this Government to the contrary notwithſtanding.

Signed by Order of the Houſe,

JEHU CURTIS, *Speaker.*

An ACT *repealing an* Act, *entituled,* An Act for encouraging the killing of Squirrels, *ſo far as the ſaid* Act *concerns the County of* New-Caſtle.

WHEREAS it is found by Experience that the aforeſaid Act is very grievous and expenſive to the Inhabitants of *New-Caſtle* County; BE IT THEREFORE ENACTED by the Honourable *GEORGE THOMAS*, Eſq; by and with His Majeſty's Royal Approbation, Lieutenant-Governor and Commander in Chief of the Counties of *New-Caſtle*, *Kent* and *Suſſex* on *Delaware*, and Province of *Pennſylvania*, by and with the Advice and Conſent of the Repreſentatives of the Freemen of the ſaid Counties in General Aſſembly met, and by the Authority of the ſame; That the ſaid Act, and every Clauſe therein contained, ſo far as the ſame concerns the County of *New-Caſtle* aforeſaid, be and is hereby repealed, made null and void, any thing in the ſaid Act contained to the contrary in any wiſe notwithſtanding.

Signed by Order of the Houſe,

JEHU CURTIS, *Speaker.*

An

An ACT *for establishing a Market in the Town of* Dover *in the County of* Kent, *and in the Town of* Lewes *in the County of* Sussex *within this Government.*

WHEREAS the Want of regular Markets in the Towns of *Dover* in the County of *Kent* and *Lewes* in the County of *Sussex* within this Government, is attended with great Inconveniencies as well to the Inhabitants as to Persons offering Provisions to Sale in the said Towns; For Remedy whereof,

BE IT ENACTED by the Honourable *GEORGE THOMAS,* Esq; by and with His Majesty's Royal Approbation, Lieutenant - Governor and Commander in Chief of the Counties of *New-Castle, Kent* and *Sussex* on *Delaware,* and Province of *Pennsylvania,* by and with the Advice and Consent of the Representatives of the Freemen of the said Counties in General Assembly met, and by the Authority of the same; That from and after the Publication of this Act, no Person or Persons whatsoever shall presume either to buy or sell any kind of Provisions (Fish, Milk and Bread excepted) on Market-Days, within any Part of the said Town of *Dover,* but in such Part of the Market-Square, as by the Justices of the said County of *Kent,* or the Majority of them, shall be appointed, until there shall be erected a Market-House in the said Town, and after the building of a Market-House, shall not sell the same in any other Place than the said Market-House, or in the said Town of *Lewes,* in any other Place but at the publick Market-House of the said Town of *Lewes,* under Penalty of forfeiting both by the Buyer and Seller, all such Provisions so sold or bought, or the Value thereof, to be levied together with Costs by the Clerk of the Market of the said Towns respectively, by Distress and Sale of the Offenders Goods and Chattels respectively, by Warrant under the Hand and Seal of any one Justice of the Peace of the respective County, and to be applied to the Use of the Poor of the same County.

No Provisions to be bought or sold, but in the Markets, except, &c.

Penalty.

AND BE IT FURTHER ENACTED by the Authority aforesaid, That if any Person or Persons shall presume to bring or carry to the said Markets, or either of them, and sell or offer to Sale any Meat or Flesh

that

Poor or unsound Flesh how to be disposed of. that shall be poor, lean or carrion, or any other Provision or Provisions not found and wholesome; every Person so offending shall forfeit the same, if too poor or lean for Sale, to the Use of the Prisoners in the common Goal of the respective County, or the Poor; if unwholesome or unsound to be burnt, or thrown into some Creek or River.

AND BE IT FURTHER ENACTED
Butchering forbid within the Limits of the Markets. by the Authority aforesaid, That no Person or Persons whatsoever shall presume to kill or slay any Cattle, Sheep, Calves or Hogs within the Limits of the said Square or Market-House or Houses, on Penalty of forfeiting the Sum of *Five Shillings* for every such Offence, to be levied as aforesaid, and applied to the Use of the Poor of the said Counties respectively.

AND BE IT FURTHER ENACTED
Penalty on Frauds in Weight of Butter, &c. by the Authority aforesaid, That if any Person or Persons whatsoever shall by themselves or others either sell or offer to Sale any Butter, Cheese, Tallow, or any Sort of Provisions, by any false Weights, or for more Weight than the same shall be found to be by Trial of the Clerk of the respective Market for the Time being, upon Complaint made, such Person or Persons shall, for every such Offence, forfeit such Butter, Cheese, Tallow or Provision so sold or offered to Sale; and the Clerk of the said Market is hereby impowered and required to seize the same, to be applied to the Use of the Poor of the said County.

AND BE IT FURTHER ENACTED
Market-Days appointed. by the Authority aforesaid, That at all times hereafter every *Wednesday* and *Saturday* in each Week, and no other Day or Days whatsoever, shall be deemed and taken for the publick and regular Market-Days of the said Towns of *Dover* and *Lewes*.

AND BE IT FURTHER ENACTED
No Flesh to be sold on Tuesdays or Fridays, except, &c. by the Authority aforesaid, That no Person or Persons whatsoever shall presume to hawk or carry about the said Towns of *Dover* and *Lewes*, or to expose to Sale on the Square in the Town of *Dover*, or in the Market-House or Market-Houses of the said Towns of *Dover* and *Lewes*, or either of them, any Flesh-Meat on the *Tuesdays* or *Fridays* in each Week, except in the Months of *June*, *July* and *August*, on Pain of forfeiting such Flesh-Meat, or the Value thereof, to be recovered in like Manner as other Forfeitures are

are directed to be recovered by this Act, and paid, the one Moiety thereof to the said Clerk for the Use of such Clerk, the other Moiety to the Treasurer of the County, for the Use of the Poor of the said County.

AND for preventing Frauds that may happen to be committed by publick Bakers of Bread for Sale in the said Towns of *Dover* and *Lewes,* BE IT ENACTED by the Authority aforesaid, That from and after the Publication of this Act, every Baker or Bakers of Bread for Sale within the said Towns of *Dover* and *Lewes,* shall and are hereby directed and required to make or impress some Mark, Letter or Name of such Baker on every such Bread as he or she shall bake for Sale as aforesaid, on Penalty of paving for every such Neglect, the Sum of *Five Shillings* to the Clerk of the respective Market aforesaid for the Time being.

Bakers shall mark their Bread.

Penalty of Neglect.

AND BE IT FURTHER ENACTED by the Authority aforesaid, That all soft or Loaf-Bread baked or to be baked for Sale within the said Counties of *Kent* and *Sussex,* shall be either white, middling or brown, and of no other Sort whatsoever: And that the Justices of the Court of Quarter-Sessions for the said Counties respectively, shall and are hereby impowered and required from time to time at their Quarterly Sessions of the Peace, to settle and appoint the Size and Weight of the several Sorts of Bread which shall be baked for Sale in the said Towns of *Dover* and *Lewes* respectively: And all Bakers in the said Towns shall conform themselves, and make the Bread by them baked for Sale, agreeable thereto, on Pain of forfeiting, for every such Offence, all such Bread as upon Trial of the Clerk of the Market, shall be found to be of lesser Weight, to be by the said Clerk seized for the Use of the Poor of the respective County, and *Five Shillings* to the said Clerk, to be recovered as aforesaid: And that no Baker shall upon any Pretence whatsoever, make any different or other Sorts of Bread for Sale, but White, Middling and Brown, under the Penalty of forfeiting the same, to be applied in Manner aforesaid.

Sorts of Bread to be baked.

Size & Weight of Bread shall be conformable to Appointment made by the Justices.

AND BE IT FURTHER ENACTED by the Authority aforesaid, That *Thomas Nixon,* of the Town of *Dover* aforesaid, is hereby appointed and constituted Clerk of the Market for the said Town of *Dover;* and *Joshua Fisher,* of the Town of *Lewes* aforesaid, is hereby

Clerks of the Market appointed.

Their Power.

by appointed and conftituted Clerk of the Market for the faid Town of *Lewes*; who are hereby ftrictly charged and commanded to put this Act and every Part thereof in Execution in their refpective Towns, and impowered to receive, demand and recover all fuch Penalties, Fines and Forfeitures as in this Act are directed to be forfeited and paid; and to enter into all fuch Places and Houfes where they fhall fufpect any fuch Bread to be, which fhall not be made agreeable to the Directions of this Act; and to examine the Weights, and try the fame, for the Purpofes in this Act before directed.

Clerks to keep fair Accounts.

AND the faid Clerks refpectively are hereby directed and required to keep fair and juft Accounts of all Fines, Forfeitures and Penalties that each of them fhall receive by virtue of this Act, and fettle fuch Accounts once in every Year, with the Treafurers of the refpective Counties, and pay to them all fuch Sum and Sums of Money as fhall by them be received for the Ufe of the Poor.

In cafe of Death, &c. Juftices may appoint new Clerks.

AND BE IT FURTHER ENACTED by the Authority aforefaid, That upon the Death, Refufal, Removal or Inability of any of the Clerks of the faid Markets of *Dover* and *Lewes*, appointed by virtue of this Act, the Juftices of the Court of Quarter-Seffions for the faid Counties of *Kent* and *Suffex* refpectively fhall, and are hereby impowered and required to appoint, from time to time, fo often as there fhall be Occafion, fome fit and proper Perfon or Perfons to ferve in the Office of Clerk of the Market of the aforefaid Towns of *Dover* and *Lewes* refpectively;

Qualification of Clerks of the Market.

which faid Clerks of the faid Markets hereby appointed, or that fhall hereafter be appointed by virtue of this Act, before they or any of them fhall prefume to enter upon their faid Office or Offices, or execute the Truft repofed in them, fhall firft take an Oath or Affirmation before fome Juftice of the Peace of their refpective County, that they fhall and will well and truly demean and behave themfelves in their refpective Offices of Clerks of their Markets aforefaid, and impartially difcharge the Truft repofed in them, by virtue of this Act.

Signed by Order of the Houfe,

JEHU CURTIS, *Speaker.*

An

An ACT *for the appointing a Corder or Measurer of Fire-Wood in each of the Towns and Villages within this Government.*

BE IT ENACTED by the Honourable *GEORGE THOMAS*, Efq; by and with His Majefty's Royal Approbation, Lieutenant-Governor and Commander in Chief of the Counties of *New-Caftle, Kent* and *Suffex* on *Delaware*, and Province of *Pennfylvania*, by and with the Advice and Confent of the Reprefentatives of the Freemen of the faid Counties in General Affembly met, and by the Authority of the fame ; That all Fire-Wood fold and bought in any of the Towns and Villages within this Government, fhall be by the Cord, each Cord to contain in Length Eight Feet, in Breadth Four Feet, and in Height Four Feet, and fo in Proportion for a greater or leffer Quantity: And that all fuch Wood fhall be of the Length of Eight Feet, or of Four Feet, to be meafured from the Extremity at one End unto the Beginning of the Cut or Carf at the other End, and fhall be laid or corded as clofe as poffible, and all crooked Pieces, if Occafion be, fhall be cut, for the more compact and better Stowage thereof.

AND BE IT FURTHER ENACTED by the Authority aforefaid, That the Juftices of the Court of Quarter-Seffions, in each of the Counties within this Government, fhall and are hereby required, from time, as often as Occafion fhall be, to appoint fome fuitable and proper Perfon to be a Meafurer or Corder of all Fire-Wood which fhall be brought for Sale into any of the Towns or Villages within the feveral Counties ; and the faid Perfon or Perfons fo appointed, upon Misbehaviour to remove from his or their Office, and fome other more fuitable Perfon to appoint in his or their room and ftead. And that there fhall be paid by the Buyer of fuch Wood unto the faid Corder or Corders, or his or their Deputy or Deputies refpectively, for each Cord of Wood by him or them corded and meafured, the Sum of *Six Pence*, and fo in Proportion for any greater or leffer Quantity, one Half whereof fhall by the Perfon felling the fame, be repaid to the Buyer, or deducted out of the Price thereof; and upon Non-Payment thereof, the fame may be recovered by the faid Corder,

Deputy and Buyer refpectively, in like Manner as Debts under *Forty Shillings.*

Corders may appoint Deputies;

AND BE IT FURTHER ENACTED by the Authority aforefaid, That it fhall and may be lawful for the faid Corder of Wood for any of the Towns or Villages within this Government, to appoint one or more Deputy or Deputies to be his Affiftant or Affiftants when and fo often as he fhall fee or have Occafion. But before the faid Corder or Corders of Wood, hereafter to be appointed by virtue of this Act, enter upon the Execution of the Truft hereby repofed in him or them, every Corder

Corders to be qualified.

and Deputy fhall be qualified upon Oath or Affirmation before fome Juftice of the Peace of the fame County wherein fuch Corder or Corders, Deputy or Deputies fhall be appointed; which Oath or Affirmation any fuch Juftice is hereby impowered and required to adminifter; That he or they will well and truly, to the beft of his or their Knowledge and Ability, fairly and impartially cord and meafure all fuch Wood as he or they fhall cord. And no Perfon or

Penalty on other Perfons meafuring of Wood.

Perfons whatfoever, without Deputation from the Corder, fhall cord or meafure any Fire-Wood hereafter to be fold or brought to Sale into any of the Towns or Villages aforefaid, upon Pain of forfeiting the Sum of *Ten Shillings* for each Gord of Wood by him or them corded or meafured, and in Proportion for any leffer Quantity, to be recovered together with Cofts by Diftrefs and Sale of the Offender's Goods and Chattels, by Warrant under the Hand and Seal of any Juftice of the Peace of the fame County, and paid, the one Moiety thereof to the Corder for the Time being, the other Moiety to the Informer.

Signed by Order of the Houfe,

JEHU CURTIS, *Speaker.*

An ACT to prevent Swine running at large without Rings and Yokes in certain Parts of Kent *County in this Government.*

WHEREAS the Inhabitants of the Parts of *Kent* County within this Government, lying between *Delaware* Bay and the King's Road leading down the

the said County, have heretofore suffered great Damages. and Inconveniencies by Swine rooting and turning up their Lands; For Prevention whereof for the future,

BE IT ENACTED by the Honourable *GEORGE THOMAS,* Esq; by and with His Majesty's Royal Approbation, Lieutenant - Governor and Commander in Chief of the Counties of *New-Castle, Kent* and *Sussex* on *Delaware,* and Province of *Pennsylvania,* by and with the Advice and Consent of the Representatives of the Freemen of the said Counties in General Assembly met, and by the Authority of the same; That from and after the *Tenth* Day of *December,* which shall be in the Year of our Lord, *One Thousand Seven Hundred and Forty-two,* no Swine shall be allowed or permitted to run at large (unless sufficiently ringed, to prevent them from rooting, and yoked, to prevent them from creeping or breaking through Fences) on any of the Lands or Marshes lying between *Delaware* Bay and the King's Road leading from the Town of *Salisbury,* down the said County of *Kent,* to the Bridge on *Murtherkill,* commonly called the *Draw-Bridge,* and from thence to the Three Runs. And if at any time after the said *Tenth* Day of *December,* in the Year of our Lord *One Thousand Seven Hundred and Forty-two,* any Swine shall be found at large within the above-mentioned Limits, not as aforesaid sufficiently ringed and yoked, except upon the Lands or Marshes of the Owner thereof, it shall and may be lawful for any Person, being a Freeholder or possessing some Tenement or Farm within the said Limits of the yearly Value of *Thirty Shillings,* to take up or kill any such Swine found upon his or their Lands or Farms, and shall give Notice to the Owner or Owners thereof, or, if the Owner or Owners thereof be not known, shall inform the next Justice of the Peace of the same County, whereupon the said Justice shall cause the same immediately to be appraised by Two creditable Men of the Vicinage, upon their Oath or Affirmation, and sold to the highest Bidder; and after Deduction of Charges, the Residue of the Money arising by such Sale, shall be paid, the one Moiety thereof to the Person or Persons taking up or killing such Swine, and the other Moiety to the Owner of such Swine, if known, and if not known, to the said Justice for the Use of such Owner, if within Six Months next after such Sale, he or she shall claim the same, and to the Satisfaction of such Justice, prove his or her Right thereto: And the said Justice shall cause an Advertisement to be set

up

up in fome publick Place of the Neighbourhood, fetting forth the Number and Marks of all fuch Swine, and the Time of their being fo taken up or killed as aforefaid. But in cafe no fuch Owner fhall within the faid Six Months appear, and make out fuch his or her Right as aforefaid, then the faid Refidue fhall by the faid Juftice be paid to the Treafurer of the County for the Ufe of the Poor of the faid County ; and the faid Owner fhall for ever after be foreclofed and debarred from any Title or Claim thereto.

AND BE IT FURTHER ENACTED by the Authority aforefaid, That no Perfon or Perfons inhabiting within the Limits aforefaid, fhall be allowed or permitted to drive or carry any Swine out of the Limits aforefaid, which were raifed or bred therein, with Intent that the faid Swine may run at large without Rings and Yokes in any other Parts of the faid County of *Kent*, under the Penalty in this Act before provided againft Swine running at large within the faid Limits, to be difpofed of in Manner aforefaid, unlefs the Perfon or Perfons fo driving or carrying any fuch Swine, fhall at the Time of his or their doing thereof, be Owner or Owners or Poffeffor or Poffeffors of Land near the Place whereunto fuch Swine fhall be fo driven or carried, whereupon he or they fhall have a Tenant or Tenants, Servant or Servants, Slave or Slaves refiding or inhabiting.

AND BE IT FURTHER ENACTED by the Authority aforefaid, That if any Perfon or Perfons fhall be fued for doing any thing according to the Direction or Permiffion of this Act, he or they may plead the general Iffue, and give this Act in Evidence as a Bar to fuch Suit or Suits, and fhall recover of the Plaintiff or Plaintiffs double Cofts, any Law, Cuftom or Ufage to the contrary notwithftanding.

Signed by Order of the Houfe,

JEHU CURTIS, *Speaker.*

An

An ACT *repealing an* Act *to prevent Swine running at large without Rings and Yokes in certain Parts of* Kent *County within this Government.*

WHEREAS it is conceived, that if the aforesaid Act should be continued and remain in Force according to the Tenor thereof, it will prove very prejudicial and grievous to a great Number of the Inhabitants of *Kent* County aforesaid; For the Prevention whereof, BE IT ENACTED by the Honourable GEORGE THOMAS, Esq; with the King's Royal Approbation, Lieutenant-Governor and Commander in Chief, under the Honourable JOHN PENN, THOMAS PENN and RICHARD PENN, Esqrs; true and absolute Proprietaries of the Counties of *New-Castle, Kent* and *Sussex* upon *Delaware,* and Province of *Pennsylvania,* and with the Advice and Consent of the Representatives of the Freemen of the said Counties in General Assembly met, and by the Authority of the same ; That the said Act, and every Clause therein contained, be and is hereby repealed, made null and void, any thing in the said Act contained to the contrary in any wise notwithstanding.

Signed by Order of the House,

RYVES HOLT, *Speaker.*

An ACT *for raising County-Rates and Levies.*

WHEREAS it is necessary yearly and every Year, to raise several Sums of Money for the defraying and paying the publick Charges of the respective Counties of this Government ; Therefore for the more easy and regular laying and raising the same,

BE IT ENACTED by the Honourable GEORGE THOMAS, Esq; with the King's Royal Approbation, Lieutenant-Governor and Commander in Chief, under the Honourable JOHN PENN, THOMAS

R r r   PENN

PENN and RICHARD PENN, Efqrs; true and abfo-
lute Proprietaries of the Counties of *New-Caftle, Kent* and
Suffex upon *Delaware*, and Province of *Pennfylvania*, and
with the Advice and Confent of the Reprefentatives of the
Freemen of the faid Counties in General Affembly met,
and by the Authority of the fame ; That the Freeholders

Freeholders to chufe Affeffors yearly. and Inhabitants of the refpective Counties of this Govern-
ment, who are legally qualified to elect and be elected
Members of Affembly, fhall yearly and every Year on the
Firft Day of *October*, at the Place appointed for making
fuch Elections, by a Majority of Voices of the Electors as
aforefaid for each Hundred, chufe One fubftantial Freeholder for every Hundred in the Counties aforefaid, to be the
Affeffor for the enfuing Year ; and when fuch Affeffor or
Affeffors fhall be fo chofen, the Sheriff of the refpective
Counties fhall take down their Names in Writing, under
the Hands and Seals of Six or more of the Freeholders of
the refpective Counties where they fhall be fo chofen, and
certify the fame to the Juftices of their General Seffions of
the Peace in each of the Counties next after fuch Election,
which Return fhall be entred on Record in the Seffion's
Minutes ; and fuch Affeffor or Affeffors being fo chofen as

Penalty on Af-feffors not fer-ving. aforefaid, fhall ferve in faid Office, under the Penalty of
Twenty Shillings, to be recovered by a Warrant under the
Hand and Seal of any one Juftice of the Peace of the County, to be paid to the Treafurer for the Ufe of the Poor of
the County. And if any fuch Affeffor or Affeffors fo
chofen as aforefaid, fhall happen to die, or remove out of
this Government, or be otherwife difabled to ferve in the
faid Office ; the Juftices of the refpective County-Courts
fhall fo often as it fhall fo happen, nominate and appoint
another fit Perfon to ferve in the faid Office, until a new
Election fhall be made in Manner aforefaid. But before
any of the faid Affeffors fo to be chofen or returned as
aforefaid, fhall take upon themfelves the Service and Duty
by them to be performed and executed under the Directions
of this Act, they fhall be qualified, by taking an Oath or
Affirmation, to the Effect following, *viz.*

Their Qualifi-cation. I A. B. *will well and truly lay, or caufe the Rates and Sums
of Money by virtue of this Act to be impofed or raifed, duly
and equally to be affeffed and laid, according to the beft of my
Skill and Knowledge ; and herein I will fpare no Perfon for
Favour or Affection, or grieve any for Hatred or Ill-will.*

                Which

WHICH Qualification may be administred by any Justice of the Peace of the respective Counties, where such Assessor or Assessors shall be chosen as aforesaid. And if the Inhabitants of any of the said Counties neglect or refuse to chuse or elect such Assessor or Assessors (after Assessors shall be once chosen by virtue of this Act) then and so often and when it shall so happen, the Assessor or Assessors of the next preceeding Year, shall continue to officiate in their respective Station as Assessor or Assessors, until a new Election shall be made pursuant to the Direction of this Act.

No new Choice being made, the old Assessors shall continue, &c.

AND BE IT FURTHER ENACTED by the Authority aforesaid, That the Justices of the Peace of the respective Counties within this Government, or any Three of them, at their respective Courts to be held in the Month of *November* yearly and every Year for laying the Levies, together with Eight Grand-Jurymen, or such of them as will attend, and the Assessors, or the Majority of them, shall meet at the Court-Houses within the said Counties, on the next *Tuesday* following their respective County-Courts held in the Month aforesaid, and shall then and there proceed to calculate and settle the publick Debts and Charges of the respective Counties, allowing all just Debts and Demands which now are or hereafter shall be chargeable upon the said respective Counties, and shall settle and adjust the Sum and Sums of Money, which ought of Necessity to be raised yearly, to defray the Charges of building and repairing Court-Houses, Prisons, Work-Houses, or for destroying Wolves, Crows and Blackbirds, with such other Uses as may redound to the publick Service and Benefit of the said Counties respectively; and shall also ascertain and set down such competent Sum and Sums of Money, as shall be yearly applied toward every of the said Duties and Services; together with such Sum or Sums as may be needful to make good Deficiencies in County-Rates assessed and not yet collected, and to enforce the Collection thereof as Need may require.

Justices, eight Grand Jurymen, and Assessors, to meet & settle the publick Debts, &c.

AND BE IT FURTHER ENACTED by the Authority aforesaid, That the Clerk of the Peace in each County, shall and is hereby required, at every *August*-Sessions to issue forth Precepts directed to the Constables of every Hundred or District, requiring them to bring to the said Justices at the *November*-Sessions next after the Date of such Precepts, fair and true Lists or Accompts in Writing, upon their Oaths or Affirmation, of the

Lists of Taxables, &c. to be brought in every August-Sessions.

Names

Names and Surnames of all and every the taxable Persons refiding or dwelling within the Limits of thofe Hundreds or Diftricts, with which they fhall be charged, and the Names of all the Freemen, Inmates, hired Servants, and all other Perfons refiding or fojourning in every of their Hundreds or Diftricts aforefaid; upon Pain of forfeiting any Sum not exceeding *Five Pounds*, at the Difcretion of the Juftices aforefaid, to be levied by Diftrefs and Sale of the Delinquent's Goods and Chattels, to be paid to the Treafurer of the County for the Ufe of the Poor of the County, and for want of fuch Goods or Chattels, then to take the Body of fuch Offender or Offenders in Execution, to be committed to the County-Goal, there to remain until Debt and Coft are fully paid, or be otherwife legally difcharged. And every of the faid Conftables fhall have and receive of the Treafurer of the refpective Counties for the time being, the Sum of *Five Shillings* each, for their Care and Trouble in taking and returning the faid Lifts in Manner aforefaid.

Penalty on Neglect.

AND BE IT FURTHER ENACTED by the Authority aforefaid, That after fettling and allowing all juft Debts and Demands chargeable upon the refpective Counties, and adjufting and fettling the Sum and fums of Money of Neceffity to be raifed as aforefaid, to be allowed by the Juftices, Grand-Jurymen and Affeffors aforefaid, it fhall and may be lawful for the Affeffors of the refpective Counties, and they are hereby required to meet together, and by the Conftables Returns, or any other lawful Way or Means, inform themfelves what Perfons and Eftates in their refpective Counties are rateable by virtue of this Act; and fhall forthwith equally and impartially affefs themfelves and all others as aforefaid (exempting out of fuch Affeffments all unfettled Tracts or Parcels of Land, and having due Regard to fuch as are poor and have a Charge of Children, the poorer fort of fuch not to be rated under *Eight Pounds*:) and no fingle Man who at any time of Affefsment is under Twenty-one Years of Age, or hath not been out of his Servitude or Apprenticefhip Six Months, fhall be rated by this Act; and as to thofe fingle Men who have no vifible Eftates, they fhall not be rated under *Twelve Pounds*, nor above *Twenty-four Pounds*.

Affeffors to affefs themfelves and others impartially.

AND BE IT FURTHER ENACTED by the Authority aforefaid, That the faid refpective Sums of Money, with the Names of the Perfons to whom payable, and the particular Ufes to which they are appropriated, **fhall** shall be entred on the Minutes kept by the Clerk of the Peace of each respective County; who is to officiate as Clerk of the Levy-Court, which said Clerk is to transcribe from said Minutes, fair and true Duplicates of all the Proceedings of said Court, to be delivered to the Treasurer of each respective County for the Time being; who is hereby required to provide good and sufficient Books, at his own Cost and Charge, where he shall make Entries of the said Duplicates accordingly.

Fair Duplicates to be delivered to the Treasurers.

AND BE IT FURTHER ENACTED by the Authority aforesaid, That after the making such Rates and Assessments as aforesaid, the Clerk of the Peace in each respective County, shall set up, or cause to be set and published in the most publick Places of the respective Hundreds of the said Counties, in Writing under his Hand, a true Copy of such Rates and Assessments as aforesaid, together with Notice of the Day appointed by this Act for holding the Court of Appeal; and for every Neglect or Refusal to forfeit and pay the Sum of *Twenty Shillings*, to be paid to the Treasurer for the Time being, for the Use of the Poor, to be recovered by Warrant under the Hand and Seal of any Justice of the Peace of said County, by Distress and Sale of the Offender's Goods and Chattels.

Copies of Assessments to be published.

Penalty on Neglect.

AND BE IT FURTHER ENACTED by the Authority aforesaid, That after the Justices, Grand-Jurymen and Assessors, or a Majority of them, shall have made such Rates, Calculations and Assessments as aforesaid, the said Justices shall appoint that Day Four Weeks from the Time of their meeting in each of the respective Counties, to meet again at the same Place to hear the Complaints, and redress the Grievances of such Person or Persons as shall be unequally or over-rated, and upon just Cause shewed, they are hereby impowered to add or diminish to such Person's Rate or Assessment as to them shall seem just and reasonable; and they may then and there call before them such Person or Persons as they find are omitted in the said Assessment, and rectify such Omission or Omissions; and if the Person or Persons so omitted refuse or neglect to appear, to give an Account of his, her or their Estate or Estates, he, she or they so offending, shall forfeit and pay any Sum under *Twenty Shillings*, at the Discretion of the Court, to be paid to the Treasurer for the Use of the Poor of the County, and on Default thereof, to be recovered by

Justices, &c. to meet & hear Complaints, &c.

Omissions to be rectified.

S f f a Warrant

a Warrant under the Hand and Seal of any One Justice of Peace of the said County, by Distress and Sale of the Offender's Goods or Chattels.

AND BE IT FURTHER ENACTED by the Authority aforesaid, That on the Day the Justices, Grand-Jurymen and Assessors do meet to hold their Court of Appeal, as before is directed, in each of the respective Counties aforesaid, or so many of them as will be present, they shall and are hereby required to nominate and appoint One substantial Freeholder at least in every Hundred, to be Collector of the publick Tax or Assessment from time to time, and immediately after such second Meeting or Days of Appeal as aforesaid, shall cause Duplicates of the said Assessments of each Hundred to be transcribed from the Records of the Court by the Clerk, and by him delivered to the Collector of each respective Hundred, with a Warrant from the Justices aforesaid or any Two of them, impowering such Collector in his proper District to demand and receive of the Persons assessed, the respective Sums of Money wherewith they shall stand charged in his List or Duplicate as aforesaid. And if any Person or Persons so rated or assessed by virtue of this Act, shall refuse or neglect to pay the Sum or Sums so assessed or any Part thereof, by the space of Ten Days after Demand made, such Person or Persons, being a Freeholder, it shall and may be lawful for the said Collectors respectively, to levy by Distress and Sale of the Goods and Chattels of the Person or Persons so neglecting or refusing to pay as aforesaid, the said several Sums of Money that the said Person or Persons stand chargeable with, and to make Sale thereof, rendring the Overplus (if any be) to the Owner or Owners thereof, after all reasonable Charges be deducted; but if no Distress can be found by the respective Collectors, and the Party assessed refuse or neglect to shew Goods or Chattels of his own forthwith to be levied upon to satisfy such Assessment with reasonable Charges, then such Collector shall take the Body of every such Person or Persons so neglecting or refusing to pay as aforesaid, and bring him to the County-Goal, and deliver him to the Sheriff, or Keeper of the said Goal, who is hereby required to receive and detain him in safe Custody, until Payment with Costs be made.

Collectors to be appointed.

Their Power.

AND BE IT FURTHER ENACTED by the Authority aforesaid, That the said Collector shall once in Ten Months at least, from such Day or Court of Appeal

Collectors to render Accompt.

Appeal as aforesaid, render a just and true Account of, and pay unto the respective County-Treasurer for the Time being, all such Sums of Money as they or any of them shall have then received, and shall pay all and every the Sums of Money aforesaid in their respective Duplicate, within the space of Eleven Months after such Day of Appeal as aforesaid; and the Treasurer's Receipt to the Collectors shall be a sufficient Discharge from such Collection or Assessment. And if any of the said Collectors refuse or neglect to pay the Sum or Sums of Money, or any Part thereof, that they shall be accountable for as aforesaid, according to the Directions of this Act (retaining such Sum or Sums as are herein after allowed for collecting and paying the same) then such delinquent Collector shall be fined by the respective County-Court, in any Sum not exceeding *Five Pounds*; and the said County-Court shall appoint another Collector or Collectors as the Case may require, to act in his or their stead until the next Court of Appeal.

Penalty on Delinquents.

AND BE IT FURTHER ENACTED by the Authority aforesaid, That the Fees of the respective Collectors within this Government, shall be as followeth, *viz.* For collecting and paying to the Treasurer any Sum or Sums of Money by him or them so collected and paid as aforesaid, at the Rate of Ten *per Cent.* and so in Proportion for any greater or lesser Sum or Sums of Money; and for taking and selling the Goods or Chattels by virtue of their Warrant in Execution, or making Distress as aforesaid, shall be *Three Shillings and Six Pence*, and no more; and for taking the Body of any Person, and delivering him to the Sheriff or Goaler as aforesaid, shall be *Four Shillings*, and no more, any Law, Custom or Usage to the contrary notwithstanding.

Collectors Fees.

AND BE IT FURTHER ENACTED by the Authority aforesaid, That the respective County-Treasurers for the Time being, or any others to be chosen by virtue of this Act, before they enter upon their respective Offices according to the Directions of this Act, shall give Bond to the Justices of the Court of Quarter-Sessions, in the Name of the Governor for the Time being, with one or more sufficient Sureties, in the Sum of *Five Hundred Pounds*, conditioned for the true Execution of their respective Offices and due Observation of this Act; which Bond shall be immediately recorded by the Clerk of the Peace, in the Minutes of the aforesaid Court: And in case of Death

County Treasurers to give Bond.

Vacancies how to be supplied. or Removal of any of the said Treasurers, then the Justices of the Peace of the proper Counties for the Time being, or the major Part of them, shall appoint others to supply the Places of such as shall so die or be removed from time to time, which said Treasurers shall give Security in Manner aforesaid; and shall keep a distinct Book in eachCounty, containing a particular Account of all the Rates and Assessments made or to be made as aforesaid, as also of all Disbursements and Payments made by Order of the Justices and Grand-Jurymen, or other lawful Authority. And the Treasurers *Treasurers Allowance, &c.* shall be allowed for their Trouble in receiving and paying all such Sums of Money as shall come into their Hands respectively by virtue of this Act (or any other lawful Authority) the Sum of *Four Pounds* for every *Hundred Pounds*, and so in Proportion for any greater or lesser Sums of Money, to be allowed him at settling his Accompts, as is hereafter directed. And where any County-Treasurers shall be removed from their Office of Treasurer, they shall deliver up to his or their Successor or Successors all the Books belonging to or concerning such respective County or Counties where he or they acted, whole, intire and undefaced; and upon the Death of any County-Treasurer, his Executors or Administrators shall deliver up in like Manner, all the Books and Papers relating to the publick Accompts of the said Office, to the succeeding Treasurer or Treasurers.

AND BE IT FURTHER ENACTED *Persons to be appointed to settle Treasurers Accounts, &c.* by the Authority aforesaid, That the Justices, Grand-Jurymen and Assessors, at their respective Courts, to be held in the Month of *November* yearly and every Year, shall nominate and appoint out of their own Number, Three fit Persons to settle Accounts with the Treasurer, who is hereby required to lay before them the true and just State of all the Accounts, relating to the Publick, in his Hands; which Three Persons shall proceed, or any Two of them, to adjust and settle the said Accounts, and make their Report to their next Court of Appeal after their Appointment as aforesaid; which Settlement, when so made, shall be signed or subscribed by the Parties as aforesaid, and then received and filed among the Papers of the said Court.

AND BE IT FURTHER ENACTED *Allowance to Justices, Grand Jurymen and Assessors.* by the Authority aforesaid, That the Justices, Grand-Jurymen and Assessors of the several Counties within this Government, shall be allowed and paid for their Trouble, Attendance and Expences in executing and performing **what**

what is required of them in this Act, the several Sums of Money following, *viz.* To the Justices, Grand-Jurymen and Assessors of the County of *New-Castle*, the Sum of *Eighteen Pounds*, and no more. And to the Justices, Grand-Jurymen and Assessors of the County of *Kent*, the Sum of *Fourteen Pounds*, and no more. And to the Justices, Grand-Jurymen and Assessors of the County of *Sussex*, the Sum of *Twelve Pounds*, and no more. And to the respective Clerks of the Peace of the said Counties for their Pains in officiating as Clerks of the Levy-Court, and for writing Duplicates, Warrants and Precepts as aforesaid, relating to the Premisses, such Fees as the aforesaid Justices, Grand-Jurymen and Assessors shall from time to time think proper to allow.

AND BE IT FURTHER ENACTED by the Authority aforesaid, That the several Collectors of the aforesaid Counties respectively, shall each of them, before he enter upon his Office, give Bond to the Justices of the Court of Quarter-Sessions, with such Security as shall be required, in the Name of the Treasurer of each respective County, for the faithful Performance of the Trust by this Act in him reposed. *Collectors to give Bond, &c.*

AND BE IT FURTHER ENACTED by the Authority aforesaid, That all the Laws or Acts of Assembly heretofore made in this Government for the raising County-Rates and Levies, and every Matter, Clause and Thing therein contained, shall be and are hereby declared to be repealed and made null and void; any thing in the said Acts or any of them contained to the contrary notwithstanding. *Repeal of former Laws.*

Signed by Order of the House,
RYVES HOLT, *Speaker.*

An ACT *for regulating and establishing Fees.*

FOR preventing Extortion and undue Exaction of Fees, by the several Officers and Practitioners of Law within this Government, and to the End that all Fees may be reduced to a Certainty, and limited;

BE

BE IT ENACTED by the Honourable
GEORGE THOMAS, Efq; with His Majefty's Royal
Approbation, Lieutenant-Governor and Commander in
Chief of the Counties of *New-Caftle, Kent* and *Suffex* upon
Delaware, and Province of *Pennfylvania,* under the Honou-
rable JOHN PENN, THOMAS PENN and RICHARD PENN,
Efqrs; true and abfolute Proprietaries of the Counties and
Province aforefaid, by and with the Advice and Confent of
the Reprefentatives of the Freemen of the faid Counties in
General Affembly met, and by the Authority of the fame;
That the Fees of the feveral Courts, Magiftrates, Officers
and Practitioners of Law within this Government, fhall be
as herein is afcertained, limited and appointed, *viz.*

That the FEES *belonging to the Governor's Secretary,
fhall be as followeth,* viz.

Governor's Se-
cretary.

R Eading and Entring every Petition to the Governor, and the Order or Anfwer thereunto, *Two
Shillings.*

A Mediterranean-Pafs, or Let-Pafs, if required, **each**
Three Shillings.

A Regifter of every Veffel, *Four Shillings.*

Writing of the Supream Judge's Commiffion, a Commiffion of Oyer and Terminer, or for the Trial of
Negroes, each *Eight Shillings.*

A General Commiffion of the Peace, to be paid by
the County, *Eight Shillings.*

A fingle Commiffion for a Juftice of the Peace, to be
paid by the County, *Four Shillings and Six Pence.*

A Commiffion for a Sheriff, Clerk or Coroner, to be
paid by the Party, *Ten Shillings.*

Writ of Affiftance, to be paid by the Sheriff, *Ten Shillings.*

A Warrant under the Seal at Arms of the Governor
for the time being, to affix the Great Seal to any
Body of Laws or fingle Law paffed here, Judge's
Commiffion, Commiffion of the Peace, or any other
Commiffion, Proclamation, or other publick Inftru-
ment, each *Two Shillings and Six Pence.*

A Warrant for the Seal to a Pardon, to be paid by
the Party, *Four Shillings.*

And that the FEES *belonging to the Mafter of the Rolls for
each County in this Government, fhall be as followeth,* viz.

Recording

FOR {

REcording the Laws of this Government (if requi- *Master of the* red) in a fair clofe Hand, Parchment or Book in- *Rolls.* cluded, for every Line not lefs than Twelve Words (one with another) *One Half-penny.*

An Exemplification of any Law under the Seal of the Office, either for the Royal Affent, or for the Ufe of any County in this Government, *One Half-penny per* Line, and no more.

Recording Deeds, Writings and Inftruments appertain- ing to the Inrollment-Office, for each Line, and finding Paper or Parchment, as aforefaid, *One Half- penny.*

A Copy or Exemplification of any Record in the faid Office, *One Half-penny per* Line, to be paid by the Party demanding the fame.

Searching any Roll or Record, *One Shilling.*

An Indorfement or Certificate on each Deed proved and acknowledged, and his Hand and Seal of Office thereto, *One Shilling and Six Pence.*

And that the FEES *of the Juftices of the Supream Court, fhall be as followeth, viz.*

FOR {

ALlowing and Signing the Allocator of every Cer- *Juftices of the* tiorari, for removing of Indictments, Orders, &c. *Supream Court.* *Four Shillings.*

Every Caufe brought into Court by *Certiorari,* or Writ of Error, *Eight Shillings.*

Taking Bail to profecute a *Certiorari, Two Shillings and Six Pence.*

Judgment on every Writ of Error, *Noli profequi,* or other Matter, Bench-Fees, *Eight Shillings.*

Every Rule of Court, Imparlance, Continuance, by Advifement or otherwife, *Two Shillings.*

The Juftices when they fit by a Commiffion of Oyer and Terminer in Capital Cafes, to be paid by the County where fuch Court of Oyer and Terminer fhall be held, viz.

THe Chief Juftice, *Forty Shillings per Diem;* and each of *Oyer and Ter-* the Affiftant Juftices, the Sum of *Thirty Shillings per miner.* *Diem,* befides *Six Pence per* Mile for their Travelling-Char- ges; and for their Expences during the Sitting of the Court, *Ten Pounds.*

And

And that the FEES *belonging to the Attorney-General, shall be as followeth,* viz.

Attorney-General.

FOR

EVery capital Cause, where Life is concerned, *Twenty-four Shillings* for the Prosecution, to be paid by the Party (if able) otherwise by the County.

But if the Bill be not found by the Grand-Inquest, *Twelve Shillings*, to be paid as above.

Every other Matter by Bill of Indictment, if found by the Grand-Jury, *Eighteen Shillings*; if not found, *Nine Shillings.*

Every Information brought into Court, by Leave thereof, *Eighteen Shillings.*

And that the FEES *belonging to the Sheriff of each County of this Government, shall be as followeth,* viz.

High-Sheriff.

FOR

SErving every Writ of Arrest, and taking into Custody, *Four Shillings and Six Pence.*

Serving a Summons, *Four Shillings.*

Return of a Summons, Arrest or Attachment, *One Shilling.*

Delivery of a Copy of Declaration, *One Shilling.*

Every Bail-Bond, *Two Shillings and Six Pence.*

Travelling-Charges to and from the Place where the Writ or Summons shall be served, *One Penny per Mile.*

Summoning or serving a Witness with a *Sub pœna, One Shilling,* and Mileage as above.

Summoning and returning a Jury in every Cause where Issue is joined, *Two Shillings.*

Returning an Execution for Land, *Six Shillings.*

Returning an Execution for Goods and Chattels, *One Shilling and Six Pence.*

Selling the Lands or Goods executed, or delivered to the Creditor, and returning the *Venditioni exponas* or *Liberari facias,* for any Sum not exceeding *Twelve Pounds, Six Shillings.* And for all other Sums, at *Four Pence per Pound,* and no more. And that no Poundage be paid for more than the real Debt or Damage due to the Plaintiff named in the Execution.

The Turn-Key's Fees, to be paid on the Discharge of a Prisoner, *Three Shillings and Six Pence.* If on a Debt under *Forty Shillings, One Shilling.*

Executing Writs of Enquiry of Damages, Attesting the Jury and making Returns thereof, *Ten Shillings.*

A Copy

A Copy of a Pannel when demanded, *Nine Pence.*

Executing every other Writ of Enquiry, and all other Writs or Orders of Partition of Lands or Tenements, Attesting the Jury for any Matter or Thing to be done by him about such Partition, and making Return thereof, *Fifteen Shillings.*

But if the Business of the Partition exceed what the Jury can perform in one Day, then the Sheriff for every Day more that he shall attend on the Jury about such Partition, shall have *Six Shillings per Diem.*

Summoning the Grand-Jury to attend for One Year, *Thirty Shillings.*

Every Judgment in civil Causes, *One Shilling.*

Assigning every Bail-Bond, *Two Shillings.*

Every criminal Cause brought into Court, *Ten Shillings.*

Every capital Cause, *Twenty Shillings.*

Levying Fines, Forfeitures and Amerciaments ordered to be estreated and paid to the Governor or to the Treasurer of the County, *One Shilling per Pound.*

Whipping every Person by Judgment or Order of Court, *Five Shillings.*

Branding and Pilloring a Person, *Ten Shillings.*

Pilloring only, *Seven Shillings and Six Pence.*

A N D that the Cryer of every Court, shall have for every Action called in Court, *Nine Pence.*

And that the FEES belonging to every Coroner of the Counties of this Government, shall be as followeth, viz.

Coroners.

Viewing a Dead Body, *Ten Shillings.*

Summoning the Inquest, entring the Verdict, and returning the Inquisition, *Ten Shillings.*

Summoning or Arresting the Sheriff, or any other Person for him, *Four Shillings and Six Pence,* besides Mileage as allowed the Sheriff in like Cases.

And that the FEES belonging to the Justices of the Peace of the Counties of this Government, shall be as followeth, viz.

Justices.

WRiting, Signing and Sealing every Warrant of Complaint in criminal Matters, *Mittimus,* Recognizance, Certificate, Pass, or other Instrument, *One Shilling and Six Pence.*

V v v   Writs

FOR

Writing, Signing and Sealing every Warrant for Debt, Attachment, Arreft or Summons, *One Shilling*.

Taxing every Bill of Coft, and Signing every Judgment of Court, *One Shilling*.

Every Judgment of Court, upon Confeffion, Default, *Noli profequi*, Difcontinuance in Court, Bench-Fees, *Four Shillings*.

Adminiftring and certifying an *Affidavit*, or Affirmation in proving Accounts againft dead Men's Eftates, *Six Pence*.

Refpiting a Recognizance, *One Shilling*.

Writing the Affignment of a Servant, Signing it, and keeping a Record thereof, *One Shilling and Six Pence*.

Taking a Depofition or *Affidavit* out of Court, drawn in Form, *One Shilling and Six Pence*.

Adminiftring every Oath or Affirmation in any Judicial Proceedings in all Matters concerning the *Five Pounds*- or *Forty Shillings*-Laws, to be done *ex officio*.

Writing and Signing the Summons for Witneffes in any Complaint of Debt founded on the *Five Pounds*- or *Forty Shillings*-Acts, *Six Pence* for One Witnefs, and not exceeding *One Shilling* for Two or more.

Judgment, *Nine Pence*, and Execution thereon, *One Shilling*.

And that the FEES *belonging to the Clerk of the Supream Court within this Government, fhall be as followeth,* viz.

Clerk of the Supream Court.

FOR

ENtring every Action or Caufe there, *One Shilling*. Filing the Errors affigned in every Caufe, *One Shilling*.

Every *Retraxit*, Difcontinuance or Quafhing a Writ of Error, *One Shilling*.

Entring every Appearance, *One Shilling*.

Filing and Entring any Demurrer, Plea, Replication, and every fubfequent Plea and Iffue; Calling the Jury and Attefting them, *One Shilling and Six Pence*.

Attefting each Witnefs in every Caufe, *One Shilling and Six Pence*.

Recording every Verdict, *One Shilling and Six Pence*.

Entring every Judgment, *One Shilling*.

Every Continuance, *One Shilling and Six Pence*.

Entring an Arreft of Judgment, *One Shilling and Six Pence*.

Entring every Warrant of Attorney, *Committatur*, or Rule of Court, *One Shilling*.

Reading

F O R

Reading the Record, with all the Proceedings below and above, *Two Shillings.*

Every *Noli profequi, One Shilling.*

Filing a Declaration, *One Shilling and Six Pence.*

Reading every *Affidavit, One Shilling.*

Acknowledging Satisfaction upon Record, *One Shilling and Six Pence.*

Every *Sub pœna* to give Evidence, *One Shilling and Six Pence;* and Affixing the Seal thereto, *One Shilling and Six Pence.*

And that the FEES *belonging to the Clerk of the General Quarter-Seffions of the Peace, fhall be as followeth,* viz.

F O R

EVery Warrant of the Peace or good Behaviour, requiring to bring Sureties, if drawn by the Clerk, *Nine Pence.* — Clerk of the Quarter-Seffions.

Every common Warrant or *Mittimus,* if drawn by the Clerk, *One Shilling.*

Every Recognizance, if drawn by him, *One Shilling and Six Pence.*

Every Indictment of Felony, Trefpafs, Affault, Battery, Riot, &c. if drawn by the Clerk, *Three Shillings.*

A Copy thereof, *One Shilling.*

Entring an Appearance to every Indictment or Information, *Nine Pence.*

Difcharge of every Perfon upon Bail for the Peace, good Behaviour, Contempt, or the like, *One Shilling.*

Making out Procefs againft the Defendant upon an Information or Indictment, and fixing the Seal, *Three Shillings.*

Difcharge of every Indictment upon *Ignoramus, Nine Pence.*

Every Plea of Not-guilty, *Nine Pence.*

Entring every fpecial Plea or Demurrer, *Nine Pence.*

Entring every Submiffion, *One Shilling.*

Calling the Jury and Attefting them, *Nine Pence.*

Attefting each Witnefs on every Trial, *Six Pence.*

Entring every Verdict, *Nine Pencce.*

Entring every Judgment, *Nine Pence.*

A Copy of every Judgment, *One Shilling and Six Pence.*

Refpiting a Recognizance, *Nine Pence.*

Every Writ of Reftitution, *Two Shillings.*

Entring every Order of Seffions, *Nine Pence.*

A Copy of the fame, *Nine Pence.*

Reading

FOR

Reading and entring every Petition, *Two Shillings and Six Pence.*

Entring the Return at large of a Road, *Two Shillings.*

A Copy thereof, *One Shilling and Three Pence.*

Entring a *Similiter* to join Issue, *One Shilling.*

A *Venire facias* and the Seal, *Three Shillings.*

Reading the Indictment and arraigning the Criminal, *Nine Pence.*

Continuing the Cause, *Six Pence.*

Reading every Evidence upon Trial, *Six Pence.*

Entring the Allowance of *Certiorari*, Writ of Error, or *Procedendo*, *Six Pence.*

Entring a Rule upon a Motion to arrest Judgment, *One Shilling and Six Pence.*

Entring the Arrest of Judgment, *One Shilling and Six Pence.*

An *Habeas Corpus*, *Three Shillings.*

Drawing up and examining every Record of all the Proceedings upon Indictment or Information, in Rolls of Parchment, not less than Ten Inches wide, for every Line containing Twelve Words, *One Half-penny per* Line.

A Copy and signing thereof, if required, *Half-penny per* Line.

Making out the Estreates for the levying of Fines and Forfeitures of each Sessions, *One Shilling.*

Writing every Recommendation for a Licence to keep a Publick Inn, Tavern or Ale-House for selling Provisions and all sorts of Liquors, *Two Shillings.*

And that the FEES *belonging to the Prothonotary or Clerk of the Common-Pleas in every County in this Government, shall be as followeth, viz.*

Clerk of the Common Pleas.

FOR

EVery Arrest, Attachment or Summons, if drawn by the Clerk, *Four Shillings and Six Pence.*

Every Replevin, if drawn by the Clerk, *Four Shillings.*

Entring any Action, *Eight Pence.*

Filing every Declaration, *Eight Pence.*

Copy of a Declaration in an Action of Account, Debt, Detinue, Trespass or *Assumpsit*, *One Shilling.*

Copy of a Declaration in an Action of Slander, Covenant or Waste, *Two Shillings.*

Withdrawing or discontinuing every Action, *Six Pence.*

Entring every Appearance, *Nine Pence.*

Filing

Filing every Demurrer, Plea, Replication and Pleas subsequent, and Issue in every Action, *Eight Pence.*

Entring every General Issue, *Nine Pence.*

Copy of every Plea, *Six Pence.*

Replication, or Plea subsequent, *One Half-penny per Line.*

Calling the Jury and Attesting them, *One Shilling and Six Pence.*

Attesting each Witness which shall give Evidence on every Trial, *Six Pence.*

Recording every Verdict, *One Shilling.*

Entring the Judgment, *One Shilling.*

Every Imparlance or Continuance, *Nine Pence.*

Entring a *Committatur*, *One Shilling.*

Admission of every Guardian or next Friend, and Copy, *Two Shillings.*

Entring every Warrant of Attorney, and Filing, *One Shilling.*

Entring every *Committatur* for Debt or Damage, *One Shilling.*

Drawing the Bill of Costs at large, *Nine Pence.*

Acknowledging Satisfaction of a Judgment on Record, *One Shilling.*

Acknowledging a Deed in Court, *One Shilling.*

Affixing the County-Seal to a Deed or other Writing, *One Shilling and Six Pence.*

Reading a Deposition and *Affidavit* in Court, *Nine Pence.*

Recording a Mark or Brand, *One Shilling.*

Search of a Record, *One Shilling.*

Entring an Appeal, and taking a Recognizance, *Three Shillings.*

A Transcript of Recognizance on Appeal, when the same is drawn up at large, *Four Shillings and Six Pence.*

And that the FEES belonging to the several Registers of this Government, shall be as followeth, viz.

GRanting and making Letters of Administration, with the Seal to them, and the Registring, *Thirteen Shillings;* But if the Estate be under *Fifteen Pounds*, then Half Fees, and no more.

Proving a Will, with Copy under the Seal, and recording the same, *Seventeen Shillings.*

Every Citation to Court, *Three Shillings.*

Register.

FOR

Filing an Inventory, *Nine Pence.*

Copy of an Inventory, and certifying the same, *An Half-penny per* Line.

A Search, *One Shilling.*

A Copy of Letters of Administration, *Four Shillings.*

A *Quietus*, with the Seal, *Four Shillings and Six Pence.*

Every *Caveat*, *One Shilling.*

Every Renunciation entred in the Office, *One Shilling and Six Pence.*

A Copy of an Administrator's Account, *One Half-penny per* Line.

A Copy of a Will under the Seal, to any Person requiring the same, *An Half-penny per* Line.

And that the FEES *belonging to the several Clerks of the Orphans-Court within this Government, to be as followeth,* viz.

Clerks of the Orphans Court.

FOR

Reading a Petition, and Filing, *One Shilling.*

Reading a Will, *Nine Pence.*

Reading an Inventory, *Nine Pence.*

Making an Order of Court, *One Shilling.*

Entring a Judgment of Court, *One Shilling.*

Reading Letters of Administration, *Nine Pence.*

The Seal of the Office to any Writing, *One Shilling.*

Chusing a Guardian, recording the same, and Copy, *Four Shillings.*

Binding an Orphan, with the Copy and Seal, *Five Shillings.*

Taking Bond, *Two Shillings.*

AND the Constable attending the Orphans-Court, for every Judgment of said Court, *One Shilling.*

And that the FEES *belonging to the Attornies at Law in this Government, shall be as followeth,* viz.

Attornies at Law.

FOR

Every Replevin, if drawn by the Attorney, *Four Shillings.*

All Actions that they shall undertake for Plaintiff or Defendant, with Declaration or Plea, *Twelve Shillings.*

Attending every Writ of Enquiry, *Four Shillings.*

Every Action brought to Judgment, and Execution, *Eight Shillings.*

Writing every Writ of Enquiry, *Scire facias*, *Venditioni exponas*, or Execution, *Three Shillings.*

Drawing

FOR

Drawing the Recognizance for profecuting a **Writ of** Error, or *Certiorari*, in the Supream-Court, *Two Shillings and Six Pence.*

Every Writ of Execution in that Court, *Six Shillings.*

Drawing every Warrant of Attorney, *One Shilling.*

Giving Oyer of a Bond, or other Oyer, *One Half-penny* per Line, Twelve Words to a Line.

Drawing out the General Iffue, *Nine Pence.*

Every Replication, Demurrer, Joinder in Demurrer, or any fubfequent Plea, every Line of **Twelve** Words, *One Half-penny.*

Drawing out the Record of all the Procefs and Pro-ceedings, in Parchment or good Paper, every **Line** of Twelve Words, *One Half-penny.*

An Injunction, Prohibition, or *Audita querela*, **Six** *Shillings.*

And that the FEES *belonging to the Conftables of this Government, fhall be as followeth,* viz.

Conftables.

FOR

SErving every Warrant, *Nine Pence.*

Travelling Charges, *One Penny* per Mile to and from the Place of ferving a Warrant, to the neareft Juftice.

Summoning every Evidence, *Nine Pence*, and Mileage as above.

Serving every Execution againft the Body, *One Shil-ling*, and Mileage.

Every Execution againft Goods and Chattels, **Selling** the fame, and making Return, *Three Shillings.*

Serving every Warrant of Attachment in the **Hands** of One Garnifhee, *One Shilling*, and Mileage.

Every other Garnifhee, *Six Pence*, befides Mileage.

Whipping a Criminal by Order of the Juftices, *Four Shillings and Six Pence.*

Putting a Perfon in the Stocks, and attending, *One Shilling.*

Conveying any Perfon to the County-Goal by *Mitti-mus*, *One Shilling*, and Mileage.

And that the FEES *belonging to all Juries, Inquefts and Evidences within this Government, fhall be as followeth,* viz.

Trying

Juries.

FOR

TRrying all Actions on Issue joined, each Juror, *One Shilling*.

Every Inquisition on Writ of Enquiry of Damages, *Eligit*, Partition, Inquest of Office, or any other Enquiry, each *per diem*, *Two Shillings*.

Every Inquisition made by the Coroner, or other proper Officer, on the View of a Dead Body, to each Juror, *Two Shillings*.

AND that every Witness legally summoned to attend, shall have for every Day that he or she is obliged to attend in order to give Evidence, *Two Shillings*.

And that the FEES *belonging to the Deputy-Surveyors of this Government, shall be as followeth, viz.*

Surveyor.

FOR

SUrveying every single Hundred Acres of Land, or lesser Quantity, *Seven Shillings and Six Pence*.

Surveying any Tract of Land above One Hundred Acres, *Seven Shillings and Six Pence* for the first One Hundred Acres, and for every Hundred more, *Three Shillings per* Hundred.

A Town-Lot, and Return of the Plot, *Six Shillings:* Which Fees respectively shall be paid on delivering up the Draught or Plot, and Return of the Survey, signed by the Deputy-Surveyor's own Hand to the Possessor or Owner of the said Lands or Lots, and not before.

Searching for a Warrant and Return, and Copy thereof, *One Shilling and Six Pence*.

Search for a Warrant, if not found, *Nine Pence*.

Travelling-Charges, *per* Mile, *One Penny*, to and from the Place of Service.

And that the said Deputy-Surveyors shall in fair Books record the Warrants, and shall duly prove the Draughts or Plots, and then record them.

Which Fees as aforesaid are to be in full of all Manner of Fees that the Deputy-Surveyors by any Means whatsoever may hereafter pretend to claim or take for any Matter or Thing relating to his or their said Offices.

Chain-carrier. AND that the Fees belonging to the Chain-Carriers, shall be *Two Shillings and Six Pence per Diem*, with their Accommodations.

AND

AND BE IT FURTHER ENACTED by the Authority aforesaid, That if any Magistrate within this Government, in putting in Execution the *Forty Shillings-* and *Five Pounds-*Acts, or any other Officer or Officers herein before mentioned, shall by Colour of any Law, Custom or Usage of this Government or that Part of *Great-Britain* called *England,* take, directly or indirectly, any more, greater or other Fees, than is herein before limited and appointed, for the doing, acting or performing any of the Matters, Duties or Things herein before enumerated, or shall make Demand of any Fees, without giving the Party of whom such Fees shall be demanded, a Bill of Particulars (if required) or shall refuse to give the Party or Parties a Receipt under his Hand for the said Fees (upon Payment thereof;) every such Magistrate, Attorney, or other Officer, shall forfeit and pay, for the first Offence the Sum of *Ten Pounds,* current Money of this Government, and for the second Offence, *Twenty Pounds,* current Money as aforesaid, the one Half to the Governor for the time being, and the other Half to him, her or them that shall sue for the same; which Penalties and Forfeitures shall and may be received in any Court of Record within this Government, by Action of Debt, Bill, Plaint or Information, wherein no Essoign, Protection or Wager of Law, or more than one Imparlance shall be allowed; and for the third Offence to be displaced or removed out of Office; any Law, Custom or Usage to the contrary in any wise notwithstanding.

Penalty on Breach of this Law.

AND BE IT FURTHER ENACTED by the Authority aforesaid, That all Laws or Acts of Assembly heretofore made in this Government for regulating and establishing Fees within the same, and every Matter, Clause and Thing therein contained, shall be and are hereby declared to be repealed, made null and void; any thing in the said Laws, Acts, or any of them, to the contrary notwithstanding.

Former Laws repealed.

PROVIDED NEVERTHELESS, AND BE IT ENACTED by the Authority aforesaid, That an Act of General Assembly of this Government, entituled, *An Act for establishing a Great Seal for this Government,* be, and is hereby declared to continue and remain in full Force and Virtue, to all Intents and Purposes whatsoever.

Act establishing a Great Seal continued.

Signed by Order of the House,
RYVES HOLT, *Speaker.*

An

An ACT for erecting Publick Bridges, Causeways, and laying-out and maintaining Highways.

WHEREAS nothing more contributes to the Ease, Safety and Conveniency of Travellers, than the erecting of Bridges, Causeways, and keeping in good Repair the Highways and Roads of each particular Government;

BE IT THEREFORE ENACTED by the Honourable *GEORGE THOMAS*, Esq; with His Majesty's Royal Approbation, Lieutenant-Governor and Commander in Chief of the Counties of *New-Castle*, *Kent* and *Sussex* upon *Delaware*, and Province of *Pennsylvania*, under the Honourable JOHN PENN, THOMAS PENN and RICHARD PENN, Esqrs; true and absolute Proprietaries of the Counties and Province aforesaid, by and with the Advice and Consent of the Representatives of the Freemen of the said Counties in General *King's-Roads* Assembly met, and by the Authority of the same; That *to be laid out by* all King's-Roads, and Highways, and all such other Roads *Justices,* as may be deemed necessary for the Ease and Advantage of the Inhabitants of this Government and Travellers, shall be laid out by Order of the Justices of the Peace, at the Court of Quarter-Sessions within each respective County, where Application shall be made.

Who shall also AND BE IT FURTHER ENACTED *appoint Over-* by the Authority aforesaid, That the Justices of each re-*seers of High-* spective Court of Quarter-Sessions within this Government, *ways, &c.* are hereby impowered and required, in *May*-Sessions yearly and every Year, to nominate and appoint in each of the Hundreds of their respective Counties, one or more discreet and substantial Inhabitant or Inhabitants, to be Overseer or Overseers of the Highways, Causeways and Bridges of the several Parts of their respective Hundreds for the ensuing Year, by Warrant from under the Seal of the said Court, signed by two or more of the said Justices.

Highways to be AND BE IT FURTHER ENACTED *40 Feet wide.* by the Authority aforesaid, That all King's-Roads or Highways within this Government, shall be of the Breadth of Forty Feet, whereof Twenty Feet shall be grubbed and cleared,

cleared, and the Branches and Limbs of Trees adjoining to the said Roads or Highways, shall be cut down, at least Ten Feet from the Ground ; and all dead Trees standing near the said Roads or Highways, if by falling they might reach the same, shall be cut down. And that all publick Roads, which are not properly King's-Roads or Highways, shall be of the Breadth of Thirty Feet, Twenty Feet of which shall be grubbed and cleared in like Manner as King's-Roads or Highways. *Other publick Roads 30 Feet wide.*

AND BE IT FURTHER ENACTED by the Authority aforesaid, That all Roads into and out of all Swamps, Creeks, Runs and sunken Lands, that fall within the Limits aforesaid, shall be made open, secured by Causeways or otherways. And that all Causeways and Bridges shall be of the Breadth of Twelve Feet at least, and Bridges standing over deep Water shall be railed in, at the Distance of Ten Feet from Rail to Rail, and of the Height of Three Feet from the Plank or Floor of the Bridge. *Causeways to be made, and Bridges, their Breadth.*

AND BE IT FURTHER ENACTED by the Authority aforesaid, That all Bridges over Creeks and deep Waters, lying on the King's-Highways leading through any of the Counties aforesaid, shall be repaired and maintained at the common Expence of the respective County wherein such Bridges are erected. PROVIDED nevertheless, That such Persons who are legally entituled to the Benefit of any Bridge or Bridges lying over deep Waters or Creeks, and the Causeways leading thereto, built at their own Expence, or at the Expence of their Predecessors or Assignors, shall enjoy all and every the Privileges and Advantages already granted them, they maintaining and keeping in Repair such Bridges and Causeways as aforesaid. *Bridges how to be maintained. See below.*

AND BE IT FURTHER ENACTED by the Authority aforesaid, That if any Person, who for his own Benefit already hath or hereafter shall cut through the King's-Road, or any other publick Road, a Race, or by any other Means obstruct the Passage of Travellers in any of the aforesaid Roads, such Person shall at his own Expence support and maintain a convenient Passage for Men, Horses and Carts, over the same. *Passage to be made good over Races, &c.*

AND BE IT FURTHER ENACTED by the Authority aforesaid, That all Bridges heretofore erected

erected in the several Hundreds in this Government, or publick Roads which are not properly King's-Roads, shall be repaired and maintained by the Inhabitants residing in the respective Hundreds where such Bridge or Bridges are erected. PROVIDED nevertheless, That where any Bridge is already erected over any Creek or deep Water, which is bounded by two Hundreds, the Inhabitants of each Hundred shall and are hereby obliged to support equally the said Bridge and the Causeway leading to the same on either Side.

AND in order that Bridges and Causeways may be easier built and supported, BE IT ENACTED by the Authority aforesaid, That it shall and may be lawful for the Overseers in their respective Hundreds, to fall, cut down, and carry away all such Timber and Trees as stand within the Limits of the Roads aforesaid, for and towards the Support of the Bridges and Causeways of the same: And in case no such Timber or Trees there be found, then it shall and may be lawful for the respective Overseers, to cause such Trees or Timber as shall be necessary for building and repairing Bridges and Causeways, standing or growing on any Lands that are most commodiously situated for such Use, to be viewed and appraised by Two impartial Freeholders of the Vicinage, nominated and appointed by the said Overseer or Overseers, they being first sworn or affirmed before some one Justice of the Peace, to duly appraise the same in Presence of the Owner thereof, if he will attend (after Notice given him by the Overseer) to be cut down and carried off for the Use before mentioned, and the Value thereof to be paid to the Owner or Owners in Manner as is herein before directed; and if the said Overseer or Overseers shall be sued for doing as above directed, he or they shall plead the General Issue, and give this Act in Evidence; and if the Plaintiff be non-suited, discontinue, or a Verdict pass against him, he shall pay the Defendant treble Cost.

Overseers may cut Timber for Bridges, &c.

AND BE IT ENACTED by the Authority aforesaid, That when any Road or Roads after Application being made to the Justices as in this Act before directed, by the said Justices is or are ordered to be laid out, then the said Justices are hereby required and directed to nominate and appoint Five substantial Freeholders of the Neighbourhood, to lay out the same; and the said Freeholders, or any Three of them, Return thereof shall make to the Justices of the Court of

Justices to appoint Freeholders to lay out Roads, &c.

Quarter-

Quarter-Seffions, to be held in the County where fuch Application is made next after fuch Proceedings, from under their Hands in Writing; and the faid Juftices fhall caufe the fame to be entred on Record, and from thenceforth fhall be deemed, taken and allowed to be a lawful Road or Roads. And whenever it fhall be found neceffary and convenient by fuch Five Freeholders, or any Three of them, that fuch Road or Roads fhall run or go through the improved Lands of any Perfon or Perfons, then and in fuch Cafe fuch Five Freeholders, or any Three of them, fhall, together with the Return of the View of fuch Road or Roads, make Return to the refpective County-Court aforefaid, upon Oath or Affirmation, to be taken before any Juftice of the Peace of the County where fuch Lands lie, of the Damages that may be fuftained by fuch Perfon or Perfons as fhall be Owners of fuch improved Lands, by reafon or means of laying out fuch Road or Roads through the fame. And the Road or Roads fo returned, fhall not be confirmed until the Perfon or Perfons petitioning for the fame, fhall pay to the Owner or Owners of fuch improved Lands, all fuch Damages as he, fhe or they fhall have fuftained, by the Valuation of fuch Freeholders or any Three of them, as aforefaid. And the Petitioner or Petitioners of fuch Road or Roads, fhall pay and fatisfy all Cofts and Charges whatfoever that fhall or may happen to accrue for laying out fuch Road or Roads. And the faid Freeholders or any Three of them, fo nominated and appointed by the Juftices as aforefaid, neglecting or refufing to comply with the Directions of this Act (unlefs hindred by Sicknefs or other unavoidable Accidents,) every fuch Freeholder fo neglecting or refufing, fhall for fuch Neglect or Refufal forfeit the Sum of *Ten Shillings*, to be levied together with Cofts by Diftrefs and Sale of the Offender's Goods and Chattels, by Warrant under the Hand and Seal of any one Juftice of the Peace for the County where fuch Offender fhall refide.

Penalty on Freeholders not complying with this Act.

AND to the end that Highways may be kept in good Order and Repair, BE IT FURTHER ENACTED by the Authority aforefaid, That all and every Overfeer and Overfeers of every Hundred within the refpective Counties of this Government, being firft by the Juftices appointed as aforefaid, may and are hereby refpectively impowered and required to give Notice to every taxable Perfon within their refpective Diftricts, in Manner and Form

Roads how to be kept in Repair.

Z z z   following,

following, *That is to say*, Every Overseer appointed as aforesaid, shall fix publick Advertisements in Writing, at Five of the most noted Places in his District, at least Ten Days before the intended Meeting, advertising and requiring each and every Person in his said District taxed or rated at any Sum not exceeding *Thirty Pounds*, to find One sufficient Man to be and appear at the Place he the said Overseer shall in the said Advertisement appoint, in order to do and perform such Services as the said Overseer in the Performance of his Duty shall require : And every Person taxed or rated at any Sum not exceeding *Sixty Pounds*, nor under *Thirty-one Pounds*, to find Two sufficient Men for the Purposes aforesaid : And any Person taxed or rated at any Sum exceeding *Sixty Pounds*, to find Three sufficient Men for the Purposes aforesaid. Which said Notice shall be deemed a sufficient Warning. And every Taxable who neglects, refuses or delays to appear, after Notice given as aforesaid, or to send a sufficient Man or Men according to the Directions of this Act, with proper Tools and Instruments, to do and perform such Services as the Overseer or Overseers shall require and direct, from one Hour after Sun rise, until one Hour before the setting of the same, Meal-Times excepted ; shall forfeit for the Delinquency or Non-performance of the Duties and Services above required and directed, any Sum not exceeding *Five Shillings*, nor under *Two Shillings and Six Pence*, to be levied as aforesaid ; and the Overseer's Return of each and every the Delinquent or Delinquents, upon his Oath or Affirmation to any one Justice of the Peace of the County where he resides, shall be deemed sufficient Proof for the Conviction.

Work-men by whom to be provided.

Penalty on Delinquents.

AND BE IT ENACTED by the Authority aforesaid, That any Person appointed Overseer as in this Act is directed, refusing or neglecting the Performance of his Duty as Overseer, shall forfeit for such Refusal or Neglect, the Sum of *Four Pounds*, to be levied as aforesaid.

Penalty on Overseers.

AND BE IT FURTHER ENACTED by the Authority aforesaid, That all and every the Fines and Forfeitures in this Act laid and to be recovered as aforesaid, shall be paid to the Treasurer of the County where such Fines and Forfeitures shall be hereafter levied, for and towards the defraying the Charges in repairing and maintaining the Bridges lying on the King's-Highways as aforesaid.

Fines how to be disposed of.

AND

AND to prevent any Difference that may arise amongst Neighbours about Roads or Causeways already laid out by Order of the Governor and Council, or any of the County-Courts of this Government, and which are or shall be en-tred upon Record, either before or after the making and publishing this Act; All such Roads and Causeways as aforesaid, shall be taken, deemed and allowed to be free, open and lawful Common Roads and Cart-ways, from the Time of their being so laid out and recorded as aforesaid. *Roads on Re-cord are Com-mon Roads.*

AND BE IT FURTHER ENACTED by the Authority aforesaid, That all Acts of General As-sembly of this Government, for laying out Roads, and for erecting, repairing and maintaining Bridges, Causeways and Highways within this Government, and every Matter and Thing therein contained, shall be and are hereby repealed, made null and void, to all Intents and Purposes. *Former Acts repealed.*

Signed by Order of the House,

RYVES HOLT, *Speaker.*

An ACT *for the better settling Intestates Estates.*

Vid. sup. p. 27.

BE IT ENACTED by the Honourable GEORGE THOMAS, Esq; with His Majesty's Royal Approbation, Lieutenant-Governor and Com-mander in Chief of the Counties of *New-Castle*, *Kent* and *Sussex* upon *Delaware*, and Province of *Pennsylvania*, under the Honourable JOHN PENN, THOMAS PENN and RICHARD PENN, Esqrs; true and absolute Proprietaries of the Counties and Province aforesaid, by and with the Advice and Consent of the Representatives of the Freemen of the said Counties in General Assembly met, and by the Authority of the same; That the Registers of the several Counties of this Government, having Power to grant Let-ters of Administration unto the Widow or next of Kin to the Intestate, and upon their or either of their Refusal to the principal Creditor or Creditors of the said Intestate, as the Register for the Probate of Wills and Testaments, and granting Letters of Administration within the Counties aforesaid, shall think meet and convenient; and the said **Registers**

Registers shall thereupon take Bond in the Name of the Governor for the Time being, with one or more sufficient Sureties, in Manner and Form following, *mutatis mutandis,* viz.

Form of the Bond.

THE Condition of this Obligation is such, That if the above bounden A. B. Administrator of all and singular the Goods and Chattels, Rights and Credits of C. D. deceased, do make or cause to be made a true and perfect Inventory of all and singular the said Goods and Chattels, Rights and Credits of the said Deceased, which have or shall come to the Hands, Possession or Knowledge of the said A. B. or unto the Hands and Possession of any other Person or Persons for him; and the same so made, do exhibit or cause to be exhibited unto the Register's Office of the County ---------- at or before the ------- Day of ------- next ensuing; and the same Goods and Chattels, Rights and Credits of the said Deceased at the Time of his Death, or which at any Time after shall come to the Hands or Possession of the said A. B. or into the Hands and Possession of any other Person or Persons for him, do well and truly administer according to Law; and further, do make or cause to be made a true and just Account of his Administration at or before ----------- Day of ------------ And all the rest and Residue of the said Goods and Chattels, Rights and Credits which shall be found remaining upon the said Administrator's Account, the same being first examined and allowed of by the Orphans Court of the County where the said Administration is granted, shall deliver and pay unto such Person or Persons respectively, as the said Orphans-Court in the respective Counties, by their Decree or Sentence pursuant to the true Intent and Meaning of this Act, shall limit and appoint: And if it shall hereafter appear that any last Will and Testament was made by the said Deceased, and the Executor or Executors therein named, do exhibit the same into the Register's Office, making Request to have it allowed and approved accordingly: If the said A. B. within-bounden, being thereunto required, do surrender and deliver up the said Letters of Administration (Approbation of such Testament being first had and made in the said Register's Office;) Then this Obligation to be void and of none Effect, or else to remain in full Force and Virtue.

Which Bonds are hereby declared and enacted to be good, to all Intents and Purposes, and pleadable in any Court of Justice within this Government. And also that the said Orphans Courts in the respective Counties of this Government, shall and may, and are hereby enabled to proceed, and call such Administrator or Administrators to Account for,

for, and touching the Goods and Chattels of any Person dying Inteftate; and upon the hearing and due confidering thereof (the Deceafed's juft Debts and Funeral Expences being firft paid and allowed) the faid Orphans Court fhall and are hereby fully impowered to order and make a juft Diftribution of the Surplufage or remaining Part of the perfonal Eftate of the Deceafed, in Manner and Form following, *That is to fay*, One Third Part of the faid perfonal Eftate to the Wife of the faid Inteftate for ever, befides her Right of Dower, or Thirds in and to the Lands, Tenements and Hereditaments of the Deceafed's perfonal Eftate during her natural Life, where fuch Wife fhall not be otherwife provided for by Marriage-Settlement; and the Refidue of the Deceafed's perfonal Eftate fhall be diftributed by equal Portions to and among the Children of the faid Deceafed, and fuch as fhall legally reprefent them, if any of them be dead (other than fuch Child or Children who fhall have any Eftate by Settlement of the Inteftate, or fhall be advanced by him in his Life-time by Portion or Portions equal to the Share which fhall by fuch Diftributions be allowed to the other Children) to whom fuch Diftributions are to be made.

Orphans Court to make Diftribution, &c.

Manner of Diftribution of perfonal Eftates.

AND in cafe any Child or Children who fhall have any Eftate by Settlement from the Inteftate, or fhall be advanced by the faid Inteftate in his Life-time by Portion or Portions not equal to the Share which will be due to the other Children by fuch Diftribution as aforefaid; then fo much of the Surplufage of the Eftate of fuch Inteftate, fhall be diftributed to fuch Child or Children as fhall have any Eftate by Settlement from the Inteftate, or were advanced in the Life-time of the Inteftate, fo as fhall make the Eftate of all the faid Children to be equal, as near as can be eftimated.

Cafe of Children that have been advanced in the Inteftate's Life-time.

AND in cafe there be no Children, nor any legal Reprefentatives of them, then one Moiety of the faid Eftate to be allotted to the Wife of the Inteftate, and the Refidue of the faid Eftate to be diftributed equally to every of the next of Kin to the Inteftate who are in equal Degree, or to thofe who legally reprefent them.

Where there are no Children, the Widow to have one Moiety, &c.

PROVIDED ALWAYS, That there be no Reprefentatives admitted amongft Collaterals (after Brother's and Sifter's Children.)

Where no Wife, the Estate goes to the Children, &c. AND in case there be no Wife, then the said Estate to be distributed equally to and amongst the Children of the Deceased, and their legal Representatives as aforesaid.

AND in case there be no Children, then to the next of Kindred in equal Degree of or unto the Intestate, and their legal Representatives as aforesaid, and in no other Manner whatsoever.

PROVIDED ALSO, And to the End that a due Regard be had to the Creditors of the said Intestate, That no such Distribution of the Goods and Chattels of any *No Distribution* Person dying Intestate, shall be made as aforesaid, until One *to be made till* Year be expired after the Intestate's Death; and that every *after One Year,* one to whom any Distribution or Share of the said Estate *&c.* shall be allotted, shall give Bond, with sufficient Sureties, to the Orphans Court, in the Name of the Governor for the Time being, That, if any Debt or Debts truly owing by the Intestate, shall be afterwards sued for and recovered, or otherwise duly be made appear, that then, and in every such Case, he, she or they shall respectively refund and pay back to the Administrator or Administrators, his, her or their rateable Part of the said Debt or Debts, and Costs of Suit and Charges of the said Administrator or Administrators by reason of such Debt or Debts, out of the Parts or Share so as aforesaid allotted to him, her or them, thereby to enable the said Administrator or Administrators to pay and satisfy the said Debt or Debts so recovered or made to appear after the Distribution made as aforesaid.

AND BE IT FURTHER ENACTED by the Authority aforesaid, That if any Person or Persons shall die Intestate, being Owners of Lands and Tenements within this Government at the Time of his or her Death, and who shall not have disposed of the same in his or her Life-time by Will in Writing or otherwise, that then all and every such Lands, Tenements and Hereditaments shall be subject to a Division, and be alike distributed, according to the Rules herein after expressed, *That is to say,* One *Manner of Dis-* Third Part of the said real Estate to the Widow of the said *tribution of In-* Intestate during her natural Life, where such Widow shall *testates Lands.* not be otherwise provided for by Marriage-Settlement; and the Residue of the said Deceased's real or landed Estate shall be distributed by equal Portions to and amongst the Children of the said Deceased, and such as shall legally represent them (if any of them be dead) other than such

Child

Child or Children who shall have any real or landed Estate by Settlement, or shall be advanced by the said Deceased in his or her Life-time by Portion or Part of such real Estate, equal to the Share which shall by such Distribution be allotted to the other Children, to whom such Distributions are to be made. And in case any Child or Children who shall have any real Estate by such Settlement from the Intestate, or shall be advanced by the said Intestate in his Life-time by Part or Portion not equal to the Share which shall be allotted to the other Children by such Distribution as aforesaid, then so much of the Surplusage of the real Estate of such Intestate shall be distributed to such Child or Children as shall have any such Settlement from the Intestate, or were advanced in the Life-time of the Intestate, as shall make the real Estate of all the said Children to be equal as near as can be estimated ; except the eldest Son, or his lawful Issue (if any be) who shall have Two Shares, or a duble Portion of the Whole of the real Estate of his, her or their Ancestors : And where there are no Sons, the Daughters shall inherit as Co-partner in the Division of the Intestate's Lands, Tenements and Hereditaments.

Children to share equally, except the eldest Son, who shall have Two Shares.

AND BE IT FURTHER ENACTED by the Authority aforesaid, That the said Division shall be made by Five sufficient Freeholders, or any three of them, to be appointed by the Orphans Court, and sworn or affirmed by the said Court for that End and Purpose; unless where all the Parties interested in any such Lands, Tenements and Hereditaments, being legally capable to act, shall agree of and make Division among themselves, and mutually give each other Releases in Writings under their Hands and Seals, which said Releases shall be allowed and accounted valid in Law, being first acknowledged by the Parties subscribing the same in open Court of Common Pleas for the aforesaid respective Counties, and duly enrolled.

To be divided by 5 Men, unless, &c.

PROVIDED NEVERTHELESS, That where any Estate in Lands, Tenements and Hereditaments cannot be divided amongst all the Children of the Intestate, without Prejudice to or spoiling of the Whole, the same being so represented and made to appear to the Orphans Court of the County where the said Lands or Tenements lay ; then the said Court may order the Whole unto the eldest Son, if he accept it, or to any other of the Sons successively, upon the eldest Son's Refusal, he or they paying to the other Children of the Deceased, their equal or proportionable

Where Lands cannot be divided, the eldest Son to have the Whole, &c.

Parts

Parts or Shares of the true Value of such Lands, Tenements and Hereditaments, as upon a just Appraisement thereof, to be made by Three sufficient Freeholders to be appointed by the Orphans Court and qualified as aforesaid, or giving good Security to pay the same in some reasonable Time as the said Orphans Court shall limit and appoint: And the Person or Persons, whether Minors or others, to whom, or for whose Use, Payment or Satisfaction shall be made for their respective Parts or Shares of the Deceased's Lands by the Heir at Law or others, in Manner aforesaid, and shall be for ever debarred of all the Right, Title and Demand, which he or they can or may have of, in or to such Share or Part by virtue of this Act; and the same shall be held and enjoyed by the Heir at Law, or other Purchaser, as freely and fully as the Intestate held the same.

AND if any of the Children happen to die before he or she come to Age or be married, the Portion of such Child or Children shall be equally divided amongst the surviving Brothers and Sisters, or their legal Representatives.

Where no Children, who to inherit the Lands, &c.

AND in case there be no Children, nor any legal Representatives of them, then one Moiety of the Intestate's Lands, Tenements and Hereditaments, shall be allotted to the Widow of such Intestate, during her natural Life; and the Residue of the Deceased's real Estate shall be equally divided to every of the next of Kin of the Intestate in equal Degree, and to those who legally represent them; no Representatives to be admitted amongst Collaterals after Brother's and Sister's Children.

Where no Wife, &c.

AND if there be no Wife, the same shall be distributed amongst the Children; and if no Children, to the next of Kin to the Intestate in equal Degree, and their legal Representatives as aforesaid, and in no other Manner whatsoever.

AND every one to whom any such Distribution or Share shall be allotted, shall give Bond with Sureties in the said Orphans Court (if required) That if any Debts afterwards be made to appear against the Deceased, to refund and pay back to the Administrator his or her rateable Part of that Debt or Debts, and of the Costs of Suits and Charges of the said Administrator by reason of such Debts, out of the Part or Share so as aforesaid allotted to him or her, thereby to enable the said Administrator to pay and satisfy the

the said Debts so recovered, after the Distribution made as aforesaid. And that the Widow's Part or Portion in the real Estate of the Deceased, shall at the Expiration of her Term, be alike divided as aforesaid: Saving to any Person aggrieved, at any Order, Sentence or Decree of the Orphans Court, made for the Settlement and Distribution of any Intestate's Estates, their Right of Appeal unto the Supream Court of this Government, to be held for each County respectively; every Person so appealing, giving Security to prosecute the said Appeal with Effect. *{Widow's Part to be also divided, &c.}*

AND BE IT FURTHER ENACTED by the Authority aforesaid, That if any Person or Persons dying Intestate, being Owners of Lands and Tenements within this Government at the Time of their Death, and leave lawful Issue to survive them, but not a sufficient personal Estate to pay their just Debts, and maintain their Children; then and in such Case it shall be lawful for the Administrator or Administrators of such Decedents, to sell and convey such Part or Parts of the said Lands or Tenements for defraying their just Debts, Maintainance of their Children, and putting them Apprentices, and teaching them to read and write; and for the Improvement of the Residue of the Estate (if any be) to their Advantage, as the Orphans Court of the Counties where such Estate lies, shall think fit to allow, order, and from time to time direct. *{Personal Estate not being sufficient to pay Debts, &c. Lands may be sold;}*

PROVIDED ALWAYS, That no Lands and Tenements contained in any Marriage-Settlement, shall by virtue of this Act be sold or disposed of contrary to the Form and Effect of such Settlement; nor shall any Orphans Court allow or order any Intestate's Lands and Tenements to be sold before Administrators requesting the same do exhibit one or more true and perfect Inventory or Inventories, and conscionable Appraisement of all the Intestate's personal Estate whatsoever, and also a true and just Account, upon his or her solemn Oath or Affirmation, of all the Intestate's Debts which shall be then come to his or her Knowledge. And if thereupon it shall appear to the Court, that the Intestate's personal Estate will not be sufficient to pay the Debts, and maintain the Children, until the eldest of them attains to the Age of Twenty-one Years, or to put them out to be Apprentices and teach them to read and write; then and in every such Case, and not otherwise, the Court shall allow such Administrators to make publick Sale of so much of the said Lands, as the *{Except Lands contained in Marriage-Settlements.}* *{Proceedings in Sale of Lands directed.}*

Court, upon the beſt Computation they can make of the
Value thereof, ſhall adjudge neceſſary for the Purpoſes a-
foreſaid, reſerving the Manſion-Houſe, and moſt profitable
Part of the Eſtate, till the laſt. But before any ſuch Sale
be made, the Court ſhall order ſo many Writings to be
made by the Clerk, upon good Paper, as the Court ſhall
think fit, to ſignify and give Notice of ſuch Sale, and of
the Day and Place where the ſaid Sale will be, and what
Lands are to be ſold, and where they lie; which Notices
ſhall be by the Adminiſtrator or Adminiſtrators affixed in
three of the moſt publick Places of the County and in the
Hundred where the Land lies, at leaſt Twenty Days before
the ſaid Sale is to begin; and the Adminiſtrator that makes
ſuch Sale, ſhall bring his or her Proceedings therein to the
next Orphans Court after the Sale made; and if it ſhould
happen that any Lands be ſold, by virtue of this Act, for
more than the Court's Computation of the Value thereof,
then the Adminiſtrator or Adminiſtrators ſhall be accountable for the Surpluſage of the ſame, to be paid and divided
as by this Act is before required and directed in reſpect of
the Inteſtate's perſonal Eſtate.

A N D   B E   I T   F U R T H E R   E N A C T E D
by the Authority aforeſaid, That the Surpluſage and remaining Parts of the Inteſtate's Lands, Tenements and Hereditaments, not ſold nor ordered to be ſold by virtue of
this Act, and not otherwiſe limited by Marriage-Settlement,
ſhall be divided, as aforeſaid, between the Inteſtate's Children, or the Survivors of them, or their Repreſentatives,
as aforeſaid.

Surpluſage upon Sale, to be divided.

A N D in caſe the Inteſtate have no known Kindred, but
a Wife, then all his Lands, Tenements and Hereditaments
ſhall deſcend to his ſaid Wife during her natural Life, and
after the Death of the ſaid Wife, then all the ſaid Lands,
Tenements and Hereditaments ſhall eſcheat or go to the
immediate Landlord of whom ſuch Lands, Tenements and
Hereditaments are held, his Heirs and Aſſigns; and all the
Goods, Chattels and perſonal Eſtate whatſoever, of ſuch
Perſons dying Inteſtate and without Wife or Kindred as
aforeſaid, ſhall go to the Governor or Commander in Chief
for the time being. But if any of the ſaid Inteſtate's Relations ſhall appear, and make their Claim or Claims to
ſuch Inteſtate's perſonal Eſtate within Seven Years after
the Deceaſe of the Inteſtate; they ſhall be reſtored thereunto.

If the Inteſtate have no known Kindred but a Wife, the Land to be hers during Life.

Perſonal Eſtate goes to the Governor; but ſhall be reſtored if Relations appear in 7 Years

A N D

AND if the lawful Heir to any such Lands or Tenements shall at any Time within Twenty-one Years after the Intestate's Decease appear, he may traverse the Inquisition, or Office found for the Lands so escheated, and recover the same, paying the Lord or Person in Possession for the Improvements thereupon, according to the Valuation of a Jury of Twelve Men, to be appointed by the Court of Common-Pleas for that County in which the said Lands and Tenements lie.

If an Heir at Law appear in 21 Years, he may recover the escheated Lands.

PROVIDED ALWAYS, AND BE IT FURTHER ENACTED by the Authority aforesaid, That in all Cases where the Register hath used heretofore to grant Letters of Administration with Testament annexed, he shall continue so to do; and the Will of the Deceased in such Testament expressed, shall be performed and observed in such Manner as it should have been as if this Act had never been made.

AND for lessening the Charge of dividing the Lands of Intestates amongst their Children, BE IT ENACTED by the Authority aforesaid, That the Justices of the Orphans Court of the County where the Lands lie, upon Application made to them by the Heir at Law or any other Child, when he, she or they shall attain to the Age of Twenty-one Years, shall and are hereby impowered to appoint Five sufficient Freeholders of the County, who, upon their Oaths or Affirmation, shall take with them a skilful Surveyor, and go upon the Lands of the Intestate, and divide the same equally amongst the Children or other Heirs of the Intestate, according to the Directions and true Intent and Meaning of this Act; which said Five Persons, or any Three of them agreeing, shall make Return of such Division to the next Orphans Court; and if such Division be approved of by the said Court, the same shall remain firm and stable for ever.

Division of Lands to be made by 5 Men, &c.

PROVIDED ALWAYS, That such Division shall not debar the Eldest Son, or others as aforesaid, for making a Purchase of the Share and Parts of his Brothers and Sisters, in the Manner before directed by this Act.

AND BE IT FURTHER ENACTED by the Authority aforesaid, That all Laws or Acts of Assembly heretofore made in this Government for the settling Intestates Estates, and directing the Descent of

Repeal of former Laws.

Lands

Lands of Persons dying Inteſtate, and every Matter, Clauſe and Thing therein contained, ſhall be and are hereby declared to be repealed, made null and void ; any thing in the ſaid Acts, or any of them, to the contrary in any wiſe notwithſtanding.

PROVIDED NEVERTHELESS, AND BE IT FURTHER ENACTED by the Authority aforeſaid, That all Settlements and Diviſions of any Inteſtates Eſtates, either real or perſonal, heretofore made purſuant to any former Laws of this Government, are hereby ratified, confirmed and approved of.

Signed by Order of the Houſe,

RYVES HOLT, *Speaker.*

THE

THE
T A B L E.

An

An